What Racists Believe

SAGE SERIES ON
RACE AND ETHNIC RELATIONS

Series Editor:

JOHN H. STANFIELD II

College of William and Mary

This series is designed for scholars working in creative theoretical areas related to race and ethnic relations. The series will publish books and collections of original articles that critically assess and expand upon race and ethnic relations issues from American and comparative points of view.

SERIES EDITORIAL BOARD

Volumes in this series include

What Racists Believe

Race Relations in South Africa and the United States

Gerhard Schutte

Sage Series on Race and Ethnic Relations

v o l u m e   8

SAGE Publications
International Educational and Professional Publisher
Thousand Oaks   London   New Delhi

For information address:

 SAGE Publications, Inc.
2455 Teller Road
Thousand Oaks, California 91320

SAGE Publications Ltd.
6 Bonhill Street
London EC2A 4PU
United Kingdom

SAGE Publications India Pvt. Ltd.
M-32 Market
Greater Kailash I
New Delhi 110 048 India

Printed in the United States of America

Library of Congress Cataloging-in-Publication Data

Shutte, Gerhard.
    What racists believe: race relations in South Africa and the
United States / Gehard Schutte.
        p. cm. — (Sage series on race and ethic relations; v. 8)
    Includes bibliographical references and index.
        ISBN 0-8039-5785-8. — ISBN 0-8039-5786-6 (pbk.)
1. South Africa—Race relations. 2. United States—Race
relations. 3. Racism—South Africa. 4. Racism—United States.
5. Whites—South Africa. 6. Whites—United States. I. Title
II. Series.
DT1756.S38   1994
305.8'00968'09049—dc20   94-36220

95 96 97 98 99   10 9 8 7 6 5 4 3 2 1

Sage Production Editor: Astrid Virding

Contents

For my parents and Andries and Stephan—in South Africa.

Series Editor's Introduction

The study of whiteness is becoming an important fad in 1990s race and ethnic studies. We now have growing numbers of scholars who are studying whiteness as a racialized category in the United States, Great Britain, the Netherlands, Brazil, and South Africa.

Gerhard Schutte has written a fascinating book on the social, cultural, and political construction of white consciousness and racialized visions of nationhood in South Africa, with some comparative remarks regarding the same in the United States. Given the political transformations occurring in contemporary South Africa, what he has to say about the construction of white consciousness and the changes it is undergoing is quite timely. Also, the unique case of whiteness in South Africa, which has been a matter of minority demographic presence, sets Schutte's analysis apart from whiteness studies conducted in nation-states where European-descent populations are in the majority.

Another thing that sets this book apart is that whereas most studies on whiteness have been published by cultural and literary studies scholars and by historians, Schutte is a sociologist. His approach, which draws heavily from phenomenology, critical discourse theory, and grounded theory in ethnographic and long interview data, offers a methodological strategy for other sociologists interested in exploring the fascinating question of whiteness in nation-states and regions dominated by persons of European descent. What this means is that he has attempted to examine the roles of institutions and other social organizations (the state, political parties, organized religion, media, economics, ecosystems) in shaping the racialized consciousness of whites and their visions of their multiracial nation.

The rich interpretive perspective on the study of whiteness that Schutte offers is a model for other sociologically oriented scholars to emulate and expand.

John H. Stanfield II
Series Editor

Acknowledgments

This book is the culmination of an idea that first occurred to me in 1985 during my sabbatical on an Alexander von Humboldt Fellowship in Bielefeld, Germany. On March 21, 1985, 19 mourners were indiscriminately killed by police at Langa in the Eastern Cape. It was also the twenty-fifth anniversary of the Sharpeville massacre. In the intervening years, numerous killings of blacks occurred as a result of the actions of police and other whites. Since 1985, even more have died in the context of resistance to apartheid. Both whites and blacks, frequently assisted or directed by whites, were involved in these killings. These violent reactions to resistance to an iniquitous system prompted deeper questions: What forms of consciousness among whites could give rise to such actions? How was the "other" conceptualized to make him or her a target of elimination? These questions gave rise to even more broader ones that caused me to reflect on racial thinking in general within the community in which I grew up.

During the course of my investigations, which first concentrated on the Afrikaners, it became clear to me that it was necessary to create a broader ethnographic description of Afrikaner "culture" than simply concentrating on sensational incidents of racial violence. The then director of the South African Council of Churches (SACC), C. F. Beyers Naudé, who for decades endured the persecution and harassment of the government because of his stance on race relations, encouraged and inspired the study. The SACC's Asingeni fund made it possible for me and my coinvestigator at the time, Diana E. Forsythe, to conduct a preliminary study on the Afrikaners. During the course of this study it became clear that substantial shifts had occurred in the white community that indicated that the old ethnic divide between English and Afrikaans speakers was less noticeable in the light of the urgency of South Africa's race problem. In 1987 I decided to refocus the whole study on the issue of white solidarity. The John D. and Catherine T. MacArthur Foundation made a generous award to cover the cost of the ethnographic research and the transcriptions underlying the study. Without the assistance of the MacArthur Foundation this study would not have been possible.

I need also to acknowledge the contribution many colleagues, assistants, and students made to this work. I am indebted to Anselm Strauss, with whom I had discussions in San Francisco at the time his major methodological work on qualitative analysis appeared. In Evanston, Illinois, Howard S. Becker not only became a friend, but opened my mind to new perspectives on fieldwork. The fieldwork itself was a daunting task. The scope of the study was too large for me to gather all the information personally. The heads of the anthropology departments at the University of the Witwatersrand, David Hammond-Tooke, and the Rand Afrikaans University, Boet Kotze, helped me get in touch with advanced-level students who helped me in the interview phase. Anthropologist At Fischer, at the Rand Afrikaans University, helped me select Afrikaans-speaking students. He was especially helpful in putting me in touch with rural contacts through his brother, Dirk Fischer. I will not easily forget the pain and concern with which he spoke about his fellow rural people.

I gratefully acknowledge also the help I received from Charmaine de Fortier, Gail Emby, Annemarie Grindrod, Carol Schoeman, John Simmonds, Harold Thompson, and Tessa van Riet-Lowe. Tessa van Riet-Lowe and Harold Thompson invested great effort in providing extensive material, and Annemarie Grindrod did brilliant work in sorting, reading, and coding hundreds of schoolchildren's essays. Sandra Brady and Ashley Lammers helped me transcribe the interview material recorded in English and Afrikaans. They invested hundreds of hours in the often-frustrating labor of listening, typing, reviewing, correcting, retyping, and printing. Only those who have done this kind of work can really appreciate the effort involved.

The Program of African Studies at Northwestern University in Evanston hosted me as visiting scholar from 1988 to 1992. Through the program's support, I gained access to the superb Africana Collection in the library. The curator at the time, Hans Panofsky, not only proved to be an invaluable resource in tracking down material but, more important, impressed me with his humanitarian concern for Africa. During most of the research period, Marilyn Green of Palo Alto, California, provided me with a newspaper clipping service that kept me informed about South African events as viewed by the U.S. press. I thank her for her effort. Finally, I wish to mention Marjorie Benton, who helped me get in touch with resource persons in the Chicago area. Her support at a very difficult time in my career will not be forgotten.

I undertook this project out of my personal concern for the country of my birth and the well-being of everybody who resides there. I approached it also with the knowledge that a substantial gap exists in our qualitative knowledge about white South Africans. Whether this book will help to fill that gap, time will tell. I also have the practical intention of providing, to some degree, usable knowledge to anyone interested in the minimization of violence in a South Africa undergoing dramatic structural changes. Writing these lines on the day of the first democratic election ever held in South Africa, I realize that the contents of this book attempt to describe white attitudes and values at the start of a new era for that country. May they change and may peace be maintained and lives spared in the new South Africa.

Gerhard Schutte
Chicago

1

Introduction

This book is about South African whites during a period of rapid social change. The legal system that enshrined their privilege is rapidly disappearing. They are faced with adjusting to a new situation in which their traditional senses of identity, purpose, and place in society have largely become obsolete and in need of substantial modification. Yet many, clinging to the past, meet the undeniable reality of change with disbelief and resistance. Others adopt strategies of coping with the new reality. I will argue that permeating these diverse responses is a sense of solidarity and unity shared by a broad spectrum of whites. On the surface, the evidence suggests that they are torn by a divisiveness that sometimes borders on civil war. However, on a different level there are many unspoken and tacit agreements about their hopes for the future and the nature of interracial relations.

The material presented in this volume is largely descriptive, but it raises important theoretical points with regard to the issue of social solidarity. I would therefore suggest that the reader whose interest in the topic is general and relatively nonacademic start at Chapter 2. The current chapter deals with the general theoretical and methodological framework underlying the study reported here, and is therefore more technical in conceptualization and style.

GOALS OF THE STUDY

It is my purpose to present in this volume a systematic and analytic investigation of the social origins of those structures of consciousness that persistently give rise to attempts to preserve and consolidate whites as a group in the rapidly changing political environment of South Africa. I consciously do not want to frame the initial statement of the problem in terms of racism, paternalism, fascism, or any other preconfigured explanatory judgment. It may well prove to be one, or a combination of these, but, methodologically speaking, I will adhere to the principle of examining the evidence first before proceeding any further. The avenue of examining evidence of social solidarity first puts the investigation within the framework of a classical theme of sociology.

It is very tempting to look at the problem in terms of racism, as many studies about South African realities have done. From a comparative perspective, Teun van Dijk (1985, 1987, 1992a, 1992b) and his colleagues have conducted extensive work on the discourse of race and racial differentiation in a number of Western democratic societies. They have taken their point of departure from the common observation that, regardless of its illegality, racism is still rife in the United States, Great Britain, and various European countries. In these societies, racism tends to assume a relatively covert form, disguising itself in neutral and subtle ways. However, if one looks at the social structures of these societies, at the distribution of power, health, and wealth resources, blatant inequalities simply stand out. This racism is borne by covert and disguised sentiments of superiority and entitlement and has real and disabling consequences for minorities in these societies. Under the conditions of white majority domination found in these societies, these mental images of the racial and ethnic "other" are perpetuated and reproduced on two levels. Van Dijk and others have demonstrated how the reproduction of racism is achieved on the macro level in the dominant discourse encountered in the press, electronic media, and political and educational arenas. At the same time, this discourse provides legitimation for the existing societal structure by providing "rationales" for inequalities or by denying their existence. Discourse on the macro level informs group attitudes and dispositions. On a micro level, the reproduction of racism operates on the level of everyday situated interactions of individuals.

The relationship between the micro and macro levels is a complex one. On the micro level, group members engage in practices governed by cognitions and values that are publicly mediated in the dominant discourse. Yet individually shared values and attitudes cannot simply be seen in a deterministic framework, as if the dominant discourse would successfully inscribe itself in, and determine, the individual mind. The interrelationship is a dynamic one. Group members experience the world individually and collectively and attach meaning to it. The public discourse, in whatever form it may take, would lose its relevance if it did not orient itself toward these shared meanings and expectations. On the other hand, individual experiences and expectations may be shaped and guided by the public discourse. We fully recognize the interplay between the micro and macro levels of discourse. However, in the existing literature on South African race relations, very little attention has been paid to the micro level (I review some of these studies in Chapter 2). One-sided attention has usually been given to the role of the political elite and leaders in South Africa. This volume is designed to give more weight to the neglected perspective from below. It is structured in such a way that it accounts for the ongoing public discourse but emphasizes how members of the white public attach meanings to current events and political and economic pressures.

The mere fact that the current dominant discourse is not very successful in shaping white minds may be a peculiarity of South Africa. In my experience over the past two decades, a large proportion of the white public has become disillusioned with the dominant discourse controlled by the National Party and the captains of industry. The steady decline in the standard of living of the middle class and the seeming rudderlessness of the political process have caused a large section of the white citizenry to drift away from their traditional leaders and the dominant discourse, in both political and economic senses. Dominant discourse and public discourse therefore do not necessarily overlap. Although public discourse is still greatly influenced by the interests of the dominant, there is a domain of this discourse that is less formal. Description and analysis of this informal domain is crucial if we are to come to a better understanding of the values and cognitions that underlie white actions and verbal practices. The evidence for this type of discourse is found in everyday talk, gossip, rumor, anecdotes, and symbolic interaction. In shifting the focus toward a grassroots perspective, we are guided more by the evidence itself and less by populist considerations.

WHITES AS A "MINORITY"

South Africa presents a unique situation with regard to race relations. In no other country has a numerical minority dominated for so long in the postcolonial era. Where race relations do constitute a problem in the West it is usually within the context of relations between a white numerical majority and racial and ethnic minorities perceived by whites to be different and/or unequal. Those in the numerical majority, of course, also happen to have the greater share of power and wealth in their respective societies. This is the pattern found in the United States, Great Britain,

Germany, Holland, and other nations. During colonial expansion, people of European extraction settled as minorities in a great variety of places around the world. In some areas they were highly successful in reducing indigenous populations to powerlessness (or in decimating those populations). As a result, they emerged as dominant majorities in those countries. In the United States, Australia, and New Zealand, British settlers became the majority. British colonies in Africa and Asia produced powerful settler minorities. As a proportion of the total population they were small, and eventually they had to integrate or return to Britain after national independence was achieved in the former colonies. Southern Africa was an exception, however. The farther south in Africa the territory was situated, the longer it took to establish participatory governments. After Zimbabwe and Namibia gained their independence, South Africa was the last territory to move toward a democratic form of government.

The dominance of the white section of the population in South Africa must be understood historically. The British took over a preexisting Dutch settlement when they arrived, and it was these settlers who never enduringly emancipated themselves from colonialism until the whole territory of South Africa was surprisingly granted independence after the colonial Anglo-Boer War. Britain disempowered the black majority of the population by ratifying a South African constitution for the country that would entrench and safeguard white power. As a result, the white minority monopolized political and economic power. Today whites remain a sizable numerical minority, making up about 15% of the total population. In comparison with the dominant majority in the United States, whites in South Africa stand in almost exact inverse proportion to blacks. In the United States, African Americans number approximately 12.5% of the population, which is close to the percentage whites represent as a proportion of the South African population. Though numerically a minority, South African whites are a "majority" in terms of the political and economic power they wield. We can expect that, unless blatantly racist, the rationales whites produce for the structure of their society and the nature of their culture would differ from the rationalizations and self-justifications of their counterparts in white America. Arguments based on the "will of the people" or "the South African way of life" simply lack credibility in light of the overwhelming presence and visibility of the black majority. I am sensitive to this difference, and this volume examines how whites endow their privilege and domination with a sense of plausibility under the historical circumstances they find themselves in during the last decade of this century. The construction of plausibility in the presence of so much evidence to the contrary is an interesting theoretical problem in itself. In essence, the way whites manage the cognitive dissonance between the reality they perceive and the reality they idealize deserves special attention.

INTERSUBJECTIVITY
AND EVERYDAY LIFE

This study is theoretically informed by the phenomenological perspective Alfred Schutz and Thomas Luckmann (1974; Luckmann, 1983) adopted in their analyses of the social construction of reality. In the words of Luckmann (1978), this is an "egological" and "reflexive" perspective. The "egological" perspective takes "the individual human being as the center of a system of coordinates on which the experience of the world is mapped." It is "reflexive" because it reinstates "human experience in its place as the primary datum about the world and it describes this experience by turning and returning to the intentional features of experience" (p. 8). This theoretical orientation implies a methodology with which it is closely integrated, thus I will raise methodological issues while discussing theory.

Studies from a phenomenological perspective tend to celebrate the creativity and constructiveness of humans within their social contexts. The nature of the material analyzed in this book does not leave much to celebrate about the way in which many whites construct their reality. The depressing nature of the evidence does not exonerate the inquirer from attempting a subjective understanding of their constructions. This understanding implies the "reflexivity" referred to above, especially in the sense of turning toward the intentional features of whites' experience. As an exercise in sociological understanding, the research required that I capture, as much as possible, an internal view of the world from the perspective of my subjects. Having lived in South Africa for most of my life and having been socialized in the Afrikaner section of the society were both advantages and drawbacks. I was, or am, one of them. Being a "native" of a society means that one takes for granted what the other members take for granted. As Schutz (1973, pp. 207-229; 1976, pp. 20-26, 226-249) points out, taken-for-grantedness is the mode of consciousness typical of everyday life, or of the commonsense world. This mode of consciousness is an unquestioning one that tends to suspend doubt about itself and its assumptions about truth and justice. Scientific investigation amounts to just the opposite insofar as it adopts a critical attitude toward its own cognitions and suspends belief about social construction claims. Translated into research praxis, the consciousness of everyday life is a decided disadvantage and amounts to a form of blindness. However, in order to understand subjectively what is going on, one must share the axiology of the everyday life of one's subjects. The biggest strain in my research was therefore to migrate between the familiarity of everyday life and the "strangeness" of the scientifically objectified reality in a constantly oscillating way. I had to make strange what was familiar to me. I had to approach my own "tribe" as an anthropologist would approach a strange culture.[1] I had to make strange my own family and friends in order to thematize properly what they were doing and saying. Although this procedure of making the familiar strange was taking place in my mind, I had to act "normal" so as not to disturb the plausibility of the everyday-life constructs of my subjects. Through carefully managed silences, I censored my disagreements in order to maintain rapport. I felt uncomfortable with my lack of intervention, but I had to maintain it until I was finished with the fieldwork phase of the research.

My objective in bracketing myself in the research process was to diminish possible inhibitions to the spontaneous actions of subjects I wished to place on record. I have no illusions about my own or my assistants' intrusiveness and potential distorting influence on the material produced. Nevertheless, this is an attempt to capture meanings and motivations white South Africans might share about their world of experience and their future in it. These meanings and motivations are shared in an intersubjective manner.

Intersubjectivity is essentially social in nature, for it sets boundaries for its membership and shares a sense of mutual belonging to a community. How these boundaries are set and justified occupies the greater part of this book. The sense of belonging subjects experienced demonstrates the subjective dimension of the central theme of this inquiry: social solidarity. Because solidarity is indicative of an in-group/out-group distinction, members have developed interpretive schemes to make sense of outsiders and of political processes that affect them. They also develop typifications with regard to themselves and the outsider. These typifications have consequences in the realm of social interaction. Typifications inform both strategies and rationalizations of interaction. The undeniable and historical power differential between black and white is an important dimension of white social solidarity. Typifications of the other and of the self are important indicators of the sense of white identity, and also unlock some of the reasons a major change in the distribution of power and social boundaries is viewed with so much resistance.

METHODOLOGY

The fieldwork underlying this study provided most of the evidence of whites' experience and construction of reality. Social interactions and symbolic manifestations were documented through participant observation. Public meetings and everyday social interactions were videotaped or photographed. The bulk of the evidence is verbal. Most of the verbal materials were collected in 69 lengthy interviews. Some verbal materials are derived from speeches and sermons. Video- and audiotapes were meticulously transcribed. The transcriptions record hesitations, silences, and emphases, but are not as elaborate as those usually used in the fields of ethnomethodology or conversation analysis. My field assistants and transcribers were carefully trained not to edit or correct respondents' utterances, and I checked the transcriptions for accuracy. In addition to interview material, I used printed material reflecting features of the dominant discourse. The discovery of children's essays and drawings was a bonanza.

My choices regarding research methods were guided by the assumption that they would produce evidence that contains indications of cognitive processes and schemata whites use in constructing their social world and their place in it. I am aware that interviews with 69 individuals cannot produce material that is representative of all whites in the country. Unfortunately, the scale of the project did not allow for more. However, the choices of subjects were not random. I decided to stratify the set of interviewees according to residence in rural or urban areas. In urban areas, I selected respondents in upper- and lower-middle-class areas. All but 1 of the 11 rural interviewees were Afrikaans speakers. They lived in a district of the Eastern Transvaal. The urban set consisted of 28 Afrikaans speakers and 30 English speakers. I stratified the urban set into lower- and upper-middle-class respondents on the basis of the reputations of residential areas. More lower-middle-class people were Afrikaans, and the ratio was reversed for the upper-middle-class category. The lower-middle-class selection was done on the basis of residence in the suburbs of Triomf and Mayfair and the southern suburbs of Johannesburg. Upper-middle-class subjects were assumed to live in Linden, Emmarentia, and Parktown. A few came from Auckland Park and Randburg. There is a serious imbalance as far as gender is concerned: Only 15 respondents are female. Public discourse in South Africa is heavily male dominated, however, and I am not sure this gender imbalance has a distorting effect on the overall picture.

Interviews were open-ended and subjects were encouraged to speak freely. Intervention by the interviewer was kept to a minimum. In order to minimize obtrusiveness, microcassette recorders were used in interviews as much as possible. Interviewees were invited to tell stories and anecdotes that would illustrate their views. The interviews were conducted in informal settings, and it was considered more important to record spontaneous talk than the responses to questions. In a way, this method may be described as the ethnography of everyday talking. My assistants and I therefore also made a special effort to listen to spontaneous talk wherever it might be overheard.

The transcripts of the interviews, discussions, speeches, sermons, and fragments of everyday talk were coded and indexed on computer. Two coding levels were used. I first indexed "manifest" lexical items. Only after I was thoroughly familiar with the contexts of these items did I proceed to identify and label the connections, associations, and typifications subjects made. These labels were entered as codes in the text. The procedure I followed was strongly influenced by the precepts of grounded theory as expressed in Anselm Strauss's *Qualitative Analysis for Social Scientists* (1987).[2] His notion of theoretical sampling was useful because it takes account of the complex process of qualitative analysis. In theoretical sampling, the researcher, "after previous analysis, is seeking samples of population, events, activities guided by his or her emerging (if still primitive) theory" (p. 16). In the course of analysis this emergent theory, or set of theoretical constructs, is refined, modified or rejected, and replaced. The theory is built up in a forward and backward movement in which the researcher moves between the material and its theoretical conceptualization. The theory constantly interrogates the data.

The development of the theoretical construct of "white solidarity" can serve as an example of theoretical sampling. In the study of published literature as well as in the verbal texts, I was looking for a theoretical construct that would capture the nature of the bond that unites the white population. In succession, I examined the concepts of race, ethnic group, caste, class, language group, and political orientation, and in each instance I encountered the problem of "fit." Interrogating the evidence repeatedly failed to produce a satisfactory fit between concept and evidence. Yet each of these emerging theories performed valuable heuristic functions. Some of these concepts—such as ethnic group, culture, political orientation, and language community—highlighted divisions rather than unity. Yet there were overarching cognitive schemes and typifications that reflected a common "understanding" of their situation among whites (see Chapter 2).

PLAN OF THE BOOK

This volume falls into two parts. The distinction is guided by neo-Weberian approaches such as that used by Berger and Luckmann (1972), which view society as objective and subjective reality without dissolving the domain of the social into one or the other. The dynamic and dialectical relationship between these two aspects will also be upheld in the presentation of my analysis in this book.

Following this introduction of the theoretical rationale and methodological aspects of the research, I review briefly in Chapter 2 various categories of literature on South African whites. I then explain the perspective of the book and introduce the central theme of white solidarity by reviewing how conventional and traditional ethnic, cultural, linguistic, and political divisions have yielded to a wider in-group awareness and self-definition.

In the first major section of the book, Chapters 3-5, I deal with the objective aspect of South African society viewed from a white perspective. These chapters address the dominant discourse in South African society. In Chapter 3, I discuss how the discourse on history has changed over the years and review the development of white ethnic reconstructions of the past in the forms of historiographies, public debate, and artistic representations. The reception of these reconstructions by the public is traced through popular myths about descent and divine election. Chapter 3 highlights the genesis of typifications of the self and blacks as far as historical roles and destinies are concerned.

In Chapter 4, I examine how the present is constructed in public discourse. I trace how racial, ethnic, and cultural divisions of South African society have been entrenched through the manipulation of the legal system, the media, and the church. I explore how the structure of South African society channels the consciousness of the white population and analyze the privileges these manipulations have bestowed upon the white population. I then attempt to place these privileges within the contexts of the bureaucratic and moral rationales they provide for social inequalities.

During the past decade, political divisions among whites seem to have deepened. In Chapters 5 and 6, I take up the difference in political orientation between conservatives and reformists by looking at public discourse, in both its dominant and white populist forms. Chapter 5 examines how right-wingers and conservatives view the political situation and the distribution of power in South Africa. Detailed material is drawn from political speeches and rallies. Right-wingers tend to draw hard-and-fast lines between black and white, but attempt to underplay the fact that their distinctions are based on race. Chapter 6, in turn, looks at those political cadres that actually wield decision-making power: the recently "enlightened" reformist government and the large corporations. Their voices are privileged in the media and propagate a "new" South Africa in which the old "ideological" irrationalities of the past will be replaced by a new rationality.

The second part of the book analyzes the ethnography of talk as evidence of society as subjective reality. Its main purpose is to conceptualize the cognitive schemata and typifications of white South Africans. In Chapter 7, I primarily examine symbolic structures and everyday linguistic and interactive conventions as objectifications of the way whites construct blacks and their future. Detailed attention is given to a collection of schoolchildren's essays and drawings as renderings of past, present, and desired human relations in South Africa.

Rural whites—more specifically, farmers and those dependent on agriculture—have a world of experience that differs in fundamental aspects from that of their urban counterparts. Chapter 8 is concerned with attitudes of whites in areas where blacks are mostly perceived to be laborers.

Chapters 9 and 10 deal with whites in town, differentiating between those with conservative perspectives and those with more moderate views. Conservatives have fewer face-to-face encounters with members of other groups, especially blacks. They construct strong stereotypes of blacks that center on differences of culture and civilization, but barely bother to disguise the racial overtones in their discourse. Moderates draw social boundaries between white and black less rigidly, but do seem to be worried about the maintenance of civilized standards in a future South Africa under black rule.

Chapter 11 is devoted to a synthesis of the findings of the study. I explore patterns in the construction of present and future group relations and place them within a theoretical framework that attempts to account for the type of social solidarity and identity whites share. In the final chapter, I explore possible future trends in intergroup relations in South Africa and reflect on the differences and similarities in white racial attitudes between the United States and South Africa.

NOTES

1. I have elaborated elsewhere on the theme of familiarity and strangeness while doing fieldwork in South Africa (Schutte, 1991).

2. Grounded theory as an approach was first formulated by Glaser and Strauss (1967).

2

Perspective: White Solidarity?

There is a great bitterness [between Afrikaners] as we had this morning here . . .
that a [National Party] candidate—when I made a little joke this morning—
almost cursed me. A candidate! I'm not talking about . . . The only thing I
asked him was, "Pal [pointing to blacks playing football on a nearby field],
isn't this the thing we are fighting against? This sort of integration, this
noise, this lack of self-discipline. These people have their own facilities."
He then replied: "Man, what's going on in your own backyard?" [meaning
that all whites have live-in servants]. Then the man launched into a personal
attack, and one word followed the other. And [if] you call this person a
candidate, then I prefer to respect my garden boy more.[1]

The man I was talking to had a serious expression on his face. He was an
electoral officer of the Conservative Party. We were standing at the polling
booths on October 26, 1988, municipal election day. It was one of those
glorious South African spring mornings where the air was filled with the
smell of blossoms and freshly mown Kikuyu grass. The polling station
consisted of two marquee tents on the corner of a rugby field of a nearby
school. Some young men were kicking a soccer ball on the field. We were
in Mayfair, a suburb of Johannesburg. The men on the field were black.

This was an auspicious day. Municipal elections were usually not that
important to white South Africans anyway. This time it was different. The
National Party (NP), which had been ruling the country for forty years,
had spun a formidable net of legislation entrapping the entire population
in a system of oppressive structures. Now it was backing off under pressure
and slackening the enforcement of its laws, notably the Group Areas Act.[2]
As a result, people of "racial" heritages different from that of whites had
gradually moved into areas set aside by law for exclusive occupation by
the white group. This happened in poorer white areas, one of which was

Mayfair. Since 1983 the Conservative Party (CP) had fought against the reform, liberalization, and relaxation of racist legislation in an attempt to restore the system of racial domination prevalent in the 1960s.

The CP official at the polling booth knew his party's policies very well. The CP wanted to restore Mayfair to the whites but also desired to clean up the city by removing all "nonwhites," including the young black men playing on the field, to their "own" areas. He confronted the NP candidate in what he thought was a joking way. But even in paraphrasing his own words when he told me the story he revealed a serious tone, an irritation built on his "negative" experience. He maintained that blacks had their own facilities and should not share space with whites. The Nationalist, in response, homed in on the ambiguity and contradiction of white lifestyles: Whites were dependent on black labor, but refused to share equally with blacks everyday-life spaces and facilities. Many of the legal and interpersonal intricacies involved in the brief interaction sequence recounted above will be explained below.

The theme of the above quotation reveals the problem and perspective of the study reported on in this volume. The problem, according to the speaker and his National Party counterpart, was the presence of blacks in a "white" country. Should blacks be accommodated in a system shared by black and white, or should they be accommodated in a dispensation separate from that of the whites? Both the Conservative Party man and the Nationalist assumed that the solution to that problem lay in the hands of the white section of the population. Building on their assumptions, I wish to reformulate the issue by problematizing their unquestioning attitude that the power to change South Africa lies in the hands of whites only. It is this attitude that underlay their reluctance and, in the case of the Conservatives, their intransigence toward power sharing and their refusal to negotiate with the black majority or its leaders. It is the taken-for-granted notion that whites move history in South Africa that transcends the divisions of political orientation (conservative/liberal), cultural difference (immigrant, Afrikaans/English heritage), and language (Afrikaans/English as language communities). It is also the dimension of power that provides a key to understanding the pervasiveness of social solidarity among whites. After explaining the rationale for the study and reviewing the literature, I will argue that a convergence has occurred among the various white subdivisions and has cohered around the issue of power in recent years.

South Africa has been a focus of international attention more than ever during the past 10 years. Its racial conflicts have inspired many inquiries, fanned by the concerns of groups with moral, political, economic, and academic interests. Most of the attention has been devoted to the problems of the victims of oppression. Major funding has been provided to projects that highlight the plight of these victims and what can be done about it.[3] The main rationale of this inquiry is closely tied to the observation that it is hard to anticipate the nature of any possible transformation of South African society, violent or less violent, without an intimate knowledge of white values and white predispositions to political action. It is also extremely difficult to understand how such a powerful minority as the whites will fit into a postapartheid society without more knowledge about how they think about and construct boundaries vis-à-vis other groups. I do not claim to provide clear answers to such questions in this volume; a separate book is therefore planned to address the policy implications of issues raised here.

Looking at the available literature, one is struck by the great number of publications dealing with South African whites. Few, however, express at the same time both insider and social scientifically informed perspectives. Insider perspectives provide fascinating and revealing insights into the forms of white consciousness. Authors abound across the total political spectrum, and their work tells us as much or more about the authors themselves, as South African whites, as it does about the political situation. I will refer to these works and use them in my subsequent analysis. Among Afrikaans authors, titles range from the right-wing, optimistic *The Third War of Liberation Is Being Waged: We Can Win!* (Bruwer, 1986) to the liberal, hesitant *What Happens After Apartheid? Young Afrikaners Speak Out* (Landman, Nel, & van Niekerk, 1988) and the terminal *The Last White Parliament* (van Zyl Slabbert, 1985). The mere fact that these works have been published presumes that they are considered worthwhile as descriptions, opinions, and ideas. They give voices to emerging or real opinion leaders. The ordinary person and supposed consumer of these ideas and visions seldom gets a word in. On the other hand, many whites seemed to be preoccupied with a quest for the historical meaning of their presence in Southern Africa (I will elaborate upon this later). The South African emigré Marq de Villiers should be singled out for producing a most illuminating family history in his *White Tribe Dreaming: Apartheid's Bitter Roots as Witnessed by Eight Generations of an Afrikaner Family* (1988). It is less an academic treatise than a careful personalized attempt to reinterpret a history that has so often been reconstructed as a charter for oppression. Rian Malan's *My Traitor's Heart: A South African Exile Returns to Face His Country, His Tribe and His Conscience* (1990) is written in a similar vein, though it is more anecdotal in style.

Among English speakers there is a less prolific record of self-presentation of the kind referred to above. The reason may possibly be found in these authors' tendency to write either analytic (i.e., academically inspired) works or serious literature. Nadine Gordimer's name is the first that springs to mind in this category. A large part of her work deals with the lives of social actors and their experiences in a world dominated by inequality. The analytic works are not specifically written from a "tribal" (i.e., parochial English-speaking) point of view, although it is hard to divorce them from the social framework of their creation. These authors tend to regard themselves more as members of a community of scholars than as ex-colonials or colonials. English-speaking authors tend to problematize other groups, notably the Afrikaners and the Afrikaner-led government, rather than whites in general as causes and explanations for the country's misery. Afrikaner racism or ethnocentrism is blamed for South Africa's moral, political, and economic decline. The growing body of Marxist scholarship among young South African intellectuals deviates from this tendency by singling out capitalism rather than ethnocentrism as the root of the country's problems. This discourse will be discussed in Chapter 6.

Highly illuminating and informative are the works of journalists who have managed to document in most vivid fashion their day-to-day experiences in South Africa, intertwining them with a wealth of data about leaders and social structures. One of the best examples in this category is the work of Joseph Lelyveld. In *Move Your Shadow* (1985), Lelyveld presents a very good investigative account of white roles in race relations, but he essentially remains the outsider looking in at South African society from the privileged vantage point of a senior journalist for the *New York Times.* He had access to both the chic liberal white cocktail circuits and to some government officials and black leaders willing to talk to him. His observations are sometimes stunningly sharp, documenting in captivating prose realities that mostly escape the attention of even the trained social scientist. James North, author of *Freedom Rising* (1985), actually lived in a white South African community and thus familiarized himself with the values and interactive styles of the members of that community. William Finnegan, an American like Lelyveld and North, taught at a coloured school and was thus in a unique position to observe from close quarters the interaction between white and coloured teachers and their pupils, which he describes in *Crossing the Line* (1986). In a subsequent work titled *Dateline Soweto* (1988) he describes his experiences in accompanying black journalists to areas of political unrest.

Quite a number of accounts such as those described above exist, and they tend to be published with increased frequency when South African news captures headlines in the international press. Their main value lies in their documentation of their authors' personal experiences, and they thus rank as eyewitness accounts in the directness of their reporting. One drawback of journalistic accounts is their lack of methodological and theoretical rigor, but this sort of rigor might have killed the attraction these works have had for a wide readership.

I now wish to give substance to the perspective of this study discussed in Chapter 1. This volume focuses on the everyday experiences of whites in South Africa in order to make sense of the ways in which they talk, make their choices, and construct their actions in a complex arena of racial and ethnic interaction. It is in the world of everyday life that people from various backgrounds and legally defined statuses interact and interpret each other's intentions and acts. It is also in the everyday context that iniquitous laws made themselves felt, both as advantaging and disadvantaging mechanisms. My inquiry therefore focuses on daily life in contemporary South Africa. It is on this level that unequal treatment occurs, that discrimination is practiced by whites without being perceived as abnormal or morally reprehensible. This is the level of uncritical acceptance of actions and interaction patterns, modes of address, reference, and talk about nonwhites and about themselves. It is a universe largely invisible to the individual immersed in it and rarely articulated by him or her. The study of the world taken for granted by whites is thus beset by difficulties and pitfalls reluctantly faced by many social scientists, who would rather aim at documenting the much more verbalized opinions and attitudes of people or their demographic profiles. Yet looking for the unquestioned constructs and values held among a population is of great importance in making sense of, or anticipating, spontaneous actions. For example, how can we explain the lack of resistance, or even the willingness, of white police officers ordered to shoot into a crowd of people running away from them? How are we to understand the ease with which white officials could uproot centuries-old black communities, bulldoze the homes, and "resettle" the residents under extremely harsh conditions on the barren, infertile veld? These questions cannot be properly addressed unless we first engage in a serious effort to make visible and to articulate the realm of unquestioned constructs adhered to by these actors, the realm of implicit meanings they share.

It is not my intention here to dwell on the sensational and outrageous aspects of racial discrimination. Rather, I will examine the mundane and routine lives of "ordinary" whites. In recent studies much attention has been devoted to the words and actions of leaders, opinion makers, the intelligentsia, rulers, politicians, and other manipulators and articulators of what is known as the "dominant discourse." Researchers have tended to collect interviews and speeches of party leaders and academics in the hope of discovering patterns in the unfolding political process. Authors favoring both the reformist and conflict models of change have seemed to agree on the assumption that the spokespersons' formulations of ideologies and strategies are the data that really count for making an assessment of political developments in South Africa. Antonio Gramsci has attained a lively following among neo-Marxist scholars, especially his work on the "collective will formulation" and the intellectual and moral leadership of intellectuals (see, e.g., Gramsci, 1971). Similarly, among more conservative and right-wing authors there has been a hope of achieving change in South Africa through consensus and negotiation politics. One-sided attention has been devoted to the role of the political elite and leaders. In itself, this inclination may reveal an authoritarian, less democratic attitude on the part of these authors.

In my view, the relationship between leaders and their constituencies in any given society is always a dynamic, if not a dialectical, one. Leaders rise from the ranks of their potential followers, and followers are "brought to life" by their potential leaders. To view leaders one-sidedly as agents of change is misleading. Formulated in a classical sociological way: The probability of leaders' (the wielders of authority) finding and inspiring a following depends on their constituencies' willingness and interest to obey them.[4] Leadership and authority make sense not only through the claims of the leaders themselves, but even more so through the predisposition of ordinary people to lend support and loyalty to such leaders. It is important to examine the social preconditions that produce political and ideological leadership. These preconditions are traceable to the everyday context of interaction and typification encountered among real or potential followers.

Numerous works critical of the apartheid system deal with whites' roles in historical rather than ethnographic fashion. Other publications analyze the concentration of political power in white hands. The Afrikaner section receives the most attention, if not, as I have mentioned, the blame for the system of racial inequality. These studies are too numerous to review here individually. Some of the more prominent works include those by Adam and Giliomee (1979a, 1979b), Thompson (1985), and Frederickson (1981). Moodie's *The Rise of Afrikanerdom* (1975) still remains an important contribution to the historical sociology of the Afrikaner. Vernon February

(1991), a native speaker of Afrikaans, undertook an analysis of language use in Afrikaans literary, legal, and political texts. He examined how oppression and inequality became embedded in and perpetuated through the language. The objectives of his study come pretty close to my own, because he was dealing with meaning structures embedded in texts. My emphasis, however, will be on verbalizations in talk and nonverbal aspects of interaction.

THEORETICAL INTERLUDE

I have attempted an ethnographic investigation of currently held meanings and values that guide political and economic actions among broad layers of the white South African population. Apart from the fact that whites have been neglected in recent studies, the question of the nature and boundaries of *South African whites* as the unit of analysis requires attention: Are we dealing with whites as a racial, ethnic, or class entity? As analytic tools, the concepts of race, ethnicity, and class provide separate and illuminating perspectives on the South African dilemma. The analytic categories should be distinguished from empirical labels. As Max Weber (1978) has incisively pointed out, both *race* and *ethnicity* are theoretically ambiguous terms (pp. 385-395). I wish to distinguish between the terms *ethnicity* and *ethnic group*; *ethnicity* will be used here in an analytic sense, whereas *ethnic group* will describe the empirical, subjectively experienced reality of an in-group. Weber foresaw that the "collective term 'ethnic' would be abandoned, for it is unsuitable for a really rigorous analysis" (p. 395). What he referred to were empirical and subjective self-constructions of groups in "ethnic" terms. These are commonsense, everyday, and taken-for-granted constructions. We simply cannot elevate them to the status of analytic—that is, scientific—constructs. Ethnic groups can therefore construct themselves on the basis of language, religion, culture, descent, or a combination of these and other features. An ethnic group may even shift the basis on which it constructs its identity from one feature to another. Historical ethnic groups may merge and found their solidarity on a new basis. It is this dynamic conception of an ethnic group that is used in the text.

I wish to highlight how whites in South Africa recently moved from self-definitions that blurred the old ethnic distinction between English and Afrikaans speakers on one level and, on another, rendered less distinct the line between racial and ethnic groups by redrawing ethnic boundaries along racial lines. From the outset, I have to state that any discussion of ethnicity or ethnic groups in South Africa is necessarily highly emotion laden. The black population learned through the experience of many decades that the ethnic group, as an ascriptive and enforced category, had dire consequences for their lives. It was in terms of this categorization that they were uprooted from their residential areas and lost their jobs, their nationality, and a host of other things valuable to them. On the other hand, in the eyes of the dominating and exploiting white minority, the concept of the ethnic group had a positive connotation and served as an objective justification for their separate privileged existence and for the measures they employed to uphold it.[5] These emphases may sound strange to the ears of members of ethnic minorities in large, complex societies, such as in the United States, who embrace their ethnic identities with feelings of pride and as places of refuge in a mass society.

HISTORICAL WHITE ETHNIC GROUPS

It was not without reason that the Afrikaner section of the white population was blamed for the institutionalized inequality in South Africa. However, the Afrikaners' initially ethnically based party, the National Party, inherited much of its structural racism from the Afrikaners' predecessors. When they assumed political office, they perfected an existing system of segregation. This perfected system became known as *apartheid,* and it did indeed serve the interests of Afrikaners, who continued entrenching it by legal and constitutional means. Before the constitutional deliberations of the 1990s, Afrikaner racist policies were severely criticized and condemned by liberal English-speaking South Africans, but these liberals tacitly and gratefully acquiesced in the awareness that these policies served some of their own deep-seated economic interests. They needed the order and stability of NP rule to continue their pursuits. This symbiosis of apparently opposing groups frequently escaped the attention of serious inquiry. This cannot be said of the prolific Marxist scholarship on South Africa, which has unearthed a wealth of historical material in its pursuit of class analysis. In Marxist analyses, all whites are usually lumped into the ruling class or the propertied classes (see, e.g., Murray, 1987). The research underlying the present study, however, focuses on subjective processes rather than on the objective forms of class. Another approach looks at how Afrikaners mobilized ethnic power for political purposes (Adam & Giliomee, 1979a, chap. 3; Adam & Moodley, 1986, pp. 30-31). As a broad analytic concept, ethnic mobilization has its uses, and I believe that also applies to the present case, where ethnic boundaries are being redrawn. However, looking at the ethnic mobilization of the Afrikaner alone in the present situation is not appropriate anymore. In my view, using the concept of ethnic group consciousness in the broader sense of a strategic self-identification by South African whites may prove to be more useful in the final analysis.

Cultural organizations such as the Federation of Afrikaans Cultural Organizations (FAK) and the 1820 Settlers (Association) staunchly uphold the historical differences between the two language groups. However, the growing awareness among whites of the political aspirations of the black majority in the country has led to a political realignment bridging many of the older cultural boundaries between the two main white components of the South African population. In the years immediately following World War II, white voting patterns were largely split on an ethnic basis. Those Afrikaners who still supported the old opposition United Party, comprising both English and Afrikaans speakers, were gradually swayed to join the National Party. The NP grew in strength during the 1950s and 1960s, mobilizing the support of Afrikaners and some English speakers for the idea of a Republic of South Africa in 1960. The strong anticommunist stance of the government in the aftermath of the Rivonia trial of African National Congress (ANC) leaders accused of attempting to overthrow the state by violent means (1963-1964) added to the popularity of the government among a broad segment of the white population. Economic and political interests of both Afrikaners and English speakers converged strongly during the 1960s. The old notion of a "black peril," so assiduously propagated by Afrikaner politicians since the 1950s, now gave way to its redefinition as the "communist peril." Black nationalism, resistance to apartheid, and almost every other form of protest were associated with communism or communist instigators. This served members of the English-speaking commercial and industrial class well as they dealt with their black laborers' growing resistance to low wages and exploitation. The anticommunism of the 1960s thus had the function of cementing Afrikaans and English speakers. English public rhetoric denied the existence of such a community of interest, however, because it was bad publicity at the time.

Looking at the available literature on the everyday lives and perceptions of ordinary whites, it strikes one how little has been written. The work of Vincent Crapanzano (1985) stands out in this regard. He describes a rather atypical white community in the Cape Province, which, he concedes, is isolated and immobile (p. 14). An experienced anthropologist, Crapanzano has produced a remarkable, vivid documentation of everyday life in a rural town. However, he remained an outsider, and he tends to underestimate the influence his strangeness to the community had on the account he gives of it. He displays more understanding of the lives of English speakers than of those of Afrikaners, whose language he obviously does not speak. The misspelling of numerous Afrikaans and Sintu (a black language) words and names in the book only reinforces the impression that his understanding and interpretation of the meanings of many of his informants may be less than trustworthy. His speculations about the cultural dimensions of the Afrikaans language (pp. 30-34) tend to sound hollow. In all, however, his work is methodologically interesting and, in a sense, pioneering.

The Afrikaner-dominated government's ruthless suppression of the black youth revolt of the mid-1970s encountered vociferous protest from a waning minority of English speakers. Their protest tended to be articulated more strongly by elitist voluntary organizations, such as the South African Institute of Race Relations and the Black Sash, than by any political party represented in Parliament. The weak opposition to the introduction of a new race-based constitution in 1983 by the predominantly English-speaker-supported Progressive Federal Party is a further indication of the declining significance of an ethnic basis to party politics. Many English speakers and the largest English-language newspapers came out in support of the new constitution.

In the mid-1980s, black political dissidence triggered the state of emergency declared in 1986. After its renewal in 1988, the state of emergency was lifted in June 1990. This move was made largely in response to pressure by the ANC and the international community. The government was also concerned with creating a favorable atmosphere for negotiating the country's future. Strict media controls in place at the time I was conducting my research prevented me from gauging the strength of white opposition. There was ample evidence, however, that the strong-arm methods of the government in the maintenance of "law and order" and the manipulation of information were seen largely as necessary though "unfortunate" means of ensuring the survival of the economy and thereby the political order in South Africa. Whites in general were furthermore unified in their condemnation of internationally imposed sanctions.

Among a broad spectrum of whites, then, there has occurred over the past few years a convergence of economic and political interests. I discuss below the factors that have contributed to the greater solidarity based on "whiteness" in recent times.

THE EROSION OF
AFRIKANER ETHNIC SOLIDARITY

During the past half century, three occasions highlighted Afrikaner socio-cultural solidarity very clearly. The first was the 1938 reenactment of the Ossewatrek (Great Trek) of 1838. Afrikaners from all walks of life joined in the celebration of their "most wondrous divine election and predesti-nation" to conquer the country and subject its inhabitants to their "Christian," "civilized" rule. Much of the enthusiasm and pathos of these celebrations derived from the Afrikaners' sense of being an oppressed people in their own land. The momentum and messianic fervor generated by the Ossewatrek of 1938 helped the ethnically based National Party to victory in 1948. The election victory of 1948 was the second time Afrikaners experienced unity, but this time it was combined with the political triumph of a self-righteous nationalism entitling them to privilege in "their own country." The third occasion at which Afrikaners experienced a high degree of solidarity was the declaration of a republic in 1961. At this time Afrikaner power consolidated itself and found support in both rural and urban contexts. The political foundations were by now laid for establishing South Africa as the whites'—more specifically, the Afrikaners'—country by excluding blacks more than ever from the political process through the creation of Bantustans. Bantustans were marginal territories in which blacks were expected to find their "own" cultural and political identities. Afrikaners established a moral rationale for the exclusion of blacks from South Africa in a massive and ascriptive projection of the matrix of their own people-hood onto the different language groupings among blacks, but the neces-sary economic infrastructure and political awareness to support such mini-ature nation-states were nonexistent. The Bantustan policies can be viewed as indicators and reflections of the relevance that cultural and political identity had for the ruling Afrikaners. In the process of enforcing white exclusivity through a series of humiliating laws, the government elicited protest and resistance from a black population whose impatience was growing. One such act of protest led to the Sharpeville massacre of March 1960.

The Sharpeville massacre was a watershed for both Afrikaner and black politics. The black nationalist ANC now turned away from the passive resistance and peaceful protest of previous decades to a strategy of limited violence. At the same time, the first cracks appeared in Afrikaner sociocul-tural and political solidarity. A number of Afrikaans church leaders and laypeople voiced their shock and moral revulsion over the Sharpeville incident. On the literary front, figures such as N. P. van Wyk-Louw (1972) expressed their careful doubts about the moral purity of some Afrikaner historical heroes, only to be publicly and savagely rebutted by then Prime Minister H. F. Verwoerd. A new dissident Afrikaans literary genre produced by the *sestigers* (authors of the sixties) divided a readership that, until now, had largely been nurtured by romantic novels about a nostalgic rural past. English speakers also experienced diversification. In 1959 the Progressive Party was founded to cater to the more liberal minded, whereas conservative English speakers sustained their allegiance to the successor of the old United Party.

A process of political, and in a sense cultural, realignment was set in motion in the 1960s. In the wake of the anticommunist scare of the mid-1960s, the government took great care not to move too close to some liberals. However, it was in this period that W. J. de Klerk, editor of an Afrikaans newspaper, made a distinction between two sorts of Afrikaners: *verligtes* and *verkramptes.* The *verligtes,* or enlightened Afrikaners, took a less hard-line and more pragmatic attitude toward race relations, whereas the *verkramptes,* or traditionalists, held on to their ideology of domination and racial exclusiveness. The enlightened Afrikaners dominated the white political culture of the 1970s. This development was not unrelated to the fact that some members of the white (traditionalist) labor class became so disillusioned with the government that they founded their own party, the Herstigte Nasionale Party (Reestablished National Party) (HNP), to the right of the Nationalist government in 1969. During the 1970s the Nationalists also carefully planned the co-optation of the members of the mostly English-speaking business community. They were not only deemed indispensable for the future economic development of the country along apartheid lines, they were also incorporated into the administrative framework of Nationalist labor policies. In the process, the onus of the execution of labor apartheid fell on the mainly English-speaking business community, which, if at all, voiced only weak opposition to its new role. The convergence of government and the business community continued right into the 1990s, when the government took its cue from business practice itself in its effort to privatize many quasi-government institutions, such as transport and the postal system. Some commentators see this trend as an attempt by the ruling whites to consolidate their interests, thus corroborating the argument that white solidarity across the linguistic divide is increasing.

ORGANIZATIONAL MANIFESTATIONS OF
SHIFTS IN WHITE ETHNIC ALLEGIANCES

In early 1982, a major split occurred in the National Party when the Conservative Party broke away. It gained an unexpectedly high degree of support in the 1987 elections and made a near clean sweep in the Transvaal and in Northern Natal during the white municipal elections of October 1988. It created a major political upset through its successes in by-elections. The most spectacular of these was the party's success in the Potchefstroom constituency in February 1992. Potchefstroom was considered a safe seat by the National Party, yet the CP unseated the NP by a wide margin. The CP drew additional support from other splinter movements, such as the Afrikaner Resistance Movement (AWB). Apart from its political clout, the CP is a manifestation of the revival of the spirit that prevailed among Afrikaners in the period leading up to the 1960s. The ideal of a state where whites, under the cultural and political hegemony of the Afrikaner, would predominate expressed itself in the notion of a *volkstaat* (people's state) or *Boerestaat* (Boer state). Blacks would be tolerated in this state only insofar as they sold their labor. Otherwise they would have no right to be there. The country as a whole would be partitioned into one white area and a number of black areas. Generally, promoters of the white state assumed that Afrikaners would remain the dominant group there. Asked whether their insistence on whiteness as criterion for citizenship was not racist, they explained that the Afrikaner was the dominant ethnic group in the white community. Those in the English-speaking group had close cultural and religious affinities with Afrikaners. They had no such affinities with any other group in South Africa and therefore belonged to the white community on ethnic grounds. Their self-legitimation thus ultimately rested on the argument of ethnic identity as the foundation for their *Boerestaat*. Even the ultra-right-wing Afrikaner Resistance Movement insisted that the English speakers who came out in support of the *Boerestaat* "were truly our brothers."[6]

In the municipal elections of 1988 the NP, as the mainstream political party, lost considerable support to the right, but gained many votes from white Anglophones to the middle and left of the political spectrum. Apart from some influence the Progressive Federal Party (PFP) retained in the metropolitan areas, it dwindled virtually into insignificance elsewhere. Its insistence on multiracialism and individual human rights went too far for many Anglophone whites, who, in recent years, had come to share fears of an impending chaos believed to be inherently linked to democratic majority (black) rule. The National Party, in contrast, successfully managed its image of a reasonable and responsible government. It made use of its well-entrenched power base to manipulate voters through public media such as the state-owned television and various daily newspapers owned by private corporations sympathetic to the government.

Without relinquishing the premise of group rights and separate political representation of blacks, the NP nevertheless acknowledged the interdependence of the various sectors of the South African population. Until 1991 the NP held power sharing with blacks to be a long-term political ideal, but how it was to be achieved was left unclear. The rhetoric surrounding this ideal assuaged many Christians whose consciences had been activated by disclosures about the living conditions of blacks in the country as well as by international pressures. The NP, I will argue, is just an organizational manifestation of a wider in-group consciousness of whites.[7] During the four field trips I undertook between 1988 and 1991 I was amazed at the degree of solidarity that existed among Afrikaans- and English-speaking elites. Their educational qualifications and financial standing enabled them to influence large sectors of the white middle class. A new national pride was manifested in the unanimous rejection of foreign interference in South African economic and political matters and the self-congratulatory attitude that they were "making it" regardless of pressure from outside the country's borders. However, the deteriorating economy and the effects of international sanctions left their mark. Toward the beginning of the 1990s, they started using arguments of economic rationality to justify the abolition of certain apartheid laws. They refused to concede that their change of attitude was a result of external pressures. These whites were aware of their rootedness in South Africa, and their economy of survival was a symbol of it. They generally professed an "understanding" of the South African situation that the politically and economically interfering foreigners did not have. It was this understanding, this sharing of meaning, that distinguished this category of whites from their European and American critics. Their "understanding" informed them that majority rule was not the rational solution for the country because of the chaos that might ensue when black interethnic war and competition would engulf the black population in a postapartheid situation. In fact, the strife between members of Inkatha and the ANC was seen in exactly this light.

Whites assumed that they, as a politically and culturally cohesive group, were a powerful force whose know-how and sense of order guaranteed the relative stability of the country and the life chances of the various groups inhabiting it. The new white left-wing coalition assembled at the beginning of 1989 as the Democratic Party (DP), though representing a small minority of white liberal intellectuals, still was ambiguous about protecting group rights rather than individual rights. After the government released Nelson Mandela, legalized the previously banned ANC, and abolished some cornerstone laws of apartheid in 1991, the DP was largely outflanked and lost much of its support to the National Party.

DISCUSSION

Whereas the "ethnicity" of the conservative groups rigidly emphasized "white nationhood" in a separate territory,[8] more liberal whites had an open approach to territorial boundaries. The boundary to them was a cultural one, but it also involved, at least as far as the present was concerned, some form of legal protection for maintaining group identity. "Whiteness," as an ethnic group identifier, was used more explicitly by the conservatives than by the reformists. The reformists, however, made it abundantly clear in their reform initiatives that they considered their own in-group to be white. The disagreement between these two segments was not about whether or not white group identity should be preserved, but about how to go about it. The conservatives were very resentful of reformist policies, which they considered the beginning of an irreversible process of integration. In their eyes, reformists were naive and shortsighted, unable to understand that they were putting whites on a road to racial assimilation that would result in integration and the disappearance of their group and the values it stands for. On the other hand, reformists deemed conservatives to be crudely racist. They gave the country a bad name and reinforced the worst stereotypes foreign countries had of South Africa. From the viewpoint of reformists, conservatives fanned racial hatred and increased the probability of violent conflict and the destruction of a white power base. In the short term they hampered the reform initiatives of the present government, which were meant to improve South Africa's image abroad and were designed to attract foreign investment. Reformists felt ashamed about the pronouncements and actions of conservatives.

Both reformists and conservatives, however, felt themselves to be united by a "brotherhood," and the bitter differences between the two sides were regarded as *broedertwis* (strife between brothers). Conservatives were angry with the reformists and considered using limited violence against their brothers in order to bring them into line. On August 9, 1991, these threats and smaller acts of violence culminated in the deaths of two AWB members. The AWB tried to break up a political meeting addressed by the state president in Ventersdorp. Shots were fired, and two AWB members were killed by the police. The minister officiating at the funeral of one of these men symbolically stated, "When brother is menacingly pitched against brother, [God] intervenes as the Elder Brother—not to keep us apart, but to bring us together in a new way" (quoted in *Beeld,* August 15, 1991).[9] However divided these brothers might be with regard to the means, it is my argument that both sides agreed that the strife was motivated by a common concern: the survival of whites as a group.

Whereas such strong emotional values as group survival reveal group boundaries clearly, there were a number of other indicators that demonstrated, though less blatantly, the same tendency. The ethnography of speaking about others disclosed a consistent pattern of in- and out-group linguistic conventions among whites (see Chapters 7-10). Another important indicator of white solidarity is the "understanding" whites believe they have about the nature of South Africa's problem. This shared set of meanings distinguishes this understanding from opinions held by groups that I will call *external outsiders* and *internal outsiders.* External outsiders are the foreigners of the United States and Europe; internal outsiders are radicals and blacks in South Africa who, for obvious reasons, have different "understandings" of the situation. Lifestyle is another area that whites shared and in which they experienced comfort and familiarity. In fact, lifestyle is one of the realities they explicitly wished to preserve, with regard to the standard of living and its reliance on cheap black labor.

Two other problems require attention here. First, whites in South Africa speak two different languages. Given that it is my hypothesis that whiteness is a form of ethnicity, can I still argue that both language groups belong to one ethnic group? The question poses a genuine problem, and academic discourse fails to throw much light on the matter. A great deal of published material on ethnic groups deals with disadvantaged minorities within larger societal frameworks. The next unit larger than the ethnic group is the nation within which language groups can be accommodated (e.g., the Belgian nation, with its Flemish- and French-speaking components). Substituting *nation* for *white ethnic group* in the South African situation is highly problematic (although certain conservatives do exactly this).[10] To me, whites are a subgroup within the South African nation. For the moment, I will not enter into a discussion of the labels and the ideologies surrounding them. It is clear, however, that "white" ethnic consciousness has an intersubjective basis. It therefore cannot be argued that it is merely a figment of the analyst's imagination. I believe it is possible to conceptualize this entity as an ethnic group. Though it lacks one important common symbolic system, language, there seems to be sufficient evidence that, as a group, it subjectively shares a culture along a number of identifiable dimensions.[11]

Second, we have to consider the position of white integrationists and radicals. They had very little influence on dominant white politics during the 1980s. They were regarded as a traitorous nuisance to be dealt with within the context of security legislation, that is, through bannings, imprisonment (with or without trial), or straightforward assassination by official bodies such as the Bureau of Civil Cooperation.[12] At present this component of the white population is minute, but it is growing because it recruits from a dissenting and increasingly critical stratum of young intellectuals at universities.

Conservative and reformist whites alike deny that they are racists. They maintain that the differences between South African population groups are of a cultural and religious nature. However, it would be irresponsible to take these ideological pronouncements as sole evidence for the "mere" ethnic nature of the white group. There is ample evidence of the presence of a strong racial component in their judgments of, and actions toward, ethnically different outsider groups. Racial (like sexist) language pervades the talk of everyday life of both reformists and conservatives. It is most blatantly evident among the latter. In social interaction, the treatment meted out to blacks in the workplace, whether in the domestic or the industrial sphere, reveals subtle and unsubtle instances of racism. In the following chapters I hope to demonstrate this situation by using concrete evidence from my field material.

"Whiteness" as a self-identifying term has been used openly by ultra-right-wingers. Recently, Conservative Party officials and reformists have been hesitant to use the term because of its racial overtones and resultant bad publicity. In the absence of explicit verbal evidence, the way they draw the ethnic boundaries of their group in word and action evidently follow the lines of race. The context of inequality and oppression in which whites justify their separate existence exposes their argument that their ethnic consciousness is culturally and not racially based. Racism thus masquerades as cultural ethnic awareness. Whites' self-definition of their status as an ethnic group should be clearly distinguished as their own creation, as a social construction. Thus it should not be confused with the anthropological and sociological discourse on the heuristic and analytic significance of the concept of ethnicity when we are reflecting on and making social scientific sense of the way whites achieved social and cultural solidarity in South Africa.

NOTES

1. Unless otherwise noted, all translations in this book from Afrikaans to English are my own. The Afrikaans original of this man's remarks follows:

Daar is baie bitterheid, daar is baie bitterheid soos ons vanoggend hier . . . dat 'n kandidaat toe ek vanoggend 'n ligte grappie maak, my feitlik vloek. 'n Kandidaat! Ek praat nie van 'n . . . Al wat ek vir hom gevra het: "Kyk ou maat, is dit nie waarteen ons baklei nie? Hierdie tipe integrasie [Hy verwys hier na die Swartes wat op die voetbalveld langs die stemtente gespeel het], hierdie lawaai, hierdie onbeheersdheid. Die mense het hulle eie geriewe." Toe sê hy vir my: "Man, hoe dink jy lyk dit in jou eie agterplaas?" Toe raak die ou persoonlik en die een woord op die ander woord. En as dít 'n kandidaat is, dan wil ek so waar as wragtig my tuinjong meer respekteer, eerlikwaar.

2. This is formally known as the Group Areas Act No. 41 of 1950.

3. This type of research project finds it hard to acquire funding because, understandably, foundations feel morally obliged to support research for "action" projects among the underprivileged black masses. Requests for support for research among the privileged white minority have been met with embarrassment and apologies in the past. In one instance, a foundation expressed anxiety that such support might be misunderstood by the black community. Ironically, it was the South African Council of Churches' (SACC) Asingeni Fund that gave limited support for a project proposal submitted by D. E. Forsythe and me on Afrikaners. The SACC has been involved in numerous action projects helping local black communities to help themselves under the apartheid system.

4. This is a somewhat modified formulation of Max Weber's (1978) notion of authority, which "is the probability that a command . . . will be obeyed by a given group of persons" (p. 53) and further, as far as legitimate authority is concerned, it "implies a minimum of voluntary compliance, that is, an *interest* (based on ulterior motives or genuine acceptance) in obedience" (p. 212).

5. For an extended discussion of the South African definitions of ethnic groups, see Sharp (1988).

6. The Conservative Party had its greatest successes in the Transvaal. Humphries, Schlemmer, and Stack (1990, p. 25) found that the CP had the following support in urban constituencies in the Transvaal (their poll is not dated, but it seems to have been conducted at the beginning of 1990). In large urban constituencies, the breakdown was as follows: upper-middle class areas, 10%; areas with English constituencies with substantial apartments, cosmopolitan residents, students, and young families, 11%; English-speaking middle-class areas, 26%; Afrikaans-speaking or mixed middle-class areas, 41%; Afrikaans or mixed lower-middle working-class areas, 52%. In rural and small urban constituencies, the CP gained 56% of the vote, and in small town areas, 57%. The findings of this poll seem to be corroborated by the results of a by-election in the predominantly English-speaking constituency of Umlazi in the port city of Durban. The CP gained 44% of the vote in a formerly very safe seat of the NP (Humphries et al., 1990, p. 27).

7. The National Party still had the support of the majority of whites toward the middle of 1990. A poll by the Afrikaans newspaper *Rapport* conducted before and after the general election of 1989 and after the unbanning of the ANC and PAC in February 1990 reveals a slight shift of support toward the NP. Most commentators agree that the Democratic Party lost support to the NP, which, after the unbanning of the ANC, started to take over aspects

of DP policy. The DP drew support predominantly from middle- and upper-middle-class English speakers. The NP, in turn, lost support to the CP (see Humphries et al., 1990, p. 24).

8. The quotation that opens this chapter, taken from an informal talk I had with an organizer of the CP on the day of the municipal elections, captures the difference between the "separatists" and the "reformists."

9. Ook as broer dreigend teenoor broer staan, tree Hy tussenbeide as oudste Broer. Nie om ons van mekaar weg te hou nie, maar om ons op 'n nuwe manier na mekaar terug te bring.

10. Stein and Hill's (1977) study on the new white ethnic movement in the United States unfortunately throws very little light on the current problem, because it deals with responses of subsections of the white American population to dominant culture.

11. Native Americans, for example, do not share a common indigenous language, yet may identify with each other as an ethnic minority.

12. The assassinations of Richard Turner, a political scientist, and the social anthropologist and antiapartheid activist David Webster by still-unidentified gunmen are cases demonstrating the extremes to which the elimination of "traitors within the gates" can be driven. Jacques Pauw (1991), a journalist with the *Vrye Weekblad,* has published a book revealing the underground activities of the Civil Cooperation Bureau. In it, he lists hundreds of black and white dissidents and civil rights workers who have been assassinated or who disappeared mysteriously.

3

The Emergence of the Past

[A people (*volk*)] has the need for myths to help support its ethnic existence. Even in those cases where their content is incongruent with the objective external historical or contemporary reality, they may yet mirror certain internal values and ideals that bind the community together through their acceptance of and faith in it. The point isn't whether myth is objective, true, or fictitious, but whether a community accepts it as a veritable rendering of what they regard as a truthful and authentic value or ideal. Such a myth has an inspiring value in a people's life. It has the value of creating ideals, positing norms, and integrating the people. . . . To debunk or to demythologize such a conviction can have a debilitating and destructive effect on a people. (Viljoen, 1978, p. 70)[1]

Gerrit Viljoen used these words in a speech delivered in 1971. At that time he was the rector of the Rand Afrikaans University in Johannesburg. He was later to become minister of national education and, still later, vice president. Viljoen stressed the importance of "myth" as an integrating factor in the life of a people (*volk*), more specifically, the Afrikaner people. He acknowledged, if not confessed, that reconstruction and falsification were necessary in order to achieve solidarity. In a cynical way, he was right. The reconstructions of the past were indeed functional falsifications. Their function lay in the present and the future. Historical reconstruction thus becomes the legitimation for the existing institutional order as well as a charter for future actions. Legitimation, as Berger and Luckmann (1972, p. 111) have pointed out, has both cognitive and normative dimensions. Legitimation thus implies values and knowledge as well as justification and explanation.

This chapter will look at the consecutive historical reconstructions made by whites in South Africa and the legitimations they provided for the institutional order. In Chapter 2, I made a distinction between reformists and conservatives, arguing that those in both categories share an understanding of the position of whites as a group. Turning now to history, it is striking how divisive the various renderings of the past have been. Historical reconstructions made by English speakers diverge widely from those made by the Afrikaners. Conflicting interpretations of South African history have served as ethnic boundary markers between Afrikaners and English speakers. I will now take a differentiated and diachronic view of how they have both reconstructed South African history in the past before looking at trends in the present. I particularly wish to examine whether the same convergence toward white solidarity suggested in Chapter 2 with regard to politics and social life existed in the historical self-reconstructions of whites.

Perspectives on history, and on historiography for that matter, reveal much about the time they were written, about the authors, and, above all, about the audiences to whom they were addressed. Before turning to audiences and the ways they have appropriated various versions of history at different times, I wish to give a brief account of both English and Afrikaner historiography. I will focus on those aspects that have actual or potential social and political relevance, in other words, on interpretations that have had consequences for the organization of human relations and interaction. Both historiographies, I argue, have been socially coconstructed by their respective audiences.

AFRIKANER HISTORIOGRAPHY

The first history written in Afrikaans was du Toit, Hoogenhout, and Malherbe's *Di Geskiedenis van Ons Land in di Taal van ons Volk* (The History of Our Country in the Language of Our People) (1877). This history was conceived in the context of the First Afrikaans Language Movement. This movement signaled the awakening of a cultural and ethnic consciousness among settlers of Dutch descent who no longer spoke pure Dutch but a local variant of it, Afrikaans. The movement strove to elevate the language from its humble, nonliterary status as a "kitchen language," or patois, to that of a respectable means of communication and expression. It therefore propagated the rule that people should write as they talk. The history du Toit et al. published in 1877 was born in a colonial situation where British cultural pretensions to cultural superiority were more and more resented by Afrikaners. Du Toit et al. articulated the need to instill among Afrikaners pride in their own language, history, and culture.

The First Language Movement was born of cultural resistance, and historiography was co-opted in the process. Political emancipation of the Afrikaner from British rule was not yet a dominant theme. However, du Toit et al., and others like them, maintained that histories written in English distort the image of the Afrikaner. They insisted that the record be set straight. It was their purpose to enhance the reputation of Afrikaner heroes among schoolchildren. *Afrikaner* in this context referred equally to inhabitants of the Cape and the two Boer republics. Their positive image was derived from the Voortrekker (emigrant pioneer from the Cape) and from the Boer (farmer). In these idealized descriptions of the lives and actions of pioneers one unfailingly encounters themes of martyrdom and suffering at the hands of imposed British rule. Du Toit et al.'s rendering of the Slagtersnek episode is emotional and contains the notion that God is on the side of the suffering Afrikaner.[2] The British annexation of the Transvaal in 1877 and the war waged by the Boers against the British in 1880-1881 prompted Afrikaner historians to elaborate further on the Afrikaner's role and mission in South African history. The theme of military conflict inspired historians to dwell on the justness of the Boer cause and on the justification of the Boers' presence in Africa as civilizers of the dark continent. C. P. Bezuidenhout, in his *De Geschiedenis van het Afrikaansche Geslacht van 1688 tot 1882* (The History of the Afrikaans People 1688 to 1882), published in 1883, drew an analogy between the Afrikaners and the Jews of the Old Testament (cited in Smith, 1988, p. 61). This analogy was to recur in the work of many Afrikanercentric histories to follow.

The aftermath of the Anglo-Boer War reinforced Afrikaner historians' zeal to place the Afrikaner in the center of South African history. This war, waged between the two Boer republics and Britain, led Afrikaners to make a clearer distinction between Cape Afrikaners and the Boers of the two republics. Cape Afrikaners, aside from a few rebels, were not involved in the struggle against England. They were accorded the image of a tolerant, easygoing, urban bourgeois population prone to suffering from "English-sickness," that is, liberalism. Because the Cape colony was not involved in the war, its population escaped suffering. The Transvalers and Free Staters bore the brunt of a brutal colonial war. In its final phases, the British followed a scorched-earth policy in order to destroy the Boer armies' food supplies and support. Crops were burned, animals destroyed, and homesteads torched. Women and children were removed to concentration camps, where almost 27,000 perished before the end of the war. Approximately 3,000 Boers fell in the war.

After the war, the British introduced an Anglicization policy, which added humiliation to Afrikaner suffering. It was in this context that the Afrikaner historiography of the first years of this century was produced. Afrikaner historians felt the need to restore a feeling of self to the Afrikaner, and they consciously engaged in the construction of glorifying myths of origin. For many years historians concentrated on the period from 1836, the start of the Great Trek, to 1902, the end of the Anglo-Boer War. It was as if those years and the Afrikaners' experience of them contained the meaning of the Afrikaners' existence and the formation of their identity. These historians maintained that a thorough knowledge of the history of one's people is prerequisite to the development of a sense of identity. Gustav Preller, who had fought in the Anglo-Boer War, saw the history of South Africa as the clash "between Afrikaner nationalism, British imperialism and black 'barbarism' " (Smith, 1988, p. 68). His serious concern was to restore Afrikaners' courage and self-esteem at a time when they felt dejected and demoralized. His first works described the heroism, leadership, courage, endurance, and moral character of Voortrekker leaders. The emphasis on great men as exemplars to subsequent generations has remained a feature of Afrikaner historiography to the present day. During the 1930s, Preller seemed to have absorbed some of the racial ideologies then fashionable on the European continent under national socialism. He explained the worldwide dominance of whites on the basis of their inherently superior intelligence. Preller's work coincided with the Second Afrikaans Language Movement, which was born in the wake of the bitterness following a colonial war. The literary products of this movement centered strongly on the pathos of an unjust war. The suffering of Afrikaners as a group was vividly and poetically portrayed in the works of J. F. E. Celliers, Eugène Marais, and J. D. du Toit. This emphasis was a far cry from the reactions to the colonial cultural imperialism addressed in the First Language Movement. Descriptions and poetic renderings of Afrikaner suffering were now anchored in the experiences of a generation and added a political emphasis to the cultural. Histories and literary works furthermore provided Afrikaners with a means of coping and living with the past by situating it in a moral context.

The moral and religious underpinning of history was an even greater hallmark of Afrikaner historiography in the second decade of this century. G. B. A. Gerdener, in his history of the "great man" Sarel Cilliers, combined a number of traditions about the clash between Boers and Zulus at Blood River and its aftermath in order to demonstrate how a covenant between God and the Voortrekkers was established. According to his version, the

Voortrekkers under Cilliers entered into a covenant with God in which they promised to build a church to his glory should they win the battle. At the same time, they allegedly solemnly undertook to celebrate the day of their victory as a "sabbath." Much to the chagrin of right-wingers, Gerdener's version of this event, connecting the covenant, the building of a church, and the notion of a sabbath, was later exposed as a fabrication.[3]

The Afrikanercentric view of history, with its strong emphasis on the Great Trek and the Anglo-Boer War, exposed yet another dimension as the Afrikaner struggle toward national political hegemony began. Not only was it necessary to address the problem of English domination, but the ubiquitous presence of the vast black population in a country perceived to be "white" received increased attention by historians. All white interest groups seemed to have agreed on the principle of territorial segregation of white and black after the unification of South Africa's four territories (provinces) in 1910. It was not until the 1930s that apartheid was contemplated as the solution to the "black problem." P. van Biljon published his Ph.D. thesis of 1937, *Grensbakens Tussen Blank en Swart in Suid-Afrika* (Boundary Markers Between Black and White in South Africa) in 1947 (cited in Stals, 1974).[4] This work found wide acclaim among Afrikaans audiences and especially among National Party politicians, who had insisted on its publication. They were on the point of taking over the government in 1948, and the thesis was a useful document. Van Biljon argued that racial segregation, or apartheid, typified the Afrikaner's national race policy at its best. In his recommendations he pleaded for an intensification of territorial segregation and pointed out that such a policy would have legal implications over a wide spectrum of affairs, including education and administration. This was quite a prophetic view for 1937. The punch line of the work states: "With the creation of territorial separation [literally, separating lines] South Africa rejected forever the principle of equality [*gelykstelling*]. May she [literally, he] construct her future on a firm foundation" (p. 465).[5]

To Afrikaner Nationalists this apartheid was not the same as the pragmatic segregation practiced before 1948. Apartheid constituted the final solution to the "racial question" (van Jaarsveld, 1979, p. 9) and was justified not only in religious and cultural terms but also in terms of history and tradition. However, before 1960, the complete segregation of white and black was regarded as only an ideal by Afrikaner pragmatists. Around the 1960s, however, historians such as G. D. Scholtz (1957) and H. J. J. M. van der Merwe (1961) insisted that total territorial segregation was necessary if Afrikaners wished to avoid the downfall and disappearance of whites in South Africa. Any halfhearted approach to segregation would be detrimental to Afrikaner, and therefore white, survival.

In his book *Het die Suid-Afrikaanse Volk 'n Toekoms?* (Does the Afrikaans People Have a Future?), Scholtz (1954) lamented the fact that the Afrikaners were a small and relatively powerless nation. He blamed the Dutch East India Company's immigration policy for this. The company halted white immigration in 1706 and allowed the settlers to practice agriculture only, instead of granting them permission to trade. The Afrikaner were thus both numerically and economically weak. In contrast, these restrictions did not apply to immigrants to America. Scholtz cited a further drawback: the Afrikaner's tendency to depend on black or nonwhite labor (pp. 72-75). He implicitly argued that, in the face of overwhelming black numbers, the Afrikaners' survival was made more difficult by historical circumstances. He conceived the Afrikaners' survival in the context of what he called "the revolution of the twentieth century" (p. 9). This was a time in which the worldwide domination of colored races by white nations was coming to an end. The Afrikaners (he seemed to use the terms *Afrikaners* and *whites* interchangeably) could not turn history back, but it was within their grasp to enhance their numbers and, above all, to make themselves less dependent on black labor. In a later work, *'n Swart Suid-Afrika?* (A Black South Africa?), Scholtz (1964) recommended strict territorial segregation and remarked about black labor, "It thus amounts to the whites having to redeem themselves from their painful dependence on Bantu [black] labor in which they find themselves" (p. 142).[6] Further, he noted, "Persisting in the habit of shifting all forms of hard labor onto the shoulders of the non-whites must, over time, inexorably lead to the decline of the white race" (p. 142).[7]

Scholtz ruled out legal curbs on labor dependence as effective measures and argued strongly for educating whites about their plight. He personally slanted history in such a way as to demonstrate to whites how they progressively made themselves dependent on black labor. Afrikaners and whites needed to be made to realize that they were set on a course of self-destruction by following the course of labor dependence set by past events. For Scholtz, the notion of survival was always connected to racial survival, to survival as a separate and self-sufficient racial entity. At the same time, racial survival would ensure the preservation and perpetuation of civilization and the values inherent to it. Economic integration of blacks would lead to political and eventually to biological and cultural integration. Integration thus would eventually draw the curtain on white civilization.

Scholtz had great influence on the Afrikaner mind. For many years he worked as foreign editor of the *Transvaler* (a major Afrikaans newspaper) with H. F. Verwoerd, who was then editor in chief. Verwoerd, as minister of Bantu affairs and prime minister, perfected apartheid as a system during the late 1950s and early 1960s. Many of the motifs and historical interpretations of Scholtz's work showed similarities to those of Verwoerd himself. Scholtz became editor in chief of the *Transvaler* in 1960 and had the opportunity to disseminate his ideas to a wide readership in the most populous province of the country, the Transvaal. He was thus able to reach the whites in order to inculcate in them those survival values he deemed important. He was unsuccessful, however, because the government itself, under the leadership of Verwoerd, his former boss, did nothing to lessen white dependence on black labor and, in fact, encouraged it through the rejection of the Tomlinson proposals.[8] Tomlinson reported that major territorial and financial sacrifices were necessary if Afrikaners were to achieve strict territorial segregation.

More than any other historian, F. A. van Jaarsveld from Pretoria made perhaps the most significant contribution to shaping South African whites' consciousness of history. His prolific scholarship over four decades produced a series of publications widely read by a slightly more informed public than the audience reached by Scholtz's editorials. Van Jaarsveld's audience was found in and around the institutions of education. In the 1960s and the beginning of the 1970s, his works exhibited the same features as the dominant nationalist discourse on the existence within South Africa of discrete groups with separate cultural and political identities. The prior existence of such separate groups, it was argued, historically justified South Africa's policy of "multinational development" (what apartheid was officially called at the time). Although van Jaarsveld's work concentrated on the Afrikaner, he, in contrast to his predecessors and contemporaries, gave ample attention to blacks. However, they figured as "wild, untamed and barbaric forces" in contrast to their "white Christian, pioneer, civilizing" counterparts (Smith, 1988, p. 84).

Van Jaarsveld also reflected on Afrikaans historiography and the folk understanding Afrikaners had of history, a theme I will take up below. In his book *The Afrikaner's Interpretation of South African History* (1964), he made a special plea for objectivity in the writing and teaching of history at schools and universities. In the last essay of the book, reprinted from an official educational journal, the *Transvaal Educational News,* he addressed the duties and responsibilities of history teachers. Apart from their obligation to be impartial and objective and to limit themselves to the "truth," he elaborated on a further duty: "The history teacher has a third duty: to the future. If he wishes to [have] his share in promoting the ideals of our leading statesmen, 'to forge a nation' or to achieve 'unity' between the language groups, he will stress their collaboration rather than their differences" (p. 199).

Regardless of what van Jaarsveld had previously said about the elimination of propaganda and politics, it is quite obvious that an implicit political agenda lurked behind the forging of unity between the language groups. Any white South African would have understood which language groups he meant. Depending on the groups to which they themselves belonged, history teachers were prone to present South African history from Afrikanercentric or English-speaking perspectives. I believe that Afrikaner teachers were more inclined to do this than their English-speaking counterparts, because of their tendency to view history as a series of injustices done to the Afrikaner. The language groups that counted in this discourse were the Afrikaners and the English speakers, and van Jaarsveld happily supported the efforts of (Afrikaner) statesmen to forge unity between the two—that is, among the whites. The black population, who in the 1950s became more and more vociferous in their protest against white rule and in demands for political rights, was the backdrop to this quest for white unity. History teaching thus had to become functional for white unity in the face of the "black peril."

In the latter half of the 1960s, van Jaarsveld went through a decidedly conservative, if not right-wing, phase. The Rand Afrikaans University was founded in 1967. To Afrikaners, the establishment of a major cultural center in the country's largest city, Johannesburg, which for so long had been dominated by English-speaking commercial culture, was a symbolic achievement. The context of the university's foundation was the *kultuurstryd*, or cultural struggle of the Afrikaner in an environment traditionally perceived as hostile. Van Jaarsveld was approached to head and build up the university's history department. The conciliatory attitude toward English speakers referred to above now made way for an increasing Afrikanercentrism, with an emphasis on identity issues. In 1970, van Jaarsveld wrote 70 talks for the state-owned South African Broadcasting Corporation. Only a selection of them were used. In 1971, in a book titled *Afrikaner, Quo Vadis?* van Jaarsveld took a number of episodes in history and turned them into moral and political lessons for the present. He romanticized the Afrikaners, as a people, as an undivided group needing to assert its ethnic identity in an aggressive manner (p. 136). He strongly supported separate development, which was the euphemism for apartheid in the 1960s, as part of the Afrikaner's struggle to preserve his own identity (p. 146). He spoke of historical ethnic components (*volkskomponente*) that had to be accommodated when South Africa was subdivided into a number of nation-states (homelands):

> We have to realize that our *future* is at stake and that it is a serious matter, a matter of life and death. Do we have the personal traits to defend ourselves and to teach our youth positive thinking and the realization how serious the situation is? Where are we going? Afrikaner *Quo Vadis*? Does the policy of separate development lead us toward the future in a way the ideal of becoming a Republic already did? If not, there is something wrong with our leadership. (p. 146)

At another turn in his career, van Jaarsveld has recently become increasingly critical of Afrikaner historiography, and he now concerns himself with the examination of some of the myths of history. He says that he reached a turning point in his career in 1976 after spending a sabbatical in Europe (personal communication, September 1986). There, he was able to examine his own work and South African society from an outside perspective. In the same year, the Soweto schools' revolt occurred, sparked off by the issue of whether the Afrikaans language should be used as the medium of instruction in black schools. In his lectures at the summer school of the University of Cape Town in 1977, he argued emphatically that it was essential for Afrikaners' survival that they change and adapt to a South Africa in which blacks are the majority. As a starting point, he said, they had to abandon their self-definition as an elect people. He subsequently lost favor at the Rand Afrikaans University and was openly attacked by the university's rector, Gerrit Viljoen (see the quote that opens this chapter).

Van Jaarsveld's critical turn is a benchmark in Afrikaner academic historiography. It was not his intention to destroy Afrikaner history; rather, as a practical matter, he felt it was important to correct or to avoid a sterile historical image that would prevent Afrikaners from meeting the future with confidence (du Bruyn, 1982, p. 59; cited in Smith, 1988, p. 85). This sophisticated turn was not grasped by gut-level white politics. On the one hand, van Jaarsveld was rejected by Afrikaans academics bent on preserving the narcissistic image of the Afrikaner; on the other, he was rejected by white supremacists who could not accept any historical self-image other than that of the *Uebermensch.*

In the process of demythologizing history, van Jaarsveld criticized as a misinterpretation and falsification the rendering of the Day of the Covenant as a sabbath. At a joint conference of the departments of theology and history at the University of South Africa in Pretoria, he explained how the Voortrekker vow taken before the battle at Blood River was erroneously taken for the institutionalization of the Day of the Covenant. Barely five minutes into reading his paper, he was interrupted by some 30 members of the ultra-right-wing Afrikaner Weerstandsbeweging (Afrikaner Resistance Movement) (AWB), who poured tar and feathers over him and read a statement (see below, where I elaborate on the popular reception of history). Van Jaarsveld thus went too far for some Afrikaners. Since these events, he has turned his attention to the reinterpretation of South African history in the context of reconciliation between black and white, and to the question of collective guilt (van Jaarsveld, 1984).

HISTORIOGRAPHY IN ENGLISH

In this section I review history written by whites in the English language. The social and political relevance of this category of historical writing is much less than that of Afrikaner historiography. In contrast to Afrikaans historiography, the audience English-language historians have addressed has been largely academic. The authors have not necessarily been English speakers, as we will see. The small body of historical literature written by blacks is significant, but it falls outside the scope of this chapter.

In this genre of historiography, material has been collected and published since the early years of the nineteenth century. Publications have been conceptualized and surrounded by controversies about the relations between white and black. In his *Researches in South Africa,* published in 1828, John Philip of the London Missionary Society maintained that whites were oppressing blacks. Donald Moodie, on the other hand, published archived material in his *The Record, or a Series of Official Papers Relative to the Condition and Treatment of the Native Tribes of South Africa* (1838-1841) indicating that relations between whites and people of color were peaceful and that the culprits in disturbances of this peace were usually nonwhite.

The most prolific and influential historian of the nineteenth and early twentieth centuries was George McCall Theal, who was procolonist and antiblack. To him, the Boers were like the Pilgrim Fathers of America. Theal was critical of the humanitarians of those times, the missionaries.

After the Anglo-Boer War, he occupied himself with reconciliation between the Boers and the British. Theal's authority was well established in the early twentieth century, and all subsequent generations of historians had to acknowledge his research. Nowhere was his influence so marked as among Afrikaner historians. Not only did he provide ample historical evidence, but his ideology of justifying white occupation and infiltration of the country suited them well. His quintessentially colonialist stance of white entitlement to land and power, combined with his anti-imperialist sentiments, suited the Afrikaners very well.

W. M. Macmillan and C. W. de Kiewiet were early liberal historians. They changed this picture. They shifted their perspective away from the "heroic" exploits of the Boers and Britons and from Afrikaans-English speaker relations to that of race relations. It was Macmillan's concern to explain to his readers how and why their society had assumed the shape it had. He also had the practical intent of demonstrating how to change it. In his works he strove to correct the negative and inferior image of blacks Theal had helped to create. He further attempted to dispel fears that a nonracial vote would endanger the political situation of whites. In Macmillan's eyes, "talk of segregation evaded the reality of the contact between 'advanced' and 'backward' peoples in one country" (Saunders, 1988, p. 69). Both he and de Kiewiet were professional scholars who reached only a limited audience of intellectuals and sometimes caused a ripple in the dominant political discourse of the 1920s and 1930s.

As the decolonization of Africa drew international and scholarly attention, historians such as Leonard Thompson turned toward the decolonization of history itself. Since the late 1950s, one African state after another had become independent. Historians in South Africa then wanted their readers to know that, after all, South Africa is part of Africa. They started looking further and further back in time to paleontological and archaeological evidence of human life in southern Africa in order to correct the white perspective on the past. Thompson paid special attention to the importance of oral evidence in black societies as a source of evidence. The new Africanist emphasis in historiography was perhaps at best exemplified by the *Oxford History of South Africa,* published in two volumes in 1969 and 1971. The editors were Monica Wilson, a Cape Town anthropologist, and Leonard Thompson. Half of the first volume was devoted to precolonial history, and the essays in both volumes made a decided effort to break away from the albocentric perspective. However, South Africa's problem was conceptualized as a predominantly racial problem. This emphasis opened the work of these "liberal" historians to criticism from the so-called revisionists.[9] This most recent generation of historians generally preferred to see South Africa's problems in terms of class rather than in racial categories. In heated debates they rejected the stance of the liberal historians. Among themselves they were also divided. Some favored the rather exotic French structuralist perspective, whereas others followed different neo-Marxist theories. Both the liberal-revisionist controversy in South African history[10] and the debates between what Bundy (1986) calls the "radical Africanists" and the "radical materialists" (p. 6) remained confined to the corridors and seminar rooms of the English-language universities. These debates' social relevance and influence on popular white thinking were minimal. The exploration of class domination and oppression provided a segment of white students who were highly critical of government policy and the political economy of the country with intellectual and moral justification for resistance to the government and solidarity with the black underdog. At present, such students constitute only a small percentage of South African youth. However, one group, the radical Africanists, became increasingly involved in writing history "from below," establishing in the process the South African version of the History Workshop movement. Afrikaans historiography, with its elitist emphasis, has largely missed the opportunity of dealing with the poor and downtrodden in the Afrikaner population. This has now been done by Marxist historians.

Saunders (1988, p. 194) correctly observes that English speakers have not regarded history as important as guidance in the present, nor have they seen history as important for their identity. Saunders quotes the South African history workshop organizer Belinda Bozzoli, who asserted that the dominant South African culture was "anti-historical" (p. 195). However, even among the black population the idea of their history being handed back to them by white middle-class Marxists did not prove to be entirely popular either (Bozzoli, 1990). In Chapter 6, I will discuss the particular dilemma of avant-garde white intellectuals' frustration with black leaders' aloofness from them. In particular, the notion that the white intelligentsia would assume an ideological leadership position in blacks' struggle for freedom proved to be distasteful, if not totally unacceptable, to black leaders.

WHITES' APPROPRIATION OF THE PAST

The connection between myth and history Viljoen establishes in the quotation that opens this chapter was most clearly borne out by popular

Afrikaner discourse on the past. In addition, the religious overtones of myth demonstrated how the past was reconstructed as a moral charter for the present. In this section I draw on some published works, my field material, and my own experience of what I was formally and informally taught within the system of Christian National Education (CNE) between 1947 and 1958.

When the members of the AWB stormed the podium where van Jaarsveld was delivering his lecture on the Day of the Covenant, their leader, Eugene Terre'Blanche, grabbed the microphone and read out the following statement:

> As young Afrikaners we have reached the end of our tether. Our spiritual heritage and everything we consider holy to the Afrikaner are being trampled underfoot and desecrated by liberalist politicians, "stray" [Afrikaner] academics, and false prophets who hide under the cloak of learning and false religion like Professor Floors van Jaarsveld. In this symposium they defile the holiest of holies of the Afrikaner being. This attitude is blasphemous and annuls the meaning of Afrikaner history. (quoted in *Beeld,* March 29, 1979)

Terre'Blanche, whose name (which translates as White Earth) had symbolic significance to his followers, claimed that the Afrikaner knew how to deal with traitors. He referred to the Anglo-Boer War hero Danie Theron, who once *sjambokked* (whipped) an English journalist who belittled Afrikaners.

This incident and its accompanying rhetoric illustrates the different meanings Afrikaner history has had for the critical academic historian on the one hand and the "folk" historian on the other. Furthermore, it demonstrates the conflict existing among Afrikaners with regard to their respective self-identifications. The ultraconservative AWB clung to a timeless and historically fixed self-image, which its members were prepared to defend aggressively against alternative interpretations. They made a clear distinction between the true brand of young Afrikaners filled with vitality and true Afrikanerness and the straying members of their group who tended to undermine the valued spiritual and moral qualities of the former. The notion of "pure" Afrikanerness and the struggle for purification have filled many pages of Afrikaner historiography on both sides of the reformist/conservative divide. Yet, whether reformist or conservative, all participants in the conflict have staunchly upheld their Afrikanerness and rarely denied it.

The Articulation of "Folk"
and "School" Versions of the Past

The tar and feathering incident happened at an important juncture in time. Afrikaner historians lamented the fact that Afrikaners lost interest in history during the 1950s. In the pre-World War II period, two factors kept an awareness of history alive. First, many of the veterans of the Anglo-Boer War were still alive, and they passed the oral tradition of the injustices and suffering inflicted upon the Afrikaner on to their children and grandchildren. Second, in the struggle for the political and economic emancipation of the Afrikaner, politicians manipulated history in order to create among their followers a psychological climate of commitment to Afrikaner moral causes.

After the National Party came to power in 1948, the significance of historically founded moral causes declined. However, this decline in interest occurred only after two spectacular celebrations brought the meaning and purpose of the Afrikaners' presence in Africa into sharp focus. It was as if these celebrations finally settled the issue of the Afrikaner's historical self-justification. In 1949, Afrikaners celebrated their triumph over black barbarism and British domination, and in 1952 they glorified the "planting of a nation" in 1652.

In 1949, the newly completed Voortrekker Monument was dedicated. Tens of thousands of Afrikaners from all over the country converged for the occasion, which climaxed in the renewal of the Day of the Covenant on December 16. The visitors lived in expansive tent villages around the *koppie* (hill) on which the Monument was built. There were church services, massive collective traditional folk dancing, and scores of wedding ceremonies. People dressed in pioneer clothes and addressed each other in pseudokinship terms customary during Voortrekker times. This event, with all its euphoria and wild optimism about the future, was at the same time a celebration of the triumph of the Afrikaner in the political field the previous year, when the National Party defeated the mixed Afrikaans-English United Party at the polls. In a sense it was symbolic of their liberation from English political and cultural domination. "History" had now delivered its promise that the Afrikaner would be truly free in a country they could call their own and in which they legitimately held power. Soon the politics of white *baasskap* (masterhood) would follow. In the years that ensued, the celebrations of the Day of the Covenant still drew sizable crowds, but as the years went by they dwindled.

The second significant occasion was the third centennial of van Riebeeck's landing at the Cape of Good Hope. This massive celebration was
held in April 1952. The Dutch commander of a contingent of three ships,
Jan van Riebeeck, landed at the Cape on April 16, 1652. He was sent by
his masters, the officials of the Dutch East India Company, to found a
halfway support station for supplying company ships with fresh food and
water. His arrival is generally seen by Afrikaners as the planting of the
nation and as the beginning of South African history. In a wider sense, van
Riebeeck was also considered to be the European cultural hero who brought
white Christian civilization to the dark continent of Africa. To most
readers of history it is less known that he despised the Cape and begged
his employers to transfer him to India, a fact that would have irritated
many whites who, two centuries later, would oppress Indian immigrants
as inferiors. The massive 1952 celebration of van Riebeeck's arrival
reinforced Afrikaners' identification with their European roots, but, at the
same time, they viewed themselves as a separate category of people in
Africa: as the bearers of white Christian civilization. In the decades that
followed, the significance of whiteness and civilization received increasing emphasis in efforts to bring about greater national unity between
Afrikaans and English speakers—but less so for historical reasons than
for political and economic expediency.

The younger generation of the 1950s and 1960s grew up without the
tradition of the Anglo-Boer War. The generation that had fought in the war
had died off. Younger people were less concerned about their political future,
which, by now, they regarded as secure and safe in the hands of their
leaders. After a brief efflorescence around the declaration of the country's
status as a republic in 1961, political consciousness was at a low ebb. In
the schools, history was only an elective subject. Historians, educationists,
and the Federation of Afrikaans Cultural Organizations (FAK) expressed
grave concern about this. A committee of inquiry, under the auspices of
the National Council for Social Research (later to become the Human
Sciences Research Council), found that the percentage of matrics (final-
or senior-year students at high schools) taking history dropped from 60%
a "few years prior to 1966 to 49% at the end of 1966" (Human Sciences
Research Council, 1972, p. 4). The committee recommended that history
be made a compulsory or core subject until the ninth school year, and that
attempts should be made to introduce it as a compulsory subject until the
final school year (p. 29). The committee stated that the teaching of history
should have the following objectives:

1. the orientation of the child in time and space
2. the equipping of the child for a future as a politically molded person
3. the national molding of the child (meaning that a child has to be influenced to "adopt" "an appreciative attitude, i.e. loyalty, honor and love for his own country")
4. the guiding of the child toward "respecting the cultural heritages of other national groups"
5. the social molding of the child ("He learns that in their co-existence all men are equal, but at the same time he also discovers the inequality of man to man that entails particular fraternal obligation and responsibilities, so that the best interests of everyone can thereby be promoted.")
6. the instilling in the child of a "realization of a historical sense"
7. the fostering in the child of "objectively critical thought" ("In this way he learns to be tolerant and will first ascertain all the historical facts or circumstances before venturing a critical opinion.")
8. the religious and ethical molding of the child (Human Sciences Research Council, 1972, p. 4)

The authoritarian tone of these objectives is blatant. Rather than viewing education in history as part of children's participation in a developmental process, they emphasize the need to mold and form children to adopt appreciative and patriotic attitudes toward their country. English-speaking members of the committee did not object to these formulations.

Once they were adopted in teaching situations where children were captives of courses steeped in a particular ideology, the practical implications of these objectives were enormous. Spontaneous interest in history among Afrikaans children was largely lacking. Now they were channeled into taking the subject. Even without the system of Christian National Education such objectives would be draconian, opening the door wide for the possibility of brainwashing.[11]

What were the students offered? J. M. du Preez (1983), who examined the contents of 53 South African high school textbooks, subjected 14 history books to thematic analyses.[12] Other textbooks he studied covered such disciplines as Afrikaans and English literature, geography, and social studies. Du Preez lists 12 axiomatic "master symbols" that recur in the books:

1. Legitimate authority is not questioned.
2. Whites are superior; blacks are inferior.
3. The Afrikaner has a special relationship with God.
4. South Africa rightfully belongs to the Afrikaner.

5. South Africa is an agricultural country; the Afrikaners are a farmer nation [*boerevolk*].

6. South Africa is an afflicted country.

7. South Africa and the Afrikaner are isolated.

8. The Afrikaner is militarily ingenious and strong.

9. The Afrikaner is threatened.

10. World opinion of South Africa is important.

11. South Africa is the leader in Africa.

12. The Afrikaner has a God-given task in Africa.

Many of these master symbols are echoed in a UNESCO study of South African school textbooks that appeared in the same year (Dean, Hartmann, & Katzen, 1983). This work embarked on an extensive content and thematic analysis of textbooks in use during the 1970s and 1980s. The fact that the study is dated does not detract from its significance today. Most people passing through the school system internalized values and attitudes based on the interpretation of history they received in class. Many of them would not read any history after finishing school. The examination of the thematic content of textbooks in circulation 10 years ago is thus significant for coming to an understanding of the historical consciousness of a certain cohort of young adults today. Similarly, an examination of works more than 30 years old reveals aspects of older adults' appropriation of the past.[13]

The UNESCO study examined both Afrikaans and English textbooks, but the researchers mostly used the English versions prescribed for Transvaal schools. It is remarkable that the majority of these textbooks were translations from Afrikaans originals. For the final school year, standard 10, only two books were available to English schools. This limited schools' choices and fostered a high degree of standardization. Special committees of the Transvaal Education Department scrutinized texts for their suitability. Texts were often submitted in manuscript form and could thus be referred back to their authors for modification. This gave the Nationalist-run Education Department even more control over content. As a consequence, even the few texts specifically written in English only marginally exhibited a more liberal character. As a whole, they largely conformed to the ethnocentric model of their Afrikaans counterparts. It is revealing that both English- and Afrikaans-speaking pupils, with few exceptions, were forced to use books written by Afrikaners. One can thus assume that, at least as far as their textbooks are concerned, most white pupils were taught the same version of South African history. Even more revealing is the fact that the history texts prescribed for black schools were written by Afrikaners. History books for black schools were not a direct concern for this particular study, but we can assume that the white-centric perspective must have caused great concern in the black community in these times. Dean et al. (1983, p. 39) observe, furthermore, that some of these textbooks were hopelessly out of date and failed to incorporate historical scholarship of the preceding 30 years.

What were the lessons contained in these books? First of all, the perspective was white-centric in general and Afrikanercentric more specifically. South African history started with the arrival of the whites. The contributions and perspectives of blacks were ignored, or the blacks were seen as a hindrance to the development of a civilized country. Some of the most important recurring themes in these books are discussed below.

Blacks are a problem. The books contained many references to the "black problem," the "Xhosa problem," the "Bantu problem." In the twentieth century, black history was treated as the history of legislation dealing with blacks as a problem and as objects of control. Indians, too, were perceived as a "national problem." Even the relatively enlightened English-speaking schoolbook author A. N. Boyce wrote about blacks' "penetration" and "infiltration" into white areas as if they had no right to do so (Dean et al., 1983, p. 81). Nowhere were the settlers or Afrikaners seen as a problem.

Blacks and other people of color are different. Elaborate accounts of racial differences and skin color were given. Some texts authored by English speakers were less prone to this emphasis, but in the rest of the books physical differences were given prominence. Racial ancestry was thus considered greatly relevant. In some cases the terms *race, tribe,* and *ethnic group* were used interchangeably. Crucially important were cultural differences. Above all, the Afrikaner's attainment of a separate cultural, linguistic, and national identity received attention. Even the coloureds were portrayed with a separate "national identity" as far back as the eighteenth century. The parallel "development" of ethnic groups was justified.

Segregation of ethnic groups is a good thing. Historical foundations were sought for establishing segregation as a solution and inhibiting factor for conflict between groups. The Black Consciousness Movement of the 1970s was erroneously seen as support for the idea of separate homelands. C. J. Joubert (1979), an Afrikaans-speaking author, argued:

> The population of South Africa has never been homogeneous. The Whites wish to retain their national identity in their own territory. At the same time

it must be acknowledged that Black peoples also wish to assert their national identities. History has shown that each nationalism cannot be artificially grafted on to another. . . . If all the different population groups of South Africa were included in one system, one or more groups would inevitably dominate the others. (quoted in Dean et al., 1983, p. 77)

This quotation could have come straight from a Nationalist political speech of the 1970s. I wish to draw attention to the implicit assumption in these accounts that "history" is neither artificial nor accidental, but that history demonstrates "natural" phenomena and processes.

Blacks offer their labor freely. Somewhat at odds with the message discussed immediately above, the notion that blacks offered their labor freely simply ignored the fact that blacks were coerced through landlessness, taxes, dislocation, and a host of other factors to enter the economic system at its lowest end and remain there. It was argued that blacks provided labor cheaply because of their numbers, that is, because of an oversupply. The abnormality of the situation and the artificiality of the oversupply were not questioned. On the contrary, it was suggested that this arrangement was acceptable to blacks (Dean et al., 1983, p. 72).

Blacks have always been the working class in South Africa. Here another quotation from Joubert demonstrates the point:

South Africa has never actually had a White working class as is the case in European countries. From the early days of White settlement in this country, Non-Whites have been the labourers. . . . and over the years it became the accepted thing for Non-Whites to do all the heavy work. This was how a Non-White working class developed. . . .

After the interior had been opened up by the Voortrekkers, the Blacks remained the labourer [*sic*]. In this way a division of labour based on race came into being in South Africa with the Blacks as labourers in the employ of the White man. (quoted in Dean et al., 1983, pp. 71-72)

Joubert forgot that Afrikaners were proletarianized laborers in the early decades of this century. This quotation demonstrates hierarchical thinking. Whites were placed in an elevated position of employer and guardian.

Black resistance is subversive and externally inspired. The black nationalist movements, the African National Congress (ANC) and Pan-African Congress (PAC), were presented as communist inspired. Their mode of operations was called "intimidation," "agitation," and "subversion." On the other hand, the resistance of the Afrikaners to British imperialism was portrayed as legitimate and moral. Sympathy was expressed for the plight of white mine workers during the strike of 1922, whereas the strike actions of blacks were seen as a threat to whites.

South Africans (whites) know best how to handle the race problem. According to these texts, outsiders propagating the ideals of the French Revolution had no knowledge about the South African context. What applied to Europe did not necessarily apply to South Africa. Uncivilized people could not be placed on the same footing as civilized ones. Humanitarian and liberal ideas were at best suspect and potentially communist. Looking at the level of knowledge the authors of the schoolbooks had about blacks, Dean et al. (1983, p. 56) observe how they tended to trivialize black motivations. To an English-speaking author such as Boyce, coloureds were savage in a childlike way. They were capering, grinning minstrels. To another author, blacks "displaced" to the city did not have the same needs and frustrations as the Afrikaners.

As far as independent black Africa is concerned, the following themes were found:

- Parliamentary democracies have failed.
- Ethnic domination of one group over the other has occurred.
- One-party states have predominated.
- Leadership has been unprepared for self-government.
- Africanization of the civil service was disastrous because of incompetence.
- The white exodus led to economic misery.
- African unity was a threat, but, because of "incompetence," was not really to be taken seriously (the works of Boyce seem to be an exception to this stereotype).

In the 1980s, educators were thus still constructing a historical self-identity for Afrikaners and English speakers, qualified by the corporateness of their groups, by authoritarianism, suffering, racial/ethnic superiority, and divine legitimation of their cause. Blacks and, by extension, black Africa were viewed as less competent to care for themselves. White initiative was needed to keep order and to manage the affairs of the country. The sense of white identity conveyed by history books was intensely alive in the hearts of the conservatives. The rhetoric of conservative politicians reinforced that self-image, and the more militant white groups, such as the AWB, expressed willingness to fight and even to die for the preservation of it.

It would be misleading to look for this self-image among conservatives only. In terms of the earlier distinction between reformists and conservatives, I would argue that many of these traits also color the self-perceptions of reformists engaged in the struggle for the preservation of their corporate identities in a future, democratic South Africa.

The Public's Appropriation of the Past

I now turn to the way in which the popular presentation of history has been appropriated by the white public. During my first field trip to South Africa in October 1988, the official media were virtually saturated with historical material staking out justifications for white presence and privilege in the country. In the first week of my stay, both radio and television were running documentaries, reports, plays, and soap operas with historical content. There were, for example, programs on the manufacture of furniture in the old Transvaal, a program about nineteenth-century Potchefstroom, and a dramatization of *Temmers van die Noordweste* (Tamers of the Northwest) by Elizabeth Vermeulen, a book dealing with Voortrekker movements into the harsh desert areas of the country. Programs on the arts and crafts of the Boers praised their ingenuity. Afrikaans radio stations featured old songs, partly in Dutch, and new ones dealing with nineteenth-century themes of courtship, *nagmaal,* and traditional sports such as *jukskei* and sack races.[14] It was the 150th celebration of the Great Trek that year, but this was not the only context for the production of such programs. Nationwide, municipal elections were to be held, and the existence of a state of emergency underscored the precariousness of white life.

Media reporting created the impression that it was Afrikaners who were bent on proving their roots in the country. The conservative parties had a heyday, because they somehow dominated the public celebrations of the Great Trek. An air of nostalgia pervaded these public events. I noticed how celebrants "escaped" into an idealized past in these confusing times of political turmoil. "History" made people feel good and allowed them to relive a better past unencumbered by the complexity and economic depression of the present.

Apart from nostalgia, the words spoken and the symbols used at the celebration I attended recalled many of the master symbols discussed above. One afternoon I went to the Waterval celebration grounds (*feesterrein*) in the northwest of Johannesburg. These parklike grounds are situated between the affluent white suburbs of Northcliff and Linden and the poorer Triomf and Waterval suburbs. This park is one of many in the country created in 1938 for the annual celebration of the Day of the Covenant. At the center of the grounds is a *feeshuis* (house of celebration). At Waterval, the celebrations followed a pattern I had witnessed on many other occasions across the country during my youth, when I accompanied my father, a minister, as he attended these events to conduct religious services. Thus the Waterval celebration evoked many memories of rural celebrations where Afrikaners congregated and camped around the *feeshuis,* creating the atmosphere of *nagmaal.* Politicians and community leaders extolled Afrikaners' past heroism while praising their tribe's achievements in the present. The evils of English cultural and economic imperialism were exposed in flowery, xenophobic language. In the evenings, plays dramatized the past and choirs sang traditional songs.

In October 1988 about 300 people assembled at Waterval. It was lunchtime when I arrived, and instead of camping around the *feeshuis* as in the past, numerous family groups sat picnicking in small circles on blankets. These groups comprised three generations; grandparents, parents, and children were enjoying the day together. An obvious effort had been made to involve not only the nuclear family but broader kin groups in this historical celebration. It was a strange, almost anachronistic, experience to observe the "communion" these extended families celebrated within the wider communion of their tribal group viewed against the backdrop of the gleaming high-rise buildings of industrial Johannesburg.

The *feeshuis* stood at the center of the grounds. On one side there were several assemblies of crossed flags, each consisting of a national and a flag of the Voortrekker movement.[15] The flags flanked a wooden wagon wheel that formed the background for a flaming torch. The text inscribed below the torch read *Hou Koers* (Stay on Course). On the other side of the building, closest to a small stage, there was an exhibit of Africana. Four wooden ox wagons with four oxen each stood next to an exhibit of quilts followed by memorabilia such as old Voortrekker movement uniforms, old Afrikaans encyclopedias, and relics supposed to have been on the Great Trek. Near the entrance there were various paintings of South African nature scenes.

Outside the building, half a dozen black men were putting up the lighting. They were disregarded by the picnickers, who seemed to view them as part of the scenery. The whites also ignored the black policemen on the periphery of the grounds, who stood near a yellow enclosed van (which in the past had been used to cart black pass offenders to jail). They were obviously there to protect the whites from terrorist attacks, bomb throwers, and hooligans.

East of the main building, food was being prepared. Thick corn porridge, or *pap,* was cooking in large three-legged cast-iron pots. Nearby, *potjiekos* (a meat and vegetable stew) was being made in a row of smaller pots suspended over the coals. Further to the south, men were barbecuing meat on a huge grill, while the women stood at a table preparing salads and bread rolls. These were all considered traditional foods to be prepared in the traditional way according to the traditional division of labor between men and women. In front of the tent where the food supplies were kept there was a large board depicting Voortrekker boys and girls handling flags, training for battle in the bush—against, I presume, (black) insurgents. On the southern end of the grounds, adults grouped children for sack races, egg and spoon races, water-balloon-throwing competitions, tug of war, and some stringing game I didn't understand.

To the west of the building an open-air oven was being prepared. It was a reconstruction of the clay brick ovens used on Boer farms in the past. The oven was first heated by a wood fire. After the coals were removed, the bread pans and dough were placed inside and the structure was closed with a piece of sheet metal and sealed with clay. Nearby, an elderly Afrikaner demonstrated how to braid and make whips.

Later that afternoon, an ox wagon was to be pulled up the hill by some schoolchildren. It was supposed to be drawn over a slab of wet concrete in which it would leave the imprints of its wheels. The commanding officer of the Voortrekker movement of the Waterval region told me that the organizers were concerned about making this an interesting occasion. Therefore, there would be no long speeches that evening. An elderly gentleman who took a leading position during the centennial of the Great Trek in 1938 was asked to unveil a commemorative plaque.

This was only a local celebration of the 150th anniversary, but it demonstrated the pertinence of the past to the participants. It was my impression that the participants sought the key to a better future from the past. To participants, the sociality, the family ties, and the symbols of the past they shared were filled with a warmth they must have missed in the greatly impersonal and plural urban environment in which they lived and worked. In the milieu of the *fees* (celebration), life was integrated, uncomplicated, peaceful, and homogeneous, if only for the reason that no blacks were present. Although a great deal of the history they were reliving was riddled with conflict and written in the blood of black and white, the blacks present were invisible and ignored. This was dream time, an ideal world full of wholesome values and trusting human relations. There were games, laughing, and children playing. There was the good company of those who "spoke your language" (*praat jou taal*).

As a groping for and reliving of the past, this celebration looked cozy. The less cozy aspects of Afrikanercentric history, however, were kept in remembrance by numerous monuments erected to the glory of a rather bloody and violent past. Perhaps the most unambiguous message was and is conveyed by the Voortrekker Monument. It is an artifact and symbol extolling the heroism of the pioneers, their suffering, and their divine election as a people. It is a sacred place to which busloads of white schoolchildren are taken to be vividly confronted with the past as inspiration and charter for the future. It is filled with emotion-laden symbols that justify white—more specifically, Afrikaner—predominance in, and entitlement to, the country as a whole. Young Afrikaner visitors viewing the scenes of "black barbarism" and white suffering are filled with a feeling of outrage and a sense of moral purity and superiority. This at least is the effect the Monument had on me when I visited it for the first time as an 8-year-old at its inauguration in December 1949.

The Monument is perched on a hilltop that forms part of Voortrekker-hoogte (Voortrekker Heights). Before the Nationalists came to power in 1948, it was known as Robert's Heights, named after a British general of Anglo-Boer War fame. The Nationalists quickly changed the name after their election victory. The Monument is a massive, almost cubic, structure built of granite blocks. Huge sculptures of the busts of four Voortrekker leaders guard the corners. Below the main entrance, flanked by two staircases, stands a sculpture of a woman and two small children, symbolizing the contribution and suffering of women and children in Afrikaner history. The structure is encircled by ox wagons molded in concrete, symbolizing the defensive structure of the laager. The wrought iron gates incorporate an *assegai* (spear) motif. On the inside, the visitor is awed by the darkened space. Huge arched windows let through a dim, amber light. High up in the shallow domed roof there is a single round window, actually a lens designed to cast a ray of sunlight on the sarcophagus, which is one level lower than the entrance. From the quiet interior one can look down from the wide, circular balustraded opening onto the sarcophagus, a solid rectangular block of marble. It is inscribed with the words "Ons vir jou Suid Afrika" (literally, We are [exist] for you, South Africa). Every year on December 16, the day the Boer victory over the Zulu is celebrated, a ray of sunlight illuminates these words. As one of the hundreds of thousands of Afrikaners who visited the monument at its inauguration in December

1949, I marveled at this wonderful phenomenon. To my 8-year-old mind it was as if God mobilized the sun to illuminate the Afrikaners' election as a people and to justify their cause. On the sarcophagus level, an eternal flame, first lit during the Ossewatrek of 1938, is kept burning in memory of many generations who have given their lives to the taming and conquest of "their" country. The walls of the entrance level are lined with white marble friezes depicting scenes from the Great Trek. Themes of black brutality and treachery on the one hand are explicitly contrasted with white heroism and suffering on the other.

Previously, blacks were allowed to visit the building only on special days. Nowadays, the Monument is open to all races. Because it is considered a shrine, special dress regulations apply. The sign at the entrance proclaims, "No bare feet, no sleeveless shirts, no shorts for women."

Outside the laager of wagons, a garden of indigenous trees and plants surrounds the total complex. It is within this garden to the east of the Monument that a most interesting reconstruction of the Great Trek is to be found. I have witnessed how white schoolchildren meticulously follow the graphically depicted history. From four directions, footpaths laid out in different kinds of stone, representing different Voortrekker parties, lead through the garden to meet and diverge at posted historical points. Various paths converge, leading to a laager at Blood River. The laager represents the site of the battle where Afrikaners believe the Zulu were finally defeated. It consists of small ox wagons made from cement. It is surrounded by rows and rows of small black stones representing the Zulu warriors. Another footpath marked by the same black stones leads to a number of scaled-down grass huts representing the *kraal,* or home, of the Zulu chief, Dingane. Next to these huts a small outcropping is topped by a black obelisk on which the names of the Voortrekker delegation sent to negotiate with King Dingane are inscribed. The history books tell us that all the members of this delegation were impaled and clubbed to death. When I visited the garden in 1989, little groups of white children came up to the obelisk and pointed their fingers to names they recognized, maybe those of ancestors or distant relatives. Though they were speaking Afrikaans, I couldn't hear exactly what they were saying, but they were surely enthusiastic about the graphic depiction of history. In the background, two blacks in overalls were glancing at the visitors while watering the garden.

Later that day, I returned to Johannesburg after picking up a collection of essays written by female high school students. The inscription "Ons vir jou Suid Afrika" rung ominously in my ears that evening as I read an Afrikaans essay describing how a young conscript lost his legs in a trench war, apparently an imagined South African border war against "terrorists" or ANC forces:

> Suddenly, in one god-forsaken moment, I know what everything is waiting for: It is as if all hell breaks loose, heaven falls, trees tip over, and birds sing their deafening war cry. Whose legs are those yonder?
>
> Then, darkness . . .
>
> Three days later, days during which I gathered I did not die, everything is too painful. . . . Days of despair, rebellion, and bitterness. Couldn't He [God] just have taken my life? Why only my legs? My precious legs for running, for riding on the prairie on Pronk [the narrator's horse]. Legs on which I wished to walk courageously into the future, stopping the enemy bent on the destruction of my country! I don't want to be a make-believe person on make-believe legs! I want to live!
>
> Then suddenly: [I heard] "We will heed your call."[16] I replied: "I will sacrifice whatever you demand." I did sacrifice. I have given up what was most precious to me. "We will live and we will die." I did die, the selfish ego deep inside died a painful death and that is why I am alive now in the fullest sense! Therefore, I joyfully realize: I love my country because I could sacrifice, could die, nay, could always reply, sacrifice, live, die. Not "we" but I am there [exist] for you, South Africa. (Essay 408)

These are very strong words and images of suffering and self-sacrifice. The author proves herself to be an individual successfully socialized into a group that deems itself the savior of a country threatened by destructive forces. A simple dichotomous model of the forces of good and evil dominates the text, and a sense of religiously motivated conviction permeates the essay. The recruit or serviceman's sacrifice is the will of God. Religious themes and patriotic justifications punctuate the rest. Being maimed for life is considered a privilege in this context and is expressed in the refrain of the national anthem, here presented in dialogue form. Many of these schoolchildren's essays in Afrikaans use the anthem as a final, historical, and patriotic cap. The anthem provided an idiom of struggle, of moral courage and destiny couched in the symbols of a pioneering people taking possession of a promised land.

The essay I quote from above is one of more than 2,000 that were entered in a competition sponsored by Women for South Africa, an organization founded by concerned Afrikaans-speaking women. The competition was open to all races, but most of the essays came from white English and Afrikaans speakers. I was able to get access to 480 essays written in Afrikaans and English (the whereabouts of the others, written in nine other vernaculars, were unknown). With the assistance of Annemarie Grindrod, one of my research assistants, I subjected these essays to thematic analysis. I subsequently selected for closer scrutiny 50 essays I considered to be typical as well as 50 more chosen on a systematic random basis.

The essay writers had a choice of three subjects: (a) "My country needs me"; (b) "I love my country because . . . "; and (c) "We South Africans can help each other . . . ." The essayist quoted above addressed the second of these themes. Afrikaans writers tended to select the first two topics; English writers, the last.

Some of the master symbols found by du Preez in schoolbooks and the themes found in the UNESCO study of history books cited above eerily found their way into these Afrikaans essays. Although there was little evidence of the theme "South Africa belongs to the Afrikaner," there were many examples of the theme "South Africa is a white country." First, blacks generally did not figure in the essays in a positive or contributing way. One essay writer describes South Africa as a dark and dreamless "embryo" in Africa until the small ships of Portuguese explorers Diaz and da Gama came, bringing light and life. South Africa's "childhood" was its existence as a (Dutch) supply station to ships on their way to the East. Then the French, British, and slaves came, followed by a "black sun that passed through the country." In another essay, "fire and spears split the country, and a bloody sun hung over Blood River." Writers mentioned black distress in the abstract, but all the places of suffering were those symbolic to the Afrikaner: Blood River, Bloukrans, Spioenkop, and Slagtersnek (Essay 3).

Another essay describes how whites brought light and warmth to the country: "The candle one lights for leading others gives off warmth to the bearer too. So be it. . . . South Africa's warm flame caused everyone to share its heat since the historical origins of the country when the white man came to settle here." Yet another writer says, "Our country has a very long history since van Riebeeck landed at the Cape."

The master symbol "The Afrikaner has a special relationship with God" is very much in evidence in the essays. One writer says: "The land is given to us. The Voortrekkers fought for their land and for their God. They fought in order to keep their land" (Essay 415). One writer draws parallels between Israel and South Africa: South Africa, like Israel, was the promised land and the land of "milk and honey." Further: "Huguenots, Germans, Scots, and Dutch were led by God to come to South Africa" (Essay 335). Without the love and support of God, "South Africa would have been like the seed that fell on rocky ground . . . without food and water facing a dark future" (Essay 391).

In the essays, the theme of Afrikaner suffering runs like a golden thread through history, connecting the hardships of pioneer life to those of war. The struggle against "terrorism" and "communism" in the present is a continuation of the struggle against barbarism in the past. The suffering incurred is the same. The Anglo-Boer War still has significance for some. The British are called by their hate-name: Khakis (Essay 101). In the same essay, a poem by Afrikaans theologian and poet J. D. du Toit, "Forgive and Forget," is quoted at length. The poem deals with a young thorn tree (Acacia) crushed by a passing wagon—a symbol of British imperialism. The tree is symbolic of the Afrikaner. It rights itself, heals, and grows into a strong and robust tree, still bearing in adulthood the scar inflicted by the wagon. The essayists assume that all members of the Afrikaner people are involved in the struggle and share in the suffering, regardless of age or gender. The writers draw on the past to develop guidelines for the present. One writer, in a mood of "total mobilization," says: "Not only men but women and children helped in past wars. They should do the same now" (Essay 357).

In comparison with the past, the present is held to be dangerous and morally deficient. One essay cites some of the evils: strikes, demonstrations, drugs, famine, and free love (premarital sex). These practices and events open the doors to "liberalism and communism" (Essay 348). After they fought so hard for their "sunny fatherland, the Afrikaner people had pride in their nationhood in the past. Today, however, they have little concern for each other." Another writer asserts that there is too much moral decay; she cites a 1949 speech by the first Nationalist premier, Malan, in which he exhorted his followers to turn "back to your people; back to the highest ideals of your people; back to the legacy you have been entrusted with; back to the people's altar on which you lay your sacrifices, and if it is required of you, yourself as sacrifice; back to the sanctity and inviolability of family life; back to the Christian way of life; back to your Christian beliefs, back to your church; back to your God!" (Essay 257).

This particular essayist chose the theme "We South Africans can help each other . . . ." The text deals with a love motivated by the hallowed values of the past. Looking more closely at who "we South Africans" are, the author targets the Boer nation (*Boerevolkie*—a term of endearment) or South Africans in general as people to love. In the examples cited, "South Africans" are people from the mostly white urban middle classes. The ethnocentrism of this essay is encountered repeatedly in others. There is agreement that South Africans/Afrikaners needed to return to the faith of their fathers, because much of their present misery has been caused by their abandonment of it. Later we will see how the theme of "apostasy" also occupies some adult minds.

The picture painted in the essays is bleak. Regardless of the limitations of the evidence,[17] most of these essays convey a message of white superiority and entitlement. Whites and Afrikaners are seen as the bearers of light and warmth. Blacks are associated with danger and barbarism. Some Afrikaans students still have a problem in coming to terms with English speakers' economic predominance in "their" country. English speakers are still viewed as quasi-colonial exploiters. Only in one instance did I find evidence of a wider inclusive attitude that encompasses all white South Africans.

In the Afrikaans essays ethnic values are closely linked to religious justifications, and the in-group is regarded as a sacred community. Ethnocentrism and its companion, xenophobia, are closely linked. Today it is not acceptable to be openly racist. However, the tone of many of these essays is xenophobic and, not too latently, racist. The essays are evidence of the appropriation of a specific reconstruction of the past, a reconstruction that is very much out of phase with recent developments in South African historiography.

The few essays in English dealing with the past have a different tone. One states, "The people of South Africa are descendants of many nations, blown there from the corners of the Earth by the winds of history" (Essay 89). The author asserts that all, regardless of descent, share the same country, but that each group considers itself to be the chosen one. They hate each other and, as a result, a scorched earth is drenched in their blood. Another essay laments the fact that the country "has not remembered her past. She has cut off her roots, her beginnings" (p. 16). Lust for power and wealth blurs her vision and causes her to forget that "all men are brethren." Both these examples, like their Afrikaans counterparts, reflect a pessimistic view of the present, but these at least show a degree of fairness and neutrality with regard to the past and demonstrate a more inclusive, nonracial view of South Africa in the present. That only two essays in the English sample deal explicitly with the past confirms the view that English speakers seem to be less preoccupied with historical issues. The different, more tolerant tone of the essays may also be indicative of the way historical material is presented at English-medium schools. As noted previously, the content of Afrikaans and English history textbooks is largely the same.

At a time when South Africa seems to be poised on the brink of a new era of democratization, the way in which whites appropriate history is of crucial importance to their sense of justice and fairness. The prevailing albocentric perspective in certain circles would regard the empowerment of blacks as unfair and unjust. It is therefore important to restore the significance and contribution of blacks to the historical image of white South Africans. Thereby whites' self-centric view of their own importance might have to be revolutionized in order to incorporate the role and perspective of the majority of the population. The Afrikanercentric view of history would resist such a transformation and would mobilize its resources to divide the social world into friend and foe, the latter usually being black and associated with hostile ideologies and philosophies.

In 1964, the historian van Jaarsveld looked into the possibility of teaching "national" history in South African schools (pp. 196-199). He chose to disregard the "nonwhite" section at that time, concentrating on the problem of forging white national unity in the country. In examining these essays, it becomes clear that some teenagers still have a problem with a common history inclusive of all whites. The same van Jaarsveld, 20 years later, despairingly noted that a general history of South Africa would be possible but would never be generally acceptable to all the country's inhabitants (1984, p. 203). In a democratic state of the future with a common educational system the issue of a historical account of the past can become as crucial as the language question was to the Soweto revolt in 1976. Instead of blacks taking to the barricades, conservative whites may revolt against the redefinition of their historical identity.

The Question of Descent

If the issue of a common history is difficult, the possibility of a common descent of whites and people of color poses an even bigger obstacle for some. At the end of 1984, H. F. Heese, a lecturer at the University of the Western Cape (an institution created to cater to the tertiary education of the so-called coloured category of the population at the time), published a work titled *Groep Sonder Grense* (Group Without Boundaries), a piece of genealogical research aimed at exploring the origins of the university's "community," the coloureds. The book came to the less-than-startling conclusion that a significant ratio of admixture existed among slaves imported from Malaysia, the Orient, and Africa, the Khoi, and the Dutch population at the Cape during the seventeenth and eighteenth centuries:

> The status enjoyed by the individual . . . in the period 1652-1795 . . . was not only determined by genetic descent, estate, residence, religion, or occupation. Combinations of these factors could contribute to the acceptance of a person of black or brown appearance in "white" society. Similarly, a person of white appearance and descent could land in the core group of the "Cape Coloureds." Cultural identification rather than racial classification admitted a coloured person to the "white" group. However, by 1795 whites had already become associated with dominance and coloureds with subservience. (Heese, 1984, p. 39)

The findings of this study created a stir when prepublication copies were circulated among white politicians. In Parliament an "enlightened" member challenged the leader of the Conservative Party to abstain from making derogatory remarks about the coloured populations. Referring to Heese's book, he cautioned that the ancestors of some of the members of the CP were "slaves from Bengal and India." The remark provoked a furor in the house (*Sunday Times* [Johannesburg], February 24, 1985). The CP leader hotly dismissed the claims as "rubbish." The book also detailed a report of Dutch males dancing with naked female slaves in eighteenth-century Cape Town. At the time Heese's book was published, the Immorality Act, which prohibited relations between the racial groups, was still in force, and statements such as these were looked upon as blasphemous, to say the least. The popular image whites had of their ancestors endowed those ancestors with pure racial homogeneity, high moral character, and loyalty to their kind. They were supposed to have been a God-fearing separate group. The Immorality Act was an attempt to preserve and protect this purity by law.

Mindful of reactions to his findings, Heese added a timid rider that the reader should not construe that all bearers of the family names of those whites who had offspring with women of color belonged to the same branch of the family. This rider became the escape hatch for many Afrikaners, who could then deny the relevance of the findings to their own family histories by simply relegating the instances of racial admixture to deviant behavior of individuals belonging to minor branches of their respective family trees. However, right-wingers reacted violently. In one instance there was a fistfight between an HNP member of the Pretoria City Council and another member. The latter raised the question of whether it was fair to exclude black and coloured entrepreneurs from the central business district of Pretoria, given that Afrikaners themselves had mixed ancestry. In another case, 16 Afrikaners threatened the editor of the *Sunday Times* newspaper, saying that unless he refrained from publishing further reports on Heese's research, they would undertake legal action and sue the paper for damages totaling R 320,000 (roughly U.S. $125,000). In their lawyer's letter to the editor, the 16 men alleged that the *Sunday Times* report suggested that they were of mixed blood, that their origins were "suspect and doubtful," that they were therefore not entitled to comment on racial matters or resist integration, and that they should be ashamed to be Afrikaners. Heese's findings were furthermore described as "defamatory." Heese himself was threatened with legal action by the same 16 people. He was reportedly taken aback by their threats; he noted that early Cape society was a "physical melting pot," and now South Africans found themselves in a "political melting pot" (*Sunday Times,* March 10, 1985).

From this episode we can distinguish three responses. First, Afrikaners denied that the findings had much relevance. This was a position taken by those Afrikaners who saw racial admixture as a deviant hiccup of the past. Therefore, the research findings did not really affect them or their sense of identity. For other Afrikaners associated with right-wing political parties, the findings deeply affected their sense of identity and racial purity. Their reactions flared up in an intense and even violent fervor to expose the findings as fabrications or at least to prevent their publication. The denial of this group was much stronger than that of the first group; it was a form of psychological repression. The right-wingers' reaction strove to annul the findings. Eventually they dropped their court action and the whole issue sank back into their cumulative resentment against Afrikaner liberals. The third reaction was that of the author, who saw himself as an Afrikaner historian in the wider context of the "political melting pot" of contemporary South Africa. He joined a number of Afrikaans historians, political scientists, and linguists who increasingly viewed the past from an inclusive rather than an exclusive, ethnocentric perspective. These historians all seemed to be caught between the diverging expectations of their different constituencies. On the one hand, they desired to do good academic work acceptable to their academic peers. On the other, they produced work that was too esoteric for the general public and that was often misunderstood when popularized in press reports.

Continuity and Community
in History, Language, and Literature

A new generation of historians with Afrikaans background is rising, and its members suffer from the same pressures as Heese. Herman Giliomee and André du Toit (1983), for example, found recognition among the revisionists of English-speaking historiography. Most of their work is published in English and addresses debates being waged at Yale and at South African English-medium universities. These authors' attempts to reach a wider Afrikaans audience have been confined to occasional op-ed newspaper articles and the glossy pages of expensive magazines such as *Die Suid-Afrikaan,* read by a few elite Afrikaners. Other Afrikaans historians have joined with liberal-minded English speakers in the publication of *An Illustrated History of South Africa* (Cameron, 1986), a lavishly illustrated collection of essays in a coffee-table edition. One of the seven sections of the book deals with black history. The book's foreword states that "a conscious attempt has been made to present and analyze, wherever possible, the motives, actions and reactions of all members of South African society" (p. 7). Of the 20 essays, 9 were written by Afrikaans historians. Throughout the work there is an emphasis on inclusiveness.

The success of *An Illustrated History of South Africa* is indicative of the increasing unease of the white middle class concerning the availability of historical material outside the university and school contexts that deals fairly with all population categories. The Reader's Digest Association of South Africa was quick to respond to this need and produced in 1989 a glossy illustrated volume that sold for R 85.00 (U.S. $30.00). Its price, which is very high by South African standards, put it in the range of the high-income-bracket middle-class white public. Within the first six months after its publication, 85,000 copies had been sold (Hamilton, 1992). The interest shown by well-to-do, liberal-minded middle-class South Africans in "alternative," inclusive history demonstrates their preoccupation with a corrective of history that not only "restores" perspective on the past but assuages their feelings of guilt about the omission of blacks.

In the field of linguistics and literature there has been a similar trend toward inclusiveness. In an essay titled *Die Eenheid van die Afrikaanse Taalgemeenskap* (The Unity of the Afrikaans Language Community), Fritz Ponelis (1987), professor of Afrikaans and Dutch at Stellenbosch University, examines the contribution of slaves and blacks to the Afrikaans language. Stellenbosch University is generally considered to be an elitist Afrikaner institution and a guardian of the Afrikaans culture. It is the institution where the architect of apartheid, Verwoerd, taught social psychology, and where National Party presidents receive honorary doctorates and buildings are named in their honor. It was also where the dissident social historians Giliomee and du Toit departed from for the more tolerant atmosphere at the nearby English-language University of Cape Town. It is therefore important that Ponelis's view be seen in context. He argues that from an early stage the unity of the Afrikaans language community was so strong that the "political dividing line of color" could not disturb it (p. 6). He examines not only the Malay (slave) contribution but also the dialect of Flaaitaal, used by urban blacks, as a valid form of Afrikaans. Afrikaans as standardized language, he argues, drew people with different dialects together into a "community of communication" (p. 8). Unfortunately, the predominance of the formal standard version of Afrikaans, propagated by the government-controlled media, led to the stigmatization of other forms of Afrikaans as inferior. This must have been "a factor in the Anglicization of especially the Brown [i.e., coloured] speakers of Cape Afrikaans" (p. 11).[18]

Ponelis's emphasis on the community aspect of language and language use is especially important as an indicator of an inclusive attitude. A similar emphasis is present in the massive tome *Suid Afrika in Poësie* (South Africa in Poetry) (van Wyk, Conradie, & Constandaras, 1987), edited by Afrikaans academics from the universities of the Western Cape and Durban-Westville. Like the University of the Western Cape, Durban-Westville was founded under apartheid legislation to cater to the Indians' (separate) needs for tertiary education. Van Wyk and Conradie (Constandaras's base is unknown to me) thus used these universities, historically created in the discriminatory context of apartheid, as launching pads for the propagation of an inclusive perspective on South African culture. The poems included in this 900-page volume are arranged in chronological order, ranging from precolonial Khoi poetry to pieces in Sintu languages, in Flaaitaal, in English, and in Afrikaans. In their selection of poems one detects that the editors were guided by an underlying assumption about a social solidarity that unites South Africans regardless of color. That solidarity is based on the shared experience of suffering and domination. Therefore, poems dealing with the solidarity between Afrikaner and black garment workers are presented next to those dealing with both black and white resistance to apartheid.

How well these attempts toward inclusiveness in the reconstruction of South African history and language are received by a wider than academic audience is still to be seen. They constitute a decided shift in the drawing of the ethnic boundaries between white and black. One important factor hampering an inclusive view will be the tendency of many whites, especially Afrikaners, to deny a common heritage, whether biological, historical, cultural, or linguistic. This repressive denial is essentially a defensive attitude adopted in the process of upholding the phantasm of ethnic purity and exclusiveness. Upholding this fantasy is becoming a very difficult and burdensome task in light of the political developments of the 1990s, during which blacks have entered every arena of social and cultural life with great vigor. Dissolving the mirage will depend to a great extent on communication between the inclusivists and the exclusivists among whites. This will not be easy, however, because, as noted at the beginning of this chapter, historical reconstruction legitimates the present order. There is still a strong common vision that unifies whites historically. Regardless of the differences between them, the historiographies produced by Afrikaans and English speakers both contain strong justifications for the presence of whites in South Africa. This message also comes across in schoolbooks that offer all white children the same fare.

The essays explored above written by high school girls point in a similar direction. Although in the essays conservative Afrikaners, sometimes guided by lingering memories of an oppressive imperial Britain, are much more vociferous in propagating an ethnocentric perspective than are their English-speaking counterparts, they largely agree with reformists on one important point: Whites have had, and still have, a civilizing and educational mission in South Africa. This idea gives their lives meaning and purpose. The common mission might be expressed as one of Christianizing, civilizing, educating, uplifting, or developing the country and its inhabitants. However it is expressed, the mission empowers its agents to control, subdue, or change whatever poses resistance to the mission. In the execution of their mandate, whites have established a tradition. In this tradition blacks do not appear as coactors in any constructive sense. They are either invisible or a hindrance to the goals of the mission. It will be no easy task to deconstruct this tradition, because it is imbued with an authority that has received very little challenge during the 350 years of white presence in South Africa.

NOTES

1. This is an extract from a speech delivered to the Rapportryers of the town Lichtenburg in June 1971. Rapportryers is an exclusively male Afrikaner organization patterned after such bodies as Rotary International, but with ethnocentric goals. The secret Afrikaner organization the Broederbond recruits much of its membership from the Rapportryers.

2. In 1815 a small uprising of white frontiersmen occurred in the Eastern Cape. It was reported that they sought an alliance with the Xhosa against the British. After a trial, five men were sentenced to death. At their execution by hanging, the ropes broke. Pleas for mercy

by those present went unheeded, and the men were hanged successfully the second time. Slagtersnek became an important symbol of oppression during the political mobilization of the Afrikaner after the 1930s (see Moodie, 1975, p. 181).

3. Smith (1988, pp. 74-75) cites a series of articles by B. J. Liebenberg in the magazine *Huisgenoot* (December 16, 1977; January 2, February 17, and March 10, 1978) in which the manufacture of the covenant celebrations is discussed.

4. This is from Stals's inaugural lecture at the Rand Afrikaans University. The addendum contains a complete (for that time) bibliography of the historiography of black-white relations in South Africa.

5. Met die daarstelling van territoriale skeidslyne het Suid-Afrika vergoed die beginsel van gelykstelling verwerp. Mog hy die toekoms op 'n hegte fondament bou.

6. Dit kom dus daarop neer dat die blankes hulself sal moet verlos van die pynlike afhanklikheid van Bantoe-arbeid waarin hulle hulself vandag bevind.

7. Volharding in die gewoonte om alle swaar vorms van arbeid op die nie-blankes af te skuif, moet op die duur onvermydelik tot die ondergang van die blanke ras lei.

8. In 1950, F. R. Tomlinson was appointed by the Nationalist government to head a commission with a brief to investigate the means necessary to stem the flow of blacks toward the cities. The commission recommended, among other things, that 50,000 jobs be created annually for blacks in the rural areas in order to keep them away from the cities and to reverse the urbanization trend. Verwoerd, then minister of native affairs, favored the creation of fewer than 1,000 jobs per year.

9. In a private communication, a noted historian who prefers to remain anonymous observed that liberal, English-speaking historians tend to share their professional interests more with the more enlightened Afrikaans-speaking historians than with the Marxists at their respective universities.

10. Wright (1977, p. 90) observes that "radicals" tend to preach to the converted. He also raises serious points of criticism with regard to their handling of historical evidence.

11. Christian National Education in South Africa originally developed around the need to provide education to Afrikaner children through the medium of their vernacular. The secondary socialization of children was to be placed in an ethnic context guided by Christian principles. After the NP came to power, the total school system for whites was transformed in the spirit of CNE.

12. Du Preez attempted to apply a specific form of content analysis to the material. He chose thematic analysis rather than lexical or semantic analysis; thematic analysis involves the classification of explicit and implicit themes as they occur.

13. Auerbach (1965) did a study of school history textbooks of the 1950s and early 1960s. The ethnocentrism, racism, and stereotypes he recorded recur in later textbooks, but less blatantly so.

14. *Nagmaal* is the Holy Communion celebrated in rural towns. Farmers and their families all trekked to the town with their ox wagons and camped on the church grounds. *Nagmaal* was held on a quarterly basis and lasted for several days. It was more than just a religious celebration; it was an occasion to meet family friends and acquaintances. It was also a time for courtship and, within the confines of Calvinist strictness, celebration. *Jukskei* is a game similar to horseshoes; it is played with bottle-shaped pieces of wood.

15. The Voortrekker movement is an Afrikaner ethnic youth movement founded in 1929. The Scout movement founded by the Boer adversary, Baden-Powell, was unacceptable to Afrikaner nationalists.

16. I have translated the last lines of the South African anthem literally to capture the meaning adequately. The official version of the first verse runs as follows: "Ringing out from our blue heavens, / From our deep seas breaking round; / Over everlasting mountains / Where the echoing crags resound; / From our plains where creaking wagons / Cut their trails into the earth / Calls the spirit of our country / Of the land that gave us birth. / At thy call we shall not falter / Firm and steadfast we shall stand / At thy will to live or perish / O South Africa dear land.

17. The representativeness of these views is a problem, however. As far as I could determine, the essays cited here seem to derive slightly more from rural schools than from urban ones. A number of the essays give no indication of their geographic origin. It is therefore not possible to say whether we are dealing with a rural bias. That there are very few urban essays that take up the topic of history may be a result of history's being regarded as relatively unimportant.

18. This essay was published in a collection edited by du Plessis and du Plessis (1987), who title one of their book's three sections "Afrikaans in the Past." Five essays in that section recognize the contribution of other groups (some nonwhite) to the development of Afrikaans. In an earlier work, Claasen and van Rensburg (1983) also give recognition to the fact that the variants of the language spoken by nonwhite communities could be considered variants of Afrikaans.

4

The Construction
of the Present: Official,
Media, and Religious Versions

> The animals in totemism cease to be solely or principally creatures which
> are feared, admired or envied: their perceptible reality permits the embodiment
> of ideas and relations conceived by speculative thought on the basis of empirical
> observations. We can understand too, that natural species are chosen not
> because they are "good to eat" but because they are "good to think."
> (Lévi-Strauss, 1969, p. 161)

At first glance, these remarks may seem quite inappropriate to describe
white South African racial thinking. Yet, in a metaphoric sense, there is a
link. Lévi-Strauss argues that, in a totemic system, animals have the perceived status of cognitive constructs that are useful in explaining and
making sense of social relationships and natural realities. These constructs
provide collective guidance and orientation in the lives of members of
preliterate societies. One most striking feature of white-dominated South
African society until the last decade of the twentieth century was its structu-
ration by legal means. In South Africa, I will argue, instead of animals
being good to think (with), "laws were good to think with," as far as most
whites were concerned in the age of apartheid. (As we will see, laws were
also good for eating in the sense that they provided whites with economic
privilege.) Not only did laws, especially those regulating relations among
people, provide a sense of order and security, they also offered explanations and understandings of the economic, social, political, and even religious
order. They assumed a "natural" character. They organized thought. Their
validity was seldom questioned by ordinary whites. The importance of

law and the rigid social and political structures it created can, in significant part, be attributed to deep authoritarianism among middle-class South African whites. I will elaborate on this point toward the end of this chapter.

Among Afrikaners, laws are to be greatly respected. This respect comes out of their authoritarian upbringing, which accords to the state a divine mandate to regulate relations among humans. According to Afrikaners' Calvinist conceptions, all authority ultimately derives from God, whose glory it exults and by whose grace it exists. In the halls of some Afrikaans universities and theological seminaries, the theocratic ideals of Calvin's Geneva still echo. Generations of ministers of religion have been sent to parishes across the country to inculcate in their congregants a specific sense of order and respect for authority and the law. The ministers themselves are subject to dual role expectations. In the popular conception, a minister has to be a *volksman* (politician; literally "man of the people") as well as a *Godsman* (man of God). Ministers have had strong peers in this regard, such as the first prime minister of the National Party, D. F. Malan. In leadership and ideology, harmony is thus established between church and state conceptions. The changing of any laws is therefore a serious matter, and when it occurs the process is difficult and slow. The Dutch Reformed Churches, for example, utilize to this day the seventeenth-century church laws established by the Synod of Dordrecht in the Netherlands as the base of church government and doctrinal control. To envisage a radical abolition of the system of laws and the overthrow of a government is thus quite unthinkable to mainstream Afrikaners. It is therefore understandable that the abolition of apartheid laws during the 1990s has met with a high degree of shock.

The Afrikaner view of the relationship between church and state is very heavily informed by the late-nineteenth-century thoughts of the Calvinist Dutch politician-theologian Abraham Kuyper. Kuyper headed his anti-revolutionary, essentially bourgeois, party in stiff opposition to the socialistically inclined labor party in his country. He was the initiator of the idea that separate organizational structures should serve different groups, especially religious groups, in one society. He therefore advocated that societies should establish separate cultural and educational institutions for different groups. This idea was called *verzuiling,* meaning that society was organized in a pillarlike fashion. His main concern was to get Calvinists and Protestants out of the clutches of revolutionary socialism on the one hand and Catholicism on the other. As far as his attitude toward political change was concerned, Kuyper saw gradual reform as the only way. Kuyper's philosophy had a profound influence on the South African concept of the state, especially his two notions of the separateness of its constituents and the necessity of reform rather than revolution as a means of bringing about political change. Among the majority of the Afrikaner population, abhorrence of revolutionary change is deeply rooted in a Calvinist theology of reform and a respect for existing social and political order, which cannot simply be overthrown or replaced. Afrikaner religious leaders and politicians alike adhere to Calvin's tenet of *reformata reformanda* (what is reformed should be reformed) in the domains of public and private life.

Of equal influence, and more radical in certain respects, have been the views of the Dutch Calvinist philosopher Herman Dooyeweerd. His views, taught at Afrikaans universities to generations of theology, law, education, and political science students, have had a trickle-down effect on the constituencies of these professions. In his central work, *Wijsbegeerte der Wetsidee* (Philosophy of the Idea of Law) (1935), Dooyeweerd's main goal was to anchor universal and cosmically valid laws in the Word of God (see Spier, 1950). He thus expanded the notion of law far beyond its jural boundaries to include every aspect of human life and of reality in general. The whole cosmos, the world, and particularly human reality are thus structured by laws ordained by God. It is as if an elective affinity exists between these ideas and the need of Afrikaners to find an intellectual and philosophical foundation for their political culture. Dooyeweerd's views had an almost immediate impact on Afrikaner thought. In the late 1930s, a major Afrikaner philosopher, H. G. Stoker, propagated and adapted Dooyeweerd's ideas on the nature of law to the situation of the Afrikaner people. The reception of this philosophy by Afrikaner intellectuals and leaders of the *volk* (people) occurred at a time of intense ethnic mobilization between 1938 (the Voortrekker centenary) and 1948 (the political ascendancy of the Afrikaner). It taught the broader population, through its ministers of religion, its teachers, and other professionals, that reality is structured by laws of divine origin and that their country's legal system must give expression to those universal laws in the jural realm. In other words, they maintained that a convergence ought to exist between the law of man and the Law of God. Such a philosophy exalts obedience as a supreme virtue and affirms that social order is inviolable.

WHITE INTERESTS AND THE LAW

It would be misleading, however, to explore only the theological, historical, and ideological aspects of whites', and especially Afrikaners', conception of order. These aspects show an affinity to a host of other white interests. I distinguish three sets that have helped sustain economic, security, and civil measures necessary for the perpetuation of the (white) South African way of life. Since 1991, some laws fulfilling these functions have been repealed and have, in some instances, been replaced by others.

First of all, there as been material interest in an economy of white privilege. A stable political and legal order was its precondition. All sections of the white population, especially the business sector, invoked the crucial importance of the "rule of law" as a sine qua non for a sound and growing economy. Since the late 1970s, the largely English-speaking business community has been increasingly co-opted by the government in upholding the system of cheap black labor. The government avoided the bad publicity attached to influx control legislation (pass laws—see below) by abolishing it in 1986. Officials realized they could achieve the same restriction on black surplus population in the cities by convincing industrialists to adopt employment practices that would exclude the "unwanted" from the cities. In this way, demographic "order" would be achieved. The government took care of remaining urbanization problems by passing laws such as the Prevention of Illegal Squatting Amendment Act of 1988.

Second, there was interest in providing security for the white lifestyle. It was necessary to uphold a sense of personal safety and property in a society riddled by racial tensions. Toward this end, a strictly regulated civil order was necessary. Many security laws were therefore designed to contain "elements" that jeopardized the order. The restriction, detention, and imprisonment of people without recourse to due process was thus justified. Both English speakers and Afrikaners generally accepted this legislation as an unfortunate but necessary safeguard and guarantee of peace. Their acceptance rested on a widespread lack of sensitivity toward civil and human rights or on the fear of the chaos that might ensue if political discourse were opened up and political protest tolerated. During 1990, the government experimented with greater tolerance toward public protest. However, this was done by easing the application of available laws, rather than by abolishing them.[1] Security has remained a major concern of whites during the 1990s, and even though the provisions of the Internal Security Act were relaxed in 1991, I cannot foresee its repeal as long as whites have a significant say in government.

Third, there was interest in the perpetuation of an undisturbed lifestyle: "the (white) South African way of life." The boundaries, both social and geographic, that the laws set suited the lifestyle of whites. By law, poor and not so poor blacks had to live far away, and consequently did not intrude into white suburbia. Even after public amenities were opened to all races in certain cities during 1989, these amenities remained the preserve of whites. They were usually built close to or within white residential areas, allowing easy access for whites but not for blacks. The legal structure also created, and business held in place, ample surplus labor at minimal wages. Thus white families could afford to employ servants to do the chores and drudgery of household labor, freeing the "masters" and "madams" to devote much of their time to leisure activities. The existing order maintained by the legal structure was thus convenient and kept blacks "in their place." Any change in this situation would disturb the peace of mind and the pattern of life of most whites.

Respect for the law among whites therefore was clearly not founded on purely ideological, economic, and political grounds, but had an intrinsic bearing on the maintenance of a very materially cozy and secure existence. As noted above, laws are also good to think with: They frame reality and bestow upon it at the same time the character of realness and normality. To most whites it was not an "abnormal" situation that blacks as a category "by nature" were destined to do menial and blue-collar work. Children were not taught that these assumptions were questionable and that there was something wrong with such a system. Their geography books told them that the physical racial separation in rural and urban South Africa was normal. Most parents did not question the arrangement, nor did they question the racial division of labor in their homes.

Having introduced the idea of an interplay of ideology and interests in the reproduction of the South African way of life, I now wish to turn to some of the more concrete structures providing the context of the everyday world experience and consciousness of white South Africans. The rest of this chapter is devoted to an examination of some of the legal markers of white intersubjectivity in South African society along two dimensions. First, how did the system of laws provide a matrix for thought? Second, what influence did the media and organized religion have in the structuring of whites' experience and thought? I will explore how the media assist in endowing the legal construction of reality with the quality of normalness. Religion has always played an important part in white South Africans' lives. What guidance and orientation has organized religion offered to the public on race relations and the South African lifestyle? Chapters 5 and 6 examine the right-wing and government-guided public discourse on the present and future situation of South Africa. Also, in Chapter 6 special attention is given to the intellectual discourse at universities and other educational institutions, and its influence on whites.

LEGAL CORNERSTONES

It was not until the 1990s that the most important legal cornerstones of apartheid began to be removed from the statute books. Their impact on white racial thinking was enduring, however. I therefore intend to review in this section the four laws that formed the pillars of legal apartheid: the Population Registration Act (1950), which established four categories of persons in society; the Land Act (1913, 1936), which determined where persons in each of those categories could own land; the Group Areas Act (1950), which allocated separate living spaces to persons in the four categories; and the Constitution Act (1983), which determined the civil rights of persons in the four categories. At the end of June 1991, three of these laws were repealed, and the government promised to negotiate a new constitution that would replace the Constitution Act. These laws were both the outcome and the perpetuators of group and racial thinking among whites.

Looking at the tremendous number of laws and regulations that regulated racial privilege and relations in the country during statutory apartheid, a certain logical structure can be seen to underlie the system. This logic was not necessarily a chronological one. The most fundamental piece of legislation underlying the whole system and reflecting at the same time the organization of South African thought patterns and categorizations is the Population Registration Act (No. 30) of 1950. This act was one of the first major pieces of legislation passed by the newly elected National Party government of 1948. Its name, in a fashion typical of South African legal phraseology, disguised its purpose as a merely administrative measure to keep track of population matters. The consequences of the act for the lives of individuals affected by it were unrelated to the mere record keeping its name seemed to imply. The act originally distinguished among "whites," "coloureds," and "natives." The coloured category initially included Indians and Asians, people descended from immigrants from India. The coloured category was subsequently further subdivided into many subgroups, such as "Cape Malay," "Griqua," and "other coloured." Indians became a category on their own. In everyday parlance, *coloureds* were regarded as descendants of mixed unions between whites and blacks, or the descendants of coloureds or of the Malay population at the Cape.

"Natives" in later revisions of the law became known as "Bantu" and still later as "blacks." They were further subdivided according to what the government held to be ethnologic and linguistic categories. There were nine such subcategories. The whites were generally regarded as a homogeneous category, without any legal provision for the wide-ranging linguistic and ethnic diversification among them. The government's main rationale for this law rested on its "recognition" of "natural" and "historical" divisions in society. Members of the white public were given the impression that these were "pure" categories. They failed, however, to reflect on their own ethnic diversity, which was not expressed in law. The failure to differentiate the white population along ethnic and linguistic lines amounted to a tacit confession by the government that race rather than ethnicity or culture was at the bottom of the act's distinctions. No separate provisions were made for English and Afrikaans speakers. The large Portuguese, German, and Greek communities were considered to be "natural" parts of the white category.

Classification into one of the legal categories occurred at the registration of a birth, when the child was automatically classified into the parents' population category. Descent was thus taken as the crucial criterion. In borderline cases the criteria of "appearance" and "general acceptance" were used. Generally these criteria reflected in a negative way characteristics that are "not white," namely, "habits, education and speech, and deportment and demeanor." Officials applied ridiculous means to determine racial classification. For example, they used measures such as the ease with which a comb could be pulled through the hair, microscopic analysis of hair, the coloring of fingernails, and the form of the nose. Needless to say, such procedures often divided families, with tragic effects on the lives of children.

As a consequence of the everyday reality of these divisions, their racist basis became widely internalized, not only by whites but by members of the disadvantaged categories. Being classified as nonwhite carried with it a stigma. Being classified black rather than coloured "degraded" a person even further. A hierarchy of racial status thus stretched from the lightest skinned to the darkest skinned at the bottom of the scale. As far as the white, coloured, and black categories were concerned, the government set officially sanctioned but often arbitrary markers to distinguish the subdivisions. More devastating, however, were the differential life chances that race classification distributed among the population.[2] By examining the parameters of infant mortality, morbidity, income, education, and welfare payments, to name but a few, clear gradations can be discerned. Whites

had and still have the best life chances: the longest life expectancy, highest
level of education, and so on. They are followed by the Indians, then the
coloureds, and finally the blacks.

The South African population was explicitly cast into legally defined
racial categories that also distributed life chances. The Population Registration Act could thus be seen as the true cornerstone of apartheid society.
Within the discourse about the "new" postapartheid South Africa, the
question of group rights keeps returning. The basic fourfold division of
the South African population into white, black, Indian, and coloured, and
its impact on the structure of everyday life, is deeply ingrained in white
consciousness. This law was the embodiment of deeply rooted ideas and
values. The distinctions it made were symbolic to whites' sense of identity.
In my view, a majority of whites, even liberals, whether Afrikaans or
English speaking, will seek legal or constitutional guarantees for the preservation of their group. If legal protection proves impossible, they will erect
other social and physical boundaries to achieve the same end.

The Population Registration Act thus made a very basic distinction
between white and black. To distinguish the privileged category from the
rest, the dividing line ran between whites and nonwhites. As far as the
geopolitical division of the country was concerned, the distinction ran
between blacks and nonblacks. Let us look at this distinction. The land
question has been a perennial issue from the earliest times of white settlement in the country. After the colonial Anglo-Boer War, when a unified
South Africa was envisaged, one of the first issues addressed after a new
constitution was thrashed out in 1908 was the land question. The South
Africa Act, passed by the British Parliament in 1909, disenfranchised
blacks, with the exception of those living in the Cape, who retained a
nominal political representation in the new South African Parliament. One
of the first tasks this Parliament set itself was to draft legislation that
would settle the land question once and for all. The system of black tribal
reservations had to be rationalized under one general law. In the early
stages of its conceptualization, the Natives Land Act (No. 27) of 1913
(later known as the Blacks Land Act of 1913) was vehemently opposed by
the black population and was the most important reason for the founding
of the South African Native National Congress (SANNC), the predecessor
of the present African National Congress (ANC). In its application, this
law logically (not chronologically) built upon the categories established
by the Population Registration Act and constituted the second cornerstone
of the corpus of racial legislation. It excluded blacks from owning land in
South Africa except in certain areas that coincided largely with the system

of tribal reservations. The area in which blacks were allowed to possess land constituted less than 8% of the country's surface. In 1936 the law was amended to increase the area to 13.6%. The "black" territories stretched in a horseshoe pattern from the northwestern to the southeastern quadrants of the country. They were extremely fragmented and were organized around what the government considered to be ethnic units. The ethnic principle was not followed consistently: The Xhosa were split into two separate territories that made up the Transkei and the Ciskei, respectively, and until the 1980s the Zulu unit (KwaZulu) consisted of 44 different pieces of land. These areas, first known as *native reserves,* were later called *Bantustans,* expressing the government's intended impression that they were separate political units. In the 1970s the government described them as "homelands," pretending they were the "homes" of blacks, in contrast to the metropolitan and other white areas. In doing this the government obviously wished to sell to the white and black populations the idea that blacks in "white" areas were temporary sojourners and "naturally" belonged in rural areas. This was done regardless of the overwhelming evidence that blacks had lived all over South Africa from the earliest times. A large proportion had lived in cities for generations and had no ties with the ethnic "homelands." Yet they were ascribed to "belong" there.

The disproportionate distribution of land, of course, did not escape the attention of the white public. The government defended its policies by emphasizing that "black" land was situated in the most fertile areas of the country and that the land could therefore support a greater population density. However, what the government did not say was that these areas could by no means support even the black population living there at the time. The government-appointed Tomlinson Commission reported in 1954 that the native reserves could potentially support only about half of the black population (see also Chapter 3, note 8), and that in order to achieve this a massive development scheme was necessary. The then prime minister, Hendrik Verwoerd, refused to authorize the financial means necessary for Bantustan development. The public was still being told that the black areas were sufficiently large, and that those blacks in "white" areas were, in fact, no different from the migrant workers in modern European states. Territorial separation and migrant labor were thus not only placed within the context of normal practice, but morally justified. Again, what was not revealed were the devastating consequences this policy and the division of land had on the population. To date, the government has relocated millions of blacks in accordance with apartheid legislation. In 1983 the Surplus People's Project calculated that more than 3.5 million blacks had been moved, most of them as a result of the provisions of the Black Land Act (Omond, 1986, pp. 131-132).[3] As recently as 1990, and in the middle of their "liberal" and "reform" masquerade, the National Party government continued to relocate thousands of blacks in pursuit of the geopolitical separation of races.

One of the most draconian pieces of legislation built upon the Black Land Act was the National States Constitution Act (No. 27) of 1970 (previously the Homelands Constitution Act). This law denationalized all blacks allocated to those homelands that embraced political independence from South Africa. There were four of these so-called independent states: Transkei, Ciskei, Bophutatswana, and Venda.[4] Their "independence" was not recognized by any state but South Africa. Denationalization meant the removal of South African citizenship and all its privileges from blacks designated by the South African government as citizens of the National States (independent homelands). Every black in the country was allocated to some homeland. Those unlucky enough to be considered citizens of the National States could be removed to the "countries of their citizenship" in accordance with international law governing the repatriation of citizens. The South African government could thus hide the implementation of its apartheid policy under the guise of internationally sanctioned legality.[5] Correspondingly, it convinced its white electorate that it was acting not only legally but normally. The electorate and the public were all too willing to believe this. For the blacks affected by this ploy, it meant that they could be forced to go to homelands they may have had no relationship with when they lost their jobs in larger South Africa or when they were arrested for minor offenses. Technically, this would have looked like deportation. Thus the misery of people so affected was hidden from the international community and from many critical-minded individuals in South Africa as just another act of international "justice."

Another consequence of the Land Act and the National States Constitution Act has to be considered. In Latin American countries, the poor have the right to seek, or eke out, an existence near the concentrations of wealth, the cities. In South Africa, urban black unemployment and poverty were exported to the rural homeland areas and thus hidden from the white public eye in both geographic and statistical senses. Official black unemployment figures thus looked ridiculously low. In the geographic sense, various laws and regulations prohibited whites from leaving the highways to enter the homelands in order to see for themselves the conditions that prevailed. A group of socially aware social scientists, for example, launched a comprehensive project to document the effects of the government's relocation policies on the black population. In its report, the Surplus People's Project (1983) mentions only cursorily that the state detained two fieldworkers for a period of 10 months and that other fieldworkers were harassed at various times (p. xv). This is only one example of the state's attempts to hide the true situation from the public. Harassment and intimidation of journalists, social scientists, and humanitarian workers have been copiously documented.

The so-called pass laws were recently abolished in the wake of the government's reform policy. Their basis was the Blacks (Urban Areas) Consolidation Act of 1954, which was repealed on July 1, 1986. Thereafter, some movement of blacks to the cities took place, and the already insufficient black housing situation in the cities was aggravated. "Shacking" (the erection of shacks next to existing houses) and squatting thus occurred in the vicinity of large cities. The best-known squatter camp was that of Crossroads, near Cape Town, highly visible right next to the highway and under the final approach to the main airport. On the surface, South Africa's urban reality now apparently gave a home to the poor and unemployed. During recent visits (between July 1989 and June 1991), I observed many more poor black people on the streets of Johannesburg and Pretoria than when the pass laws were still in force. Again, many regulations and laws controlling vagrancy and trespassing have given the government the means to expel blacks from the cities without resorting to the ignominious pass laws that brought the country so much bad publicity.[6] New laws have been enacted to control the flow of blacks to the cities. In 1988 the Prevention of Illegal Squatting Amendment Act was passed. This law made homelessness and the occupation of informal housing illegal. De facto, the same results were achieved through this arrangement as with the old pass laws. In its typical rhetoric, the government justified its action in technocratic terms, namely, to make an "attack on the 'rapid unorderly urbanization' which, the government believed, had developed since the pass laws were repealed" (South African Institute of Race Relations [SAIRR], 1989, p. 163). The white electorate was thus still made to believe that poverty was disappearing, without evidence of the mass bulldozing of squatter settlements and the sending of their occupants "back to their homelands."[7] The white public was left with the impression that order was preserved without realizing how the undeniable reality of mass black poverty was again removed from their field of awareness. In the 1990s these removals stopped abruptly, however.

The third cornerstone of legal apartheid was the Group Areas Act (No. 41) of 1950. This law was logically based on the Population Registration

Act, the categories of which it adopted. It complemented the Black Land Act by rationalizing, along racial lines, land usage in the whole of South Africa (excluding the black homelands). At its introduction, the responsible minister justified the legislation in terms of the need to minimize contact among the groups, maintaining that "the paramountcy of the white man and of Western civilization to South Africa must be insured in the interests of the material, cultural and spiritual development of all races" (Omond, 1986, p. 37). According to this law, separate areas were to be set aside for the occupation, trade, and residence of the four main population groups as defined by the Population Registration Act. A great proportion of the removals mentioned above were done in accordance with the terms of this law. In many cases residential patterns that had developed over centuries were destroyed and stable communities uprooted through the reallocation of their territory to another group. In the case of District 6, an area that had been occupied by Cape (Malay) coloureds for centuries, the whole population was moved out of the city and hundreds of historical buildings were razed to make way for the white population's business and residential interests. The same happened to the Indian community of Pageview in Johannesburg. The pattern of segregating groups in the cities repeated itself in hundreds of towns and villages. Traveling through the countryside, one notices the effects of group areas most poignantly in the separate cemeteries for blacks and whites on the outskirts of towns. As one nears the periphery of a town, one finds the Indian trading area, separate from the center.

School geography books contained lessons about town and urban development along lines and divisions established by this law. Group separation was treated as normal, and its geographic expression in the organization of urban life represented as a matter of fact. What was not emphasized was the hardship this separation imposed on poorer populations. Not only were they forced to live farther and farther away from the center of town and their workplaces, they also had to cope with long travel times and increased transport costs. Whites rarely thought about how such legislation affected the experiences of blacks. They took for granted that their laborers would turn up for work punctually and refreshed.

The Group Areas Act had implications not only for the physical location of the groups but for the location of separate schools, health facilities, churches, and so on. In 1985 two laws based on the Population Registration Act were abolished. The Immorality Amendment Act (No. 23) of 1957 forbade sexual relations between whites and members of any another population group. The Prohibition of Mixed Marriages Act (No. 55) of 1949 made marriages between whites and members of other population groups illegal. Both these laws brought South Africa a bad reputation and even ridicule from other Western societies. Their repeal would not have been much more than a public relations exercise were it not for the abolition of the Group Areas Act itself in June 1991. Very few mixed marriages took place after the repeal of the legislation, and they often had tragic consequences (see Omond, 1986, pp. 31-32; SAIRR, 1989, pp. 179-181). In 1987, 1,393 marriages took place between people of different races, or 2.1% of all marriages (SAIRR, 1989, p. 152). The effects of apartheid legislation have crystallized in physical structures, geographic arrangements, and human values to such an extent that they will guide human interaction and pattern social life in South Africa for many years to come.

In the interim period between the repeal of the Mixed Marriages Act in 1985 and the Group Areas Act in 1991, the latter attracted bad publicity both from within and from outside the country. It became one of the obstacles in the process of negotiation between the African National Congress and the Nationalist government. It is important to follow the debate that preceded its abolition, especially to note how the issue of (white) group protection was handled. First, the law was amended in 1988. The Group Areas Amendment closed some loopholes and tightened the restrictions on residents not legally entitled to live in certain areas. Fines and prison sentences were increased for people contravening the main law by buying, selling, or occupying property belonging to members of groups not qualified to live in the group areas to which the properties were designated. The courts were also forced to evict illegal occupants. In passing this law, the government was reacting to white right-wing fears and pressure before the general election of 1989. Whites were thus made to understand that nothing had changed. Some aspects of the law were subsequently revised in response to criticism by the coloured and Indian communities. While tightening up on Group Areas enforcement on the one hand, the government attempted to pour oil on the water by passing the Free Settlement Areas Act in the same year, 1988. This act allowed the creation of residential areas where people of all population groups could live. In 1989, 14 such areas were identified (but not created) across the country. In his rationale for the act, the then minister for education and chairman of the minister's council in the House of Assembly, F. W. de Klerk (now state president), declared:

> Balance is being striven for [in the Free Settlement Areas Act] because, while the basic point of departure of own residential areas is maintained, room is

also left for individuals who feel differently. . . . Individual and group rights can, in the South African context, best be protected within the context of an own community. The ministers' council also accepts the other point of departure underlying this legislation, which is the acceptance of the principle of free association for those who desire it so that they may settle in residential areas where anybody may live. (quoted in SAIRR, 1989, pp. 218-219)

Note how the "basic point of departure" and the "other point of departure" are sequenced. The prioritizing by the minister becomes much clearer if one examines who has the power to decide on the creation of free settlement areas. The state president had the final say in such deliberations, though members of the public would be heard at an inquiry. A small degree of flexibility was thus introduced by "allowing" ("room is also left") for free association. The "group" of the Group Areas Act was now described as "community" and contrasted with free association. However, in his landmark opening speech to Parliament in February 1991, F. W. de Klerk combined the notion of freedom of association with that of community:

- A community life of one's own has to be sustained by one's own inherent will and abilities and not by statutory coercion; and
- Community recognition has to be based on freedom of association, as it is constitutionally and otherwise recognized by various countries in the world. (Republic of South Africa, Bureau of Information, 1991, p. 13)

These are important shifts, but the reader may notice the preoccupation with the notion of "group." It is my argument that this notion of group essentially carries with it the overtones of the old legal definition of ascriptive social categories even after the repeal of the act itself.

In its distribution of privilege, the Population Registration Act relied on the distinction between nonwhites and whites. Political developments in the 1970s necessitated a shift in the major legislative pattern toward a reliance on the distinction between black and nonblack. Before the 1970s, white political power went largely unchallenged after the severe suppression of black nationalist movements during the 1960s. The Soweto schools' revolt of 1976 and the increased militancy of black workers, inter alia, inspired the government to co-opt not only business (see above), but also the Indian and coloured population groups into the power structure. With negligible exceptions, whites had monopolized political power since 1910. In the late 1970s the government wanted to stabilize the black urban workforce and to redistribute political power in order to entrench white domination while at the same time satisfying the political aspirations of the two other minority groups, the coloureds and the Asians. It thus drafted constitutional legislation that would drive a political wedge between blacks (Africans) and all other population groups (nonblacks). Instead of extending the general vote to whites, coloureds, and Asians, the government made use of the Population Registration legislation in distributing political rights according to preexisting ascriptive categories. It made use of the complex of legislation based on the Black Land Act such as the Homelands Constitution Act to justify the exclusion of blacks (Africans) from the political process. This legislation, government officials claimed, provided political rights to the whole black (African) population. They thus felt there was no need to give any further consideration to initiating common South African political process. It was only in the local, municipal context that mechanisms for the political participation of all populations were created.

The government solved the problem of retaining political control after enfranchising the coloureds and Asians by following a simple divide-and-rule method combined with underweighting the newly enfranchised minorities. Under the Constitution Act of 1983, three lower houses of Parliament were created, one for each population group. Fundamental to this subdivision of Parliament is the bureaucratic notion of competence. The separate houses were allowed to deal only with problems and legislation pertaining to their own population groups. The principle of "own affairs" was thus established. These separate spheres of influence included such matters as health, education, welfare, and housing. As late as June 1990, the minister for constitutional development gave the white Parliament the reassurance that the distinction of "own affairs" would remain until the constitution is changed (*Transvaler,* June 6, 1990).

The Constitution Act of 1983 also recognized the existence of "general affairs," that is, matters that concern all three population groups. The state president was given the power to determine what constitute common affairs as well as own affairs. For legislation on general affairs to become law, all three chambers had to pass it. In case of conflict, a president's council had to arbitrate. In the tricameral Parliament, the president's council, and the electoral college for the state president's office, the vote was distributed among group representatives according to the following formula: for every four representatives the whites had, there would be two for the coloureds and one for the Asians. On every level, the combined Asian and coloured vote could thus be overruled by whites. The state president was accorded wide-ranging executive powers, enabling him to manipulate the legislative process. One observer described his position as an "executive autocracy" (Murray, 1987, p. 117). In effect, then, the constitution of 1983 entrenched white power. Beyond that, it placed the ruling party in a powerful and unchallengeable position.

In November 1983 a referendum was held on the new constitution. Liberal government critics found themselves in an ambiguous situation. Opposition to the new constitution could have been interpreted as support for the status quo, that is, for the exclusion from the political process of every group but whites. Support for these proposals could be interpreted as acceptance of the disenfranchisement of blacks (Africans) and of the principle of group rights based on race. In the end, however, even semiliberal newspapers supported the new constitution as a "step in the right direction." The strongest opposition came from white conservatives, who saw the new constitution as a dilution of the "white man's power." Nevertheless, 66% of the white electorate (with 76% voting) accepted the new constitution. Even at the drafting stage, the new constitution and the philosophy underlying it deeply disturbed the more conservative elements in the white population. It directly contributed to a major split in the National Party, when Andries Treurnicht took with him a number of NP parliamentarians in order to found the Conservative Party in March 1982.

The Constitution Act of 1983 fit logically into the structure of apartheid legislation. It bound together the Land Act-based legislation, the Group Areas principle, and numerous other laws based on the group distinctions made by the Population Registration Act into one legal master edifice. Ideologically, this arrangement enabled the South African government to pride itself on its incorporation of nonwhites into a common political system and thus to counter arguments that it was racist. It achieved this incorporation without abolishing apartheid. Whites could thus believe that their political system had become more democratic without having to make the sacrifice of a redistribution of "common resources."

In this section I have argued that the abolition of legal apartheid would not make those structures in consciousness disappear that it perpetuated and helped to give rise to in the first place. Three of the cornerstone laws have been repealed; at the time of this writing, the Constitution Act is still in force. Before dealing with developments around this last act, I want first to address the aftermath of the other three. Given that white group sentiments seem to be so strong, will they not now seek new and overt legal manifestations? It would be unreasonable to expect them to take on any of the old forms; we therefore have to look for disguised forms.

In 1991, the government prepared the way to introduce the Residential Environment Bill. This act was intended to ensure that proper norms and standards would be followed in residential areas. The government would ensure that communities would have the rights and means to maintain standards they set for themselves. Because the Group Areas Act already established the residential structures of the country, this law would enable the largely racially based groups to enforce standards by excluding violators. It takes little imagination to identify the racial characteristics of the potential violators. Since the repeal of urban pass laws, blacks have "illegally" rented apartments near the central business district of Johannesburg. In order to pay the high rents, many individuals and families have banded together to live in apartments in the high-rise area of Hillbrow. The resultant overcrowding has led to "deterioration" of the neighborhood. Many whites who previously considered the area a playground have looked on in disgust. The Residential Environment Bill would address this problem in a seemingly nonascriptive group (read "racial") way. However, its effect would be to maintain the group characteristics of a residential area; that is, the result would be similar to what the old Group Areas Act achieved. The bill found strong opposition among the nonwhite sections of the population. In a brochure published by the government's Bureau of Information, de Klerk furthermore argued that the abolition of the Land Act had "constitutional implications" and that any reform with regard to the usage of land would have to take into account the principles of "free enterprise, security of tenure and *vested property rights*" (Republic of South Africa, Bureau of Information, 1990; emphasis added). Vested property rights, of course, were both constituted and protected by the Land Act and the Group Areas Act in the past. After these laws were abolished, the tendency to entrench white group privilege and wealth surfaced in the sanitized and deracialized language used in regulations replacing the old racist laws.

The debate surrounding the replacement of the Constitution Act centered on the issue of whether a new constitution should be negotiated by a constituent assembly or by a multiparty conference. The ANC favored the constituent assembly idea, membership of which would follow the lines of the ANC's declared nonracialism. The white government, on the other hand, insisted on a multiparty conference in which "the negotiation of a new constitution should be the responsibility of the representatives of all political parties who enjoy proven support and are committed to a peaceful and negotiated solution" (Republic of South Africa, Bureau of Information, 1991, p. 7). Here again, the emphasis rested very strongly on groups, now in the guise of parties as the actors at such a conference. Below the surface of these formulations those group concepts so long cultivated by the legal structures of the past lie in wait.

THE NEWS MEDIA
AND EVERYDAY LIFE

For many decades, the news media in South Africa were constrained by legal barriers that confined not only what they were allowed to report on, but also the language they could use. Radio and television services were controlled by the state. The press had to conform to a massive body of laws that restricted reporting and was subject to censorship laws that also regulated the exhibition of art, the publication of books, and theater and movie productions. The act protecting censorship was the Publications Act (No. 42) of 1974, which empowered the state to declare publications "undesirable" mainly on the grounds of indecency, blasphemy, racism, and threats to the security of the state. *Publication* was broadly defined to include art in all its form as well as news of every kind.

Most of the publications submitted to the Directorate of Publications, the administrative body dealing with censorship, came from police or customs officials.[8] The largest category of material submitted was political in nature and ranged from Friedrich Engels's *The Condition of the Working Class in England,* a nineteenth-century account of life during the Industrial Revolution, to modern novels with political themes, such as André Brink's *A Dry White Season,* dealing with black liberation and the role of the secret police. A wealth of literature, cinematographic material, and academic works dealing either with South Africa or with racial and political themes relevant to the country was thus removed from public access. Through censorship and control of the media, the progovernment political socialization of all South Africans was manipulated. In this way, whites were not exposed to alternative perspectives on their society, alternative human and race relations, or different possible social forms and values. In any future South Africa where these restrictions might be lifted, there will still remain more than one generation of whites who lived only off information and art they were allowed to see and read by the government. This generation has developed a notion of normality that is very specifically apartheid oriented, resting on an authoritarian attitude that acquiesced in the decisions made on its behalf by the government. In the 1990s this control was relaxed, however.

The fact that more than 50% of books banned in South Africa were of a political nature is no accident. The Internal Security Act (No. 74) of 1982 enhanced the Publications Act by making the possession of certain books illegal. These works were thus not only withdrawn from circulation but had to be gotten rid of by their owners. The effects on university teaching were particularly debilitating.

As if the government control of reading material through censorship and banning were not enough, there was much greater direct intervention and exercise of control over the radio and television system. The content and language of radio and television programs were carefully selected, screened, and matched to government policy.[9] The South African Broadcasting Corporation (SABC) operated 23 internal radio stations and four television channels. It is estimated that it reached well over 20 million people a day, or about two-thirds of the country's population. By contrast, total newspaper circulation among whites was below 2.2 million in 1990 (South African Advertising Research Foundation [SAARF], 1990, p. 51). Four major corporations owned 98% of the newspapers published in South Africa. Two of these were decidedly progovernment in their stance. Most of the English-speaking press was controlled by the giant Anglo American Corporation.

How did the media assist in reproducing the legally constructed realities of South Africa? As the government controlled practically all of the media, the answer is simple. The government-controlled media conferred the quality of normality and naturalness on the racial categories created by law through the Population Registration Act and its satellite laws. There were thus separate television channels for blacks that used black vernaculars. Because whites did not understand these vernaculars, the realities depicted in the programs remained hidden from them. Because of their lack of familiarity with the world of blacks, whites could barely understand whatever might be reflected in these programs. The biggest English-language daily newspaper, the *Star,* published in Johannesburg, had a special edition for the black townships. As a result, local black news did not reach a white readership. Again, this arrangement contributed to the insularity of white and black consciousness, respectively, with, of course, the one difference that blacks mostly worked in white areas and were thus much more familiar with what happened there.

It was not only that separate realities were reported upon separately; the radio, television, and progovernment press did not, or was not allowed to, question the laws and the structures that gave rise to them. Therefore, for instance, the press represented the independent homelands, unrecognized by any country other than South Africa, as full-fledged nation-states. The media accorded the leaders in the homelands the status of statesmen, and reported on relationships with them in the context of international law. The media tried to convince the public that blacks really wanted their homelands and the political structures that governed them. The endemic overpopulation, poverty, disease, and corruption in the homelands were carefully hidden from the public eye.

Whites were given the impression that, with minor exceptions, peace reigned in the country. A 1983 study, for instance, found that South African television showed 20 times more aggression in foreign contexts than in South Africa (Phelan, 1987, p. 58). The SABC was also accused of not covering the unrest in the townships during the state of emergency. Instead, it would buy occasional footage from international networks, edit it, and present it to the public. During my fieldwork visits between 1988 and 1990, I was amazed at the limited television and radio coverage given to political developments and action in black areas. Whites refused to believe that the scenes of urban unrest shown in the United States had really happened. In discussions, they frequently insisted that foreign TV crews acted as agents provocateurs in order to create scenes of unrest worthy of filming. It was their feeling that the country suffered from a few isolated incidents of violence, but that, in general, peace reigned.

Apart from receiving messages that blacks were actually peripheral to their reality, and that the legal population categories were normal in a country that was basically peaceful, a stream of impressions fostered whites' illusion that their country was a white country. The media created a selective blindness in the white population that rendered it unable to incorporate into consciousness the overwhelming evidence of the presence of blacks in everyday life. For instance, run-of-the-mill radio and television soap operas in most cases had only white characters, and even plays dealing with rural themes simply failed to mention or show the existence of the vast black labor force on which agriculture depended.[10] A recent and very popular series, *Game,* centered on rugby, a game played almost exclusively by whites. In the rare instances where blacks did appear on radio or television programs for whites, they did so in subservient roles and were addressed in condescending ways.

The release of Nelson Mandela and the unbanning of black political movements in February 1990 was a watershed not only in South African history but in media reporting. The pattern of communication in entertainment material remained pretty much the same, but the ANC suddenly received very sympathetic coverage by both the newspapers and the electronic media. The media, whether liberal or supportive of the government, kept hammering on issues of "one person, one vote" as a worrisome concern and propagated the idea of group rights. They openly favored the notion of multiracialism, which could accommodate white group rights, in opposition to the nonracial emphasis of the ANC. Two other main matters of concern were the affiliation between the ANC and the South African Communist Party and the question of the nationalization of industry and commerce. These issues had never been raised before. All news and debate about them had previously been censored. Now it was in order to discuss them, but in such a way that left the editors in control of the perspective and time allocated to the different parties. In recent times the censors have even reevaluated banned political works for release to the public (*New York Times,* July 23, 1990). This new "openness" has been fraught with contradictions, however. Afrikaans newspapers have published letters from some dissidents but have censored others whose criticisms were deemed damaging to the image of the National Party.[11] However, the media have persisted in their protectionist stance toward the white minority and its elite class of entrepreneurs and businessmen. Even with the relaxation of censorship, the media still strongly propagate the idea of group identity and privilege.[12] In this regard the Afrikaans press and English-language press do not differ substantially.

Both the government-controlled media and, to a lesser extent, those in the hands of business concerns have had to contend with the possibility of their nationalization in a postapartheid ANC-governed polity. It has been ironic to see how the government and the business world have reacted to this prospect. They hated to see the media come under the sort of control they themselves have exercised. They saw as unacceptable the prospect of a democratic nonracial party or government using the media in ways similar to those imposed by the present white National Party and government. In consultation with the commercial world, the government started to press for the privatization of the media. Privatized press, radio, and television run on the principle of popularity ratings would respond to viewer tastes. Privatized media would not be involved in the possibly traumatic venture of educating the white population about the inequalities of society and the need for the redistribution of resources. The ANC, however, was aware of these initiatives, and its national executive member, Aziz Pahad, argued that "other interests than big business should have access, through control and ownership, of the press" (Collinge & Niddrie, 1990, p. 7). By 1992 the government appointed the Viljoen task force to make recommendations on the privatization of the electronic media. The

ANC vigorously opposed the adoption of the report, and recommended instead that the South African Broadcasting Corporation be placed under the control of the proposed interim government (*South Africa News*, February 1992). I consider the privatization initiative to be another attempt to consolidate white group interest. Whites, not blacks, have the money to buy up the media and to continue to influence their editorial policies.

A small liberal critical press has bravely resisted government censorship and banning. Publishers have faced the seizure or embargo of a number of issues. Their offices and personnel have frequently been targets of threats and bombings by white extremists. The Afrikaans-language *Vrye Weekblad* seemed to pose a particular threat to the government. Its editor and some of its journalists were hounded by the government, which used the Internal Security Act to exact convictions and fines on the newspaper for quoting "banned persons" or for examining the military conscription system (*Vrye Weekblad*, June 23, 1989). The newspaper's offices were bombed in July 1990 (*New York Times*, July 5, 1990). However, *Vrye Weekblad*'s influence on the political process has been small. It appeals to, and adds to the discourse of, academic and highly educated sectors of the white group. In 1991 the circulation of this newspaper was about 12,000 (*Vrye Weekblad* editor, personal communication, June 6, 1991). The *Weekly Mail* had a circulation of less than 20,000 in 1990, compared with the daily newspaper *Star*'s circulation of 227,000 and the weekly *Sunday Times*'s of more than 500,000 (SAARF, 1990, pp. 51-54).

As circulation and viewer figures indicate, white South Africans have been informed through radio and television more than through newspapers and printed material. The SABC, a state-controlled body, has determined what images of reality should reach listeners and viewers, and the SABC view of reality has been slanted toward the status quo. In the period of rapid change the country is entering, this conservative imagery has been challenged. At the beginning of the 1990s, media conservatism was still the order of the day. The electronic media are a powerful tool to assist in the inevitable changes that need to occur in "white" values, however, so control of the media will be hotly contested in a more democratic society.

ORGANIZED RELIGION
AND SOUTH AFRICAN REALITY

The church has always played a very important role in the lives of white South Africans. In a 1980 survey, only 1% stated they had no church or religious affiliation (Republic of South Africa, Central Statistical Service, 1988, p. 10). Church attendance might have dropped off in recent years, but the church nevertheless fulfills a most important function during life crises and ceremonial occasions. As a professed "Christian" country, South Africa has traditionally prescribed religious instruction and prayer in schools, and religious leaders have filled influential positions on school boards and university councils.

In various guises, the church has entered public political discourse. In the past, Afrikaans churches have played an ideologically supportive role to the government policies of apartheid. In the 1940s, moral and theological justifications for Afrikaner political initiatives were provided during the ascendance of the National Party. The nationalistic fervor expressed at the symbolic ceremonies of the Day of the Covenant and Founders Day was given divine sanction by Afrikaans clergymen. This simple supportive role of Afrikaans churches has changed since the 1960s, especially since the massacre at Sharpeville. Afrikaans clergy have become divided among themselves, some supporting government policy and some expressing reservations. Some have been more cautious than others. The more courageous have articulated not only their protest but also their resistance to government policy. One outstanding figure in this regard has been the Reverend C. F. Beyers-Naudé, who, with others, valiantly opposed the government's policies. However, these individuals have been rapidly marginalized or pushed out of their churches. Some were hounded and banned by the government for many years. From the outset, English-speaking clergy have been more vocal and unanimous in their opposition to apartheid. Their churches have been open to all and have welcomed members from all population groups. In the 1990s, however, there was virtually no church, including among those groups that have sprung from the ranks of white supremacist movements, that identified with overt racism.

I will not elaborate here upon the theological and moral discourse surrounding apartheid. This public discourse has taken place in the forums of ecumenical movements, in learned journals, and on the op-ed pages of newspapers. It has sometimes penetrated to political platforms, but this has been rare because, among Afrikaans speakers, there is the notion that religion should remain beyond the realm of debate, especially political debate. I will remain true to the stated perspective of this study and concentrate on the messages organized religion has been sending to ordinary white members of churches, rather than on the words, discussions, and idealizations of church leaders and experts among themselves. The most significant social impact churches have had has occurred on the local level of congregations. We have seen how the local geographic life space was structured, or rather constructed, by laws such as the Group Areas Act and its basis, the Population Registration Act. It is within this legally constructed framework that churches have founded their congregations and their members have experienced communion and community life. Before exploring the impact this arrangement has had for congregants, I want to provide a brief overview of South African religious organizations and their numerical strength.

South Africa is characterized by religious pluralism. A wide variety of Christian denominations, Asian religions, and syncretistic and indigenous religions are represented. Table 4.1 provides a summary of the religious affiliations found among whites as of 1989 (it does not include any detail about the rapidly growing nonracial Rhema Bible Churches). As the table shows, the three Afrikaans churches accounted for more than 45% of the white population. The Nederduits Gereformeerde Kerk of South Africa (NGKSA) was by far the largest, with more than 37% of all South African whites belonging to it. It was this church that exemplified how the legal structure of apartheid became reflected in the "collective representation" of church organization. The Nederduits Gereformeerde Church was not one church. It consisted of the mother church, the NGKSA for whites, and three daughter churches as independent structures. They were the Nederduits Gereformeerde Kerk in Afrika (NGKA) for blacks, the Nederduits Gereformeerde Sendingkerk (Mission Church) for coloureds, and the Reformed Church of South Africa for Indians. The NG Church thus duplicated the major categories of the Population Registration Act. The Hervormde Kerk had less of a problem with racial diversity because it declared itself a whites-only church in Article III of its church law. It was therefore racially exclusive and became a haven for many whites with an apartheid orientation.

The smaller Gereformeerde Church was formed by dissidents from the NGK and the Hervormde Kerk in the 1850s. They objected to the "liberalism" and "pietism" of the older churches. This church decided that there were no biblical grounds for basing eligibility for church membership on racial or population categories. As far as the organization of the church was concerned, the members regarded language as the crucial mark of distinction among people. The sharing of a language was considered to be the condition for effectively communicating the Word of God. This church was therefore divided into four regional synods, which met every four years in a general synod. These four synods, however, although designed to follow language lines, failed to do so in fact. Two of the synods were black, one was coloured, and one was white. The white synod, it was

Table 4.1 Religious Affiliation of Whites in South Africa (1989)

Denomination	Percentage of Total Population	Percentage of Whites	Whites as Percentage of Membership
Nederduits Gereformeerd	13.5	37.3	100[a]
Gereformeerd	0.5	2.8	—
Nederduits Hervormd	1.0	5.7	100
Anglican	6.5	10.1	23.1
Roman Catholic	9.6	8.5	—
Methodist	8.9	9.2	19.6
Presbyterian	2.1	2.9	25.8
Lutheran	3.5	0.3	—
Congregational	1.9	0.3	—
Apostolic Faith Mission	1.1	2.6	—
Other Christian churches	8.0	13.4	
Total Christian churches	78.0	92.7	
Jewish	0.4	2.6	

SOURCES: Information in the first and second columns is from the Republic of South Africa, Bureau of Information (1990, pp. 114-115); information in the third column is from SAIRR (1989, pp. 722-744).
a. NGKSA only.

claimed, could in principle accommodate black members. However, in practice it was a rare exception that blacks could join the church. In fact, on the local level nonwhite membership was explicitly discouraged for the sake of "keeping peace and order" in the white congregations.

During my stay in South Africa in the late 1980s, I closely observed one particular case, that of a coloured woman who, for years, attended church in a white upper-middle-class Gereformeerde congregation in northwest Johannesburg. When she applied for membership in the church, she was turned down on the principle that keeping peace and harmony in the congregation overrode other considerations. This congregation, like many of its kind, was quite homogeneous and consisted of first- and second-generation Afrikaners who had "made it" in the business and professional world. After services on Sundays they gathered to drink tea and engage in small talk. As a member, the coloured woman would be able participate in communion, which, in itself, might have been troublesome to some congregants' senses of propriety and hygiene. However, the main reason that underlay her exclusion seemed to be the white congregation's reluctance to create a precedent for admitting nonwhites to local congregations. This was unacceptable because many black and coloured domestic servants worked for the white members of the congregation. All of them understood the language—how could they otherwise receive their instructions and report to their employers? Thus the coloured woman was not prevented from joining the church because she was not a member of its language community. Rather, on the local level of the congregation, her membership would have changed the cozy, clublike atmosphere of the church and would have allowed the further "intrusion" of blacks into the ranks of the church. This particular instance demonstrates how the Gereformeerde Kerk's official discourse on nonracialism on the national level was far removed from the racial discourse on the local level. It was on the local level that the actual decisions were made concerning the overt expression and boundaries of the Christian community.

In 1989 the Nederduits Gereformeerde Kerk came under pressure from the three "daughter" churches to commit itself to the ideal of a nonracial United Reformed Church in Southern and Central Africa. At a consultation in the town of Vereeniging, the white NG Church rejected the idea of one Dutch Reformed Church with one synod. The moderator, or chief executive, of this church, Professor Johan Heyns, maintained that church unity should start at the local level, with the individual congregations. He believed that the appropriate level for the achievement of unity was to be found where people physically congregate, that is, where "we and our domestic servants live and work together" (*daar waar ons met ons huisbediendes saam woon en werk*) (*Vrye Weekblad,* May 19, 1989). The lack of realism in his stance is typical of Afrikaans church leadership. When the NGKSA passed a resolution in 1986 condemning the ideology of apartheid as devoid of any scriptural base, 30,000 members resigned from the church (*Vrye Weekblad,* May 19, 1989).[13] If this was the effect the formulations and decisions of the church leadership and theologians had on ordinary members, it is not difficult to imagine what would have happened if increased pressure had been exerted on local congregations to integrate. Many more would have left the ranks of the church for exclusionist Afrikaans churches like the Nederduits Hervormde Kerk and the Afrikaanse Protestantse Kerk (APK; see below).

Both the Gereformeerde Kerk and the NGKSA have presbyterial systems of church government. Decisions, including those affecting membership in local congregations, lie in the hands of the church elders. It is highly improbable that a council of elders will act against their constituency, the congregants. In addition, the residential pattern created by legislation would not make large-scale black membership of "white" churches possible anyway, with the possible exception of domestic servants.

The Nederduits Hervormde Kerk and the Afrikaanse Protestantse Kerk continued to provide a haven for white racial exclusionists. The APK was founded after the NG Church condemned apartheid and racism as sinful. Forty ministers and 14,000 members left the NG Church and formed the APK. The APK protested against the politicization of the other Afrikaans churches (SAIRR, 1989, p. 733). It is well known, however, that its members were predominantly from the ranks of white supremacists. The church itself seemed to flourish in areas where poorer whites were under economic pressure and where residential mixing of the races threatened to occur.

All English-language churches were open to all races. In most cases, the leadership in these churches was black. In white urban areas, blacks freely attended English-language churches. In suburbia, domestic servants worshipped with their employers, and local congregations set up community services to cater to the needs of blacks. To what extent a sense of community developed, I cannot say. The tremendous class difference between employers and domestics in the suburbs placed limitations on the experience of Christian fellowship. Once back in the domestic situation, the egalitarianism of fellow Christians was bound to give way to the all-too-familiar paternalism of white employers toward their servants. In many cases English-speaking churches made serious attempts to foster interracial encounters between whites and blacks at different age levels. Long trips to or from Soweto (in the case of Johannesburg) had to be undertaken, pilgrimages to share time and space. At the end of the day the physical separation dictated by law reigned again. The Group Areas Act imposed an artificiality on these experiences of Christian fellowship, which were sometimes undertaken for the sole reason that members of these churches felt it was their duty to reach out. They were performing acts of resistance to apartheid rather than participating in spontaneous association with other Christians on a nonracial basis.

Most of the English-speaking churches were members of the South African Council of Churches (SACC), a body that had been in the news constantly because of its resistance to the government. Blacks and whites cooperate and support each other in this body. As in the case of the Afrikaans churches, the question arises here whether the discourse of resistance to, and the efforts to break down, apartheid structures really reached down to change not only the talk about but also the practice of race relations among the white members of local congregations and parishes.

In Afrikaans churches, members and ministers rarely resisted or protested against racism on the local level. A minister might make critical remarks from the pulpit before a student congregation, but in the overwhelming number of cases the morality and human consequences of the iniquitous political and economic structure were rarely addressed. In numerous conversations I had with ministers, they would sometimes agree with arguments against racism in society and racial exclusivity in the church. On a personal level they would make critical utterances and even display outrage. In the pulpit on Sundays, however, they drew back from their outrage and either remained silent or cloaked their criticisms in such vague and impersonal terms that nobody would recognize the issue or to whom the criticism was addressed. Their congregations had a powerful constraining influence on them. As "men of peace," they did not want to disturb their congregations and, given the fact that the local congregations were supposed to be the loci of change, nothing happened. An additional unhappy factor inhibiting clergy members from demonstrating civil courage and taking the initiative in transforming the local community's attitudes was that, in the Afrikaans churches, ministers are paid out of the voluntary contributions of their congregants.

Although somewhat atypical because of the composition and position of the congregation concerned, a disciplinary case brought against one minister will serve to demonstrate how tortuous bureaucratic procedure is used to cloak racism and to dispose of resistance against racial exclusivity. Many of the arguments the church used in this case could just as well have applied to other Afrikaans congregations and denominations. The case also demonstrates the pressures a local minister and his congregation, desirous of expressing Christian unity and fellowship, were subjected to by the higher church bureaucracy. The Dutch-speaking Hervormde congregation of Johannesburg was a branch of the Hervormde Kerk of Holland. In order to serve Dutch speakers in South Africa, the church arranged that the Nederduits Hervormde Kerk of South Africa would take this congregation under its wing with regard to both government and doctrinal matters. It was an uneasy arrangement, to say the least, because the Dutch mother church explicitly rejected racism and racial exclusionism. The South African Hervormde Kerk, however, defended and justified its racial exclusivity. The local Dutch-speaking congregation largely concurred with the critical stance of the Dutch mother church. However, the members were not unanimous in their opposition to apartheid in church and society.

In July and August 1989, the minister arranged two ecumenical services during which ministers from the Apostolic and Presbyterian churches shared the pulpit with him. One of the invited ministers was black. In addition, parts of the Belhar confession of unity were read during the services. The Belhar confession, adopted by the coloured NG Sendingkerk at Belhar in the Cape Province in 1986, rejected the moral and theological justification for apartheid as heresy and called on the NG Church to confess to the part it had played in this (SAIRR, 1989, p. 228).

A member of the church's congregation brought the "irregularities" of the pulpit sharing to the attention of the Hervormde Kerk's General Assembly, which immediately appointed a high-level commission of inquiry. In its findings, the commission concentrated on the minister's failure to adhere to the liturgy and procedures prescribed by the Hervormde Kerk. It pointed out that the church could not afford *willekeur* (arbitrariness) and lamented the fact that the congregation valued its participation in ecumenical affairs more than its obedience to church law. According to the commission, the articles of faith of the Hervormde Kerk set clear boundaries that should not be ignored because that would "disturb the order in the church." The minister was severely reprimanded and the council of elders was admonished that "commitment to truth is endlessly of greater importance than human quests for unity that transgress the boundaries set by the articles of faith."[14]

In this case the highest authority of the church argued for the reinstatement of "boundaries," for the restoration of "order," and for "obedience." It was quite unambiguous about the importance of order on the local church level. Given its exclusionist nature, it communicated to its members that the existing order was "true" and morally and doctrinally in accordance with the articles of faith—an order that, at least as far as the racial composition of the church membership and clergy is concerned, is that of apartheid.

The minister in question explicitly favored the expression of unity and communion of all Christians, regardless of race, at various public occasions. The church authority used the pretext of its essentially bureaucratic criticism of ecumenical services to censure and intimidate him. In the process, it discouraged others from engaging in similar activities and making the same pronouncements, thus suppressing civil courage among its clergy. English-speaking churches, on the other hand, seemed to do just the opposite, encouraging the clergy's resistance to apartheid.

Looking at the overall influence of organized religion on church members' awareness of the unequal structure of South African society, we have to distinguish the level of national organization from that of the local church or congregation. On a countrywide level, the English-speaking churches had integrated structures through which they gave organizational expression to Christian unity. Their respective church governments were also integrated and thus contrasted sharply with political structures around them. This was not the case in the Afrikaans churches. The NG Church resisted the idea of a common church government, the Gereformeerde Kerk split its members into various synods coinciding somewhat with official racial divisions, and the Hervormde Kerk and Afrikaanse Protestantse Kerk simply excluded population categories other than white. However, NG and Gereformeerde Kerk leaders debated the possibility of a unitary church. This debate did not change the racial practices of the local congregations, however, except in that instance where church leaders openly attacked apartheid. This caused resignations and the founding of an alternative "apolitical" church.

Turning to the local level, we observe that both English- and Afrikaans-speaking congregations were situated in communities structured by apartheid laws. For both, the separateness of black and white was the rule unless special efforts were made to travel to coloured or black communities. Although worship and ritual were integrated in English-speaking churches, everyday life was not, and here paternalism mostly prevailed. By law, blacks had not been residents, that is, members of the community. This law has been repealed, however. Previously, local churches could do little to overcome the legal barrier. Now that the legal barrier has been removed, the local congregations may realize that inequality and the lack of community have become entrenched by something in addition to the law, by an invisible hand: the social conventions white members have become used to. Legal apartheid thus cannot be blamed anymore as the interfering factor in the experience of Christian community.

Afrikaans local congregations followed a different strategy in maintaining their composition. They either found doctrinal reasons for excluding people of color or argued that the local community of Christians itself could be destroyed by the breakdown of the established order that would result if blacks were allowed to become members. Consequently, they created the impression that the structure of single-race religious communities was "normal" and could be taken for granted. To them "good order" in the church took precedence over integration that could destroy the cohesion of the local congregation. These communities, of course, were also part of the residential patterns established within the apartheid framework of the Group Areas Act. Thus the effects of the legal construction of South

African reality have endured the demise of the actual laws. Because a religious dimension has now been added to the construction of community, the younger generation may not only be prone to accept it as status quo but may also think it is right.

SUMMARY

In their classic work on the authoritarian personality, Adorno, Frenkel-Brunswick, Levinson, and Sanford (1982) talk of a carryover from the hierarchical, authoritarian parent-child dichotomy:

> A power oriented, exploitively dependent attitude towards one's sex partner and one's God may well culminate in a political philosophy and social outlook which has no room for anything but a desperate clinging to what appears to be strong and a disdainful rejection of whatever is relegated to the bottom. (p. 475)

They further argue that this dichotomy extends to the conceptualization of sex roles and moral values, as well as to "a dichotomous handling of social relations as manifested especially in the formation of stereotypes and of ingroup-outgroup cleavages" (p. 475). In the present study I was not able to investigate the nature of family relations among whites in any detail, but Adorno and his coauthors' findings assume an astonishing relevance in the context of what I have described above. Followers expect their leaders to be strong, and, as we will see in later chapters, they become frustrated and anxious when leaders seem to bow to democratic initiatives. The total legal construction of South Africa's social, economic, and political reality was done on the authority of patrimonial leaders in whom whites invested a great deal of trust and from whom they expected minimal accountability. Testing this authority was discouraged by the media and by Afrikaans churches. The legal system furthermore produced hierarchical and spatial structures that seemed to become obdurate the more they were implemented and used.

Georg Simmel (1971) contends that "spatial relationships not only are determining conditions of relationships among men, but are also symbolic of those relationships" (p. 143). This quotation contains a key for understanding the way in which white South Africans', and perhaps others', consciousness is structured by the formal-legal organization ("laws are good to think with") of spatial relationships among groups of people in the country. The spatial organization, as expressed by formal laws, was symbolic of the perceived horizontal and vertical distances between categories of people. These symbols communicated in a number of ways to whites and others an "oughtness" in society. They not only received the powerful underpinning of theological and philosophical reasoning in the past, but they were also internalized as normal. Many whites therefore had unquestioning attitudes about who belongs where. This normality was engendered by the everyday practices that the laws created and enforced. These everyday practices were reinforced, either by design or by default, in the media and organized religion. As a result of this routinization of formalized social distance and inequality, the consciousness of many whites became structured in a racial way that will outlast the abolition of many of the laws that contributed to its emergence.

NOTES

1. The Internal Security Act (No. 74) of 1982 applied in most of the cases. Legalizing the South African Communist Party involved the repeal of the Suppression of Communism Act (No. 44) of 1950.

2. Infant mortality may be examined as an indicator of life chances. In 1990, according to the SAIRR (1990, p. 36), infant mortality rates per 1,000 live births were as follows: Africans, 62; coloureds, 57.5; Indians, 17.4; and whites, 13.2 (these are official figures, however, and I do not regard them as very reliable). Figures for 1987 were Africans, 80; coloureds, 31.7; Indians, 13.6; and whites, 7.0. Black infant mortality rates in rural areas often exceed 250.

3. The Black Land Act (1913) linked into a network of other laws and regulations, notably those concerned with the administration of urban affairs and the regulation of citizenship.

4. In 1990 there were rebellions in some of the independent and self-governing homelands demanding reincorporation into South Africa.

5. Dugard (1980) exposes this strategy to the international legal community as both a deception and an infringement of human rights.

6. It was reported to Parliament that 77,458 Africans were arrested in 1986 for trespassing (SAIRR, 1988, p. 461).

7. National Public Radio reported on July 10, 1990, that a squatter settlement near Johannesburg had been bulldozed. Loss of life was reported in the wake of the residents' resistance.

8. In 1983 it was reported that 6% of items were submitted by the public. Police and custom officials submitted more than 80% (Omond, 1986, p. 238).

9. Political opponents to the government were either denied a voice or framed in a way that cast them in a bad light. The protest of the Institute for Democratic Alternatives for South Africa against the SABC's distortions of their operations is a case in point (*Star,* June 8, 1989).

10. For example, the series *Bosveldhotel* (Bush Hotel) depicts rural town life devoid of black people.

11. The case of the veteran Afrikaner critic of the National Party, Professor Willem Kleynhans, is graphic here. In letters to the editors of *Beeld* and *Die Burger* in April and May 1990, he compared the NP's past commitment to apartheid with its recent rhetoric against it. His letters were turned down for publication (*Vrye Weekblad,* June 1, 1990).

12. The government appointed a task force to look into the future role of the SABC in April 1990. More than half the members of this group had affiliations with the Afrikaner secret society the Broederbond. The conservative thrust of the task force as well as its protective attitude toward Afrikaner identity can be deduced (*Weekly Mail,* May 18, 1990).

13. This is the document *Kerk en Samelewing* (Church and Society), considered by some to be expressive of the symbiotic relationship between the NGK and the National Party.

14. "Bevinding en uitspraak van die Kommissie van die Algemene Kerkvergadering ten opsigte van die klag wat die Kommissie van die Ringsvergadering van Johannesburg teen _____ van die Nederlandssprekende Gemeente gelê het" (Finding and judgment of the Commission of the General Ecclesiastical Assembly on the accusation made by the Commission of the Circuit of Johannesburg against [name withheld] of the Dutch-speaking congregation of Johannesburg) (signed at Pretoria on November 24, 1989).

5

Public Discourse and the
Reconstruction of South Africa I:
Right-Wing Perspectives

Internationally, therefore, there is a two-fold system of protection: one in which the group is protected—which is the international political system; and the other in which the individual is protected—that is the internal political system. In [South Africa], where a number of groups live together but are not separated into their own pieces of real estate, the challenge is to have both those levels of protection inside one over-arching political system.

These are the words of Stoffel van der Merwe, South Africa's minister of information, in 1988. They were uttered in response to a question about whether minority rights would be protected in a future South Africa. The interview was published in the limited-circulation and highly expensive Leadership publication titled *The High Road*. The formulation and logic of this quotation are very characteristic of mainstream South African political thought. Group rights are visualized within the framework of the nation-state. This nation-state, presumably homogeneous in nature, is one in which one nation, one culture, and one language typically dominate. The nation-state idea is rounded off by the notion of a piece of "real estate" within the boundaries of which the group found its protection. The speaker lumps together the nation-state, ethnic group, and language community.

The whole formulation reminds one of old-style apartheid, in which all black persons were assigned to geographic units or "homelands" designed eventually to be accorded nation-state status. The government also ascribed an ethnic character to the "groups" supposed to constitute those "nation-states." This characterization was based on a static notion of a group, a closed social unit with clearly defined boundaries. It was within this group, then, and not as an individual, that the individual found his or her rights and protection. Primacy was accorded to the group because it preceded or even became the condition for individual rights, according to this view. By allying himself with a perspective from international law dealing with the sanctity of the borders of nation-states and the right they have to protect themselves, the speaker attempts to lend credibility and academic legitimacy to his argument. Turning to South Africa, however, he is faced with the dilemma that a number of groups live on the same piece of real estate. This is an important shift, because embedded in the statement is the realization that the old-style geographic separation of apartheid did not work. Thus, by extension, it could be argued that the various groups shared at least an overarching geographic context. The new South Africa was seen as a country containing all its people, not as individuals, but packaged into groups. The challenge, then, was how to accommodate them in one overarching political system. The speaker leaves the question open whether this overarching system is or is not another nation-state. The analogy, however, gets stuck on the existence of what the speaker believes to be various discrete groups within the country.

The debate on group identity, rights, survival, and protection formed the centerpiece of public discourse among the white population. The concern of the minister of information to salvage the group concept should not be understood from a pluralist sociological point of view; rather, one should look for some concrete and rather ethnocentric interests behind his concerns. In the final analysis, it was the psychology of white fears about the future that fired the preoccupation with group rights and their protection. It was a set of deep-seated fears that sprang from a lack of knowledge about the future and about their black compatriots and their intentions. Apartheid and the tradition of entitlement produced a "group-way-of-thinking." This is not the same as the concept of "groupthink," which emphasizes conformity in thinking. Rather, a group-way-of-thinking tends to construct all social actors in terms of their membership to a group. It is a typifying scheme used by whites to construct, order, and make sense of others and themselves. Two assumptions about the nature of a group may underlie this scheme: The group may be either primordial or associative. Membership in a primordial group is deemed to be permanent and governed by descent; membership in an associative group is voluntary. The mechanism of a primordial group-way-of-thinking is ascription of membership, whereas the associative concept of a group is based on choice. In South Africa, the primordial group concept was used to strip privileges and rights from blacks, and then, at a time when apartheid as system seemed to be on its way out, the notion of an associative group became a salvaging resource for whites themselves. The group is the high ground that whites seek out when the plain becomes flooded with black aspirations and demands for equality.

In this chapter and the next, I examine the central position the group idea has occupied in formal white public discourse in South Africa, investigating how white leaders have talked about the country's economic, social, and political realities. What were their visions for the future, and what strategies did they use to enhance the credibility of their renderings of reality? The right-wing discourse has been dominated by the primordial concept of group, whereas the discourse of reformists has tended to adhere to an associative concept. The public discourse discussed is set in the framework of the structured social reality described in Chapter 4. Three major categories of public discourse are discussed: the political, the corporate, and the intellectual.

Political discourse has taken place both in the constitutional context of party politics and in the context of white extraparliamentary opposition, whether to the left or the right of the current government. The main and most influential actor in this category has of course been the ruling National Party, followed by the right-wing Conservative Party and the liberal Democratic Party. The small right-wing splinter group called the Herstigte Nasionale Party (Reconstituted National Party) (HNP) was not represented in Parliament. Other right-wing splinter groups include the Boerestaat Party (Boer Nation-State Party) (BSP) and the Blanke Volkstaat Party (White People's State Party) (BVP). The last two join the other extraparliamentary bodies to the right, such as the Afrikaner Weerstandsbeweging (Afrikaner Resistance Movement) (AWB), the Blanke Bevrydingsbeweging (White Liberation Movement) (BBB), and the semisecret Wit Wolwe (White Wolves), sometimes implicated in racial killings. There was also the right-wing cultural movement, the Afrikaner Volkswag (Guard of the Afrikaner People) opposing the long-standing and government-supporting Federasie van Afrikaanse Kultuurverenigings (Federation of Afrikaans Cultural Organizations) (FAK). The Oranjewerkers (Workers of Orange) followed a policy of total separation of the races and promoted complete white economic self-sufficiency.

To the left of the parliamentary actors, political groups faded into bodies with nonracial membership, such as the Institute for a Democratic Alternative for South Africa (IDASA), the Five Freedoms Forum (FFF), the Mass Democratic Movement (MDM), the United Democratic Front (UDF), and the recently unbanned African National Congress (ANC) and the South African Communist Party (SACP).

Corporate discourse has sometimes widely overlapped with the dominant political discourse, given that the foundation of any future South Africa has been assumed to be a strong and secure economy. Industry provides a major tax base for the government and has an interest in sustaining its profitable operation in a highly politicized atmosphere. Therefore, not only has industry entered public discourse actively, but some of its leaders have also assumed political office. Foremost among corporate actors have been large mining companies, such as the Anglo American Corporation, major banks and finance houses, manufacturing giants, and petroleum companies. Other organizations that cut across individual companies, such as the Chamber of Mines, the various chambers of commerce, and ASSOCOM, have also been active.

Intellectual discourse has emanated from the universities and from such think tanks as research institutes and development agencies. Some of these have been linked to political parties or movements, and some to the corporate world. Noteworthy has been the role of the Afrikaner Broederbond (literally, the Afrikaner League of Brothers). This organization has undergone a radical change, from a male secret movement rather narrowly concerned with ethnocentric Afrikaner concerns to a body of intellectuals and politicians who recognize that a common citizenship for all South African inhabitants is inevitable and that constitutional proposals acceptable to all parties need to be thrashed out. Other research institutes close to the government are the Human Sciences Research Council (HSRC), the Development Bank, and the Africa Institute. The liberal establishment has the South African Institute of Race Relations (SAIRR), the Institute for Policy Studies, and the action-oriented IDASA. The right-wing movement took over the old apartheid research arm of the National Party, the South African Bureau of Racial Affairs (SABRA).

The arenas of discourse within and between some of these collective actors have been largely removed from public scrutiny or, conversely, have generated limited public interest because of their academic or confidential nature. In other words, discourse to a large extent has occurred in learned journals, in memoranda with limited in-house circulation, in boardrooms, at party caucuses, at secret society meetings, and in university seminars and lectures. Apart from the difficulty of gaining access to some of this material, it is not my concern here to examine how power, in the present or future, has been constructed backstage. Rather, I am concerned with illuminating what messages have reached the public, how they have been communicated, and what sections of the public they have reached. The public has access to political and mass meetings, to newspapers and television programs, and to gossip, rumor, and everyday talk.

In looking at agents with access to the public, we must inevitably deal with a selection, because all actors in the political arena do not have equal access to the public. As pointed out in Chapter 4, the government-controlled electronic media in South Africa have had the power to give voice to whomever they choose. Even in those cases where they have given time to opposition opinions, those opinions have been nested in, and framed by, party-line commentary. The English-language press has had greater circulation figures than its Afrikaans counterpart, and mostly, but not always, has represented a liberal viewpoint. The Afrikaans press has generally contained political commentary and reporting favorable to government policies. The conservative Afrikaans press has been underfunded, and has been highly polemical and critical of the government. Further, it is unclear what readership political items in newspapers have found. South African newspapers cater to a large number of tastes. In a single newspaper one may find the sensationalism and sex of a cheap tabloid as well as the philosophical and intellectual thrust of the op-ed pages. In the major-circulation newspapers editors have given preference to viewpoints favoring either the liberal or government perspectives. The National Party therefore has received more space and positive attention in the Afrikaans press.

Political parties have given themselves voices in public and mass meetings. The degree of public attendance and participation at these meetings indicates the relevance of the topics and issues at hand. Attendance at such meetings has varied from more than 100,000 people to a handful.

Finally, it should be remembered that political discourse not only consists of talk and speeches but also involves a spectrum of action, which can range from driving hundreds of miles to a rally to committing direct acts of violence against persons and property. These acts are interpreted by the media, but they also have public meanings independent of those bestowed upon them by the press. Such acts could include sabotage, assassination, and public demonstrations, for example.

We now turn to the subject of political discourse. More space is devoted to political discourse here because it largely embraces economic and intellectual dimensions. The right-wing and the recently reformist National Party are the main actors. The left, once represented by the Progressive Federal Party and more recently by the Democratic Party, has been outflanked by the National Party's opening of the political process to black nationalist movements. On the far left is a small minority of whites belonging to the South African Communist Party and other groups supportive of the African National Congress.

RIGHT-WING
PUBLIC POLITICAL DISCOURSE

The white right-wing political parties and movements can largely be grouped together. The nuances of their policy statements and visions of the future of South Africa are relatively unimportant here. Rather, in what follows we will look at these groups' common messages about group boundaries and the ways they are drawn and maintained.

During the 1960s, right-wing political discourse was contained within the National Party. In fact, the political discourse of the Verwoerd era, couched in terms of the "rationality" of ethnic pluralism, only thinly veiled white racism and ethnocentrism. After the anticommunist purges that followed the banning of the ANC, whites felt secure and protected under the Nationalist government. However, toward the end of the 1960s a more enlightened political climate developed in the wake of new economic challenges. Because these challenges also affected labor policy, a section of the National Party was upset by the emerging liberal attitude of mainstream politicians toward labor. Because of their dissident attitude, the National Party forced four of its vociferously critical members of Parliament to resign in 1969. These individuals then founded the Herstigte Nasionale Party. This party, with a mainly blue-collar, rural-based constituency, never managed to gain significant support, however. During the 1987 elections it captured only 2 seats out of 166 in the white Parliament, and in the 1989 elections its support fell to less than 1% of the white electorate.

In 1982 the Conservative Party was formed under the leadership of Andries Treurnicht, a conservative National Party cabinet minister who took with him 17 other breakaway NP parliamentarians. The main issue of the split was the proposed change in the constitution that allowed coloureds and Asians political participation through a tricameral parliamentary system. The breakaway followed in the wake of a power shift within the NP toward the slightly more liberal Cape Province leadership. This shift was largely a result of a corruption scandal within the government in which mostly Transvaal Nationalists were involved. From its beginning, the CP was very successful in rallying around it a wide spectrum of the white, especially the Afrikaner, population. Its main goal was to

attack the Nationalist government's preparedness to compromise the dominant position of whites in the country and, as a consequence, their security
and survival chances. The NP government delayed a general election until
1987. This gave the CP the necessary time to consolidate its organization
and support base. In the general election, the CP won 22 (13%) of the 166
seats. The right-wing vote was somewhat divided between the CP and the
HNP. Expressed in terms of the percentage of the white electorate that
voted CP, the picture looks different, however. The CP captured 27% of
the white vote; combined with the HNP vote, it amounted to 30% (*Weekly
Mail*, September 8, 1989). The swing toward the white conservative
parties continued and, in the municipal elections of October 1988, the CP
managed to gain control of 22% of the country's local authorities. It dominated, with 53.3% of local authorities, in the country's most populated
and richest province, the Transvaal, as against the NP's 38.5%. The CP's
successes were mostly concentrated in the rural areas and in towns with
high concentrations of the white lower-middle classes, especially in mining
towns. The 1989 general election brought further successes. The CP increased its number of seats in Parliament to 33. Its share of the vote was
31% by then. After the unbanning of the African National Congress in
February 1990 and the release of its leader, Nelson Mandela, its support
basis was further widened. It managed to draw massive crowds to its rallies
(see below), and its more extremist factions attained increased visibility
in public life, notwithstanding the attempts of the government media to
play down this development.

MASS RALLY OF
CONSERVATIVES: MAY 26, 1990

To illustrate right-wing political discourse, I describe below in detail a
major political rally of conservative groups. This occasion vividly drama-
tizes a great variety of values, emotions, and visions of the future typical
of white right-wing groups in South Africa. Subsequently, I will compare
some of the features of discourse found at this meeting with the discourse
observed at other right-wing meetings and actions.

After the government's announcement of the legalization of the ANC,
various right-wing groups, including the Conservative Party, expressed a
need for a symbolic protest against the government's liberalization policies.
These groups specifically objected to the notion of power sharing. The
protest took the form of a *volksvergadering,* or people's rally. According

to the text of the glossy program for the meeting, such people's rallies developed out of the Afrikaner's repeated loss of, and struggle for, independence and sovereignty. The rally organizers chose the weekend of May 25-27, 1990. This was the weekend before May 31, the date celebrated as the founding of the Union of South Africa in 1910 and later as the founding of the Republic of South Africa in 1961. The place, the amphitheater where the Voortrekker Monument stands near Pretoria, was highly symbolic as well. It was here that the centenary of the Great Trek and the battle of Blood River were celebrated on December 16, 1938. The Monument was dedicated in 1949, and until the late 1960s this was the scene where Afrikaner national fervor was expressed at December 16 celebrations. After the late 1960s, enthusiasm for these meetings waned, and even the AWB's attempts to revive them were not successful—only a handful of people turned out each year. Not so this time, however. Furthermore, there might have been an additional reason this particular day and place were chosen. A major rugby game between the country's two strongest teams, the Blue Bulls of Northern Transvaal and Western Province, was scheduled to be played that Saturday. Rugby is tremendously important to most male Afrikaners. Some even view it as a secular religion of hero worship and the celebration of male strength. The official program for the people's rally discreetly stated, "The main proceedings will be completed by approximately 14h30"—that is, 2.30 p.m., in time so that those attending could make it to the main rugby feature in downtown Pretoria.

According to the program, various organizations were to erect stalls at the rally site on Friday. On Friday afternoon, people could visit these stalls and also listen to the practice session of the mass choir that would be performing at the rally. There was also to be a rehearsal of a taped historical dramatization. Finally, a number of theology professors were to conduct a service of confession (*verootmoedingingsdiens*) during the evening. The main event was on Saturday. It started off with the arrival of a military unit on horseback. The mass choir sang, and the meeting was opened with a passage from the Bible read by an English-speaking clergyman. An Afrikaans-speaking professor of theology then conducted a prayer. According to the program, the rally was then to be addressed by the deputy leader of the Conservative Party, followed by the historical audio presentation that was rehearsed on Friday. Representatives from the four provinces would then hand over copies of the "Freedom Manifesto of the Afrikaner People" to A. P. Treurnicht, the leader of the CP. The main address by Treurnicht was then to follow, at the end of which he would lead the crowd in prayer. A "coffee house concert" and entertainment by "the youth" were announced for the evening. The next morning, Sunday, would be taken up by a service of thanksgiving.

The program, which was 36 pages long, contained historical material, the text of the various songs performed, and numerous advertisements. Holiday resorts advertised themselves as places where you could be "among your own people." Another described itself as *"Blank—Veilig—Billik"* (white, safe, and affordable), and a third proclaimed: "We Recognize Ethnic Realities—Right of Admission Reserved."

I arrived at the rally site on Saturday, May 26, at about 9:30 a.m. As I approached the hill on which the Monument is situated, I noticed from afar that all the access roads were blocked. I parked at the bottom of the hill, about three miles from the amphitheater where the meeting was to be held. People streamed up the hill in unending lines, walking through the long grass and creating new footpaths. There was a spirit of celebration and optimism among them as they talked and joked. Only Afrikaans was spoken. The term *kaffer* (equivalent to *nigger* in the United States) was frequently heard in informal talk. Children and young people addressed older people in kin terms although they were not related. (This is an old Afrikaans custom not generally adhered to in the modern urban context. It is a sign of respect to address an older person as "uncle" or "aunt.")

In the parking lot there were about a hundred buses. Helicopters were flying overhead. The amphitheater was absolutely full by that time. Numerous stalls lined the uphill boundary, and later I saw even more stalls behind the stage. These were staffed by local branches of the CP and other organizations. They mostly served food and drink, especially traditional Afrikaner delicacies such as *braaivleis* (barbecued steaks), *boerewors* (spicy pork and beef sausages), and *pap* (corn porridge). In the center of the upper stalls area, AWB people assembled around a large bin bearing a banner that said, "Bevry Strydom" (Free Strydom). They were collecting signatures and money for the release of Barend Strydom, who had indiscriminately killed blacks on Strydom square in downtown Pretoria. The Afrikaanse Protestantse Kerk had some stalls also (see Chapter 4 for a discussion of the origin of the APK). Some self-appointed uniformed AWB "soldiers," armed with nightsticks and handguns, were patrolling the crowd. On their khaki uniforms they bore the emblem of their movement: three 7s arranged in a three-pointed swastika fashion.

No alcohol was on sale, although a few men were drinking beer behind some trucks. The crowd was very peaceful. A picnic spirit prevailed in some areas, but the faces were mostly somber and serious. It was as if many could not make up their minds whether this was a picnic or an open-air church assembly. At best, it could be described as a *nagmaal* atmosphere (see the description of the Great Trek celebration in Chapter 3). Small groups, mostly families, huddled together. Some wore parts of traditional pioneer Voortrekker dress, such as *nekdoeke* (bandannas) and *kappies* (bonnets) for the women. They all listened intently to the proceedings. I overheard some commenting that the size of the crowd would scare both State President F. W. de Klerk and Nelson Mandela. The state president had returned to South Africa that same morning from a European tour, during which he informed foreign leaders about the impending changes in South Africa. At the rally, one announcer ridiculed the size of de Klerk's reception by some 600 people at the airport and compared it with this massive demonstration of opposition to the president's policies. On the same day, Nelson Mandela was speaking at another rally in the region. The announcer boasted that Mandela's meeting could not draw a bigger crowd than this one either.

There were absolutely no blacks around at Monumentkoppie (Monument Hill). The whole amphitheater was filled to the brim. Left and right, thousands sat between the trees, and behind the stage many more sat in reserved seats. Notwithstanding the NP and the liberal press's disclaimers, the crowd numbered at least 100,000.

During the speeches and the historical audio presentation, banners were carried through the crowd bearing slogans extolling the virtues of white autonomy. A huge AWB flag in red, white, and black, looking very much like a Nazi flag, with its three encircled swastika-style 7s in the center, unfolded in the breeze. A large poster displayed a picture of a "white tiger" being unleashed and three mice, symbolizing the NP, DP, and ANC, scrambling for safety. The sides and back of the amphitheater were lined with other banners bearing texts such as "Hang Mandela; Hy pleeg Hoogverraad" (Hang Mandela; He Commits High Treason), "Hervorm! Terug na God Drieënig!" (Reform! Back to the Triune God!), and "Communists Are Not S.A. Citizens." On the stage a huge, square canopy, between 30 and 40 feet high, provided shaded seating for the speakers and guests of honor. Along its top it bore the words: "Die Derde Vryheidstryd Het Begin" (The Third War of Liberation Has Started). Facing the crowd, a mass choir sat to the right of the canopy. Behind it, and to the left, more special guests were seated.

Visually, the banners, posters, and other symbols conveyed a powerful message that was mostly negative and aggressive. It was anticommunist, antiliberal, and bellicose. Symbols were displayed within the overall contextual frame of the assembly: a religiously justified struggle. Accordingly, the "Third War of Liberation" was seen as the sequel to the Afrikaners' first two wars of liberation against British imperialism during the late nineteenth century and the early years of this century.

This was no ordinary political rally. It was the mass mobilization of a religious and moral community. It therefore conveyed the confusing impression of being both a stern-faced religious service and a joyous celebration of a moral unity of people feeling unjustly deprived of their birthright. The proceedings were both opened and closed with prayer. It was the intention of the organizers to demonstrate white unity unambiguously by engaging both an English-speaking minister and an Afrikaans professor to officiate at the opening. I arrived during the Afrikaans prayer, which appealed to God to bless the lips of the speakers. The crowd then sang Psalm 146, verse 8, which hails the God of the Covenant as the God of hosts/armies. The militaristic frame was clear.

The deputy leader of the CP, F. Hartzenberg, welcomed the crowd and extended a special welcome to Mrs. Verwoerd, the widow of H. F. Verwoerd, and to the many people who had come from as far away as Namibia. A solo trumpet played the *Song of Young South Africa* (meaning young white Afrikaners). The mass choir and the audience joined in and sang the song, which compares the youth to the roll of mighty thunder over the South African veld. It is a song that describes a people's awakening and instilling trembling and fear into other nations (I am freely paraphrasing). Military and marching music followed. The horsemen who had been assembled in front of the stage since earlier that morning began to leave, and the crowd joined in the Transvaal anthem. This is the anthem of the old nineteenth-century South African Republic, sung in Dutch: "Ken't gij dat volk . . . " Paraphrased, it runs like this:

> Do you know this nation abounding in heroic courage, yet enslaved for so long? It sacrificed its possessions and blood for its freedom and for justice. Come, burghers, let the flags fly in the wind. Our suffering belongs to the past. Rejoice in the victory of our heroes. This free nation are we.

As the song died down, a historical audio presentation was blended in. I give detailed attention to this presentation in the following pages because its content reveals a wealth of information about the values, perceptions, and future projections of white South Africans. I encountered many of the points raised in this presentation in right-wing and conservative political speeches I recorded later in my research. The audio presentation was written and in part read by Professor P. G. Nel, an archconservative professor of the Afrikaans language from Pretoria.[1]

The presentation started off by hailing the miraculous birth of the
Republic of South Africa, linking it to the glorious liberation struggle of
white heroes. The symbols surrounding the audience—the flags and the
horses—were interpreted: The latter stood for freedom, service, mobility,
and masculinity, and had played an active role in the emergence of the
people/nation. Horses had a role to play in the Third War of Liberation:

> *Male voice:* The struggle our fathers started will continue until we die or
> prevail. . . . [In order to] develop an own identity, a sense of belonging,
> a striving for togetherness and a shared faith, the Afrikaner had to struggle
> for centuries against the oppressive rule of the Dutch East India Company
> and later against the imperialists of British rule. The Voortrekkers
> founded their republics in Natal, Transvaal, and in the Orange Free State.
> But the British imperialists thwarted their striving for freedom and
> independence by the annexation of their territories.

The presentation then reviewed the history of the republics and the two
wars of liberation, to the beginning of the twentieth century. The historical
narrative was then suddenly interrupted by a woman's voice announcing:

> A people can only be great if it is true to itself. It can only be true to itself
> when it is free on the soil of its own fatherland, and when it is governed by
> itself according to its own tradition and its own nature.

The emergence of the ideal of a republic of South Africa was then
outlined. Parts of speeches made by the four "architects" of the Republic
of South Africa, J. B. M. Hertzog, D. F. Malan, J. G. Strydom, and H. F.
Verwoerd, were then blended into the presentation. Passages that called
the Afrikaners to return to the idealism and values of their past were
especially highlighted. Malan's famous call made at the 1949 celebration
of the dedication of the Voortrekker Monument was played back. He had
called symbolically for a return to tradition and to God (see the translation
in the description of Essay 257 in Chapter 3).

With triumphant eloquence, a male voice then sketched how the republican ideal was at last attained under Verwoerd. Suddenly the tone of the
presentation changed. The voice of an old man, a patriarch, announced:

> Yes, my son, I am an old man who, by the grace of God, was allowed to
> experience over decades the sacrifices the Afrikaner people had to make in
> order to achieve, retain, and restore their freedom. We fought, we suffered,
> we laughed, and we rejoiced. Our illustrious leaders, Hertzog, Malan,

Strydom, and Verwoerd—how hard have they fought, how hard did they work and sacrifice for our freedom, sovereignty, safety, and self-respect. But now . . . now? During the last decade or so, anxiety and fear gripped our hearts. Scores of laws were abolished by the simple stroke of a pen. Our community life was affected and is now in danger of being destroyed. The self-determination of the Afrikaner is being sacrificed on an altar in order to buy some peace without us knowing what it means and at what price. The government creates anxiety because they appoint communists and terrorists as joint rulers over us whites. We have to live behind walls, bars, and razor wire. I feel like a stranger in my own fatherland.

I tell you, my son, we are going to lose our freedom and our fatherland totally, because—where is this all going to end?

Young male: We demand our freedom. We will take our freedom back.

Young female: Ours is a struggle and fight until death for our white freedom, sovereignty, and land.

Young male: Our own government! People's education [*Volkseie onderwys*] is not negotiable!

Mature male: The Afrikaner lives and will live!

Mature female: —for freedom, people [*volk*], and fatherland! [mass applause, 15 seconds]

Mature male: —and now the Lord sent unto us again another Moses, another Joshua, in this hour of crisis. We followed his career—from the pulpit, from journalism and politics, and—into the cabinet. He was always struggling, fighting, and doing battle—fearlessly—against the attacks of liberalism that, like a cancer, were consuming his fellow Afrikaners in the cabinet and in Parliament. Power sharing and many other intolerable new policies that jeopardized the freedom and survival of the Afrikaner were the order of the day.

The emotional appeal of the speech of the grave, concerned, and bitter patriarch was strong. Piety toward the older generation is a deeply ingrained value among conservative Afrikaners. The disappointment of the old man descended on the younger generation as a mandate to do their duty. Failure to act could be seen as betrayal of the older generation, who sacrificed so greatly to bring about the republic and the white state. A strong appeal was thus directed at the consciences of the young.

The Moses, or Joshua, alluded to above is Treurnicht. The narrative went on to describe the founding of the Conservative Party as the beginning of the restoration of autonomy and self-government to Afrikanerdom. A long excerpt from a speech made by Treurnicht was then played. In religious awe, he quoted previous leaders of the Afrikaners and said he would not dare to add anything to their words, as if these words had the authority of biblical text. Much of the phraseology he used sounded biblical also:

> We strive for freedom under peace [*vryheid met geregtigheid*]. Today we want to say to each other as we sit next to each other, gazing in each other's eyes: "I need you. Your people is my people and where you go, I want to go, and your future will also be my future" [applause, 9 seconds]. No other people will fight for the rights and freedom of our people. We will have to do it by ourselves [applause, 7 seconds]. And now, we are assembled today in order to tell each other: "We belong together and we stand together" [applause, 7 seconds].

A sense of common destiny was expressed in these words. The allusion to the words of the Old Testament figures of Naomi and Ruth further reinforced the sense of a bond that tied the people (*volk*) together. After delineating the in-group, Treurnicht issued a warning to the government, placing it not inside the fold of the people, but outside,

> not to intimidate us with pressure by foreign countries [*buiteland,* literally "outside country"] or with internal threats [*binneland,* literally "inside country"] in order to blackmail us into concessions with regard to our principles and our self-determination [applause, 9 seconds]. Our road will be uphill. Of course, it will be uphill. But I think you would agree with me that it would be better to meet us on the uphill slopes than on the [downhill] slide into integration.

The audio presentation concluded with a male voice praying to God to preserve the work of the architects of the republic as a guiding light and as purifying flame. During the presentation, banners bearing messages such as the following were being carried throughout the audience (see Photo 5.1):

Do Not Fear, Dr. AP [A. P. Treurnicht] Is Fighting for You.
White Nationhood Is Greater Than Death.

The Freedom Manifesto was then read. A representative from each of the country's four provinces then handed a copy of the Manifesto to the leader, Treurnicht, after reading a message. Copies of the Manifesto were distributed beforehand. On the back of each copy there was space for signatures. It was the intention of the CP to collect 1 million signatures from persons

Photograph 5.1.
Photo by Gerhard Schutte.

13 years and older supporting the Manifesto. (The number of 1 million, the CP argued, would represent more than half of the white electorate; actually, the white electorate numbered 3.3 million.) The copies of the Manifesto were printed only in Afrikaans; my English translation follows:

Freedom Manifesto of the Afrikaner People 26 May 1990

Our people believes

that the Triune God totally controls the existence and destiny of peoples;

that our fathers were guided by Him to this land in order for us as a people to serve Him in this country;

that our history reflects His blessing and chastening;

that we ought to submit to Him in humble obedience and responsibility.

Our people rejects

an undivided unitary state in which the different peoples have to become one nation under one government;

any future domination by a black majority government or by any other political dispensation that fails to provide for the complete freedom of our people in their own fatherland.

Our people demands the right

to continue to exist as a people;

to be free;

to govern ourselves in our own fatherland without interference from outside;

to preserve our identity;

to defend our survival by all means available to us;

to fashion according to our preference our own community life, education, and society.

Our people pledges

to acknowledge the perfect omnipotence of God and to praise and serve Him in gratitude for His grace;

to live according to biblical moral norms;

to promote peace, freedom, and welfare;

to conserve the fatherland;

to promote among fellow members of our people faithfulness and the willingness to sacrifice;

to strive for peaceful relations with other peoples.

Therefore our people asserts

We will not rest unless our freedom in our own fatherland has been secured.

We call upon fellow members of our people to support each other in this hour of duress and to strengthen our unity.

We call upon fellow members to humble themselves before our Heavenly Father and to pray incessantly for the restoration of our freedom.

We request our leader in chief and our party to call the totality of our people to the struggle for liberation and to use all available means in the struggle to realize this ideal.

For our Freedom, our People, and our Fatherland

In his presentation speech, the representative of the Cape Province emphasized the fact that two meetings were taking place on this day—the one at the Voortrekker Monument and the other at the airport to welcome the state president, who was striving "toward one mixed nation." The president, the speaker argued, had for the most part lost the support of the "white man in South Africa," however. The people from the speaker's area, Cape Province, were not prepared to have the Republican flag replaced by the ANC flag. Nor were they prepared to have the anthem replaced by any other. They would work and fight for it, even if that meant dying for it.

The representative from the Orange Free State lamented that the state president, after completing his trip through Europe "on his bloodied knees," was capitulating. He feared "we will be losing our freedom totally." He stressed that the people of the Free State were convinced "that we can only be free once we free ourselves from the stranglehold other people's labor has on our people," meaning that dependence on black labor was strangling the whites.

The Natal representative was clear on the role of English speakers. Speaking in heavily Afrikaans-accented English, he asserted:

> I've got a mandate from the English-speaking people of Natal to come and stand here today and promise to our leader and pledge to our leader the loyalty of the English-speaking people, the trust of English-speaking people and the support of the English-speaking people of Natal. There are many English-speaking Afrikaners in Natal for whom the love of their dear land is as deeply embedded in their hearts as in the hearts of their Afrikaans-speaking compatriots. It is history, ladies and gentlemen, that, for not only decades, but actually for centuries there existed a certain degree of mistrust between the groups but, at last, Mr. Chairman, the two groups have come to realize that, although we speak different languages, foster different cultures, we are all whites and as such we are the enemy of the communists, the ANC, Mr. de Klerk, and his leftist puppets. But we can also be thankful, ladies and gentlemen, that we can bow our heads today and praise the Lord of Lords that this change of heart eventually came about and as such we form a force to be reckoned with.

It is important to note how this speaker played down the cultural and historical differences between English and Afrikaans speakers. The term *whites* indicates a moral community opposed to communism, "black" nationalism, and "left-wing" politics. Alternatively, and in a metaphorical sense, the term *Afrikaner* now covers English speakers too. Both are united in their love for *their* land.

Continuing his speech, the Natal representative recalled the legacy of Piet Retief, the Voortrekker leader killed during negotiations with the Zulu, and asked:

Do we not believe in the God who assisted Moses in the desert and do we not believe in the God who led Andries Pretorius to a glorious victory and who, today and tomorrow, can lead our beloved leader, Dr. Andries Treurnicht, to a glorious victory for the whites in South Africa?

This linking of Moses, Pretorius, and Treurnicht is not accidental; the three are linked not only by their leadership of an "oppressed" people but in that their leadership is an expression of a covenant between God and the people. If there was one strong undertone to the assembly that was never actually articulated, it was the expectation that the "covenant" of Blood River was being renewed there and then. Reading between the lines, I would spell out this expectation as follows: It was under the leadership of Pretorius that the Boers as the people of the covenant prevailed over the black nation of the Zulu. They thus secured their safety and freedom. Now, in these perilous times of being overwhelmed by black masses and by evil political forces bent on delivering us to chaos and annihilation, we need to renew that covenant between us and God in order to overcome the forces of darkness. Our leader, Treurnicht, being both a man of God and a leader, is the chosen one to do so.

The leader of the Transvaal did not say much except to introduce Treurnicht. The masses shouted, "KP, KP, KP," and gave a standing ovation of 40 seconds' duration. Treurnicht's speech started with these words:

Esteemed fellow citizens [*volksgenote*], the Third War of Liberation has indeed started. . . . The so-called new South Africa, in which the government forces integration upon us, leaves us no choice but to defend our rights and to secure what is our own in every domain of our people's existence. Our battle cry is, "For freedom, for [our] people and for our fatherland!" Whoever despises or ridicules this, declares himself as stranger and enemy.

He continued in English:

We are here together in our tens of thousands. We can say in all honesty this is a coming together of believing citizens and not a conspiracy against any other nations. To tell the truth, we as a nation respect the rights of other nations, not to be dominated and to rule themselves. We honor the millions of nonwhites who resist the intimidation of the terrorism of the ANC, the PAC, and the SACP. And this is . . . with the white nation. We assure those millions of nonwhites of our friendship. We wish to see in every community a resistance being built up against violence, against communism and terrorism, and against the assault on the independence of the various nations. We call upon black leaders such as Chief Minister Buthelezi of the Zulu nation to stand together with us against the intimidation and the terrorist organization like the ANC and not to let communism reign victorious in S.A.

Treurnicht thus drew clear distinctions between good whites and bad whites, and between good blacks and bad blacks. Significantly, he described those present as believing citizens, underlining their religious and moral nature. This believing community had no desire to dominate blacks. All the whites wanted was the right to their own land and the right to govern themselves. He cited the examples of Lithuania, Estonia, and Azerbaijan, whose citizens were essentially engaged in a struggle similar to that of South African whites. He further justified his stand in an international context by pointing out that the existence of Lesotho, Swaziland, Botswana, and "the four neighboring states" (meaning the four "independent" homelands) was a "normal" manifestation of independence and self-determination. He contrasted this "normality" with current political developments:

But, ladies and gentlemen, once we said that to each other we cannot help to be amazed about the repudiation and betrayal [of this arrangement] for the sake of a totally new South Africa. Where have you ever heard of a leader that denigrates his own people's status to that of a minority in order to create a new nation out of different racial groups and peoples? Which nation will give away its position of political power to become a powerless minority in its own country?

He elaborated on the betrayal by recalling what he described as the "Red Friday" of February 2, 1990, when the South African Communist Party was declared legal. The government further seemed to declare the white right-wingers a threat, while

the flags of the communists and the ANC fly in the South African sky. Those accused of high treason become fellow discussants. Those responsible for bomb murders are constantly featured on the first page of newspapers, where they are showered with humanistic conciliation. The communists are laughing, and they laugh the whole way, and the liberalists laugh with them, though they are frequently not aware what they are laughing about.

Treurnicht associated betrayal by the government with humanist and liberal ideologies. These were the markers between the government as the internal enemy and the moral community of the people. He went on to elaborate on the hate the ANC had for the Boer people (*Boerevolk*), the hate for the white nation: "[The ANC] demands our land." He expressed fear that under these circumstances Christian National Education may also be jeopardized and that local government would become multiracial. In propagating the "new" South Africa, he argued, the government was acting without a mandate from the people:

> Ladies and gentlemen, in spite of the state president's oath of office to uphold the Constitution and all other laws, one law after the other is being declared out of date. The imminent abolition of these laws is announced at the same time: the Separate Amenities Act, the Group Areas Act, the Population Registration Act, the Annexures to the Constitution. According to the Annexure 1 of the Constitution, education at all levels, art and culture, recreation, health services such as hospitals, clinics, control over private hospitals, and what they control are all own affairs. Dictatorially, I say dictatorially, in contradiction with their election mandate, without asking the nation, own affairs are being turned [?] off the table to make place for the integration of the new South Africa. What right do you claim . . . what, . . . [by] what right do you claim that other people must not take the law into their own hands when you yourself discard the law? [Calls of "Hear! Hear!"; applause, whistling.] We warn; it is an unreasonable government which no longer represents the nation which practices fraudulent politics. We will restore these rights of our people which have been . . . dictatorially . . . trodden upon. We will restore them [applause]. If the government wants to move away from its immoral position, it must speedily call a general election for the whites and put, and put its integration . . . abdication politics to the voters.

Treurnicht came very close to calling his followers to unconstitutional, direct action. He pounded away at the fears of his audience: that the ANC might become part of the military, that integration might be forced on the whites with the help of the United Nations, as it happened in Namibia. He then suddenly turned to motivate them by calling for a national movement. He associated this movement with God's purpose:

> We have the will and the faith. We are telling you today that our national movement, the true national movement for freedom in our fatherland, is an unstoppable one. You won't be able to hold it back as you won't be able to stop the incoming tide with a broom. We are telling you, sir, you don't have enough prisons to hold Afrikaner nationalism captive. . . . [Break in recording.] No power in heaven or on earth can thwart His long-suffering purpose. Without Him—he became—we are a wild, lawless people headed for destruction. We are telling each other: God's help is not only to be called upon in times of crisis. He cannot be nationalized, though. It is true that He divided

humanity into peoples; He nationalized humanity. We cannot force our arbitrariness upon Him. We have to confess our sins and transgressions and our people has to convert itself unto God. . . .

I implore you today: do not doubt when there is still time and we can do something. We can do a great deal when we leave here today. Do not allow yourselves to be talked out of the biblical truth that God subdivided humanity into peoples and that He set boundaries for them. This is a tremendous scriptural truth. The "globalism" and the phenomenon of "the New Age movement" [are] the erasure of ethnic identities [*volksidentiteite*] by humanistic conciliation through its so-called togetherness, harmony, fellowship. That is not the true message of the Bible. That is not the biblical view.[2]

The core of religious justification in this speech is contained in the phrase "He [God] nationalized humanity." According to Treurnicht, the National Party betrayed nationalism, or rather, the party's political reforms that deny nationalism are blasphemous, rebellious actions because nationalism is part and parcel of a divine plan. To act against nationalism, in this sense, is to act against God. The national movement envisaged by Treurnicht thus became an instrument in the execution of a preordained divine plan.

Treurnicht then turned to some immediate practical concerns and exhorted the audience to assist the Conservative Party during the by-election in the Umlazi constituency of Natal. He also encouraged audience members to join in the "1 Million Action," the attempt to collect a million signatures as endorsement of the Freedom Manifesto mentioned earlier. He also asked them to buy bonds, the funds from which would be used to set up a conservative newspaper.

Finally, Treurnicht expressed confidence that his party would be able to sell the idea of "separate freedoms for various nations" internationally. He emphasized that this was a modern idea, and not just an old-fashioned idea of *verkramptes* (archconservatives). To him, the principle of doing one's own work was of great importance in the context of separate freedoms and security. The strikes by black workers demonstrated that whites could and should do forms of labor usually done by blacks. In addition, being independent of black labor was important for security reasons. He underscored whites' right to take steps in order to protect themselves.

In closing his speech, Treurnicht mentioned that a number of people had requested that a new covenant be made with God on the day of the rally. He backed away from this, saying that it was a tremendously serious task that he approached with great care, if not hesitation. He referred the crowd to the Manifesto, which expressed their "strivings" and "undertaking." He was careful not to attempt to create a new covenant or renew the old one. Instead, he urged the crowd to make a public pledge to God. He recited the following, in English:

> We solemnly pledge before the Lord and each other: "We shall be a nation of the Lord. We will [encourage] our children and their children to be one with us as servants of the Almighty, free [against] the entire world; a Christian nation in our own fatherland."

As he tried to get the crowd to say these words in unison, either in Afrikaans or in English, there was confusion, and a few people mumbled, "I pledge." He told the crowd to go forth and mobilize the people. He then concluded with a prayer:

> Lord, our God, great and fear inspiring, merciful and loving. May the grace of our Lord Jesus be with us. It is that grace that recognizes and saves man from being lost; that bridges the separation and alienation of a sinner through the conciliation of your death on the cross; that transforms a worthless life into a life of service; that calls forth the elect from every people into an assembly of the people of God from the whole world.
>
> The grace that makes us into children of God and that gives us eternal life. May grace be with us.
>
> May the love of God our Father be with us; the love that nobody kindles or rejects; the love that was in your eyes when you looked onto us in sympathy like onto the prodigal son; the love of the God of the Covenant that lasts forever; the love walking hand in hand everyday with forgiveness, again and again; the love that takes back a remorseful human and a people, transforming them into servants of the highest God.
>
> May the communion of the Holy Spirit also be with us; the Spirit that inspires and nobody can stop or neutralize it; your Spirit that renews us and re-creates us in the image of our Savior; that heals us from degeneration; that brings us back after being lost; that works in us the fruit of love, the joy, the peace, the patience and tenderness, goodness and faithfulness and self-control.
>
> Oh Lord, our Lord, do not relinquish your work. Do not abandon or reject us for our lawlessness, our remorselessness and offensiveness among the nations [peoples]. Fashion us into a witness-bearing people in which the effects of your grace, your love, and your presence could be seen.
>
> Be with everyone present here today in the name of the only Savior, our Lord. Amen.

At first glance, the wording and structure of this prayer resembled those of any ordinary prayer offered by any Dutch Reformed minister at a

Sunday church service. The prayer was devoid of direct references to the political concerns and fears of the day, and remained abstract and formulalike. Treurnicht obviously was careful not to bring politics openly into religious formulations, thus the ritual use of standard Calvinist phraseology. (One of the main reasons the Afrikaanse Protestantse Kerk split off from other Afrikaans-speaking denominations was the politicization not only of their policies, but also of rhetoric.) However, one should not be deceived by the surface of Treurnicht's language. The structure of the prayer displayed a threefold division, calling upon the grace, love, and spirit of God. The words depicted the people (*volk*) as humble, but did not fail to remind the audience that very humble people are also the elect by the grace of God. The political message was subliminal but powerful. God was further called upon as the God of the Covenant. Although the original context of this appellation is the Old Testament, Treurnicht had only shortly before starting his prayer referred to requests that he renew the covenant between the Afrikaner and God. He had prepared his audience during his political speech for a political understanding of his prayer. The implicit meaning conveyed by the prayer should thus have been clear to the audience.

The boundaries hammered out during the speech reappeared in the prayer: The elect, being the children of God, are distinguished from the rest. A strange verticality pervaded the prayer. The relationship between God and the elect human community received one-sided emphasis. The separation and alienation mentioned referred to the relationship between God and humans. "Love" is the love between God and humans. The notions of "degeneration" and "service" were not brought into the context of horizontal, interpersonal, or interracial relationships. They were left hanging in the air, unconnected to the real world of human relationships in South Africa. Treurnicht's main message in this prayer was clear: God accepts "His people," and therefore their existence is not only morally but cosmologically justified.

The prayer brought to a close the formal part of the rally, and the audience started to disperse. Without any appeal being made, people spontaneously cleaned up after themselves, filling the trash receptacles and, when they were full, making neat stacks of refuse. Needless to say, there were absolutely no blacks in sight at any time during this occasion. Cleaning up was a symbolic act of *selfwerksaamheid* (doing your own work), to which Treurnicht had exhorted the audience in his speech. Behind the stage, a farmer and his adult sons, clearly unaided by black laborers, were loading buggies that had been used earlier in a parade onto a large truck. They worked quickly, almost defiantly, with rapid, precise movements, exchanging curt phrases to coordinate their task. The stalls were busy now. Young girls were selling T-shirts with the picture of a Boer and the words, in Afrikaans, "The Boers are here to stay." A huge poster in front of the stall of the Afrikaanse Protestantse Kerk advertised a petition against the opening and privatization of white schools. Some aggressive young men were carrying posters that had English text on them. This struck me as strange at this predominantly Afrikaans gathering, but then I realized they were positioned near the place where the foreign television crews were working. The posters read as follows:

> *REMEMBER! THE MAU-MAU*
> *KAFFIR—BASTARDS*
> *REMEMBER! THE CONGO*
> *REMEMBER! RHODESIA*
> *REMEMBER! PIET RETIEF*
> *CHROME-DOME DE-KLERK*
> *DO'ES [sic] NOT REMEMBER*

The associations were clear: Blacks were viewed as murderers, they were called by the most insulting term—kaffirs—and F. W. de Klerk was ridiculed. The other side of this poster proclaimed:

> *BETTER DEAD THAN RED*
> *STOCK UP WITH PLENTY OF LEAD*
> *LETS [sic] GIVE THIS KAFFIR*
> *FROM THE TRANSKEI*
> *AN ARMED STRUGGLE.*

The "kaffir from the Transkei" is Nelson Mandela. Note how important his origin was to these demonstrators. To them Mandela was a "tribal" man from a homeland. Another poster read:

> *JUDAS DE KLERK*
> *HOW MUCH WAS*
> *THE PAY OUT*
> *FOR THE SELL OUT?*

A general carnival atmosphere prevailed. Not far from the demonstration, Willem Kleynhans, a liberal Afrikaans academic, was talking to some BBC journalists, highlighting the government's unrealistic expectation of acceptance of its reforms by Afrikaners who had been brainwashed by them for 50 years. His views did not attract much attention, however, nor did the journalists bother to take notes. More people were gathered around nearby stalls that were selling books and mementos. There were recipe books for making traditional Boer food and history books for adults and children extolling the heroism of the Boers in wars against blacks and Britons. Lead figurines of Boer men and women, dinner plates with traditional designs, bandannas, and other objects were being sold. An old man dressed in rags, with unkempt, dirty hair, shuffled by and was greeted in Afrikaans. He reminded me that all Afrikaners do not belong to the middle class. Extended families were assembling on the open space in front of the stage, getting ready to depart for home. Children lugged large garbage bags to the nearest trash bins.

I left and returned home. That evening, I watched the SABC television news. Extensive time was devoted to the arrival of the state president from Europe. At the airport, de Klerk remarked: "Through no mustering of large meetings can anybody stop the process of the new South Africa. We will not be intimidated." A Soweto choir was shown singing, "Glory, glory hallelujah," and another speech was made by the acting state president. The news then switched to the rugby stadium and showed de Klerk looking at a plane towing a banner with the lettering "Thank You—Dankie FW." At the end of the news program about 45 seconds of coverage were given to the Conservative rally; Treurnicht was shown giving his speech, but there were no pictures of the mass attendance.

GENERAL FEATURES
OF RIGHT-WING DISCOURSE

The conservative rally in Pretoria provides very rich and multidimensional evidence about right-wing political discourse. I have presented it here in great detail because it contains most of the features found at other political events and in the literature disseminated by representative groups. The structure of the event in itself communicated a powerful message, but some elaboration is necessary on the structure and content of the many symbols and conceptualizations that were used. There were some variations in this regard; for example, different ideas existed about partitioning the country into white and black areas. In their broader thrust, however, these ideas tended to be similar in the message they conveyed to the white public. In the following pages, I will concentrate on the main themes addressed by right-wing rhetoric. In selecting these themes, I am guided by the ways in which social boundaries are drawn. Who is considered to belong to one's own group? Who are the outsiders? Who is a friend and who an enemy? Themes of leadership, the economy, and internal and external security also receive special attention.

Insiders

The structure of the Pretoria rally was similar in many respects to that of other related types of events, such as political party meetings and the Great Trek celebrations of 1988. As events, these all constitute special times. Each was ritually opened with a religious ceremony: An appropriate text from the Bible was read, song and prayer followed, and, at the end, prayer closed the event. The opening not only set the tone for the event but also bounded it. Speakers and public figures were therefore careful to use words or formulations in harmony with the spirit of that tone. Yet, below the surface of tempered language, there lurked much resentment, prejudice, and hostility. It was in this time bracketed on both ends by religion that public discourse was formulated. These brackets also, temporarily, defined a religious community. In Chapter 3, I mentioned the atmosphere of *nagmaal* (rural holy communion) that prevailed during the Great Trek celebrations. The same was true for the meeting at the Voortrekker Monument, and, to a lesser extent, at political meetings. Both the structure and the content of these meetings addressed those present as members of an in-group that shared a sense of community, a sense of common purpose and calling, and, above all, a sense of pious communion. The rationality that pervaded these public spheres had less to do with secular considerations than with religious self-justification and self-elevation. Speakers called those present *gelowige volksgenote* (believing citizens), "a Christian people," "a witness-bearing people," and "a suffering people." Such features placed these meetings in marked contrast with those of the National Party, or of parties to the NP's left. After the close of the official proceedings, the tone of speech among those present changed remarkably. I heard white supremacist small talk and observed the open display of racist posters.

Turning to the content of the symbols and speeches at the rally, the first striking feature is the way speakers struggled to find an overarching label to describe those present. The most inclusive label was that of "whites." The HNP, at a political meeting in the city hall of Johannesburg, displayed a huge banner proclaiming, "Whites Unite for Truth & Right" (see Leadership, 1988, p. 22). Similarly, at AWB meetings a special effort was made to include English speakers in this category by using their language on posters and in speeches. At a political meeting in the East Rand city of Benoni in July 1989, the leader of the CP, speaking in English, described the relationship as follows:

> Ladies and gentlemen, it is a wonderful privilege not to welcome you but to say we are glad you're with us in this struggle for the survival of the white man in his own fatherland and under his own, own government. . . . This party is not exclusively for the Afrikaner. It is for the Afrikaner. . . . join the party and say this is the political leader that will take us to victory on the 6th of September. . . . We will hear you plead with the Afrikaner: "Please don't leave us alone." We will not leave you behind. You are with us. You will be part and parcel of the victory of this young party [applause].

The collective, sexist term for whites, "the white man," was used often at the Pretoria rally to describe the actors united in a common destiny and struggle. The Afrikaner seemed to be the leader in the struggle, but the struggle was also seen as that of white English speakers. Speakers at the rally were not absolutely clear about the relationship between the Afrikaans and English language communities within the moral community. The Afrikaner, however, was seen as the leader. Therefore, *Boerevolk* (Boer people) was sometimes used in a parallel sense with *blanke nasie* (white nation). The clearest formulation of the relationship occurred in the Natal CP representative's speech when he referred to the English as "English-speaking Afrikaners." In this way he bridged the historical and cultural gap by reducing the difference between the two to that of dialect. In fact, such formulations implied that Afrikanerness stands for the moral, cultural, and political fiber of true whites in general.

In conservative political discourse the population of the world is not an agglomeration of individuals but is made up of various ethnic groups or peoples. I deduce, therefore, that the so-called white nation qualified by Afrikanerness is one such people. Thus a shift occurred away from the notion of an autochthonous Afrikanerdom, with one language, culture, history, and genealogy. By extension, English speakers were now recognized as members of this "people." However, this was inconsistent in a way, because the criteria applied to the different black ethnic groups relied exactly on features such as the supposed homogeneity of language, culture, and descent.

The whites had their own symbols, of course. First of all, they had their languages. Speaking in English, Treurnicht said in Benoni in 1989:

[I wish to] plead for upholding of our own language Afrikaans as an official
language. Obviously it is not necessary to plead for the maintenance of English
as official language. But we are as Afrikaners—we are in favor of two official
languages. We don't want *Nkosi Sikelela* [the ANC anthem] to be the official
anthem [loud calls: "Hoor, hoor"]. We grant that [every people] should have
his own national anthem and his own national flag. We claim of our own that
people should recognize that right of the white man, Afrikaans or English
speakers, of the white, of the white people, to have their own symbols and
to have their own freedom and their own life.

The difficulty of conceptually integrating the two language communities
is clear from this formulation, but it makes clear also the importance of
shared symbols, even if they differ in some ways, as in language.

Perhaps the strongest force unifying whites has been the undeserved
affliction they believe they have suffered at the hands of traitors and enemies.
The continued existence of whites, in the above sense, is seen as in
jeopardy because of enemies' efforts to deny that group the two elements
crucial for its survival: its own territory and its right to self-determination
in this territory. The whites as a group thus felt compelled to defend themselves in a struggle against those forces of evil that had denied them these
components of their birthright. It is important to note how, in the rhetoric
of public right-wing discourse, the notions of natural and divine right
converge around the idea of a birthright.

Finally, as far as the in-group self-definition is concerned, this defiant
people, locked in a struggle for their divinely willed identity and preservation, saw themselves as a humble people. They neither regarded themselves as racists nor wanted to deny other peoples their particular birthright. They were not the aggressors. They were the brave defenders, last
but not the least, of the faith in a world filled by the ungodly forces of the
Antichrist.[3]

Outsiders

This brings us to the outsiders. Two main categories could be discerned
in the discourse at the Pretoria rally: benign outsiders and malevolent
outsiders. In the latter category were insiders as outsiders and true outsiders. Let us turn to the true outsiders first.

True outsiders, or external outsiders, belonged to the outside world, or
the *buitewêreld* (collectively, foreign countries are called the *buiteland*).
The popular conception of the outside world covers Western Europe,

Britain, and the United States. This world was generally regarded to be hostile toward South Africa and to whites in particular because of its punitive sanctions policy. Furthermore, it was dominated by a value system that denied the importance of a collective identity for an ethnic group. This attitude was seen to emanate from a liberal and humanist orientation that values individual rights rather than group rights—meaning group rights in an ethnic context. The liberalism understood to pervade the West was not explicitly connected to left-wing movements, although Treurnicht in another Pretoria speech did identify one of its supposed tenets, "globalism," with communism and the struggle of the ANC:

> While the peoples of Eastern Europe demand their independence, our government coerces our people into a nonracial unitary state together with other races and peoples—and [thus] we move toward a black majority government, or rather, an ANC-communist government. The seeds of the so-called globalism and that of the "New Age movement" are being sown in our country.

He repeated these references in his speech at the Monument (see above).

In a pamphlet distributed at the Pretoria rally, the quasi-religious organization Operation South Africa (n.d.) was much more explicit in the associations it made. It strove to

> present the truth regarding the South African situation to believers both here and overseas, thus enabling them to stand together against the prince of darkness and his legions who are using Marxism and other ideologies and non-Christian religions and philosophies, in influencing the West to destroy us. (p. 16)

The external outsider was thus not only maintaining a foreign, hostile, and inappropriate set of values, but was thought to be under the influence of Marxism and communism. The right-wing *S.A. Observer* (December 1988) has gone even further, speaking of the "pernicious Judeo-Communist forces of change and revolution" (p. 8).[4]

It would be unfair to typify all conservative groups by this rather monolithic and paranoid view of the hostile external outsider. However, the degree of xenophobia among right-wing groups is intense. Their ultimate fears take the form of communism and Marxism. In popular right-wing discourse these two ideologies are starkly contrasted with Christian faith and morality. The perspective on Marxism, for example, is grossly oversimplified. As we have seen in some of the above quotations, Marxism/communism is placed in a dualistic, even cosmological, frame that contrasts the forces of darkness with the forces of light. As an ideology it is seen to "infect" the West, the Christian church, and even some Afrikaners (see below). The hostility toward these "forces" is acute, and is often expressed in a contradictory way against U.S. foreign policy. Robert van Tonder of the Boerestaat Party is reported to have sent the following message to Saddam Hussein during the Persian Gulf crisis of 1991: "May your weapons be blessed. What you are experiencing in your country today, the Boers experienced 92 years ago" (*Southscan* database, January 25, 1991).

By extension, whites in South Africa have believed themselves to be isolated in a hostile and godless world, surrounded by powerful adversaries with unlimited resources. This perspective of isolationism and self-defense is sometimes described as the laager mentality, a remnant of pioneer times when Boers created a defensive structure by moving their ox wagons into a circle. This enclosure provided protection against the numerically overwhelming black forces. The laager mentality is expressive of a sense of extreme isolation experienced in the face of overwhelming "un-Christian" forces. Many right-wingers thus have an understanding for the position of Israel, but their lurking anti-Semitism prevents them from making the connection publicly.

The hostile external outsider also inhabits Africa. Conservatives view Soviet influence in Africa with alarm. The implications of the end of the Cold War have yet to penetrate their minds, and the "Soviet-Cuban presence" in Africa is greatly feared. It is viewed as a surrounding force that has taken hold of the frontline states of Angola and Mozambique. Namibia, conservatives maintain, was sold out to communist forces, and Conservative party spokespeople have voiced great resentment at the South African government's role in "sacrificing South-West Africa to communist SWAPO." They have been distressed that so much "white" blood has flowed in vain in defense of a country against black "communist" forces. Zimbabwe, in their eyes, is equally communist. Until 1990, the "communist" forces were seen as external to South Africa. As ANC forces, they penetrated South African borders, but were countered by South African security forces. Conscripted young white soldiers defended their country against these forces of evil. When the ANC was declared legal in February 1990, this meant that black "communist" forces could work in South Africa. Black "communist" Africa thus extends right into South Africa now.

The choice of such words as *infection* and *penetration* is not accidental in conservative writing about boundaries. The boundary drawn between insiders and outsiders has a lot to do with infection of "innocent, healthy" whites by "diseased" blacks. In addition, the movement of blacks into white areas is looked upon as "penetration," as if a foreign object entered a body and damaged it, opened it up, so to speak, and threatened its life.

The metaphors of infection and penetration bring us to definitions of the internal outsider in public discourse. *Disease* not only has a metaphorical sense, in describing an ideological state of mind such as communism; it has in fact been concretely applied to blacks. At the conservative rally in Pretoria, the World Apartheid Movement, a South African organization with some links to white supremacists overseas, distributed pamphlets warning whites about the government's decision to open hospitals to all races. The movement looks upon blacks as carriers of the AIDS virus; the English version of its pamphlet observes:

> In spite of vehement denials by S.A. Government puppets . . . we can safely assume that the figure of one in six Black children in Soweto having AIDS is a FACT.
> While the P.A.C. and the A.N.C. cadres are dying of AIDS in Africa, and, in fact, facing extinction within the next 5 years the NP is nevertheless rushing to install these groups in a power-base in this country. . . . AIDS carries on, blithely killing thousands upon thousands of people daily.
> The ones who have not yet died are NOT obliging enough to slip off into the bush to die. They are now being encouraged by the Government to occupy every hospital and educational facility in the country, thereby guaranteeing both the infection of every patient unfortunate enough to occupy the same building, AND the collapse of all medical and educational services.
> . . . [Quoting a British White Paper of 1987] The same report also uncovered the fact that AIDS is transmitted by lice and bedbugs, which bodes ill for any patient unfortunate enough to enter a hospital which also houses AIDS infected sufferers with a less than usual regard for personal cleanliness. (World Apartheid Movement, 1990)

The Afrikaans version of the pamphlet is much more explicit in its linking of AIDS to the black population and much less subtle in its formulation. The religious organization Operation South Africa, though not identifying AIDS as a predominantly black phenomenon, nevertheless lists the "AIDS pestilence" in its catalog of sins (p. 7). The associations made in these documents are revealing. Disease, sin, blackness, and, by implication, divine retribution are all linked. The ANC and PAC should have been kept in Africa—that is, outside South Africa—where they would have met their (deserved?) fate of dying of AIDS. Blacks in general are seen as dirty, lice-infested people who should be left to their fate in the bush. "The bush" metaphorically conveys a meaning of an uncivilized, uncultured, outsider way of life. The metaphor of the bush recurred in many of the interviews conducted in this study (see below).

At the Pretoria rally, the leader of the Conservative Party was very careful to avoid expressing himself in the blatant way of these pamphlets. This is understandable because of the care he took to uphold the pious tone of the meeting and to avoid any racist labels. The pamphlets were less careful and clearer in their drawing of boundaries. They were more explicit in their terminology.

A most important, if not ambiguous, category of internal outsiders is that consisting of the government, the National Party, and other white and racially mixed political groups. I will concentrate here on the NP and the government, which are mostly lumped together in right-wing political discourse anyway. It is interesting to note that the audio presentation at the Voortrekker Monument in 1990 also used the paradigm of disease. The old man ruefully recalled that liberalism started to consume his fellow Afrikaners in the cabinet like a cancer. This cancer was the spirit of liberal humanism that now captured the minds of fellow Afrikaners. The Democratic Party, which stood for one person, one vote, was taken to task by Treurnicht at the Benoni meeting of the CP in 1989. He accused the DP of being undemocratic by favoring a system that would subject whites to the will of the black majority. He remarked that there were a number of Afrikaans-speaking individuals in the DP. This, to him, was not unique because it happened in the past that Afrikaners supported parties not in line with Afrikaner interests. However, a year later in Pretoria, after the government declared the ANC and other related organizations legal, released Nelson Mandela, and embarked on preliminary negotiations, the CP's tone turned more aggressive toward the NP. The NP, by now, was outflanking the liberal DP. There was now open talk about the nefarious spirit of liberalism and humanism that had entered the government's policies. In a spirit of humanistic reconciliation, they were alleged to have become discussion partners to murderers, terrorists, and communists. F. W. de Klerk was not only weak to "capitulate" to the pressures of liberalism exerted by the external outsider, the *buiteland,* but he and his followers somehow seemed to have absorbed the foreign ideology. Proof of this was the fact that he acted "dictatorially" in implementing his reforms. The government, the NP, and their followers were hostile to the interests of the true Afrikaners. NP supporters were essentially misguided. The posters at the Pretoria rally, of course, were much more explicit, calling de Klerk a Judas who sold out his people.

As far as the internal outsider is concerned, right-wingers insisted that a middle or neutral position was untenable. You were either for or against the cause; either an insider to the community of fate or an outsider. Conservative activist S. E. D. Brown described the situation in 1988:

There are three forces involved, as follows:

(1) The activists of change; liberals, do-gooders, communists, Zionists and so-called Christian humanists.

(2) On the other side, those who are aware of the disasters which will follow and who set out to oppose the change, or at least change on essential points.

(3) In between, a big mass of people, in leading positions everywhere, who will not face facts, who would prefer to live in a conservative atmosphere, but rather than face up to the aggressive dynamism of the Left will either remain silent or will even try to persuade the real conservatives to compromise with the extreme forces of destruction in some blind hope that this will appease and at least gain for them some respite from the strain of making decisions.

The third group, is the most pernicious of all the traitors. (*S.A. Observer,* December 1988, p. 8)

Perhaps Brown was referring to the white business community. His remarks apply equally well to the rest of the white population.

Finally, there were the benign outsiders, both close and distant. The distant ones were individuals and organizations sympathetic to the white cause in South Africa. Politicians in this category included the Bavarian politician Franz Josef Strauss; the American president, Ronald Reagan; and the British prime minister, Margaret Thatcher. They were, however, a passing generation, and their successors were looked upon with much more suspicion. Groups such as the World Apartheid Movement, based in Pretoria, established links with white supremacist organizations in Europe and the United States. Closer to home, anticommunist leaders and forces in Africa found favor in the eyes of right-wingers. Dr. Hastings K. Banda of Malawi has for many years been idealized as a "good" African leader. The commander of the anticommunist UNITA guerrilla movement in Angola, Jonas Savimbi, has similarly been held in positive esteem. Homeland leaders such as Buthelezi have been praised as supporters of the idea of separate ethnic states that would help form a bulwark against communism and the ANC (see Treurnicht's speech, above).

It is not very clear what the outsider status of homeland citizens is in conservative political discourse. On the one hand, certain conservative policies have preferred to view them as a South African labor pool without political rights, whereas others would regard them as strangers or foreigners. The Oranjewerkers have been most consistent about referring to all non-Afrikaners as strangers in discussions of exclusive Afrikaner "heartlands." They call them *vreemdes* (foreigners) (Oranjewerkers, 1990).

Conservative groups have attached a high priority to defining social boundaries explicitly in public discourse. Not only are social and cultural boundaries of utmost importance to them, but their physical manifestation, or rather their territorial expression, is crucial. The boundaries are negatively rather than positively defined. Therefore, it is more a matter of excluding categories of people. As noted above, the CP and other right-wing political organizations sometimes have had difficulty defining English speakers as members of the in-group. Yet it is possible to bridge the historical, cultural, and linguistic gap with reference to an overpowering marker, namely, skin color. In the end, it is this one racial feature of whiteness that has been endowed with cultural and historical attributes to make it look convincing as an ethnic catchall for a community of interest. In discourse, then, outsiders are told it is not race that unifies whites, but ethnicity. The ethnic boundary thus established is a firm one. It was constructed in the context of whites' defense against hostile outsiders. Therefore, as bulwark or rampart, it needs to be impenetrable.

Leadership

At the Pretoria rally, the CP leader was described as a Moses or Joshua. He was presented in a biblical paradigm to convey to the audience that he is both *volksman* and *Godsman*—a man of the people and a man of God. In other sections of the public presentation he was elevated to successor status at the end of a line of prominent figures in Afrikaner mythology. The audio presentation named him as successor to Hertzog, Malan, Strydom, and Verwoerd. He thus represented traditional Afrikaner leadership. When he was pressured to renew the covenant, he was compared to the Voortrekker leader Andries Pretorius. Traditional legitimation was an important component of his leadership. His career was furthermore described as one of suffering and struggle on behalf of his people. These descriptions added a charismatic component to his image. Some of the posters at the rally stated, "In the Hands of Dr. A.P. Your Future Is Safe." In newspaper articles, his party presented his political career as a heroic struggle. The combination of traditional and charismatic legitimation outweighed other considerations. Treurnicht had a personal lifestyle in conformity with traditional values.

The importance of charismatic legitimation to right-wingers is illustrated by the figure of Eugène Terre'Blanche, the leader of the AWB. He was allegedly implicated in an affair with a journalist and engaged in behavior deviating from the Afrikaner norm. Yet, despite both the NP and the English-speaking press's widespread coverage of the events, the scandal did not affect his leadership position. He had consciously styled himself in charismatic terms. On the occasion of the fifteenth anniversary of the founding of the AWB, he said:

> The struggle of those fifteen years was worthwhile: my comrades supported my arms, kept my exhausted feet on the road, and kept idealism burning inside me—and God protected me and forgave my weakness and failings. Sometimes He Himself was the voice that spoke in me during meetings. (Afrikaner Weerstandsbeweging, 1988, p. 1)

Terre'Blanche presented himself as the suffering leader. Even the image of Moses, whose arms were supported during the crucial moments of battle, crept in. He styled himself as a military leader, sometimes using the model of Boer generals. He thus placed himself in the line of a heroic, military tradition. At other times he emulated a fascist model, using, for example, a straight-armed salute reminiscent of Nazism.

These styles of heroic leadership were starkly different from the descriptions conservatives reserved for the leaders of the National Party and political organizations to its left. They were depicted as villains who had betrayed the people who put them into power. They allegedly hung onto their power by illegitimate, if not illegal, means—"dictatorially," as Treurnicht said. They surrendered to their enemies in a cowardly manner in an effort to placate them, without knowing that they were selling out their own people for small gains. In caricatures, even the rather conservative NP leader P. W. Botha was depicted as a skull and crossbones, a sign of death.

Security

Securing the borders from foreign penetration is a high priority in conservative discourse. The mixing of "foreigners" and whites is considered to be a safety risk. Incidents such as murders of elderly people are related by conservatives to underscore the necessity of increased security measures. Conservatives thus have argued for the reinstatement of control over blacks in "white" areas, asserting that the reintroduction of a pass system for blacks is necessary in order to identify them ("99% of elderly employers don't even know their gardener's name or where he lives"; *Die Patriot,* December 2, 1988). Blacks would be allowed into white territory only under strict controls. Their numbers would be limited to the minimum required for white labor needs (Konserwatiewe Party van Suid-Afrika, 1989). Whites are presented as if they are locked in a struggle for survival. Blacks as residents in their neighborhoods are regarded as threats to white survival. Therefore, right-wing politicians argue that whites have the right to "defend" themselves (against a largely powerless black population). At a May 1990 meeting near Pretoria, the CP leader was cautious, urging whites to cooperate with the police for their security needs. The more militant AWB's rhetoric, however, skirted legality and advocated the arming of whites. The AWB formed paramilitary units to defend the "white man" and established a security guard that, by law, was allowed to carry arms in public.

Given a rhetoric and discourse that speak about the presence of blacks in white areas as "occupation" and "infiltration," it is not surprising that right-wingers have adopted a militant stance in politics.

The Economy

Conservatives paint a very bleak picture of the South African economy. The government is blamed for gross mismanagement of resources. Conservative politicians have expressed resentment that whites contribute 91% of the total income tax collected, whereas blacks contribute only 3% and total "nonwhite" contributions amount to 8.6% (Konserwatiewe Party van Suid-Afrika, 1989). On the other hand, Treurnicht quoted statistics at a political rally on July 11, 1989, which said that "nonwhites" controlled 45% of the buying power of the total population. Only the tax burden is seen as a grave injustice. Statistics are shrewdly manipulated. When it suits the politicians, they cite the low average income of all South Africans regardless of color in comparison to other Western countries. When they discuss tax contributions to the state coffers, they distinguish whites' contribution from that of blacks. They make the point that whites are being "unjustly" impoverished by an incompetent government that spends too much on black development. The principle that right-wing politicians want to advance is that those who generate the state's income should also be its beneficiaries; blacks should have to look after themselves in their separate states.

Visions of the Future

Conservative public discourse on the future is dominated by the idea of securing a distinct peoplehood for whites. The key element in this is ownership of a "piece of real estate" (in the words of van der Merwe in the quote that opens this chapter) on which whites could exercise their own sovereign rule. A number of models have been proposed. In the CP, for example, the Verwoerdian ideal of South Africa as an essentially white country prevails, with party members maintaining that the homelands provide enough territory for the "ethnically distinct" black "peoples." This ideal is flexible in the sense that borders could be readjusted. CP leaders have repeatedly emphasized that the issue of the exact borders between the white state and the black states is still open. This is the notion of "partition." CP politicians have pointed out that precedents for their policy already exist in the forms of Lesotho, Swaziland, and Botswana. They maintain that the government has strayed from the original idea of separation as a result of liberal tendencies and pressures from outside the country. They believe that a policy of strict territorial separation between black and white has not been given a proper chance—in their view it has not failed. There is enough land for every group. They also have suggested that separate territories be set aside for the Indian and coloured population categories. Partition, to conservatives, is a modern and respectable policy. It is also realistic, because they calculate that between 68% and 80% of blacks already live in, or adjacent to, their own "states" (homelands) (Konserwatiewe Party van Suid-Afrika, 1989, p. 7).

Smaller splinter groups, such as the Boerestaat Party, have envisaged a state comprising the territories of the historical Transvaal, Free State, and Vryheid Republic.[5] The ideal is that this state would grow out of economically self-sufficient ministates (Grobbelaar, 1990, p. 39). The Oranjewerkers (1990) have proposed four possible self-sufficient white territories: Wesland (West Country), stretching over most of the Northwestern Cape Province; Hartland Hoëveld (Heartland Highveld), covering the Northern Free State and the central part of the Transvaal; Hartland Sentraal (Central Heartland), consisting of the Western Free State and the adjacent Northern Cape; and Hartland Mosselbaai (Heartland Mossel Bay), including the Southern Free State and the Eastern Cape. The Oranjewerkers have been most radical in their insistence on complete white self-sufficiency in these states. No "foreign" labor would be allowed.

Some other variants of models for a separate and sovereign white state exist. The models presented varied mainly in size, how they would be implemented, and the degree to which they would be self-sufficient with regard to labor and the economy.

Conservatives have embraced the vision of a separate white state with great fervor. On this point there is no compromise in the political discourse.[6] To them the only alternative to a separate white state is a unitary state in which whites and Afrikaners would become a minority. This is an outrageous thought; it is unthinkable. In fact, the possibility of a unitary state with one common citizenship evokes extreme hostility and is regarded as a denial of the birthright of whites, or, more specifically, of the Afrikaners. The most bellicose language heard in my research was registered in the rhetoric dealing with the current government's "treacherous" policies, which will inevitably lead to such a unitary state. Conservatives believe that a unitary state will be riddled with conflict and revolution—conflict emanating from, first and foremost, the white section of the population. Political speeches repeatedly mentioned the possibility of whites' taking up arms and "defending" what is theirs. Blacks' presence in so-called white areas is held to be a hostile act, an "occupation" of whites territory. The response of whites to integration would therefore be violent. The mere fact that the government had to declare a state of emergency for such a long period is seen as proof that the government's reform policy is a failure. Partition would militate against a revolution (Konserwatiewe Party van Suid-Afrika, 1989, p. 6).

NOTES

1. As he started speaking, I was disconcerted to recognize the voice of my high school Afrikaans teacher.

2. In a speech during a political rally on July 11, 1989, in Benoni, east of Johannesburg, Treurnicht gave a more detailed elaboration on the biblical and ecclesiastical justifications for his policies:

The world isn't just a population of four or—how many is it now—billion humans. It [consists of] peoples [*volkere*] with their own languages and cultures. It [consists of] racial groups. If you tell me it is un-Christian to refer to different peoples, to different ethnic areas, then I assert just the opposite. When I read my Bible it tells me, and I summarize, that the diversity of peoples and their settlement on different areas of domicile across the world is the preordained will of God. I will give you two instances, one from the Old Testament and one from the New Testament. Moses of the Old Testament, when God [*die Voorsienigheid*] gave to the nations their heritage and their property, divided humanity into peoples [*volke*] and set their boundaries, He also created space for Israel. He made humans part of peoples [*volkere*] and set boundaries for them. In the New Testament, years afterward, centuries afterward, the great apostle of love, of I Corinthians 13, the great apostle of the conciliation between human being and human being, the great apostle who spoke of breaking down the wall that separates human being from human being, he comes along and tells us: God created all the nations of humanity out of one human being in order for them to spread out and inhabit the earth. He set their times and boundaries for them. And accordingly, dear friends, a most important ecclesiastical meeting [determined] that the diversity of peoples and their distribution over their different habitats was due to the preordained will of God.

3. Boshoff, Jooste, Marais, and Viljoen (1989) explore the spiritual decline that surrounds the Afrikaner and manifests itself in the liberalism of the day. They describe the essential nature of the Afrikaner as opposed to the individualism and freethinking of ungodly liberalism.

4. The *Argus*, a Cape Town newspaper, reported on February 9, 1990, that 4,000 AWB supporters had assembled in the Church Square of Pretoria. They burned a flag with a Star of David and carried a banner that read, "Jews are communists."

5. The Vryheid Republic was situated in the north of Natal.

6. The Stigting Afrikanervryheid (Foundation for Afrikaner Freedom) (1990) proposes and justifies the occupation and defense of a growth point in the Northwestern Cape. Raath (1990), in a publication sponsored by the same foundation, argues for secession from the rest of South Africa, whereas Boshoff et al. (1989) see a separate Afrikaner people's state as a matter of destiny.

6

Public Discourse and the Reconstruction of South Africa II: Government, Corporate, and Academic Perspectives

> We have to construct a nonracist community in which color would not be the criterion for political division [*verdeling*] but [one in which] the diversity of our population would not disappear.
>
> . . . I do not have in mind that minority rights should mean an entrenchment of minority privilege, or an entrenchment of the domination of a minority over majorities. I am talking about the protection of minorities against the abuse of power by the majority. (F. W. de Klerk, quoted in W. J. de Klerk, 1991, as serialized in *Beeld,* February 25-26, 1991)

In the above remarks, de Klerk strikingly avoids the terms *white* and *people* (*volk*). Rather, he speaks of "our population" and steers clear of the dilemma of accommodating discrete "nations" in an "overarching political system" such as the nation-state that Minister of Information Stoffel van der Merwe was struggling with in the quotation that opened the preceding chapter. De Klerk's words are typical of the dominant political discourse of the early 1990s. The pronouncements referred to here came into wider circulation when the influential Afrikaans-language newspaper *Beeld* summarized and serialized the contents of de Klerk's biography, written by his older brother, Willem. The rhetoric of this quotation consciously skirts racial overtones and uses carefully sanitized language, yet nobody familiar with this discourse would have had any doubt that the minority referred to is the whites and the majority, the blacks.

Purging the language of racial terms would not necessarily change the understanding of de Klerk's constituency. The denial of race and color as powerful, emotional, and historically felt anchor points of white identity did not detract from their force and relevance in human relations. However, the phraseology was important because of two factors. First, terms such as *minority* were used in other international contexts to describe social and cultural diversity in nonracial terms. These were accepted and respectable terms. The conceptualization of South African society was thus brought into line with that of other, more democratic, countries, such as the United States. In applying the term *minority* to the South African situation, de Klerk conveyed the implicit understanding that whites constitute such a minority, a possibility that right-wingers abhorred in the strongest terms.

Second, de Klerk's terminology had a social scientific base and therefore claimed legitimation beyond the immediate context of South African politics. In addition, de Klerk advocated the construction of a "nonracist community." He used the term *nonracist* in contrast to *nonracial*. He said: "I do not believe in a nonracial community in the literal sense of the word." He justified his view by looking at other countries with diverse populations. He argued that race still played a role in intergroup relations in the United States and Great Britain. Race and racism were thus two distinct categories to him. Reflecting on the basis of membership of "minority" groups in the "new South Africa," he explicitly used the criterion of "free association" in contrast to "racist groupings" (*rassistiese groeperings*). The social scientific convention of distinguishing between "ascribed" and "achieved" status lay at the base of his categorization. Although there are many problems associated with his distinctions, such as association-based membership in a racially defined group, this is not the point here. Rather, what is important is the difference between the way de Klerk legitimated his views and the justifications adopted by right-wing groups. De Klerk did not resort to mythical justifications based in the Bible, in the past, or in nature. Instead, he made an appeal to reason and invoked social scientific categories to support and promote his vision. This point will be taken up again later.

De Klerk's constituency and audience was far greater and more diverse than the one that Treurnicht addressed. De Klerk used terms he hoped would be acceptable to an international community as well as to the South African population at large. He was therefore very careful in selecting his words and phraseology.

It is interesting to look at how the above quote shows de Klerk's view of social groups. In the first instance, he described them as minorities. To de Klerk, South Africa is a country populated by minorities. The criterion for political differentiation—which I read to mean political parties—

would not be based on color, but, carefully and negatively formulated, would be one in which "the diversity of our population would not disappear." Minorities, we must deduce, would then find political representation qua minorities. Yet later de Klerk talked about the protection of minorities against the abuse of power by the majority. Thus, in his vision, it was possible that a majority would emerge. What could the basis of such a majority be? Here again, we detect the sanitizing of language and an avoidance of the unutterable color word: *black*. De Klerk was, of course, addressing white fears without breaking his self-imposed taboo on racial terminology. Yet these fears, and also his fears, were expressed in the word *abuse*. What paraded in the early years of National Party rule as *swart gevaar* (the black peril) now appears in the guise of "the abuse of power by the majority."

In his biography, de Klerk was also quoted as saying that the "ethnic political consciousness" of the nonwhites waned while they were united against white rule, but that, in a time when nonethnic politics was being planned, differences between them crystallized again—meaning ethnic differences. He gave assurances that his strategy would not use these differences, or exploit conflicts, to divide South Africans politically on an ethnic basis. A political division along ethnic lines would have suited the conservatives, but when de Klerk spoke of ethnic minorities he argued that they would embrace their ethnicity through free association and not through the legally ascriptive procedures of old-style apartheid. There would be no legal privileging or disadvantaging of any group. He had a clean conscience that he followed a road that would also ensure the survival of Afrikaners. The basis for the coherence of ethnic and other communities might be shared ideas about autochthony, descent, and heritage.

Although de Klerk adhered closely to the language of minority-majority relations and the principle of free association in the future of the new South Africa, there was a deeper level to his thoughts. He was struggling to repackage the old ascriptive connotations of color, race, and ethnicity in a way that would immobilize them as generators of inequality in the South African political process. His perspective was much more open, refined, and sophisticated than that of Treurnicht and his colleagues. It was open because of its emphasis on association rather than on racial and ethnic ascription. It was refined because it endowed his definitions with the respectability of reason and science. However, for those having been socialized as whites, enough space was left in his vision to accommodate some of their old, implicit racial and ethnic categories, albeit in a different guise. Because of the strangeness or novelty of the terminology and their own lack of political sophistication, many less-informed whites might not have been able to grasp the subtlety of the connections he made. As a result, they might have experienced a heightened sense of insecurity and anxiety about the future.

In light of conservatives' dependence on the past as a psychological and political resource, de Klerk's break with the past meant a break with the security it promised. This was most disturbing to them. Referring to white privilege, he was quoted saying: "We are working on a clean page." Further:

> I believe I have an obligation to lead South Africa into a new era of its history because it is definitely an era. *The old one has finally passed.* Nobody should find this strange because the lesson of history is that dynamic renewal always has to occur in order to survive. (F. W. de Klerk, quoted in W. J. de Klerk, 1991, p. 173; emphasis added)

In stressing the break with the past, the irreversibility of a new era, and the turning of a new page, de Klerk might have been unrealistic. Considering the numbers of whites who attended the rally at Pretoria in May 1990, an occasion marked by its almost atavistic symbolism and tone, it is hard to believe that this new perspective would be popular. Breaking with the past was placed within the context of survival. This inverts the conservative perspective. At Pretoria, a return to the past, to the values and social solidarity it symbolized, was seen as the guarantee of white survival. On that occasion there was no talk of a clean page. In fact, the page of the present was block printed, or rather engraved, by the past and its restoration both as remote and recent (white) republican past, in the guise of both the old Boer republics and the Verwoerdian images of the 1960s. In a certain way de Klerk's turning away from the past was necessary. The break was a logical consequence because there was no way in which the retreat from apartheid could find an anchor, or even a precedent, in the established thought of the National Party. Yet this link with the past remained a contradictory element in de Klerk's rhetoric. He spoke of his view as if it were the logical consequence of NP policy: "I emphatically hammered out the idea that the logical consequence of our policy is that blacks have to become part of a new political system" (quoted in *Beeld,* February 25, 1991).

De Klerk thus tried to establish a continuity, not through history but through logic. We may ask, Through what logic? The logical consequence he drew obviously had something to do with the perception within NP leadership that a dead end had been reached, that apartheid, separate development, or whatever it was called did not work. Thus it was pragmatism rather than ideology or self-mystification that gave impetus to the change.[1] The external pressure of sanctions and of disinvestment certainly played a role in forcing the government's hand. Right-wingers labeled the turn toward pragmatism as weakness and traitorousness. Nevertheless, de Klerk was not alone in his change of heart. The inner circle (*binnekring*) of the National Party also had been critical of the impracticality of old-style apartheid. As far as he personally was concerned, de Klerk said, "As soon as we emerged from the reorientation process, I made a mental jump [*'n sprong in my gemoed*]—clearer than many other National Party politicians— that power sharing with black people was the right course for the new dispensation" (quoted in *Beeld,* February 25, 1991).

Old-style apartheid might not have been feasible because of economic reasons, international pressure, or security considerations. Yet, given all the traditional ballast of irrefutable assumptions about the social and cultural makeup of South Africa and the mission of whites, de Klerk had little choice but to throw it overboard. His brother has remarked that he was definitely never part of an enlightened (political) movement in South Africa. He was a conservative in National Party circles who, at one time, was supposed to recapture the loyalty of traditionalists within the Transvaal branch of the party. De Klerk thus chose to make a moral and pragmatic quantum jump toward the "right course." Members of the Conservative Party doggedly disputed the argument that Verwoerdian apartheid was impractical or that it had failed. They maintained that it never had been given a proper chance to work. They clung to their biblically justified arguments about the morality of segregation. Now, de Klerk combined the pragmatic with the moral by arguing the opposite. In a sense, he turned Treurnicht's approach on its head by applying science and pragmatism instead of mystified history.

Though brief, the words of de Klerk quoted above reflect some basic assumptions of National Party thought. They were widely publicized in the press and in Willem de Klerk's book.

NATIONAL PARTY MEETING
IN MELVILLE, JOHANNESBURG:
MAY 18, 1990

I now wish to turn to a description of a public occasion that will serve to illustrate National Party discourse. The occasion was a widely publicized political meeting held by the National Party in the Johannesburg-

West constituency to report on the government's reform initiatives in May 1990.

Weeks beforehand, posters announced that the acting state president, G. van N. Viljoen, was to address the meeting, which was to be held in a church hall with a capacity of about 400 people. On the appointed evening, there were about 300 people present. The Johannesburg-West constituency comprises middle-class Afrikaners from the Rand Afrikaans University and the media community, some professionals, businesspeople, clerical workers, and retired persons from both language groups. The event's organizers extended an open invitation to the public to attend. Most of the audience came from the vicinity, as far as I could tell, but about a quarter to a third came from an adjacent constituency, Mayfair. Mayfair, as has been noted, was at that time becoming a racially mixed area, and its white residents were upset about this development. Their representatives traveled to the meeting site in minibuses and in cars. They sat at the back of the hall. Most of the people present were Afrikaans speakers.

The stage was decorated with the orange, white, and blue colors of the NP, the same colors as the national flag. Looking from the perspective of the audience, there was a huge photograph of F. W. de Klerk on the wall to the left of the stage. The lectern stood below the photograph. From there, a long table stretched to the other side of the stage. Flower arrangements in the colors of the party adorned the table. The functionaries entered the room and took their seats on the stage without much ceremony. The chairman and the speaker sat near the lectern, and then the local member of Parliament, with his wife; the municipal alderman, also a National Party representative; and the *dominee* (a clergyman) took their places.

As discussed previously, Conservative Party and right-wing political meetings had a churchlike atmosphere. In contrast, the atmosphere and tone of this meeting was that of a school or a lecture hall. As we will see later, the tone was one of instruction, and participation by the audience was tolerated only to a limited extent. As in a school meeting, the proceedings were opened by the *dominee*. In the name of those present he thanked God for the country and its opportunities and prayed for the members of Parliament, who "are also your sons." The prayer was in English. The use of the word *also* struck me as peculiar. The frequency of its occurrence in both its English and its Afrikaans forms (*ook*) was remarkable. Its abundant usage in speech is typical among Afrikaans clerics and academics, and seems to express a reluctance on the part of the speaker to overgeneralize. The term therefore is intended to specify and isolate through its emphasis. However, in the context of the discourse of this meeting, its usage indicated a shrewd manipulation of inclusiveness. Two contexts of inclusiveness could be distinguished: that of adding something to an existing core entity and that of contrasting some essential aspect with another in order to arrive at a more complete formulation. In English usage, the latter is achieved by the formulation *not only . . . but also . . . .* I will elaborate on the specific usage as it occurs in the description of the meeting's discourse below.

The chairman, in his introduction, and Viljoen, in his speech, used expressions of humility. They talked about what a privilege it is to live in present times; the chairman remarked on the privilege of having the acting state president present, and Viljoen called it a privilege to be part of history. These formulations are in line with the Calvinist notion of grace, which is a deeply rooted part of Afrikaner upbringing. Afrikaners are taught that humans are undeserving and sinful in the eyes of God. Whatever good they receive in life accrues to them solely through the grace of God. Personal merit or performance does not count and must be underplayed. This interpretation may seem exaggerated, but I believe that an examination of the Calvinist backgrounds of the speakers and audience at this meeting would bear it out. The notion of a "calling" also has Calvinist roots. Viljoen told his audience that they would be called upon (*geroepe wees*) as voters to judge or decide upon a new constitution.

In his speech, Viljoen used the same arguments de Klerk put forward in the quote that opens this chapter. He maintained the following:

- that policy change was a normal feature of National Party philosophy
- that the idea of ethnic separation and separate privileges in the country did not work, and that therefore reorientation was necessary
- that the existence of minorities should be recognized and that their rights should be protected
- that membership of these groups should be based on association rather than ascription

With regard to power sharing, he said:

> The National Party is convinced that there should not only be power sharing for all—also for the black people—in a new constitutional dispensation, but that there should also be provisions for the protection of minorities or groups, as I mentioned previously. This is a matter about which there are sharp differences of opinion and that leads to the very difficult marketing task of the National Party, which I would like to say something about tonight.

Significantly, he maintained there should be power sharing for all, and used the phrase "also for the black people" (*swartmense*). *Also* is used here in the first sense pointed out above, that is, indicating that blacks had to be added to the existing core of people who already shared power. Blacks were thus not part of, or were not automatically implied in, the notion of "power sharing for all." (Viljoen repeated this particular formulation six times during his speech, reflecting, in my opinion, his view of the rather exceptional nature of blacks' inclusion and, possibly, an attitude of condescension about their marginality.) Within the same sentence, *also* appeared for a second time, in this instance used in the second way described above, expressing contrast. It was used to correct any misunderstanding that power sharing might imply the swamping of minorities (read "whites") by the majority (read "blacks"). Viljoen repeated this somewhat nervous mention of minority rights in other places where he mentioned power sharing.

Viljoen recognized that strong differences of opinion existed about minority rights, but he felt that the emphasis on minority rights was not an insuperable problem—the idea simply had to be promoted using the proper "marketing" strategies.[2] This metaphor is important. Viljoen did not take on the role of the religious fundamentalist, hammering upon an inflexible notion of truth that "speaks for itself," as Treurnicht maintained at the right-wing rally. Rather, he realized that a reorientation was necessary, and that both blacks and the whites needed to be prepared to accept the new situation. Marketing strategies were the means or instrument for achieving this. National Party leaders understood that their policies would no longer be accepted on faith only, but needed to be marketed. The corollary of the idea of marketing, of course, is the notion that the electorate would be buyers of the new product. If they were not potential buyers, then the marketer, the party, also had to create a need for the product among the potential consumers. This particular instrumental way of reasoning is important; it distinguishes the public discourse of the National Party from that of the Conservative Party on yet another plane.

However, moralistic qualifications played an important part too. Viljoen noted:

The decision about the need for a new constitution has been taken in the course of a fairly lengthy period of time. In the first instance it was necessitated by the demands of fairness and justice in South Africa. It was also necessitated by the basic requirements for democracy. Because neither fairness and justice nor democracy could tolerate indefinitely, or much longer, a situation in which the majority of South Africans are effectively excluded from the politically ... eh ... decision making, ... from the political exercise of power in the government at all levels in this country. ... But it is not only a matter of principle, ... it is also a matter of practical experience.

Viljoen repeatedly appealed to practicality and practical reason. Practicality, justice, fairness, and democracy were thus harmonized. He also argued that practical experience taught the National Party not to impose a new constitution, as it tried to do in 1983. He said that the time for making decisions on behalf of others was past, and that practical experience taught that one could "achieve meaningful policy changes in South Africa only by *also* involving those affected by it" (emphasis added). (Here again, *also* is used in an additive sense, expressing the idea that internal deliberations forge policies, but then those affected need to be involved too.) Pragmatism was thus elevated to a political value. Principle was important, too, but was overshadowed by the exigencies of practicality. This is an interesting turn in the thinking pattern of leaders so strongly imbued with the Calvinist tradition. How this would be marketed to whites with similar background and upbringing in Calvinism will be explored below.

As far as the definition of social boundaries was concerned, Viljoen had a much more positive attitude toward the "outside world" (*die wêreld daarbuite*). The outside world was the international community at large, whose "reasonable" expectations had to be taken into account. Internally, a boundary was set between "moderate" leaders and "elements organized around the ANC," who insisted that the political process in the country had to be "normalized" first. Given that many black leaders' freedom was still restricted at the time of this speech, no "normal" political activity was possible. The dilemma of the government, according to Viljoen, was the (temporary?) impossibility of, yet dire need for, normalization. It was impossible to lift all restrictions and normalize the political process as long as "violence, intimidation, and destabilization" reigned. The speaker one-sidedly blamed these hindrances on the ANC's notion of an armed struggle, without referring to the white extremists and their avowed violence. The following quotation illustrates the internal boundary Viljoen was drawing:

> Moderate leaders like Chief Minister Buthelezi told the government that they were unable to sustain their credibility among their supporters as long as other black leaders and black parties were still banned by the government.

And Chief Minister Buthelezi said that the only way you [meaning the government] could effectively expose [*aan die kaak stel*] the ANC and its policy was to bring them into the dust and sweat of the political arena so that they were forced to defend their policy and so that *we* can attack them and so that they could, so to speak, be plucked bare in the presence of the world with regard to their policy. (emphasis added)

Note the switch from the pronoun *you* to *we*. This might have been a slip of the tongue, but it clearly indicates how the boundary drawn by Buthelezi was adopted by the speaker. The outsider pronoun *they* was used to identify the ANC. Even stronger evidence comes from the next lines, in which Viljoen made Buthelezi's reasoning his own:

These are the reasons why the government now decided . . . and there is a certain risk . . . but it is a risk leaders had to take with courage and conviction in order to make negotiations possible in South Africa.

This risk was taken earlier in 1990 when the state president declared the ANC and other organizations legal, released political prisoners, and, later, allowed political exiles to return. The whole process of "normalization" was, however, in the hands of the government, which took the initiative. Viljoen impressed upon his audience that the government negotiated from a position of strength and resolve to go ahead and leave by the roadside, so to speak, those who wished to withdraw from the political initiative of the government. This speech provides a great deal of evidence that the government was firmly resolved to take the initiative in the process of change—the government, and nobody else, would call the shots. It alone would create the space for the ANC to expose itself. This attitude cast a shadow over the idea of freely negotiating partners.

Viljoen went out of his way to discuss the issue of protecting minorities and their rights. Although he stressed that the principle of free association would determine membership of minority groups, he was soon faced with the dilemma of whether people could join minority groups of their own free will. He said that in a future South Africa, "there will also be the freedom of association to enable persons to move from one group to the other should they be acceptable in the other group." There were thus definite limits on the practice of free association. Membership in groups established on this principle was made subject to the approval of other members. This naïveté with regard to membership in minority groups, of course, introduced an element of insecurity and doubt to whites or Afrikaners, who did not have any idea how their group boundaries would be sustained once the ascriptive barriers were removed. Coloureds, on the other hand, who, for reasons of language, religion, culture, and so on, might desire to join the Afrikaners might not be able to do so, because the current members of that group might demand the right to reserve or restrict admission.

The principle of free association as propagated by the government caused a great deal of confusion. Furthermore, the new vocabulary of minority groups and rights rendered a number of implicit assumptions opaque. The language—that is, the form—was new, but what about the content? The rhetoric looked different from before, but what was actually being said? Blacks might have suspected the worst from this lack of clarity; so could whites. Although assurances were given that the new diversity of voluntary groupings would never be used to advantage one group over another, as had happened in apartheid, the intention appeared to be to give the groups statutory recognition. Given that it would be very difficult to establish the boundaries of these groups, how would resources be proportionally allocated? The circumlocutions of "minority group" talk did not make it explicit that (as pointed out in the discussion of de Klerk's formulations earlier) the term *minority* referred first and foremost to an interest group, in this case, to whites or Afrikaners. The assumption that "voluntary" groups had discrete and solid boundaries added to the impression that they were to be given legal recognition as collective political actors and corporate qualifiers for (civil?) rights. This assumption exposed the hidden layer of meaning deriving from a pattern of reasoning described previously as a group-way-of-thinking. It relied heavily on the idea that groups have firm and permanent boundaries. Free association, however, does not work like this in practice.

Viljoen further contended:

You know, many people think democracy is simple decision making by the majority. But there are other aspects of democracy that are almost more important than majority decision making. I think, and many authors on democracy think, that representation is a very important element of democracy. In other words, all components of a population, large and small, should have the sense that they are represented by some of their leaders in those halls where decisions are made. If parts of a population are excluded through simple majoritarian rule without being represented in reality, then there cannot be democracy because a large part of the people [*volk*]—of the concept of people's government—because that is what democracy actually means—is excluded. And so we believe that we have to press for the meaningful representation of minority groups in both the legislature and the executive branch of government.

This quotation reveals the National Party's redefinition of the people (*volk*). The people was now inclusive of all inhabitants of the country. This stands in stark contrast to the right-wing use of "white people" (*blanke volk*) and the plural, "peoples," to indicate other inhabitants of southern Africa. A *people,* in this sense, refers not to an aggregate of individual citizens but to an aggregate of "components," or, in other words, to an aggregate of minorities. Viljoen then justified representative democracy as more democratic than "majoritarian rule." Representative democracy, he argued, is the prevalent form in the Western world. However, the way in which he depicted it was misleading. In addressing a lay audience, he attempted to get away with the idea that representative democracy is the same as the representation of minorities. This is clearly not so; in the United States, for example, African Americans and Native Americans are not represented in government *qua* minorities (although districting of electoral constituencies along minority lines may point in the opposite direction). They vote in their capacity as citizens in constituencies along with members of other minority groups. This distortion of the concept served Viljoen's purpose of framing the National Party vision of the future in political science terms and thereby adding to its legitimacy (see, for example, his reference to "many authors").

As constituencies in a representative democracy, minority groups would require legal definitions. Therefore, membership in these groups would, by implication, be formal—not based simply on free association, which might allow individuals to drift in and out of these groups. By my reasoning we are back to that established and obsessive tendency in South African government thinking of conceiving of groups as legally defined categories. The "associative" principle, so firmly insisted upon in the public rhetoric, has a definite hollow ring to it, because it barely disguises the typifying scheme that maintains a static, essentialist conception of the group.

It was the issue of minority rights that immediately evoked discussion after Viljoen completed his speech. A well-dressed middle-aged man, obviously prepared and surrounded by people who later were proved to be right-wing supporters, got up and said:

All along the National Party changed its points of view. They failed us in the commitments they made in order to get our support. Roelf Meyer [the former member of Parliament from the area and now deputy minister of constitutional affairs, seated on the stage with Viljoen] made a commitment here in Mayfair which he later summarily abandoned [applause and shouting, 4 seconds]. I can recall at least a dozen such cases. . . . My point is merely this: Dr. Viljoen, it is your point of departure that these people, that we should support the National Party on the basis of certain speculative assumptions. You cannot tell us—you gave us a whole presentation on minority rights. You did not answer me what that protection of minority rights is going to be. You say it has to be negotiated. Dr. Viljoen, you are not negotiating with equals. You're negotiating with criminals! [People shouting, "Hear! Hear!"; applause, 7 seconds.]

The man spoke in a disciplined way, but toward the end he became very emphatic on the topic of negotiation. The chairman interrupted him at this point, telling him, quite unnecessarily, to be considerate of others. Although the questioner made his point briefly, the chairman insisted that only questions were to be asked, and that this was not a forum for discussion because, should he give everybody as much time for their questions as this man had taken, he could allow only three questions. This response was typical for National Party political meetings. Little room was left for challenge. The speaker was to remain in charge, providing answers to the uninformed public from his wisdom.

Disorderly behavior and shouting then erupted at the other end of the hall, and the chairman shouted at somebody to sit down. The same questioner then continued:

In all fairness you cannot expect the Afrikaner—and let me forget the rest for the moment—who regarded you Mr. Meyer as their top man—left [us] in the lurch. When I recall your 1974 speech to SABRA [the South African Bureau of Racial Affairs, the former National Party think tank on racial policies] and I listen to [you] tonight then I do not have the same human before me [applause, 7 seconds]. Perhaps you will have to tell us a little bit more about minority rights because the way you have put it, it is totally unacceptable.

An elderly gentleman then interrupted, shouting:

You are Arminians because there is neither equality nor inequality before Christ! There is no inequality between white and black Christians. The doctrines of Dordt tell [us]. . . . You are Arminians! What is the horizontal and what is the vertical? You are an Arminian!!

The old man blustered into silence as a young man rose. The chairman, big, burly, and overweight, was losing control, his face growing redder by the moment. Many people looked embarrassed. They did not know who Arminius was or what the name Arminians meant here. The young man was telling the speaker that the National Party was losing votes because "things happened in Mayfair." Meanwhile, a woman raised her hand, and it was with great relief that the chairman interrupted, "Here is a lady!" counting on the audience's sense of chivalry. The audience calmed down and the woman expressed, in English, her concerns about the possible nationalization of the economy and about the brain drain that was occurring. As soon as she was finished, another young man put up his hand:

Mr. Chairman, Comrade [English term used] Viljoen! You are saying that the National Party took a new direction and that they did not simply make adjustments. As a new comrade in the country I was reading in the *Vrye Weekblad* . . . from H. Serfontein [a journalist] who spoke to an ANC member. Now, Comrade Viljoen, he says . . .

The use of the term *comrade* was too much for the chairman, who interrupted:

Mister, can you be quiet for a moment. Should you in any way insult the dignity of the acting state president and the office of the state president here, I shall have you removed from the room [applause, 6 seconds].

The young man then wanted to know whether the journalist correctly reported that the ANC and the government would constitute a broad front against the conservative Afrikaners as the enemy.

Viljoen then replied, after ridiculing those supporters of the Conservative Party he considered were present. He dismissed the last question as being based on "senseless remarks":

I cannot vouch for the impressions other people, especially people from that quarter he mentioned, care to publicize. I want to make very clear that the fact that the ANC and its fellow travelers is no longer a banned organization and that its leaders are no longer arrested, does not make them less opponents to the NP. [The difference is that] the National Party is now fighting them in the political arena. [Interjections: "Ouch! Ouch!"—ridiculing the notion of "fighting" the ANC politically.]

Viljoen then assured the audience that a free market economy was essential and that nationalization would amount to "sharing out poverty," ending any meaningful investment in the country. Not one word was said in reply to the question on the protection of minority rights. The authoritarian demeanor of Viljoen and the chairman left little room for accountability. Questions of clarity and information were addressed, but those that required accountability were just ignored. The audience seemed to acquiesce in this treatment. During the question-and-answer period the meeting reminded me of a classroom where the unquestioned truth was spoken from the lectern and pupils were talked down to.

The National Party had much to account for. Some decided shifts had occurred in its policies. During the 1988 municipal election, the National Party's posters proclaimed it was against "open" areas where blacks and whites could freely settle. Now, however, during the period after the unbanning of the ANC, the NP started moving in the direction of repealing the Group Areas Act. Viljoen also created the impression at this meeting that the coloureds and Asians had agreed to the 1983 constitution once they were properly consulted. The extremely low turnout at the polls belied this rendering in unequivocal terms.

The nature of (non)accountability in NP public discourse highlights the type of leadership found in the party, or rather the self-styling of the party's leaders. I mentioned previously that an inner circle of the NP had expressed reservations about past policies. It was this inner circle, highly confidential and secret, that made decisions and devised policies. Leadership, accordingly, had a dual base. On one level it rested in the electorate; on another, it lay in the membership of the inner circle. The members of the inner circle shared secret knowledge among themselves. The electorate, or rather NP supporters, supposedly accepted the fact that their leaders possessed and guarded a higher form of knowledge. They would therefore entrust leaders with the making and executing of decisions over the heads of the electorate. Secret information or knowledge could not be shared, but the leaders were believed to be handling their privileged situation responsibly. Over many decades, during which there was a perceived communist threat as well as perceived undermining of the state and the security of its white citizens, this belief in the leaders' secret knowledge, entrusting of decision making on behalf of the voter, and acquiescence to the leaders' will not only psychologically relieved supporters of a great deal of stress, but, more important, bred an attitude of uncritical acceptance of authority.

THE BACKSTAGE OF
NATIONAL PARTY POLITICS

The male Afrikaner secret society the Afrikaner Broederbond (Afrikaner League of Brothers) (AB) was the core of the NP inner circle. The AB was founded in 1919 in the context of the national awakening of the Afrikaner. Its original purpose was to bring together serious-minded young Afrikaners on the Witwatersrand. Its objectives were as follows:

a. To accomplish a healthy and progressive unity amongst all Afrikaners who actively seek the welfare of the Afrikaner.
b. To arouse Afrikaner national self-consciousness and to inspire love of the Afrikaans language, religion, country and People.
c. To further every concern of the Afrikaner Nation. (du Plessis, 1951, p. 9; quoted in Moodie, 1975, p. 50)

AB membership was restricted to Afrikaans-speaking Protestants who accepted South Africa as their fatherland, were of sound moral character, and stood firm in their defense of Afrikaner identity (Moodie, 1975). In its early years the AB concerned itself with equal treatment for the Afrikaans language in urban areas, but it soon coupled itself to republican ideals. It denied, however, that it was involved in party politics and affirmed that it was essentially a cultural organization concerned with the political progress of the Afrikaner people (*volk*). By 1933, the broader political commitment of the Broederbond included such ideals as seeking the full international independence of South Africa, overcoming the sense of inferiority among Afrikaners, and promoting the use of the Afrikaans language in state organizations. It envisaged the segregation of all the colored races in South Africa without sacrificing white guardianship over them. The AB opposed the exploitation of South Africa by foreigners and promoted the ideal of nationalizing finance, coordinating economic policy, and "Afrikanerizing" public life (*Volksblad* [Bloemfontein], January 2, 1945; cited in Moodie, 1975, pp. 112-113).

Avoiding direct political involvement was impossible for members of the AB; as early as 1934, the group's chairman, van Rooy, exhorted members in a secret circular: "Brother, our solution for South Africa's troubles is not that this or that party shall gain the upper hand, but that the Afrikaner Broederbond shall rule South Africa" (Vatcher, 1965, p. 147; quoted in Moodie, 1975, pp. 113-114). Nothing could have been clearer than this. It should be remembered that the Broederbond's political involvement was never supposed to be a direct one. In the South African government, the Executive Council reported its views to the cabinet after sounding out the feelings of its members; the final decision lay with the cabinet. Given that the prime minister and virtually all the members of the cabinet belonged to the Broederbond, however, the distinction was largely formal.

During my years at the University of Potchefstroom, we students noticed when a large number of cars were parked at one of the professor's homes on a Thursday night. It was a relatively small community, and we knew who those cars belonged to and why they were parked there: Their owners were attending the meeting of the local chapter of the Broederbond. The cars belonged to the professors living in the area, the pastor, the school principals, and some teachers and businessmen. In later years, a senior member confided to me some of the topics that came up for discussion at those meetings: They concerned broad future government policy. It is interesting to see how AB members used newspapers and other public forums available to them to prepare the public for the introduction of new measures. The members, carefully selected for their loyalty to the Afrikaner cause, occupied key positions throughout the country, many of them with direct access to the public; they included politicians, public officeholders, teachers, professors, newspaper editors, journalists, and clergymen. Preparing public opinion was thus facilitated through this widespread network.

During the past two decades, the Broederbond has increasingly became a think tank for liberalization and reform in government policy. This began after the Conservative Party broke away from the National Party in the early 1980s. The members who left took with them what had been, up to that point, the research arm of the Broederbond: the South African Bureau of Racial Affairs. From that time on, liberal-minded academics seemed to provide most of the intellectual input in the AB. It is therefore significant that its two most recent chairmen were principals of the urban and, speaking in terms of the Afrikaner spectrum, relatively liberal Rand Afrikaans University. Gerrit Viljoen later became minister of constitutional development and acting state president, and J. P. de Lange continued to fulfill an important behind-the-scenes function. The agenda of public discourse was set in the secret meetings of the Broederbond, but, more important, the content was determined by the Executive Council.[3]

During the 1980s the inner circle realized that its political constituency had a too narrowly defined ethnic base and that somehow the way had to be prepared for discussion with community leaders and influential persons not only across the Afrikaner ethnic boundary, but also across racial boundaries. De Lange therefore set out to find strategies that could mobilize existing groups and organizations in order to create the necessary structures for dialogue among various sectors of the population. His work was partly shrouded in secrecy, and it is unknown to me how or by whom he was funded.

De Lange openly assisted organizations such as KONTAK, an elite women's group working for greater understanding among sectors of the population by creating self-help projects and joint business undertakings between blacks and whites. Some of De Lange's other projects were more covert. When I spoke with him, he justified the secrecy of his efforts as follows:

> It includes [fostering] talks with people who are sometimes too scared to have talks in South Africa. . . . They cannot be seen here . . . eh . . . that they are talking to each other and to me . . . ehm . . . eh. My view is the following . . . that nothing is going to happen on the level of politics unless there is adequate dialogue [*gesprek*] in many ways and that it occurs on many levels that will, so to speak, exert pressure (hm) on the . . . politicians . . . to start engaging in talks and dialogue and negotiations. Currently the attempt is, is too isolated up there. [They] remain . . . it happens somewhat in a vacuum and it is not enough [to listen] only to one of the camps. That is what I am promoting . . . and I am fashioning instruments to widen the talks more than I am able to do on my own (hm). In fact, I, I was amazed when this idea was disseminated about the thick files of people from all population groups who were immediately interested or offered their help. (hm) . . . cannot use everybody [here the recording is indistinct]. A second, second thing is; this kind of dialogue has to take place outside the media. It will be dead, totally dead when it occurs through the media (hm). It is a useless, most useless avenue to pursue . . . what van Zyl-Slabbert is doing. . . . He works through the media and this year he is constantly in the forefront. He is unsuccessful and he doesn't want to do anything without the media knowing about it. . . . I do not mention this as a criticism but point it out for contrasting it with the effective way I am trying to follow.

De Lange informed me that there are about 1,000 such groups in the country. The important point he made in his justification of secrecy concerned the pressure often exerted by conflicting racial or interest groups to keep individuals from talking to the "enemy." Such individuals might feel an urgent need for such talk but are prevented from doing so openly. This new confidential network of "discussion groups" thus serves the purpose of sounding out a much wider constituency regardless of race within the confines of a space hidden from public eyes and ears.

De Lange created the impression that he had heard from many people who had "volunteered" to participate in this network. I have my sincere doubts about this. A more convincing scenario would be that the more enlightened Broederbond members had used their existing interracial contacts in the business and other worlds to build up such groups. In fact, a Broederbond acquaintance of mine from the business world described to me how he and like-minded whites had pooled their contacts across racial lines and devised strategies to invite more black businessmen to regular monthly breakfast meetings. These groups should thus rather be considered as conscious creations arising from the perceived need to bridge a communication gap between white politics and the aspirations of black elites. The underlying idea of the Broederbond as a *gespreksgemeenskap* (community of dialogue) was thus extended through this initiative without exposing its Afrikaner community interest.

De Lange's comments on the necessity of keeping these activities away from the media—more specifically, from the press—underscore the inner circle's tendency to withdraw from public discourse in an attempt to manipulate it more effectively. It has also typically been assumed that the elite constitute the cadre of real and effective actors in the political process. The leaders, not the individual votes, are important. There has been a degree of contempt for the public, who should be kept out of the fray by denying them access to developments important for their own future and that of the country through the media. The prevailing concept of leadership emphasized its capacity for manipulating rather than for representing and accounting for its actions. This is authority exercised from above, a principle inherent in the Broederbond philosophy, which, by now, was extended to other racial communities. It was the old notion of the *volksman* who spoke the language of his followers, who spoke on their behalf on the basis of the intuitive relationship he had with their deepest aspirations, hopes, and suffering. In olden times the legitimation of this kind of authority was strongly charismatic—that is, based on the assumption that the leader's authority came from his (divine?) calling and the gift of leadership. In its more recent manipulative form, however, there is a decided shift toward the autocratic and authoritarian exercise of power. On a wider plane it is therefore not accidental that the negotiations between the ANC and the government, viewed from the government's perspective, rested on the same premise of elite-guided change.

The report back to the Johannesburg-West constituency described above should be viewed against this background. Viljoen and his fellow party representatives were not keenly interested in accounting for policy changes. They were interested in telling the voters what had happened and what had been decided on their behalf. In the process of doing this, they provided some tenuous explanations that sidestepped or smoothed over the basic contradictions between present and past policies. In an authoritarian manner they talked down to the audience, especially to those who questioned government policy. When they were challenged on what "the protection of white minority rights" exactly meant, they gave no reply or detailed explanation. Such questions were virtually ignored, dismissed as "senseless remarks."

The reason this report back was made may be better understood against the background of what de Lange said in an interview the previous year (January 1989). He was talking about the crucial importance of *veranderingstyd,* or change-time—the period of time necessary for the achievement of changes in South Africa. He spoke of the dramatic steps that were necessary and how a leader should take those steps with courage, perhaps risking being blamed and losing influence. This period of change would immediately become visible or tangible:

The process of change has to start moving in a highly visible way. But, because expectations will be rising very high in the wake of that dramatic step, whatever form it might take . . . they will rise through the occurrence of actual changes that are undertaken or made—for example, large part of the Group Areas Act . . . ehm . . . [Changes] will demand an enormous reorientation that people would be unable to accept in a short period of time and it is then important that a second and third step be undertaken . . . the protection of change-time [*veranderingstyd*]—now a word I have created—the time in which changes are made—you know—from four to five years.

. . . The most important aspect of such a concept as change-time is that you, instead of leaving people to speculate about what was coming their way this time again . . . eh . . . creating insecurity and, on the one hand, expectations and, on the other, fear—you say what is going to happen . . . and you say in what period of time and then you execute actions to assist people to handle it, which is a much more positive thing than letting things go their own way. You execute action A but you don't look at its effects in terms of emotionality.

Viljoen's report back to the Johannesburg-West constituency should be seen against the backdrop of the concept of change-time. The poor attendance at the meeting, in contrast to the masses of whites who assembled at the Voortrekker Monument in Pretoria, was indicative of the extent to which the conservatives addressed the very real issue of white fear. The most active members of the audience at Viljoen's meeting were also fired by their fears. The rest of the audience had milder fears, about the brain drain and the possibility of nationalization. There were only a few National Party supporters present, however. Was this an indication of the trust of supporters, or was it merely apathy? Neither of these alternatives applies. For reasons to be discussed in subsequent chapters, a large sector of the white population was suffering from a kind of political paralysis. They withdrew and waited for the crisis—or, in de Lange's terms, the change-time—to pass. Many fled into their private spheres behind the high walls of their suburban homes.

According to de Lange, change-time has to be protected in two ways: through economic means and through security measures. These measures are meant to guarantee a relatively smooth transition from the old system to a new one. As far as security measures are concerned, a nightmarish thought forces itself on the observer. The almost weekly occurrence of black-on-black violence since 1991, and the hundreds of deaths that have resulted, might be connected to the engineering of change-time. As long as blacks were engaged in conflict among themselves, it gave some breathing space to whites who were reorienting themselves. The liberal press alarmingly documented how police and/or security forces were involved in both instigating and supporting black factions opposed to the ANC. The security forces were well known for their success in the external destabilization of Mozambique, Angola, and Namibia. It requires little imagination to grasp what they could do for the internal destabilization of the black population. In fact, in 1994 the Goldstone judicial commission of inquiry confirmed that top police officers were involved in the support of Inkatha and its conflict with the ANC.

When de Lange spoke to me about change-time in January 1989, he gave its duration as four to five years. However, within two years major changes in the legal structure of the country were made. Apart from the Constitution Act, the most important legal cornerstones of apartheid had been removed, including the Population Registration Act. In little more than three years after de Lange spoke these words, a referendum was held among whites to test their approval or disapproval of the government's initiative to negotiate a new constitution. The turnout at the polls was astounding, and de Klerk received more than two-thirds of the white vote in support of his policies. The urgency of the times obviously did not leave much room for a protracted change-time (see also Chapter 8).

Let us now turn to the sphere of the economy in order to look at corporate discourse in South Africa. Not only was the preservation of the economy important for achieving the transition of one sociopolitical state to another, but the satisfaction of definite long-term corporate interests underlay the continuing functioning of the economy.

THE CONVERGENCE OF CORPORATE AND GOVERNMENT INTERESTS IN PUBLIC DISCOURSE

The importance of the "normalization" of the political process was touched upon previously.[4] In the speech discussed above, Viljoen mentioned the necessity of lifting restrictions on "normal" political activity by unbanning organizations and leaders. The "normalization" process was, however, kept firmly under government control. The concept of normalization has a long history in public discourse. During the 1970s the term gained increased circulation around economic issues. The prime minister's economic adviser, recognizing that state control over the black population needed new terminology, wrote in 1978:

> South Africa must "normalize" the character of its socio-economic regime. . . .
> If . . . the maintenance of order requires discriminatory provisions in our legal system, these provisions must be defined in terms of other character-istics correlated to the maintenance of order. To declare or imply that racial differences as such are, in themselves, a threat to political order or socio-economic stability is simply no longer accepted. (quoted in Posel, 1987, p. 425)

In these terms *normalization* meant that an adjustment of terminology was necessary if discriminatory measures were to be packaged as "normal." This political sleight of hand involved the depoliticization of the language in which measures of control were couched. In the late 1970s, the idea of a "total strategy" evolved to galvanize various sectors of society into a joint effort to solve the problems of South Africa. One of the most influential sectors to be co-opted was, of course, the corporate world. The government by now had adopted the principle of free enterprise that the corporate world ran on as one of its own legitimating tenets. It adapted the notion of free enterprise to its policy of total strategy. In previous chapters we have seen how business was used to help the government execute its labor policies. The logic through which this co-optation was achieved is interesting. Instead of stressing the ideological justifications of political measures, the government now reconceptualized this justification in pragmatic terms. It was presented as a new realism that pervaded government thinking. On this basis it was fairly easy to establish common ground with the business community.

For many decades the corporate, or business, world had objected to the government's interference in free enterprise. The large para-statal enterprises, such as the transport system, postal and communications services, steel production, health services, and radio and television, reserved for themselves a protected and monopolized position in the economy at the expense of free enterprise. In the late 1970s and the beginning of the 1980s, a reevaluation of this form of state intervention was undertaken. The government therefore showed more and more concern with depoliticizing not only its language but also its economic practices. It became more willing to adopt business practices in the running of its own enterprise. In view of the rising costs of sustaining the apartheid bureaucracy and the financial burden the internal and external security measures imposed during the 1980s, the government demonstrated greater concern for the effective use of resources. Labor legislation was recast, and workers were no longer defined primarily in terms of their race, ethnicity, or homeland citizenship but instead were viewed as "labor units."[5]

The discourse of the corporate world was thus adopted by the government. However, the adoption of more effective methods cannot disguise the fact that very real sectional interests were served by the new rationalization procedures. As the prime minister's adviser said in the last quotation, "Discriminatory provisions must be defined in terms of other characteristics correlated to the maintenance of order." The way was thus prepared for ensuring an adequate (black) labor supply without invoking overtly discriminatory laws. Supply and demand could now be manipulated through urban housing policies and the management of unemployment and vagrancy. Race or apartheid need not be mentioned, and regulatory practices could be defined in the terms any other Western nation would use. Both the business world and the government were happy. One had an adequate labor supply and the other managed racial separation without discriminatory rhetoric. In fact, the government was able to abolish the Black Urban Areas Act in 1986 without too much risk of a sudden population surge toward the cities. The lingering doubts that certain loyal critics had about the feasibility, efficiency, and rationality of apartheid since the 1970s thus found a solution. A new system based on technical rationality and effectiveness had the potential of achieving largely the same objective of preserving the status quo with much less cost and bad publicity. Toward the latter half of the 1980s, the idea of a rationalized economy was the yeast that gradually fermented and penetrated the total sociopolitical system.

The tendency toward technocratic rationality that Posel (1987, p. 423) has so lucidly described for the period between 1978 and 1983 intensified in the later 1980s and spilled over into the early 1990s when some other legal cornerstones of apartheid were abolished. "Reason," "rationality," and "efficiency" became the keystones in the political edifice of the 1990s. One can justly ask whether this change in emphasis was an admission of the inefficiency, lack of realism, irrationality, and unreasonableness of past National Party policy.[6] Anyway, the shift toward a policy based on technical rationality meant that the layperson would not be knowledgeable enough to be able to judge what was happening in the new system and why it was happening. The ordering of the economy and the fashioning of policy now became matters for the experts. Public accountability would take a backseat during such a shift. Large sectors of government's economic and public policy could thus be withdrawn from public political debate because they had become technical issues beyond the competence of the general public.

These points were underscored in a different context in an interview President de Klerk had with the American ABC news program *Nightline* on February 13, 1990. He mentioned the importance of depoliticizing the issue of a new constitution for South Africa. About reaching consensus, he said:

Because we realize that this will be difficult, we have instructed the South African law commission, which is a powerful juridical body, *absolutely depoliticized,* to make a study of different models, constitutional models, which can be regarded as suitable to accommodate the needs arising from the type of community which we have in South Africa. (emphasis added)

The reliance on experts is clear in this case. The reliance on a depoliticized body gave "objective" scientific credibility to the evolution of a constitutional model.[7]

A significant convergence has occurred between the notion of expert knowledge on the one hand and the secret knowledge of the Broederbond inner circles on the other. This convergence amounts to what is conventionally known as *elective affinity*.[8] It is as if the inner circle, with its claim to a higher order of political knowledge, sought out the technical and scientific economists and legal experts, with their exclusive and complex "efficient" knowledge, in order to produce a new sociopolitical system. The technocrats, in turn, sought out the wielders of political power in order to realize their dreams. The language the two parties used and shared was symbolic of their mutual attraction.

The government and its inner circles furthermore had the power to define what was technical and what was political. After the Carlton Conference in Johannesburg in 1979 and the Good Hope Conference in the Cape Province in 1981, both called by the government, leaders from the business community were increasingly incorporated into cabinet committees and thus drawn into the policy-making process. The prime minister even declared government and business to be a team. The process of co-optation not only took the wind out of the sails of many businessmen who had been critical of the government; it turned them into accomplices. For corporations whose top executives came predominantly from English-speaking and more liberal backgrounds, the shift toward a technocratic rationality to justify free enterprise had an additional implication. The notion of free enterprise had deep moral roots in the liberal tradition and was interwoven with the principle of respect for the rights and freedoms of the individual. To these executives, at least initially, the shift was morally acceptable. However, the justification of scientific rationality left little space for morality. In its purer forms it instrumentalized human beings rather than generated respect for their individuality.

The field of ethics was thus to a large extent abandoned, and the critics of capitalism sought to fill the space it left. Various Marxist scholarship-inspired groups now felt vindicated in their class analyses, for, obviously, with the convergence of government and corporate interests it was easier to find evidence for the existence of a powerful exploiting class of capitalists who happened to be white in South Africa. However, because the government had the power to define what was technical and what was political, it was in a favorable position to counter its critics' efforts by labeling them as "unscientific" and "ideological." "Ideological" approaches to South Africa's problems were at the same time unproductive and unrealistic and might, under certain conditions, even be regarded as security risks. This power of definition the state appropriated for itself cut both to the right and to the left. The breaking away of the CP could therefore be blamed on ideological rather than rational considerations. Similarly, dissident scholarship could be labeled and neutralized in the same way. Even the ANC could readily be subjected to scrutiny in these terms.

In an editorial with the title "Promising the Earth," the leading South African business magazine, the *Financial Mail* (February 8, 1991), responded to the ANC's intention to make a case for reparations and affirmative action. The editorial argued that the ANC was essentially unrealistic to assume that the educational gap between whites and blacks could, for example, be rapidly eliminated. It quoted the Human Sciences Research Council's findings that a tripling of expenditures for education was necessary. This was unaffordable because—and here the editorial directed blame at the ANC itself—sanctions weakened the economy and increased government expenditure would increase inflation. It is significant that the *Financial Mail* placed so much trust in a quasi-government research agency. The HSRC typically engaged in positivistic, scientific, and "objective" social and economic research instrumental to the needs of the government, industry, and the business community (see below). The editorial argued that reparations were "a tricky problem" and that affirmative action in the United States had not been "a happy experience." It concluded that "there can't be affirmative action for blacks in a legally non-racial South Africa or conscription for whites" (*Financial Mail,* February 8, 1991).

This editorial is an apt illustration of the convergence of corporate and government interests. Not only did it find justification for government decisions, it tended to look at black claims rather negatively—not in racial terms or in terms of overt white privilege, but in terms of economic rationality. Affirmative action, accordingly, could also be excluded on grounds of "efficiency" and technical rationality. Looking below the surface and contemplating the effects of policies guided by these "neutral" and "scientific" concerns, it is not very difficult to discern how white group interest and privilege were served by them. The urgency of black economic catch-up in a situation of an extremely unequal distribution of resources was accorded a lower priority than preserving the balance of the system.

The process of "normalization," by implication, defined past "unrealistic" policies and measures as deviant and abnormal. In the process of reconstruction there was thus a serious attempt to have the new principle taken for granted by the population. What came to be regarded as normal could be taken for granted and would not be questioned. An awakening occurred. Politicians thought they were emerging from a cave of darkness and, with relief, embraced this new light of "normality." It was with relief that the government adopted the free market concept, free enterprise, and lack of state intervention. It is especially important to realize at what juncture in South Africa's history this "discovery" and relief occurred. This was at a time when the full political and economic participation of the black majority was being discussed. It is not at all remarkable that state intervention in the economy under a government where blacks have the majority vote might not be looked on by the white rulers and white-owned corporations as a good thing. The black majority had a great interest in redressing certain imbalances. In fact, the ANC made it quite clear at a certain point that it was interested in nationalizing sectors of the economy, such as the banks and mines. The state's gaining control over telecommunications (including radio and television), transport, steel production, electricity supply, health services, and some other sectors might not have worked out to the advantage of the privileged whites. In Chapter 4, the case of radio and television was discussed. Whites feared that a future black government might use or misuse those media much as the white government had. Similarly, as far as transport, electricity, health services, steel production, and so on were concerned, there were fears of reverse institutional discrimination and policy decisions detrimental to white lifestyles and standards of living.

Because it would be impossible to perpetuate white control of these bodies, another way had to be found. That way was "privatization." Privatization could be defined as a form of "normalization," and this definition allayed a lot of fears while at the same time fanning the hope that those enterprises would become profitable and thus provide a larger tax base. Beyond allaying fears there was a tacit awareness that the potential buyers and stockholders of privatized state enterprises would require generous amounts of capital. This capital was overwhelmingly concentrated in white hands. White stockholders would thus be able to control the destinies and policies of these companies for many years. This reality was, of course, not articulated in the justifications for privatization. In August 1987, the *White Paper on the Privatization and Deregulation in the Republic of South Africa* was published, and in February 1988 State President P. W. Botha announced that his new fiscal policies centered on privatization (SAIRR, 1989, p. 333). In the debate that followed, white chambers of commerce and bank and insurance company presidents were united in their praise for this "rational and efficient" policy. Except for the black chamber of commerce, NAFCOC, blacks in general and their trade/labor unions in particular opposed the move for the main reason that it benefited the wealthy only (SAIRR, 1989, p. 350).

INTELLECTUALS, UNIVERSITIES, AND PUBLIC DISCOURSE

In this section I will argue that intellectuals were largely marginal to the public discourse unless they joined in with the dominant discourse outlined above. There was a tendency to label dissident intellectuals as "ideological" and therefore not really to be taken seriously. In contrast to more repressive times, when dissident scholarship was sometimes viewed as potentially subversive, a greater tolerance was shown toward scholars in the early 1990s.

With the shift from exclusive, "inner circle" politics based on secret and confidential deliberations to a more inclusive incorporation of a wider circle of businesspeople and experts, some dissident Afrikaner academics were drawn back into the political debate. In previous decades these dissidents were alienated from the government and National Party policy because of its lack of reason and realism. With the shift toward pragmatic rationality and scientific reason, however, the economists especially drifted back in critical loyalty.

Afrikaner academic political dissidents occupied a difficult position in Afrikanerdom. After the Sharpeville massacre in 1960, some Afrikaner academics joined the outcry against the tragedy, but soon found themselves isolated and ostracized. Their position was further made untenable because of the Broederbond's reprisals against individuals with a potentially corrupting influence on students. As indicated above, the Broederbond's influence was centered strongly in the Afrikaans universities. The group had a tradition as a think tank for Afrikaner ideology, and its ranks produced a number of politicians. In other cases, there was a very narrow tolerance for criticism. A high degree of political loyalty was expected of Afrikaner academics during the 1960s and 1970s. The 1960s was the period in which South Africa had its communist scare, and criticism and dissidence were frequently viewed as "liberalism." To many political leaders and university administrators, liberalism was some form of communism, a pernicious influence from which students had to be protected. These attitudes persisted into the late 1970s, and frequently resulted in a rather conformist stance on the part of many lecturers, especially in the social sciences. The pressure varied from university to university, however. Stellenbosch University was, relatively speaking, more tolerant than Pretoria University. My own career at the Potchefstroom University underwent a rather dramatic change because of allegations that I had a liberal attitude—as did the careers of a number of my colleagues. There was one case in which an eminent law professor was fired, reportedly on instructions of the prime minister to the principal of the university. The editor of a rural Afrikaans newspaper had asked the professor to write an op-ed article on security legislation in order to stimulate discussion, but the professor's mildly provocative opinions were apparently too radical for the politicians. This case illustrates how efficiently the inner circle, with its numerous crosscutting ties, could bypass the professed "autonomy" of universities to get rid of a perceived dissident.

Afrikaner academics who were forced out of Afrikaner universities, those who left of their own free will, and those who refused to join these institutions shared a similar fate. They were mostly ignored and led an existence outside, or on the margins of, the political process. English-medium universities absorbed them or they left the country.

Louw-Potgieter (1988) interviewed a number of dissident Afrikaner academics, writers, and clergy between 1982 and 1985. She found them to be isolated as individuals, seemingly investing most of their considerable political energies in their respective professional organizations. When they arrived at English-medium universities they found themselves in unfamiliar environments, without the necessary resources and competence to deal with the liberal subculture for which those universities stood.

Those who remained loyal to Afrikaner universities eventually joined in the government's self-legitimation process of the 1980s, adding to the dominant public discourse by acting like experts or by being used as experts by politicians. It is this category of academics who had no scruples about cooperating with the HSRC. The HSRC established a reputation for its positivist perspective and its claims to objective scientific knowledge of South African social reality in its research. It failed, however, to gain the trust of many liberal-minded academics and was held to be especially suspect by Marxist scholars. During the 1980s the HSRC attempted to co-opt a broad band of academics in discipline-oriented committees. One of the main purposes of these committees was the allocation of research funds. The HSRC was funded by the government in this period. Toward the 1990s, the pressure for privatization also made itself felt in the HSRC. It was now expected to generate its own funds by contracting research in a "privatized" manner from the government and private companies. The HSRC's de facto dependence on the government thus remained and, under these circumstances, the contractor (read "the government") could more openly and unhindered by liberal and dissident criticism direct research for its own technocratic interests. The HSRC is still having great difficulty in rebutting the criticism that it provided the "scientific" legitimation for government policy decisions. In its new guise it claims to deliver depoliticized, "objective" findings by using, at least as far as social research is concerned, statistical and quantitative measures generally accepted in the Western world.

In order to establish its "scientific" credibility further, the HSRC commissioned an "expert," an American quantitative sociologist, to do a brief assessment of sociological research and teaching in South Africa (Olzak, 1990). Predictably, she came up with some mild praise for Afrikaans-speaking universities, which "appeared to be most open to recruiting and/or upgrading faculty research skills" (p. 65). The skills referred to were quantitative, technical research skills.[9] The researcher gave the HSRC some advice on how to engage in conflict research, and heavily criticized South African universities in general for not absorbing more American sociology. She castigated sociologists who decide to become politically involved, and strangely disregarded the substantial debate in American circles around the issue of "on whose side" anthropologists and sociologists chose to be in their research. Little more than a superficial reading of South African social science would have revealed a very rich tradition of research struggling to be relevant to its disadvantaged subjects. There is also much evidence of research motivated by a great deal of compassion for the victims of apartheid.

Before embarking on a short discussion of social science and its relevance to South African society, I wish to emphasize that the dominant political discourse needs social science data and analysis for its own legitimation. In a period of transition from one sociopolitical system to another, this is more true than ever before. Through the creation of privatized research structures maintaining an objectivist and functionalist perspective, it will be easy to find such legitimation. Empirical social research from a different perspective, especially from a more interpretive and qualitative angle, could easily be dismissed as ideological, soft, or unscientific. Yet it is exactly this type of research that is crucially needed if we are to understand the social and cultural dynamics of a South Africa in transition.

Research designed to let the voiceless speak for themselves has hardly been characteristic of South African social science during the past few decades. On the one hand, the dominant forces in the political and corporate world have favored the "hard, objective" approach with scientistic claims.[10] On the other hand, however, the concern for social history evident since the 1970s has started to displace much of the conventional sociology and anthropology and has left little space for interpretive approaches.

Whatever the social considerations were that motivated a whole generation of mostly English-speaking young intellectuals to assail and correct
the colonial and liberal account of the past, this emphasis in social science
had a devastating effect on the development of a viable, nonpositivist,
empirical social research discipline within the South African context.
Social historians unearthed valuable historical material, but more as professional historians than as sociologists. Already weighted down by the incredible lack of trained black sociologists and anthropologists, many white
social researchers chose to stay at home, doing documentary research
(there are notable exceptions). White social scientists in research and
teaching positions seldom bothered either to learn the vernaculars spoken
in black communities or to venture into the demanding business of doing
fieldwork, establishing face-to-face relations in black communities, living
there, participating in their affairs, documenting their lives, and hearing
them out on the problems they faced on a day-to-day basis (see Schutte,
1991). White social scientists and historians who avoided fieldwork by
using underpaid black assistants to gather, transcribe, and translate oral
traditions cast themselves in the image of colonial masters who, from their
armchairs, take credit for the work of others. Generally speaking, dissident social scientists blamed their lack of fieldwork (if the need for it was
perceived at all) on difficult access as a result of government gatekeeping
and harassment. However, doing fieldwork under these adverse conditions provided an important opportunity to resist the oppressor by using
some cunning and ingenuity in order to collect evidence exposing the
tyrant.[11] This dimension escaped the awareness of many white academics
who preferred to do intellectual reflecting on black reality in the safety of
seminar rooms.

A large part of historical social research focused on the history of class
conflict. Documentary and archival research was as popular as the collection of oral traditions. Rich material was thus uncovered, but it rarely reached
an audience beyond the university culture. Participants in seminars spent
hours situating evidence, whether oral or documentary, in appropriate theoretical contexts provided by European intellectuals such as Louis Althusser
and Antonio Gramsci (see Chapter 2). The animosity between theoretical
camps sometimes seemed to surpass their resentment of the iniquitous
social and political system in which the government's repressive tolerance
allowed them to work. Yet, despite their differences, they staunchly adhered
to a historical materialist orthodoxy that discouraged the use of alternative
paradigms.[12]

It would be harsh to use a colonial model to try to make sense of the intellectual culture of some liberal South African universities. There have been some worrying indicators of the insularity of these universities and their resident intellectuals within South Africa's social and cultural context. Consider, for example, the fact that African literature failed to find a place in English departments. Instead, it had to be housed in the interdisciplinary Comparative Literature Department at the University of the Witwatersrand for many years. The English and French departments found it difficult to build the African context of their teaching into their syllabi. Instead, they exhibited a purist Eurocentric approach. These were departments situated in an African university that had to teach an annually increasing percentage of black students. In a similar vein, a separate African Studies Institute existed at this African university. What reasoning underlay the creation and maintenance of a separate research institute for African realities when those were the realities surrounding it and in which it was embedded? Other African countries have institutes for social, economic, or historical research, but until 1994 the leading liberal/critical university in South Africa still housed Africa in a separate institute.[13] These are colonial remnants whose survival I can only explain as contingent on a frame of mind that perceived itself as external to Africa. Africa seemed to be a separate reality, to be studied separately. I do not wish to single out one university for comment here because I believe there is ample evidence of similar situations elsewhere.

In an earlier chapter I referred to the existence of a local South African version of the History Workshop movement. Apart from its role in writing history from below and holding conferences heavily sponsored by foreign foundations, it intended to bring "history" back to the people. In a series of popularizing ventures (later known as "open days") between 1978 and 1987, the workshop sought to popularize working-class history. The procedure was to bus black people to the shrine of (white?) learning, the University of the Witwatersrand. One of the organizers of these events described in a remarkably revealing document published in the *Radical History Review* how historians guided by class concepts external to the populations they were talking about were forced to come to terms with the cultural dimensions of the human subjects with whom they were confronted: "The fact that a culturally vacant, economistic Marxism is unappealing to most black South Africans in the face of a culturally, experientially, and historically rich nationalism is not surprising" (Bozzoli, 1990, p. 260).

The element of surprise was, of course, taken away by the organizers' experience that the categories the impoverished black people used to make sense of the occasion were far removed from those of the organizers. Blacks tended to take over the meetings. The *Radical History Review* article described the attending workers' behavior at the 1984 meeting as "sleazy," "raucous," and "drunk" (Bozzoli, 1990, p. 253). The organizers were amazed that Zulu workers demanded that the films they showed should be translated into Zulu, and so on. As a documentation of the lack of communication between well-meaning researcher-teachers and subjects, this article is a superb example. On the one hand were the rather naive middle-class English-speaking white academics aspiring to political hegemony in the process of black self-emancipation; on the other were the black masses, being bused in, coming from diverse backgrounds, but nevertheless sharing an idiom of resistance rooted in the day-to-day experience of oppression and exploitation. This was a world very far removed from that of the white organizers. The surprise they experienced was symptomatic of their lack of firsthand experience of, and familiarity with, the forms of spontaneity of their black counterparts. Last but not least, this was engendered by their neglect of empirical field research, which may have exposed them to those life worlds. Had they had closer prior acquaintance with their subjects' worlds of experience, they would hardly have been surprised and might have been imbued with that amount of cultural relativism that would have obviated their use of judgments such as "sleazy." The positive side of their experience was the eye-opener that a face-to-face confrontation with a spontaneous black audience resulted in. The organizers wittingly or unwittingly provided an opportunity for participants to give free expression to their feelings and views.

Various black constituencies refused to accept white intellectuals' leading role in the interpretation of their history, let alone in the mediation of their liberation struggle. This was true for those communities invited to the History Workshop and maybe more so for the black labor union movement. The mostly white-led women's movement experienced a similar rebuff. IDASA's newsletter, *Democracy in Action,* reported in its February/March 1991 issue that the white organizers and delegates to a conference on women and gender held at the University of Natal (Durban) came under fire from both black activists and professionals. A black delegate lashed out at white participants, saying she resented white women academics championing the cause of black women—black women needed to speak for themselves. She maintained that black women should conduct their own inquiries and campaigns together, and not in isolation or on anybody's behalf. The perceived maternalism or paternalism of liberal and critical white academics was thus rejected. In their own minds, white academics believed their intentions to be benign, but they gave the impression that they were entitled to lead the liberation of oppressed South Africans on the grounds of their assumed wider, more educated perspective. In a cynical moment this reminded me of the "civilizing" pretensions of the colonial "white man" in Africa. In fact, reading Bozzoli's (1990) assertion about the populist (read "nonwhite" and "proletariat") intelligentsia's leadership, one is confronted with the author's fears that such a leadership could get out of hand unless historical materialists took the initiative:

> To ignore this fact [of a rich nationalism] would be to repeat the mistakes of the German socialists who, in Wilhelm Reich's words, "were offering the masses superb historical treatises . . . while Hitler was stirring the roots of their emotional being." (p. 260)

Further:

> Indeed, it seemed from the experience of 1987, that a culturally informed Marxism disseminated by an independent group of intellectuals is more likely to be accepted by ordinary people than it is by nationalist and populist intellectuals who seek to lead and organize them. (p. 261)

The naïveté is stunning. Intellectual Marxists in South Africa were overwhelmingly white. "Nationalist and populist intellectuals" among the majority of the population were overwhelmingly black. In the article an implicit association is made between them and figures such as Hitler. They are contrasted with the culturally informed Marxists. Is this the perception of *swart gevaar* formulated in the arcane language of historical materialism? Are the culturally informed Marxists the rational and reasonable force that would inaugurate the "new South Africa"? Are the forces they oppose the same as the totalitarian tendencies among those blacks who claim to represent the "will of the (black) people" so intensely feared by the liberal establishment? Are those forces similar to what the business community and the Nationalist government fear—forces they wish to counter with scientific and technocratically rational strategies? Are those forces similar to the crude racist formulations of black peril found in the white supremacist groups? In a strange way, through different idioms and conceptualizations, they all shared a fear of chaos. It is this fear that unites whites on the level of public discourse. Using the conventional spectrum of left and right, one can confidently argue that the element of fear is present at both ends and in whatever lies in between. The one real difference between left and right lies in the ways in which danger and potential chaos are defined. On the far right, they are barely disguised as race. The government and business community contrast totalitarian ideology with pragmatism and normality, and, among the relatively uninfluential left, scientific Marxism is opposed to "populist nationalism."

DISCUSSION

The typical scheme employed in right-wing discourse with regard to groups is based on the premise of the primordial nature of group membership. It has to modify the primordial nature of Afrikanerness in order to accommodate English speakers and other white groups. It denies that in-group/out-group boundaries are drawn along racial lines. Right-wingers prefer, instead, to use cultural or heritage categories, although in the end this amounts to the same thing. The leader of the Conservative Party made a most symbolic statement when he spoke of God as having "nationalized" human beings. Establishing that the existence of groups is a product of divine will legitimates them forever. The social boundaries drawn by right-wingers are therefore clear and unambiguous in their own minds. Group categories are "pure" categories. Polluting these groups in various ways is morally reprehensible, if not blasphemous. A future is therefore projected in which these groups will be preserved.

The public discourse in government and corporate circles seemingly deviates radically from the above. However, looking below the surface of the lexical decisions of public speakers, the group concept survives in a strong form. In order to specify this form, we must look into some of the implicit meanings that are conveyed to the public in speeches and other utterances of public figures. First of all, leaders stress that groups' rights should be protected. These groups should not be based on race but on association. Making use of international analogies, van der Merwe gets tangled up in an attempt to draw a parallel between nations in an international context and internal groupings in South Africa. Viljoen sounds equally unconvincing when he tries to persuade his constituency that South African groups are "minorities" whose basis is associational without explaining how the open boundaries would work if blacks should voluntarily decide to become members of white groups. These inconsistencies of argument cover up implicit assumptions about the center from which these apologists are arguing. The legitimation for their construction of groups is sought in pragmatism and reason and framed in internationally accepted terms. From their perspective, no divine origin is sought for the group. Rather, they entertain the enlightened vision of a social contract. However, if one looks at the extension of this reasonableness to other domains, such as the economy, one can detect a set of clearly defined interests. Those in power found they did not have to resort to racial politics to advance their interests and at the same time perpetuate white group privilege. Capital, political power, and expertise are concentrated in white hands anyway. The same ends could be achieved through the seemingly neutral means of rationalization, through privatization and other technocratic solutions. Of course, the ability to govern such a complex economy and pluralistic society requires the specialized knowledge of experts. In this oligarchy the members of the white power establishment know they can hold on to power for a long time by defining themselves as indispensable. The antidemocratic tone of government/corporate discourse is borne out by the elitism of a decision-making cadre of insiders.

Considering the future consequences of both the right-wing and government discourses, we can discern a distinctly authoritarian strain. The beneficiaries in both discourses are the same too—the whites. The interpretive scheme referred to previously as a group-way-of-thinking underlies both sets of discourses. In one it is manifest; in the other it is covert. The government/corporate discourse in the long run does allow for a "trickle-up" effect of qualified members of other groups into the ranks of the experts. Those already there, however, are the gatekeepers. One important difference between the two sets of discourses is the composition of the beneficiaries as a group. Right-wingers see their group as inclusive of all whites, whereas in the government/corporate discourse it is white elites who are deemed fit enough to survive the new challenges.

NOTES

1. The chief researcher of the Human Sciences Research Council, N. J. Rhoodie, uses the same language. Referring to the white political right wing, he said: "Ultimately whites will react to the social and political realities more in a pragmatic rather than an ideological way. This pragmatism will ultimately show the way toward the postapartheid society" (quoted in *Beeld,* June 26, 1989).

2. The term *marketing* gained general currency in government circles in these times. Neill van Heerden, the director general of foreign affairs, consistently referred to his

department's task of offering and marketing a new product—meaning the policies inaugurating the "new South Africa" (*Financial Mail,* February 1, 1991).

3. Adam and Giliomee (1979b, p. 251) contend that the Broederbond acted as a secret communication channel between the government and the Afrikaner elite during the 1970s. Quoting the *Sunday Times* of September 9, 1972, the Executive Council gave an assurance to AB members that their formulations "will be reflected in official Government statements."

4. The hackneyed use of the term *normalization* occurs in every possible context of future-oriented discourse (see, e.g., Trust Bank of Africa Ltd, 1990).

5. As far as (black) labor unions were concerned, both the government and the business world were worried about, if not resentful of, their politicization. See, for example, Trust Bank of Africa Ltd (1990), where the politicization of labor unions is seen as a structural problem or obstacle to the economic performance of the country.

6. State President de Klerk maintained that the National Party realized that the arithmetic of apartheid was stupid (see W. J. de Klerk, 1991, p. 67).

7. Later in the same interview, de Klerk spoke of the depoliticization of the police as if they were henceforth merely to act in a technical way in the control of deviance, such as violence against persons and property (see ABC News, 1990, p. 7).

8. This is the concept of *Wahlverwandtschaft* developed by Max Weber in his well-known Protestant ethic thesis.

9. The choice of the term *skill* is not accidental. Research methods tend to be viewed as skills among positivistically inclined social scientists. Those who recognize the intrinsically interpretive nature of social science would not confuse skills and methods.

10. This is not the place to enter into an extensive discussion and critique of positivist social science. For decades, doubts and critiques about this approach and perspective have been formulated in the contexts of the Society for Symbolic Interactionism, the Society for the Study of Social Problems, and various influential journals in the United States. On the European continent, critical theory and the various phenomenological approaches to social reality have an even longer history.

11. There are notable exceptions, such as the Surplus People's Project, the work of David Webster and others like him, and especially the work of expatriate and emigrant scholars Shula Marks, T. D. Moodie, and a long list of others.

12. During early 1971, the coordinator of an African studies seminar at a prominent English-medium university silenced a participant who challenged the appropriateness of a historical materialist interpretation of an event with the argument that first principles could not be discussed at these meetings. This note comes from a journal I kept at the time. This was an important event that signaled the start of an orthodoxy that tended to label alternative perspectives as suspect or capitalist/government oriented.

13. The University of the Witwatersrand had an Institute for Policy Research located in its Business School. This institute, born in the late 1980s, kept itself busy with evaluating policies and strategies within the spirit of instrumental rationality.

7

The World of Whites:
Structure and Experience

In discussing the genesis of normative and legal structures and their reproduction through the communications media, I highlighted the construction of an objective social framework of white South Africans' experience. In Chapters 5 and 6, we have seen how this framework was legitimated and adapted through a "group-way-of-thinking." I now turn to the ways in which whites use, and have used, this typifying scheme in subjectively appropriating the world of everyday life in which they live and work. This chapter presents evidence of this appropriation in expressions of the group-way-of-thinking in whites' organization of the rural, urban, and domestic spatial structures typical of South Africa. Also examined are the ways in which whites' social interactions among themselves and with the racial other are structured. Symbolic representations of others as group members exemplified in children's drawings and essays receive special attention.

SPATIAL STRUCTURES

Passing over northern Botswana, the South African plane entered the airspace of the republic. Set on a gradual descending course toward Johannesburg, it first aimed for the radio beacon at the Hartebeespoort dam some 60 miles from the airport. The plane completed a long flight from Europe around the bulge of West Africa, entering the continent over northern Namibia. At the beginning of the 1990s, South African planes were not permitted to overfly the greater part of Africa because of African nations' sanctions against the apartheid-driven country. This changed in

June 1991. However, in May 1991, the particular flight path of my last field trip into the country provided an excellent opportunity for viewing its physical structure from above.

After we crossed the border between Botswana and South Africa, huge, expansive cattle ranches were visible. Set far apart from each other, single farmhouses appeared at intervals. Each had its little colony of mud or brick huts for black laborers nearby. These structures were built at a respectful distance from the main house. Sizable cornfields were not far from the houses. Soon we passed one of the portions of the black "homeland," Bophutatswana. The condition of the veld and land utilization there differed radically from that of the white-owned cattle ranches. There was evidence of large-scale overgrazing and soil erosion. There were few trees. Little square plots of land indicated agricultural activity. Population was dense and concentrated near hills. The houses were built on minute lots of land. These were examples of the government's closer settlement program, which attempted to remove blacks from the cities, settling them in greater concentrations in the homelands while providing limited access to agricultural land.

As the plane approached the Pretoria-Johannesburg metropolitan area, a black dormitory township loomed up. A concentration of huts and houses appeared to pop up in the middle of nowhere. This was another kind of rural human dumping ground of apartheid. From the township, asphalted roads led toward the big cities, and buses could be seen traveling on them. Dormitory townships housed laborers and their dependents who had to travel for hours each day to reach their places of employment. Blacks in the homelands lived, for the most part, off remittances of the wages of their migrant members. Migrants lived in hostels (dormitories), backyards of white homes, or segregated townships.[1] Dormitory township dwellers took back to their homelands the wages that remained after transport costs were subtracted.[2] The closer settlements of the homelands and the dormitory townships were evidence of the organization of white South Africa's labor needs. Blacks' labor was welcome, but not their physical presence as residents.

As we moved closer to Johannesburg, the contrast between black and white areas became even more marked. From Rustenburg to the Hartebeespoort dam, irrigated fields filled my vision. The white farmers' mansions were bigger than those to the north. The Magaliesberg passing below was dotted with (at that time) "white" recreational areas, all within easy reach of the cities. Between the mountain and Johannesburg, a patch of smaller farms, or smallholdings, was followed by what is jokingly known as the "mink and manure" belt—the residential areas of the rich, who can afford mink coats and stabled horses. Huge thatch-roofed villas, surrounded by tennis courts, swimming pools, and stables, were situated on several acres of land.

As we approached Johannesburg itself, white suburbia unfolded. Single-dwelling brick houses on adequately sized lots housed the middle-class whites of Randburg. In no other city have I seen as many outdoor swimming pools. Almost every plot of land has its emerald, shining pool. The high-rise buildings of downtown Johannesburg were now fully visible. Far to the right, enveloped in a thick cloud of smoke, the uniform patterns of Soweto houses were barely distinguishable. This was the beginning of winter, and the only fuel for cooking and heating was coal. The smoke-covered township contrasted starkly with the clean air and spacious gardens of the white suburbs. At this stage another white suburb passed under the plane. This was Triomf, a lower-middle-class white suburb. Triomf, which means "triumph," was built on the bulldozed remains of Sophiatown.[3] Sophiatown was a culturally vibrant black slum area that was destroyed by the government during the implementation of the Group Areas and Resettlement Acts in the mid-1950s. Its residents were forcibly removed to Meadowlands, an area adjacent to Soweto.

As the plane continued its descent, other white suburbs moved past—Westdene, Melville, Auckland Park. The poorer white area of the southern suburbs then followed the industrial area of the southern downtown. The plane turned from its easterly direction and approached the runway toward the north. Had we approached the airport from the north, we would have seen the contrast between ultrarich Sandton and the dirty, smoke- and shack-filled black township of Alexandra right next to it.

In viewing the physical organization of land distribution from the air it would have been easy for even the untrained eye to spot the vast difference between white and black areas. For the purposes of this study, I was looking for evidence of the world of experience of whites, a world I will concentrate on in this chapter. The physical world of whites was that of the suburban home, the shopping mall, the wide open spaces of (white) farmland and recreation. In this world, blacks appeared and disappeared as laborers. In the past, the structures that enabled and confined whites' world experience were consciously contrived by legislation and political practice. Most of the legal cornerstones of apartheid were abolished in 1991, but their physical effects remain and will be in place for a long time to come. In this way they will keep on structuring the experiences of the human beings ensnared in them.

We turn now from the macroperspective to the microperspective of spatial organization, looking at the way families live. The constitution of white households in South Africa is not much different from that in other Western societies. The nuclear family was still prevalent in suburbia at the time of this research, although the number of single-parent families was on the increase. The high-rise areas contain a large percentage of single people mixed with simple one-couple households and single-parent families. On the farms one encounters nuclear and frequently three- to four-generation families occupying a single large dwelling. The typical home in wealthier suburbs is situated on a plot of land larger than half an acre. The house is built of bricks and has three or more bedrooms, multiple bathrooms, a two-car garage, some outbuildings to house servants, a laundry room, a tool shed or workshop, and, very frequently, a swimming pool. The servants' quarters have separate bathroom facilities—usually a toilet, a shower, and a wash basin that may or may not be connected to the hot water system of the main house. The larger pieces of land sometimes accommodate tennis courts.

A very striking feature of white suburbia is the very high walls that surround the homes. Over the course of my field trips, I observed how white homeowners increased the height of the fences or brick walls surrounding their properties. Fences and walls 8 to 10 feet high line the residential streets. Some owners have affixed razor-wire coils to the tops of their walls, and most of the walls display signs warning intruders that the property is protected by some alarm system or security firm. The richer the owner, the more elaborate the security devices. This obsession with security is a relatively recent phenomenon that started in the 1980s, when the crime rate soared with the unemployment rate.

The gardens of these dwellings are in the care of part-time or full-time black gardeners, who, in many instances, live in one of the outbuildings. Legally, gardeners had the status of migrant laborers until 1987. Usually, one or more black female servants are responsible for duties inside these suburban homes, which include cleaning, making beds, washing dishes, laundering and ironing clothes, child care, and, in many cases, preparing the meals for the white family. The white families are thus freed from a great deal of drudgery. In fact, the sizes of these houses and gardens make it impossible for the white residents to maintain them by themselves. In most cases both male and female servants have families and children in rural areas whom they visit during brief holidays. The domestic setup sketched here has had an important consequence for the socialization of white children. They become used to the idea that housework "belongs" to black servants, an attitude that fosters the expectation that normal domestic routines will be taken care of, that one can always return to the home after school or work to a clean house, with beds neatly made and food on the table. After meals, the dishes are taken care of by the servants, and the white family can pursue whatever leisure or school activities they like.

In lower-middle-class areas the picture is pretty much the same, but on a smaller scale. The houses are smaller, with two bedrooms and sometimes three, one bathroom, a garage, and a servant's room. Next to the servant's room are minimal bathroom facilities, usually a small room with a toilet and shower. The toilet, in many instances, is the flush-pit type and serves as a drain for the shower. Often there is no connection with the hot water system of the main house. As a rule, black servants are not allowed to use the facilities of the main house, yet they are expected to handle the food, dishes, and babies of their employers.

People living in high-rise buildings house their domestic help in rooftop rooms or engage the services of women who come to town each morning. The owners of high-rise buildings provide apartment-cleaning services but tenants can also hire additional help.

On the farms, black labor is indispensable. Black families are housed in clay huts or, if the farmer can afford or wants to provide them, simple two- or four-room brick structures. Sanitation facilities are minimal. Wives and daughters of laborers provide domestic help to the white household at minimal wages or in exchange for food. Domestic help is in abundant supply, and it is not unusual for one household to have separate women for ironing, washing, housecleaning, and child care.

EVERYDAY INTERRACIAL CONTACT AND INTERACTION

Contact in the Home

From a very young age, the racial socialization of white children occurs in the home.[4] It is here where the baby is left in the care of a black servant, who cleans, feeds, and plays with the child in the absence of the mother. The division of labor in white South African homes tends to be very traditional, and as a rule, the father is only peripherally involved in child care. The black "nanny" stands in for the mother. Her presence, both as domestic worker and as nanny, is largely taken for granted.

For an article titled "Afrikaner Women: Breaking the Mould?" which appeared in the South African (white) women's magazine *Femina,* Pippa Green (1990) interviewed a number of businesswomen and female intellectuals. The issue of black domestic labor was seen as important for understanding the role of Afrikaner women in society. The poet Antjie Krog, for example, referred to Afrikaner women as

> a privileged species, unique on earth. We enjoy the limitless freedom of time granted by cheap, intelligent black domestic help so we can select the tidbits and specialise in entertaining, or designing clothes, or studying, or gardening, become connoisseurs in silver, and make our own pots or [write] poetry for Christmas. (p. 64)

Green observes that black women, by their servitude, have freed white women from "fractious relations" in the household because wives are spared battles with their husbands over dishes. Accordingly, there is not much soil for feminism to grow in. Green observes that Afrikaans-speaking career women are quite open about their indebtedness to domestic servants: "Apart from their grandmothers, career women almost always mentioned domestic servants as being the most important women in their lives" (p. 65).

Not only Afrikaner women but white women in general make use of this freedom. Young children grow up in the care of their nannies and become attached to them. Soon after they learn to speak, however, they learn to differentiate between the significant black person and their parents. They observe the different mode of life of the black domestic compared with their own, and it would not be unreasonable to suspect that white children think it has something to do with skin color. Children also observe the activities of their parents compared with those of the domestics. Black domestics do the hard and "dirty" work—washing floors, digging in the garden, cleaning toilets, carrying heavy loads, and so on. Many times a racial adjective is used to describe this work, that is, it is called *black work* (a term I have not heard recently because of its overt racism is *kafferwerk*). White children refuse to do such work because it pertains, or "belongs," to blacks. The work itself is considered to be below the dignity of whites; it is considered to be inferior and must be performed by people below the level of whites.

In the home, the servants are not supposed to share meals with the white members of the household. As a rule, they are also prohibited from sharing utensils or bathrooms, towels, and so on. They eat their meals separately, often sitting on the ground outside the house. White children, of course, notice these differences. They sometimes join the domestics outside, sharing their meals with them, enjoying the different fare of corn porridge or *pap* while eating with their hands. However, as they grow older children are cautioned to stop such "improper" behavior.

In other instances, black servants eat from the table of the white household. It is customary for domestics either to prepare the white family's food or at least assist in its preparation. A female servant usually brings the food to the table and waits for the family to finish the meal. After clearing the dishes from the table, she and the gardener, if there is one, can enjoy whatever remains. During a meal, members of the household are sometimes reminded to "leave something for the servant." If a meal is particularly tasty, all the food may be consumed; the servant may have no meal. I have heard white family members at such times saying, in effect, "Oh, never mind, she can take some bread."

To sum up, experiences around the table and experiences connected with sharing in general drive home important messages to white children: The servants do "inferior" work, they are black, they do not share things with us associated with body contact (inconsistencies in this regard are blatant to the outsider), their needs come last, and our "place" is not their place—although they work in it.

Terms of address are another factor reinforcing the messages summarized above. Domestic servants are called by their first names. In some households children are expected to show respect to domestic servants; in others they are not. *Respect,* in this context, has very specific meanings: Children who are respectful of servants do not verbally abuse them, attack them physically, or damage their property. It is not considered disrespectful, however, for a minor child to call adult blacks by their first names, to give them commands, or to demand their immediate attention when the servants are busy with other tasks.

The first names used by blacks are the "Christian" names they adopt in the context of selling their labor. Their indigenous African names, and what would be the equivalent of surnames, are usually unknown to members of the white household, who would not bother to learn and remember them anyway. Certain Christian names are popular among blacks, and whites who are given such names often express embarrassment. Gordon (1988) quotes an English speaker as having said about her mother: "She used to hate that name. All South African people who are named Sophia, they hate the name, because coloured kitchen girls are called Sophie. It's like my name: every second black woman you come across is Emily" (p. 70). In face-to-face encounters with blacks, standard appellations such as the generic, anonymous Jim and Annie are often used. In naming their children, whites are sensitive about upholding their sense of superiority.

Certain Afrikaners in rural areas attach the prefixes *outa* or *aia* before the Christian names of older blacks as a sign of respect when addressing them. These terms, however, are used only for blacks; they are never applied to whites. *Outa* derives from the Afrikaans *oud* (old) and *ta* from the Sotho word *ntate* (father). Sometimes the term *ta* is applied to black males, especially in reference to culprits caught in the act of committing a crime. *Aia* is a general term for an old black woman.

Black servants address white household members as master, missus, or madam. In Afrikaans, the terms *baas* (boss, master), *miesies* (missus), *nooi* (an antiquated term heard on farms, meaning something like "lady"), and, for children, *kleinbaas* and *kleinmiesies* (little master and little missus) are used. Seniority is indicated by adding *ou-* (old) to *baas* or *miesies*. Sometimes *master* or *missus* is used with the name of the individual to distinguish who is being addressed or referred to. In English-speaking households, servants frequently call the family's children by their first names; in upper-middle-class households and Afrikaans-speaking homes, more formal modes of address (e.g., Mr. Smith or *mevrou,* Afrikaans for "Mrs.") might be preferred.

The terms of reference used for blacks in the third person set them apart as a separate and lower category of being. Regardless of age, males are referred to as *boy* or *garden boy*; females are *girl* or *maid*. These terms indicate their minor status. This is also true of the Afrikaans equivalents, *jong, tuinjong,* or *booi,* and for a woman, *meid.* (*Booi* is related to "boy" and is never used for a white person. In Dutch, *meid* simply means "a young woman." It is also never used to refer to a white in South Africa. In fact, it is a great insult for a white male to be called a *meid,* meaning "lowest coward.") Recently, liberal households have begun to use terms such as *gardener* and *domestic* more frequently. In lower-middle-class Afrikaner households and in rural areas, the term *kaffer* is freely used. The term, which derives from an Arab word meaning "infidel," is highly derogatory. Its emotional impact nowadays is the same as that of *nigger* in the United States. It is rarely used in public now, but among close acquaintances it is still in circulation. The cultural elaborations and contexts attached to *kaffer* as a lexical item are remarkable. The standard dictionary of Afrikaans lists more than 300 terms that start with the prefix *kaffer-* (Schoonees, 1991). Its usage in Afrikaans originally indicated a member of the aboriginal people of Africa. The dictionary quotes numerous examples of the use of the term from popular Afrikaans literature, including youth literature. The connotations of its usage are mostly pejorative, indicating the inferiority, cowardice, uselessness, and so on, of blacks.

Finally, it is important to consider how well white employers know the blacks who work in their households. As noted above, most whites do not know their servants' personal names. When they were asked about the personal circumstances of their domestics in the interviews conducted for this study, whites could rarely give any elaborate accounts, if they were able to give any accounts at all. Some knew the areas their domestics came from, but their knowledge about the servants' families, including spouses and children, was either totally absent or incoherent. It is most remarkable that whites who are so physically close to blacks in their households on a day-to-day basis can know so little about them. Blacks, on the other hand, know much more about their employers. Whites' lack of knowledge about the lives of their black servants is a clear indication of how relatively unimportant blacks as human beings are to their white employers.

It is within this customary racial division of labor in the home, sharing of food and facilities, modes of address and reference, and other linguistic conventions that white children grow up. The pattern of human relations and the meanings that underpin it are prestructured. It is a pattern that has been repeated for generations, and, as far as children's perceptions and experiences are concerned, it is lasting and permanent. It is a world of relations that they take for granted. The pattern goes unchallenged, and it reproduces itself. It is an unquestioned construct of everyday life, and by itself it structures experience; it creates a way of seeing other human beings. This way of seeing guides whites' actions toward blacks. It is an underlying factor of white consciousness.

Contact in the Workplace

Less personal and less direct, compared with relations in the home, are black-white relations in the "white" workplace. These begin with transportation to and from that workplace. Because of the suburban sprawl of cities, most South African whites commute to work. The favored mode of transport is the automobile, because of its privacy and the degree of freedom it offers. However, more and more whites are using public transport in the cities, in part because gasoline and general upkeep of personal vehicles are very expensive.

Because of increasing costs, recent years saw economic pressure to dismantle apartheid on in public transport. Buses designated for whites in Johannesburg were running below capacity and were operating at huge losses by 1984, and buses for blacks were equally plagued by problems.[5] Although the designation "second class" was removed from bus stops for blacks in the early 1970s, separate buses kept running in Johannesburg. Until 1991, although not backed by law anymore, municipal buses for blacks were still identified by a horizontal green stripe. Before 1991, buses for blacks stopped at signs printed in white lettering on a black background, and buses for whites stopped at signs printed in black lettering on a white background. The government subsidized the Public Utility Transport Corporation to transport black laborers from their group areas to their places of work in "white" areas. White South Africans, properly socialized into the racial symbols of their society, automatically waited for buses at the appropriate signs and never dreamed of confusing them.[6] It was an unspoken code they adhered to, but to foreign tourists it was often baffling.

It is illuminating to note the reasons given by whites who were concerned with upholding bus segregation. At the time of the abolition of the mixed-marriage and immorality laws, the Johannesburg Transport Committee argued that whites would reject bus desegregation because 70% of white passengers were women (Pirie, 1990, p. 115). Implicit in this argument is the patriarchal and racist reasoning that white women needed to be protected from sexual harassment by black commuters. Although public opinion was turning more favorable toward the sharing of public facilities in Johannesburg, private resentment was great and surfaced, for example, in a letter to the editor of the daily newspaper the *Star.* The writer claimed that "frail and elderly whites were 'traumatized' by being squashed up beside black passengers, their overpowering smell, their fleas and their bugs" (quoted in Pirie, 1990, p. 115). During 1989, the Johannesburg municipality held a referendum of its white residents in order to test their acceptance of desegregated public amenities. In a 32% poll, 56% approved nonracial buses. At the end of that same year, the state president announced the scrapping of the law legalizing the creation of all separate amenities. All municipal buses in Johannesburg were thus officially desegregated in 1990. A defiance campaign against bus segregation in Pretoria sparked a wave of death threats, shootings, and bombings. When that municipality announced the abolition of bus apartheid in 1990, some white bus drivers spoke of resistance and of defying the regulations (Pirie, 1990, p. 116).

In Johannesburg, the same poll that favored the integration of buses indicated strong opposition to the desegregation of swimming pools. The municipality nevertheless went ahead and opened all swimming pools to all races. (It is not improbable that they received an okay from the inner circle of master politicians, given that, at the time, Johannesburg was governed by Nationalists.) Many whites reacted negatively to this move on "hygienic" grounds. The removal of beach apartheid at various coastal resorts met with a similar reaction. The idea of black and white bodies sharing the same private and public space and medium, whether it be water, parks, or toilet seats, seemed to be particularly abhorrent to a broad segment of the white public.

Aside from the "pollution" that blacks represented for whites, many whites viewed crowding as an intolerable experience. Before the abolition of the Separate Amenities Act, separate beaches and parks were reserved for the various population groups. Some municipalities opened parks selectively in the larger metropolitan centers. However, the capital, Pretoria, lagged far behind. It was in Pretoria where, in November 1988, Barend Strydom, a member of the militant white supremacist group the White Wolves, indiscriminately massacred blacks who were spending their lunch hour on the Strydom square in Pretoria. He claimed that whites had been crowded out of the square, which was devoted to the remembrance of a white hero, J. G. Strydom, a former prime minister (see also Chapter 5). Another incident occurred in the rural town of Louis Trichardt in late 1990, around the time of the abolition of the Separate Amenities Act. A group of black children on a Sunday school picnic in a municipal park formerly reserved for whites were viciously attacked and beaten by white right-wingers (*Southern Africa Report,* December 14, 1990). Before 1990, whites had been used to open access to the prime natural resources of the country. They were free, uncrowded, and almost limitless. The same was true of public facilities in towns; where crowding did occur, it was confined to certain areas where whites could easily avoid it.

The twin phenomena of the fear of pollution and the fear of crowding that would result from sharing facilities with the black population were even more marked in the area of health services. Driven by the scarcity of qualified white personnel and a sagging economy, private hospitals began to employ increasing numbers of nonwhite nursing staff. The government hospitals held out for a while, but the same contingencies soon caught up with them. At first, whites who objected to being cared for by blacks could go to state hospitals, where whites attended to them, but that soon became impossible. Many whites resented having their own bodies and those of their family members handled by blacks, but in the end they had to acquiesce. At one point, attempts were made at a teaching hospital to block black medical students' presence at gynecological examinations of white patients, but they were dropped when the medical school threatened to withdraw from that hospital.

In the wake of the repeal of the cornerstones of apartheid legislation, all segregation in health services technically ceased. Since 1991, hospitals previously designated as reserved for whites have admitted patients based on medical considerations only, with no race restrictions. Hospitals previously assigned to blacks now also admit whites. This means that hospital wards have become integrated, and that white patients not only might be cared for by blacks but might have to use beds blacks have used, utensils blacks have used, and so on. Many of the taboos concerning black-white contact so consistently drummed into whites during their early years of socialization are simply impossible to maintain in this situation. The old taboos cannot be upheld; the unwritten and unquestioned laws of purity and pollution are irreparably broken.

Furthermore, now that they have to share public health services with all South Africans, regardless of color, whites no longer enjoy their previous relative ease of access to uncrowded services. Priority of treatment is based purely on the grounds of medical urgency. Whites now must wait in line with blacks, sometimes for hours. Their privilege and uncrowded access have been taken away. Where available, private hospitals can still provide some of the privilege and access that whites have lost, but only at a very high price. Needless to say, the opening of health facilities to all races has affected the access of poorer whites more than that of their richer counterparts.

As in health care, privilege and priority treatment can still be attained at a price in the areas of transportation, recreation (such as at beaches, parks, and game reserves), and shopping. In Chapter 6, I sketched the tendency toward and justifications for the privatization of a whole series of industries in South Africa. Privatization has also become the motto of those who seek to provide whites with access to lost privilege. Privatization in this sense means that the rich, mostly whites, with a few affluent blacks thrown in, will be able to buy themselves into paradise lost. However, more than one generation of whites still lives with attitudes and values centering on the purity of social categories, "civilization," and "style" against the backdrop of the wide open spaces and exotic cultures of Africa.

An examination of the consumer palette of a rich white shopping mall such as Sandton City, to the north of Johannesburg, illustrates the symbolic relationship between Europe and Africa. Row after row of elegant shops, filled with imported designer clothes and jewelry, line the passages.

Expensive imported camping and hiking equipment are found in some shops; a number of others sell black ethnic art and seem to be doing quite well. These curio shops make exorbitant profits by selling individually artifacts bought by the truckload in rural black areas. Their white clientele can thus buy and bring Africa ornamentally into their living rooms while confining the African to the kitchen or garden. In contrast, a visit to the southern and western areas of downtown Johannesburg reveals a 90% black presence. These areas are shunned by whites, who resent the *verswarting* (blackening) of downtown. Here there are discount stores, Indian bargain stores, hawker supply stores, sidewalk fruit sellers, and herbalists. To the west, the glistening diamond-shaped headquarters of the Anglo American Corporation and the Johannesburg Stock Exchange sit uneasily in the presence of cheap stores and their impoverished clientele.

WHITES' EXPERIENCES AND ENCOUNTERS WITH BLACKS

Looking at the everyday interracial encounters of whites and blacks, one is struck by the different patterns found in rural and urban areas. In rural areas, the chance that whites will encounter blacks on an equal footing is relatively small. Rural blacks mostly occupy the most menial of roles. On white farms, blacks appear as laborers and domestics; they are mostly illiterate and, to some extent, more immersed in rural black folkways than are their urban counterparts. Rural whites look upon urban blacks with some suspicion as being spoiled and "uppity"; they assume that rural blacks "know their place" much better than urban ones. Whites interviewed for this study maintained that the city has a spoiling influence on blacks. The notion of "good rural blacks" versus "bad urban blacks" is also applied to blacks in rural towns, who are seen as occupying an in-between position. Apart from the sphere of farm labor, including domestic labor, rural whites may encounter blacks in supermarkets in town, as packers and cleaners; some rural shops still have separate entrances for blacks. There is almost no opportunity in a rural setting for whites to meet blacks who have other kinds of occupations or professions. Although separate amenities were no longer legally enforced at the time I was doing my research, there was tacit understanding in rural areas that blacks would not be tolerated in white movie theaters or churches, for example. When blacks did try to use public areas, such as parks, they were met with white violence, as in the case of Louis Trichardt, mentioned above. Rural blacks have become more assertive in claiming their rights since 1991, but during the research period for this study, this was exceptional behavior.

In urban areas the picture is different. Here, too, blacks appear in menial domestic roles, as blue-collar laborers in public work teams and in factories, as cleaners in buildings, and as packers in supermarkets. However, they have also become increasingly visible as supermarket cashiers, bank clerks, and other office workers. They are traffic police officers authorized to direct and ticket whites, bus drivers, and ticket sellers at theaters. In liberal, mostly English-language churches, they share religious services with whites. They can go to the theater, visit the zoo and other public places, share swimming pools to a limited extent, and, in certain professional contexts, associate freely with their white counterparts.

In cities, lower-middle-class whites have little opportunity to encounter professional blacks. Their contacts are limited largely to the laborer category and to people in formal roles such as clerks and traffic officers. It is more affluent whites who have opportunities to work with black colleagues and to encounter blacks at the theater or in restaurants. The popular press has poked fun at the tokenism that has been fashionable among white intellectuals, who demonstrate their liberalism by inviting blacks to their parties. For some whites, such black guests are status symbols. Among the more adventurous upper-class whites, "slumming" (the practice of going to *shebeens,* or speakeasy bars, in black townships at night) was the "in" thing to do in certain circles in the early 1990s.

The more liberal, well-to-do whites have experimented with black-white relations in various formal and informal settings. The political arena is one formal setting: Blacks and whites interact at the rallies and meetings of various extraparliamentary groups, such as the constituent bodies of the United Democratic Front, IDASA, and the SAIRR. More informal settings include popular sporting and musical events, where especially the younger generation of whites and blacks celebrates shared interests in, and enthusiasm for, common symbols. Public events supported by the youth are of particular interest in evoking feelings of solidarity between black and white. As yet, however, regardless of their popularity, they are still supported by only a small, select segment of liberal-minded white youths.

In this study, I expressly wished to adopt the perspective of whites in everyday life. However, as noted previously, human experience is never free of context. I therefore make one basic distinction in presenting whites' experiences of themselves, their relations with others, and their concerns: the distinction between the rural and urban worlds of experience. Whites living in rural areas share a world distinct from that of urban dwellers.

This of course is not a rigid distinction, because many variations may exist. The city is never far away in the minds of rural whites. In fact, television brings city life and culture right into rural homes. Yet there is a certain distinguishable ethos in race relations that prevails in the rural areas where I did my research. The extent of my evidence does not allow me to generalize about all rural whites, because I did my investigation among a rather conservative white population. The South African white farming population is actually quite diverse, including managers and technicians who run huge commercial farms on behalf of absentee owners, the old liberals of the family farms in the Cape Province, the sophisticated English-speaking land barons of Natal and the Eastern Cape, the inhabitants of smallholdings near cities and towns, and, perhaps the largest category, the Afrikaner owner-farmers.

Urban whites, on the other hand, share a world of experience distinct from that of rural South Africans. The differences between rural and urban Afrikaners are expressed in the names they call each other: *plaasjapies* (farm boys) and *stadsjapies* (city kids). Urban dwellers are also diverse, and I have attempted to account for this by making a rough class distinction that is, I believe, supported by subjective evidence. There are, further-more, significant geographic differences among various cities. This study concentrates on the Pretoria-Johannesburg metropolitan areas; the struc-ture of human relations in other large cities may be different. There are harbor towns that certainly have their own peculiarities. Cape Town, for example, has a very old Cape Malay and coloured population. Its black population has increased dramatically only during the past two decades. Johannesburg's black population, although it increased dramatically dur-ing and after World War II, has been a permanent component since the city's founding.

CHILDREN'S ESSAYS AND DRAWINGS

Two particularly rich and revealing sources on the attitudes and hopes of young whites in South Africa are a set of essays and a group of drawings I collected in 1989. These demonstrate how white youth internalize the values communicated to them by their parents, the institutions of school and church, and the media. I will first discuss the essays. As I mentioned in Chapter 3, the organization Vroue vir Suid-Afrika (Women for South Africa) ran an essay contest for schoolgirls in 1988. Essays could be written in 11 different languages, including most of the black vernaculars. The writers were to compete for three prizes in each language group. The available topics were "My country needs me," "I love my country because . . . ," and "We South Africans can help each other . . . ." Details of the competition were circulated in the popular press and at schools. The response was good; more than 2,000 essays were submitted. By the time of my research, however, only 480 could be traced. I selected 100 essays written by Afrikaans- and English-speaking whites on the basis of the locations of the writers' schools (white group areas at the time) and brought copies of them to the United States for further detailed analysis. No proper content analysis could be undertaken, but what follows is an analysis of recurring themes in the essays selected.

The Essays

One of the first considerations in interpreting the essays was to determine the audience they were written for. The bulk of the essays were submitted through schools, although a significant number were sent in privately. It is thus possible that most of the girls were addressing their teachers as audience, and that pressures toward conformity with teachers' expectations and ideology might have played a role in the writers' choice of content. The essays submitted privately do not differ much in style or content from those forwarded through the schools, however. All three topics evoked emotion-laden and moralistic responses from their young authors.

There is a decided difference between the essays submitted in Afrikaans and those submitted in English. The essays in English are more idealistic in tone; their authors tend to view society as inclusive of all population groups. As noted in Chapter 3, they also appear to be less concerned than the Afrikaner essayists with the past and with religion.

In contrast, the essays in Afrikaans are strongly rooted in the past, exhibiting strong and even extreme patriotism, which is manifested in the writers' stated preparedness to fight and die for their country. In these essays the enemy and outsiders are also clearly defined as the ANC and the radicals; both are regarded as communists.

Romanticism

Essays in both English and Afrikaans romanticize South Africa, listing and praising its natural beauty, its flora, and its fauna. The images thus conjured up could have been taken directly from some tourist brochure.

The way in which romantic and utopian concepts are constructed in the essays is noteworthy. In the following excerpt from an Afrikaans essay, the writer connects the natural beauty and wholeness of the country with the body politic; both are entities created and willed by God:

> South Africa, an independent republic at the southernmost point of the African continent . . . the source and origin of a most precious love . . . a love only the children of South Africa have . . . to carry this name [?] with pride. It is as if I am walking through the portals of Genesis, through the arch of triumph inscribed with the words: "In the beginning God created heaven and earth." I wander further through the music chamber of the Psalms, where the Spirit is playing the strings of nature. . . . this is my firm and true love for my country, South Africa!

She goes on:

> When I let my thoughts go and I let my magic carpet glide over the purple crags of Table Mountain then I know that the bright and shimmering colors on the horizon are a gift of God, that each tide reflects his love. South Africa in its fullness and glory, noble as a lily, disappoints no one. Everyone wishes to live in the heart of South Africa. (Afrikaans, Essay 174)

In a somewhat more secular vein, an essay in English laments the unrest and political turmoil in South Africa. The following excerpt demonstrates a similar preoccupation with the country, its people, and their minds as a pure and immaculate body spoiled by unrest but calling for restoration in the shape of "gentle geography." Writing about fears and insecurities, the author states:

> These constricting emotions cause the vulnerable body to be invaded by pathogenic germs, penetrating the sensitive depths of one's conscience, corrupting the weak immunity system, scathing the delicate tissue. Eventually the mind and soul are destroyed and become smothered in a dark shroud.

She continues:

> So rather let destiny assume the shape of gentle geography. (English, Essay 460)

Rarely are concrete references made in the essays to the structural inequality of South African society, but this sigh for a restored beautiful country is repeated over and over. The cause of the decline is often couched in terms of a question: "Why does the decadence of politics cause such discord among various creeds and colours of this land?" (English, Essay 455). (The resentment of politics spoiling the country is also encountered among adults; see below.) The sensuous utopia of sunny skies, good food, beautiful beaches, outdoor life, and sport fills the pages of many essays on the topic "I love my country because . . . ":

> Happiness quivered through me. I felt tremendous love for South Africa, my country of languid suns, blue waters and bee nectar. (English, Essay 412)

Where the topic of politics is broached, a defensive attitude is often manifested:

> [South Africa is] just as civilized and beautiful as any other country. . . .
> All in all I love this country for being just what it is and although it may have its drawbacks and room for improvement it has come a long way in the years past and who knows what is to come of the future. (English, Essay 14)

> Some overseas countries know we can stand together and they are trying to destroy this. This is where we must show our determination. (English, Essay 60)

> They do not care for the people of the land. What they care about is power and influence. This is the fundamental difference between all South Africans and them: South Africans care!
> By standing together as one—blacks, whites and Asians—and taking a stand against those aggressors who mean to steal our country right from under our noses. (English, Essay 51)

Solidarity

In the essays written in English, the notion of "standing together" is usually inclusive of other population categories, although this was highly unrealistic in view of the conflicts and divisions within the country and the pressure being exerted by foreign countries at the time. Essays in Afrikaans also address this issue of standing together under the topic of "We South Africans can help each other . . . ":

> The dark clouds on the horizon dissipated. The country was my land. Now the world threatens to overwhelm and crush [*oordonder*] us, but South Africa remains united and standing in times of duress. (Afrikaans, Essay 438)

What unity is addressed here? Many of the essays in Afrikaans equate Afrikaner with South African, but not all of them. The inclusion of all population categories found in Essay 51, quoted above, appears in a different form in an Afrikaans essay. This essay specifies historical roles of actors of different racial and ethnic origins:

> Since the earliest times the Afrikaner was dependent on his fellow Afrikaner's help: As Voortrekkers they crossed the Drakensberg together, together they fought in trenches for the preservation of what was their own and together behind their desks, ploughs, and workbenches they reconstructed what foreign elements destroyed [reference to the Anglo-Boer War].
>
> Today we learn about the heroic determination of those black boys [*touleiers*] who led the oxen [in the Great Trek], black farm laborers who for three years guarded the burned-down farmhouses [during the Anglo-Boer War], young British soldiers who protected Afrikaner women and children against aggression.... We have to acknowledge: South Africa does not only consist of Afrikaners. Various population groups are woven into one great desire—the preservation of their fatherland, South Africa! (Afrikaans, Essay 107)

The assumption underlying the solidarity propounded in this essay is the South African status quo of a society composed of unequal racial and ethnic groups. In fact, the essayist depicts blacks as serving the Afrikaners or safeguarding their interests. It is also remarkable that it only now—toward the end of the twentieth century—occurs to the young author that South Africa is not only the country of the Afrikaner.

A similar view is taken in other essays: Solidarity in the face of a common enemy, communism, is necessary and needs a broader base. Note the interplay between "we" and "they" and "white" and "Afrikaner" in the following passage:

> The enemy is communism. Alone, our small white population cannot fend off this powerful enemy in our midst. If we Afrikaners do not stand together and reach out to everyone in this country, we cannot fight this threat. It is a well-known fact that soldiers on our borders come from different population groups. They are making the highest sacrifice, possible loss of life—for our fatherland, the Republic of South Africa. (Afrikaans, Essay 253)

Is our fatherland also theirs? A similar theme is raised in an English essay that describes a hypothetical future war between South Africa and a worldwide enemy. A white woman observes how all people are suffering in this war, regardless of their racial origin. Among the explosions and the wounded, somebody suddenly starts singing the (white) national anthem:

> Voices joined in and blended. Male, female, Black, White. Labourite, Nationalist, rich, poor—all different, with one common grounding—South African. Emotion choked the room, and the woman suddenly knew, as everyone joined hands and the anthem continued, that future disaster would be prevented, that the horizon was clear and that South Africans would work together and help each other. (English, Essay 475)

This author's lack of realism is stunning. To be able to believe that all races and ideologies could suddenly achieve solidarity under a controversial white symbol while suffering in a war evoked by world hostility caused by white politics is not only naive but attests to a total lack of understanding of the reasons for foreign opposition to South Africa. The concluding phrase is therefore devoid of content. The essay ends with the white woman falling into a peaceful sleep while the others continue singing. (This essay was highly commended by the contest judges.)

In a much more ethnocentric vein, South Africans should be bound by national pride (*nasietrots*), according to another essayist:

> This word indicates a specific people characterized by a common descent, language, history, culture, and tie to the land [*landsbodem*]. (Afrikaans, Essay 391)

The essay implies that the "people" are the Afrikaners and does not elaborate on the South Africanness of other "peoples." The author clearly upholds the old conservative notion that South Africa belongs to the Afrikaner in the first place.

Diversity

The question of diversity is addressed in the essays in a variety of ways, from an extreme exclusionist point of view denying South Africans a common identity to one that foresees ethnic integration. On one end of the spectrum, an essayist writing in Afrikaans notes:

> Like Europe, South Africa also consists of a large number of different peoples. The mere fact that this essay competition had to be held in 11 languages in order to accommodate everybody is a clear indication. Apart from linguistic differences, there are also cultural differences (much larger than between Europeans) and racial differences (nonexistent in Europe). But despite all

this we are brainwashed by the government, the media, and the rest of the world to believe we are one South African nation. This train of thought is ridiculous, extremely naive, and a racist solution. (Afrikaans, Essay 481)

The author explains why this is a racist solution, saying that forcing one culture onto representatives of a number of other different cultures causes them to fear that they will be robbed of their ethnic identity (*volksidentiteit*). She asks rhetorically whether the reader has ever heard of any one people/nation that speaks 11 languages. The solution she proposes is the creation of different nation-states that might cooperate in a common market, like the European states. Her perception of ethnic diversity in South Africa is in line with views found in white conservative circles.

An essay in English addresses the diversity issue as follows:

South Africa has four races namely Black, Coloured, Indian and White. Each race has its own culture and we have decidedly different ways of life and backgrounds, but together we make up South Africa. (English, Essay 36)

This author goes on to emphasize neighborliness and how important it is that the "haves" should help those who have less. A paternalistic tone pervades this essay; the writer argues that one of the most important ways of solving South Africa's problems is for whites to engage in charitable acts toward blacks, making donations to them and providing opportunities for them. Although she tries to underplay it, the racial division always remains near the surface. Mentioning the importance of judging a person's employability on the basis of qualifications rather than color, she notes:

If we would just disregard and forget colour, which for so many years has played the most important part in our lives, and consider the individual as he/she is and what they are capable of achieving and doing for us, the company they work for and towards a better South Africa.

The contrast of "we" and "they" in the last sentence is significant. Throughout this essay, "they" implies blacks and is consistently associated with poverty, labor, and subservient status. "Their" capability is to be assessed in terms of what "they" can do "for us."

In the discussion of children's drawings, below, I note that the black-white theme occupies a very prominent place. It similarly arises in these essays. The symbolism of the zebra is striking. One writer points out that the black and white stripes of the zebra never mix, yet "shooting it in a black or white stripe will carry the same end result, death" (English, Essay 457). The organic analogy of the statement, in a very condensed way, sums up the contradictory relationship between the unbridgeable, essential difference between white and black, on the one hand, and the common destiny and fate they share, on the other. Both are united and nurtured in the organic body that is the condition of their existence. This unity, on one level, seems to imply the common economic bond of black and white. On another level, it may be an expression of the shared existential fate of black and white in South Africa.

Taking up the question of unity beyond diversity, another essay in English compares South Africa to the colorful robe of the biblical figure Joseph. South Africa has "its own multitude of colours[,] rainbows . . . from its extravaganza of landscapes to its exultant people. . . . South Africa is God's own dream robe" (English, Essay 80).

The diversity of South Africa's population is viewed by the essayists predominantly in immutable terms. Those writing in Afrikaans cannot conceive of a nonracial situation, or one in which racial or cultural difference would not matter. The English writers do not fare much better; their views of neighborliness and mutual assistance tend to reflect the traditional geographic distribution of "ethnic" groups or the traditional roles accorded to the "racially" defined groups.

The Future

In many essays the future harbors insecurity and peril. One of the worst dangers envisioned is that posed by communism. Foreign intervention in its various forms comes second. One essay in Afrikaans dwells on the peace and prosperity of the past. The writer relates how foreign countries became envious of South Africa, and communism followed a strategy of corrupting the youth, in whose veins originally flowed the blood of Voortrekkers. The youth (obviously the Afrikaner youth) have become complacent and prone to the seductions of communism: drugs, "free love" (meaning premarital sex), and alcoholism. The youth are unaware that other peoples might take their place in society:

> [They] don't know that there are other peoples [*volkere*] who would take their place with great enthusiasm. That the brown people [*bruinmense*] they are calling "damn kaffir" [*dekselse kaffer*] are working while they are sleeping. And one day they will have to call that same "stupid blackskin" [*onnosele swartnerf*] master [*baas*].

Revolution has never been nice. The history of the French Revolution makes us shudder. Wide rivers of blood always flowed when those who had been oppressed for many centuries suddenly became aware of their power and rose up against their masters.

It is often said that history repeats itself. I therefore believe that the black masses would no longer tolerate it to say "master," to swallow our insults, and to live in mud huts. They too have a fatherland for which they will live and die, true?

Isn't it better then to leave and to settle somewhere else, because when the South African Revolution breaks out we, nutshell of whites, would certainly not be shown any mercy by the half-barbaric black blood [*halfbarbaarse swart bloed*]?

Yes, it certainly is safer. But, actually, I know I will long for those humid summer days, the call of the *kiewiet* [a kind of bird] and the large cling peaches. What will I do without the nights under the Southern Cross and the smell of barbecue on the river?

No, I will stay here even if it is but a small comfort that there still exists a young person who, from her heart is singing: "I will live, I will die . . . I for you South Africa." You need me! (Afrikaans, Essay 348)

The "Revolution" is closely associated with the domination of half-barbaric people and is brought within the causal framework of the moral degeneration of the white youth. This passage is filled with a sense of insecurity, but in the end the romantic attraction of the country triumphs over the possibility of leaving. The "fatherland" of the blacks is obviously a separate one. As a perspective on the future, and reading between the lines, the vision of a black-dominated dispensation driven by revenge against whites is contrasted with one in which the black masses would have their own "fatherland."

Harking back to a morally pure past, many of the essays in Afrikaans lament the apostasy of the (white/Afrikaner) people in the present, the surrender to foreign values and practices. The essayists call on the people to return and rediscover their lost faith (*verlore geloof*) (Essay 353). When that happens, everything will be in order again, as in the days of Blood River (*alles sal regkom soos in die Bloedrivier dae*). As yet, the country is a Christian one and does not suffer the religious repression of communist countries (Essay 369). This in itself is a positive sign that the country still has not lost divine favor. A strong degree of political indoctrination is reflected in these essays. The naïveté of the utopian representation of a fictive past as the model for the future without reference to the urgent and complex problems facing the country is matched only by the pietistic idea of the reinstatement of faith as a way of dealing with the present.

In addition, and apart from the many ethnocentric statements and perspectives encountered in the essays, there is also evidence of a cosmocentric view. One writer states:

> To me it is as if the Creator had given more attention to this piece of the earth than to any other country in the world. (Afrikaans, Essay 353)

Essays in English are even more vague about the future than are those in Afrikaans, but less pious in tone:

> Let us join hands and give of ourselves, and we will receive. Let us unite in love and dignity. Let us tear away the shreds of hatred, bitterness and humiliation. We are South African citizens and if we cannot help each other, then we are not worthy of the country.
>
> And this, my fellow citizens, is going to put us on the long, glorious journey through life. Helping each other, loving each other and respecting each other is the key to a prosperous South Africa! (English, Essay 3)

Sometimes they are vacuous:

> [We reach for the future] with a sometimes unsteady, yet always determined hand [filling us] with a deep sense of pleasure and satisfaction, knowing that part of the gap of the deep crevice has been bridged.
>
> We are the present generation for the future. It is an undeniable right and privilege to have the physical and mental ability for the fulfillment of this reachable [goal?].

This author does not specify the content of the future. It is couched in some vague potential of the youth to grasp and realize it. Youth is equated with future, but the reader is never told what that future is about.

The Drawings

KONTAK, a white women's organization founded to promote interracial contact and understanding, ran a drawing contest for schoolchildren in 1988. Entrants had to depict the theme "Goodwill." The response was overwhelming; contributions from all population groups streamed in. I had the opportunity to take photographs of 200 of the submitted drawings. I selected those drawn by white children according to the names and school addresses attached, and I then included some drawings by black and coloured children for comparison. KONTAK selected 10 winning drawings in black and white and printed them as Christmas cards.

It was not easy to interpret the drawings, because there were few prior studies I could refer to that dealt with children's representations of a specific aspect of race relations. Machover (1980) provided some guidance, but she deals predominantly with deviant adults' representations of the human figure. I therefore decided to undertake a thematic analysis of the drawings. After examining them at great length, I grouped them around certain themes the young artists used to represent goodwill.

Diversity and Unity

The most striking feature of the collection of drawings is their representation of human diversity in South Africa. The four main legal population categories of black, white, Indian, and coloured appear repeatedly in a variety of configurations. For instance, in some drawings four individuals are shown holding hands or playing together, all smiling. Sometimes the diversity is expressed through balloons emerging from the mouths of individuals, identifying different languages, like Afrikaans, English, and Tswana. Hairstyles, dress, and skin color are used to differentiate the four groups. Indians wear saris, whites wear dresses, and blacks are occasionally depicted in loincloths.

In one particular image, five individuals hold hands around the national flag. Across the top of the drawing, bold letters proclaim, "We love our land, South Africa." The balloons from their mouths are not distinct, but one indicates a white male saying, "I am a cowboy." There are two females, one saying, "I am an astrol[ogist?]." The other two figures are black. One of them is proclaimed to be a "Bushman." The white male's feet are planted on the ground. Other figures seem to hover a few inches above the ground, but the black female is much smaller and appears suspended in the air. She is dressed in a sort of grass skirt and her breasts are bare. She barely has feet; her legs simply taper off into black spots. It is as if the artist wanted to get away from the fourfold representation, but racial difference persisted. The representation of this black figure is important because of its small size and floating position. I take this to express insignificance and powerlessness. Why a "Bushman" was added I do not know.

Unity in diversity is expressed in one drawing through the depiction of a hand on which numerous small stick figures are drawn. Each finger of the hand wears a different hat: the thumb, a fez; the index finger, a wide-brimmed

Photo 7.1.
Photo by Gerhard Schutte.

hat; the middle finger, a Sotho straw hat; the ring finger, a top hat; and the little finger, a flat conical hat, almost like a Chinese peasant's sun shade. The fez stands, I presume, for Asians; the Sotho hat, for blacks; and the top hat, for whites. I cannot determine what the others signify, but they surely have something to do with other population groups. The caption on the picture reads, "Unity is Great." In the background is a rainbow with emanating yellow rays in which a South African flag is placed.

Although many drawings depict four population groups, the struggle for imagery depicting harmonious unity is dominated by a black/white dichotomy. Some of the black/white images used in the drawings are listed below; many appeared in more than one drawing.

The chess board. White chess pieces stand on black squares and vice versa. The caption reads, "We can't make a move without each other."

The heart. The sheet of paper is half black and half white. A heart is drawn in the center, with a white half against black background and a black half against white background.

The black room. Two-thirds of the paper, offset to the lower left-hand corner, is covered by a black rectangle. Within this space a white figure stretches out its hand toward the edge of the rectangle. Touching this hand from the outside is a black figure on a white background. The impression created is that of a white figure imprisoned in a dark room (see Photo 7.1).

A zebra can't earn its strips without black.

Photo 7.2.
Photo by Gerhard Schutte.

The zebra. A drawing of a zebra is accompanied by the caption, "A zebra can't earn its strip[e]s without black" (see Photo 7.2). By implication, I would say the zebra is perceived as white with black stripes added. (Zebra symbolism was also encountered in the children's essays I analyzed; see above.)

Piano keys. A black right hand and a white left hand are shown playing the black and white keys of a piano. The caption reads, "Together in harmony."

Bricks in a wall. A white prisoner and a black prisoner are depicted as digging to escape from prison; the wall they have to tunnel under is made of white and black bricks (see Photo 7.3). The white prisoner is telling the submissive-looking black prisoner that they need a compass (they apparently have dug several holes, without success). The caption, in Afrikaans, reads, "Together we build a future by working and building." The prison frames the white and black figures. They share a common fate: being imprisoned by walls of black and white bricks. Can we take this to mean that they have constructed their own prison and now want to escape from it together?

The scale. A scale/balance decorated with white and black blocks weighs a black human figure (right side) and a white one (left side) (see

Photo 7.3.

Photo by Gerhard Schutte.

Photo 7.4). The black stands on a white pan; the white, on a black one. The two figures balance the scale. I take this drawing to symbolize that whites measured by black standards weigh the same as blacks measured by white standards. The message is that the two are equal.

Dice. A black die with six white dots facing upward is pictured next to a white one with black dots in the same position. The caption reads, "We could all be winners." The imagery implies that white and black are equal partners in one and the same game.

The black and white imagery used to depict unity (or the need for unity) between the two main components of the South African population carries powerful messages. The zebra emphasizes the organic unity of white and black, even though the image seems to be one of black embellishments on a basically white animal. The brick wall negatively depicts the unity of white and black in their unfree state. The chess board, the scale, the piano, and the heart all convey their own messages concerning black and white unity.

Photo 7.4.
Photo by Gerhard Schutte.

The interactions between the black and white components of these pictures stress their interdependence. The presence, or the function, of one is essential to the other. Neither the black nor the white component makes sense on its own. The two are thus locked into a meaningful framework of activity or function. Yet the dualism of this imagery is striking. Hard lines and contrasts separate the pure black and white fields in these drawings. No gray shades are present; no transitional spaces or figures appear. The pictures demonstrate the artists' dualistic conceptualization of South African social reality. (In an interview presented in Chapter 10, the absence of "grayness," of an area of experience in which the stark black/white contrast might be softened, is sadly lamented by a liberal white.)

Interactions

Many of the pictures portray children playing in settings such as school playgrounds, parks, swimming pools, and beaches. In these drawings, the participants appear as equals; frequently, black children are pictured as sad and lonely, with white kids coming to their rescue or consoling them.

The artists whose work falls in this category were approximately 10 years old and, in many cases, pupils in a private school or convent. Among teenagers' drawings, there is greater emphasis on sharing. Black and white youths are shown sitting in a cafe drinking from straws immersed in the same glass. In one picture, four young men are all sharing a single huge hot dog. Where the four population categories have been pictured together by young children, the black children in the drawings are remarkably characterized as described above, suspended in midair and with conical feet. The white children's arms are outstretched, whereas the coloured and black children's arms are kept close to their bodies.

Several drawings depict physical contact between people colored differently. Girls of different colors are shown kissing. All groups hold hands. Some blacks and whites are shown as boxers sharing a drink after a fight. There is hugging, arms on shoulders, and children sitting back to back.

One prize-winning picture has a story behind it. The white male artist originally drew a teenage white boy sitting back to back with a black boy. The white was holding a book, apparently reading, and the black was listening. The contest organizers requested that the boy who drew the picture add a book to the hands of the black boy. He did so, and the resulting drawing won a prize. The history of this picture introduces the theme of unequal exchange and sharing, as the artist had originally presented the white boy as offering his reading to the black.

Many of the pictures deal with whites giving or handing out gifts to blacks. One typical drawing consists of a white hand holding out an ear of corn from the left-hand, top side of the picture, to a black hand on the lower right side (see Photo 7.5). In another picture a white man takes the left hand of a black, saying: "You are employed. You need the money. Let us be partners." There are scenes of whites handing blankets to homeless blacks, making gifts to them, and providing medical care.

Among the drawings by children under the age of 10, many present blacks in a serving role. One 7-year-old's drawing consists of nine panels filled with pictures of Paulina, her family's servant, "holding me," "sitting in the room," "ironing clothes," "working in the kitchen" and "on the stairs," "racing with me," "waiting with me for mother," "bathing the dog," and "helping me color in pictures." Other drawings depict the typical black nanny caring for the white child. There is even one very primitive picture by a 3-year-old described (by the mother?) as "Ousie met baba op rug" (Nanny carrying a baby on her back) (see Photo 7.6). One young teenager's drawing depicts the artist in bed in a lavish bedroom filled with toys. A black girl sits in a nearby chair, reading to her from a book of jokes.

Photo 7.5.
Photo by Gerhard Schutte.

In picturing scenes of interaction, the drawings show acts of sharing space and food with blacks on an equal basis. There are, however, a significant number of pictures that deal with blacks as objects of charity or depict them in subservient roles. Younger children were more prone to emphasize the latter; this is understandable because they were probably more recently cared for by black servants. However, the theme of the "good black" as the subservient, obedient worker recurs in the drawings. As we will see later, this is also an important element in the thinking of conservative whites.

Inequality

For some of the children, the theme of goodwill and subservience seem to go together well. A number of drawings portray whites and blacks living together as unequal neighbors. Blacks are shown living in primitive huts next to the elaborate living quarters of their white neighbors (see Photos 7.7 and 7.8). The huts are black and the houses are white. In addition, as in some of the drawings described above, blacks are presented in tribal or

Photo 7.6.
Photo by Gerhard Schutte.

"primitive" garb next to white Westerners in suits and dresses. Both are smiling as a sign of the "goodwill" between them.

Conflict and the Future

Visions of the future take the form of blacks and whites, holding hands, walking toward a rainbow or climbing stairs to an open door. There are also images of blacks and whites building a common house of the future.

Though not central to the theme of this inquiry, it is interesting to note how some coloured children from the Cape Province saw the theme of goodwill. A number of their pictures depict white police officers poking guns into the ribs of darker, often smaller figures, presumably coloured persons (see Photo 7.9). In these drawings, the coloured persons are smiling. This was puzzling to me at first. Considering the theme of goodwill, I tried to understand what these smiles could mean. The only way I can interpret them is that the children who drew these pictures might have wanted to portray a situation in which a victim of violence "turns the other cheek" by being friendly toward an aggressor.

Photo 7.7.
Photo by Gerhard Schutte.

DISCUSSION

This chapter has centered on the ways in which South African whites express their group-way-of-thinking with regard to their physical and social environment. Diverse forms of evidence have been examined. Spatial expression, linguistic conventions, forms of social interaction, and the symbolization of the racial other all bear witness to the presence and importance of the group concept as a schema of interpretation. Looking at the forms this schema has given rise to, we may discover certain shared features.

The first is *distance*. Both rural and urban geography impose distance between white and black space. Distance is also emblematic of anonymity in the experience of the other. Geographically, the homelands and separate urban areas occupied by blacks are far away, inaccessible, and depressing to whites. Whites are aware of their existence, but they are largely ignorant of the conditions under which the black population lives. Geographic distance is symbolic of social distance between white and black. Not only

Photo 7.8.
Photo by Gerhard Schutte.

is there a blatant lack of detailed, personal knowledge about (any?) blacks among whites, there is also the perception that such knowledge is not really relevant. As a result, blacks attain visibility where they are needed in the workplace and otherwise are relatively invisible. Their real names and their family circumstances are therefore irrelevant. Sexually, they seemed to be neutral in the presence of whites. In urban areas they are neatly tucked away in their separate townships and areas. One striking feature of the imposition of distance is avoidance behavior. Whites spontaneously avoid physically close encounters with blacks. The closer to the body such contact comes, the more it is shunned.

In the symbolic way it is used, spatiality also implies rank. It is not a matter only of horizontal distance, but also of verticality, of a *hierarchical* organization of groups. White suburbs, homes, and wealth are symbolic of whites' status and prestige. They rank higher in terms of wealth, power, and initiative. The drawings and essays discussed above highlight whites' perceptions of the charitable handing down of gifts to blacks and the view of blacks as laborers or servants. Whites are generally believed to be more active, taking the initiative.

Photo 7.9
Photo by Gerhard Schutte.

The notion of group *integrity* and boundedness is a third significant component. The group self-concept often implies the ideal of a healthy state. Whites frequently use the analogy of the body, whose healthy state may be affected by the intrusion of foreign elements or infection. Such intrusion is viewed as coming not only from foreign (overseas) elements or communism, but significantly, from political discord and anxiety.

A fourth feature of groups is *discreteness.* The expressions of the fourfold "official" categorization of the South African population in the children's essays and drawings are striking. All along, these categories are kept quite separate and distinct. Group areas, homelands, servants' rooms, and figures in drawings all represent separate categories with definite boundaries. These boundaries have been sustained spontaneously even after some apartheid laws were abolished. Some of the children's drawings attempt to transcend these hard boundaries by representing images of sharing, touching, and kissing. There nevertheless are gradations of allowable disregard for boundaries. For many, shared facilities are still unthinkable.

As far as the future is concerned, the restoration of wholeness, peace, consensus, and intact boundaries is dreamed of by some of the essay writers. Their visions bear very little connection to the concrete world, however. Many whites realize that economic and political developments and outside pressures make such a restoration for all whites impossible. The only way whites can regain privileges in space, health, education, and so on is to buy them as commodities. The new symbols of this manifestation of a group-way-of-thinking are the game farms, resorts with exclusive memberships or admission prices that put them beyond the reach of the majority of the population. Similarly, expensive private schools and private clinics can still provide the high level of service whites are used to. Only now, much smaller numbers of whites can afford access.

The structures of consciousness according to which whites organize their everyday realities of space and interaction are manifested in the objectified forms of black areas, language use, and symbolic representations. Instead of following the objectifications of a group-way-of-thinking, we will now turn to the ways in which whites use it subjectively to endow the present and future with meaning. We will pursue this objective in the following three chapters, which present how white people in South Africa talk about themselves, others, and the future.

I will first focus on some rural whites. The interviews I conducted were unstructured and centered on two basic issues: Subjects were invited to talk about the present political and economic situation and how they situated themselves and blacks in it. They were then asked about their hopes and fears. Within these parameters, subjects could talk freely. My role as interviewer, as I pointed out in Chapter 1, was to encourage them to keep talking. The themes thus raised come from the respondents themselves.

I applied the same technique to the urban material. However, in order to generate comparative material, I had to index part of the Afrikaans transcriptions in English; they thus required translation. The Afrikaans examples I quote, of course, had to be translated too. My analysis, however, is based on the transcriptions in the original languages.

NOTES

1. Hostels are urban single-sex dormitories where migrants rent beds for overnight stay. Townships are black residential areas set aside for black occupation in accordance with the Group Areas Act (repealed in 1991).

2. In the "homeland" KwaZulu, 77% of rural household income between 1982 and 1985 derived from wages and remittances, 14% from pensions, and only 8% from agriculture and the informal sector (SAIRR, 1990, p. 626).

3. The name celebrates the "triumph" of the success of National Party policy in separating the population groups. The somewhat liberal Johannesburg City Council was hesitant about, if not resistant to, relocating the black community. Through special legislation, the government overcame the council's resistance and forced the relocation of blacks.

4. The descriptive material in this section is drawn from observations made in many white homes over recent years. My observations are biased toward Afrikaner homes, although I have not observed a fundamentally different trend in middle-class English speakers' homes.

5. Pirie (1990, p. 114) reports that the Johannesburg City Council lost R 10 million on its "white" routes in 1984 and R 1.5 million on its "black" buses.

6. There were other color codings; buses were blue and yellow, and carried instructions to stop at "white" or "nonwhite" signs.

8

Whites in the Countryside

As jy booi wegvat is dit asof jy 'n ledemaat amputeer [If you take away boy (my farm laborer) it is as if a limb is amputated]. (farmer)

These words are very rich in meaning. Not only do they contain symbolism of the body, viewing the laborer as a functioning and integral part of a body, but in describing him as such, the farmer uses racist terminology. The word *booi* literally means "boy" and is usually used to indicate a black farm laborer. It refers to his inferior status and separateness. There is a curious contradiction in this farmer's assertion. On the one hand, he expresses dependence, but on the other, he almost indicates resentment that it should be this way. This contradiction will become clearer in the following exposition. Farmers' and other rural whites' intersubjective world of experience differs in fundamental aspects from that of whites in town. Rural whites and blacks find themselves in an asymmetric but symbiotic relationship. Blacks do not leave for home after work. They are constantly in the kitchen, around the yard, and in their collective compounds near the "master's" house. Though physically close to whites, rural blacks are socially distant.

This chapter concentrates on perceptions and constructions made by conservative Afrikaner farmers. Since the 1988 municipal elections that gave the Conservative Party a tremendous victory in rural areas, the dominant conservative political perspectives have prevailed in the rural areas of the Transvaal, Northern Natal, and significant parts of the Free State and the Eastern Cape. I would therefore argue that the views recorded here are largely typical of a broad layer of white rural dwellers.

THE POLITICIZATION OF
SOUTH AFRICAN REALITY

Since the government embarked on its reform policy in the 1970s, and especially since the introduction of the tricameral Parliament in 1983, some of the old apartheid assumptions and the white lifestyles associated with it have been increasingly questioned. The introduction of reforms, no matter how limited, not only meant a redirection of official attention and resources but also introduced ideas associated with a wider sharing of those resources, whether economic, political power, or land. This has had a disquieting effect on many whites, who feel their lifestyles and livelihoods are threatened. Looking back over the past decade, a businessman and part-time farmer observed:

> Previously we talked about rugby. . . . I cannot remember exactly what all the topics were: People discussed farming. I remember when my father farmed here—they had an active social life. Dad played tennis, they played bridge with [another couple]. . . . But what are people talking about today? The only thing being discussed is politics. Politics, at present, is the topic among everybody. Then there are others; I mean, politics have so many tentacles that reach out into the fields of farming costs, anything: schools, children. All these things bring people back to politics.

Farmers interviewed for this study first of all observed that the government neglected them and that it failed to protect them. They pointed out how the numbers of bankruptcies had increased and the number of farmers had decreased over the past decade. Many attributed this to lack of care and protection by the government and lamented that the government seemed to care more about the needs of the consumer than about those of the producer. These assertions are important indicators of the spirit of dependency prevalent among farmers. They expect the government to take care of them. This attitude has been inculcated in many Afrikaans farmers since the National Party came to power in 1948. The rural vote made a significant contribution to the NP's electoral victory because the Afrikaner's self-perception at that time was oriented toward rural images. The government engaged in an active policy of preserving and supporting the Afrikaner's rural way of life. In the postwar era, demographic and economic factors propelled many rural whites to the towns, a tendency the Nationalist government viewed with alarm. Much debate was generated around the issue of the *ontvolking van die platteland* (depopulation of rural areas).

Farmers continued to receive massive government support, despite their diminished numbers. They received agricultural loans at very favorable rates, they could buy equipment and seed cheaply through a system of cooperatives, and they received price subsidization for their crops. When the government began to turn more to a free market orientation and to rationalizing the economy, it reconsidered these forms of support and care. Politically, the government also increasingly looked to its white constituencies in urban areas for support.

Farmers felt the government had betrayed them, the rural population, and the true Afrikaner, who had been the backbone of the country for so long. They thought they no longer had any say, because the government acted in an autocratic manner, giving them no voice on important decision-making bodies:

> We rural people [*ons plattelandse mense*] aren't happy at all. Take, for example—at present—I mean, I mean how do we understand this. At present the situation is that you as voter have no say in the country today. P. W. Botha simply nominates somebody to a council or to a committee and you have no say in the nomination of that person. He [Botha] nominates me [for example] and then he implements it [Botha's policy]. You see, we want the right to rule—and I don't need to tell you what the Conservative Party policy says—you should know it . . . but we simply desire the right to rule ourselves also. Isn't that true?

In addition to feeling neglected, farmers also feel they are being ignored. They have a sense of powerlessness. The government, supposedly representing them, acts in ways that run counter to their interests. The farmers interviewed raised two issues in this regard. First, they lamented the withdrawal of privileges they had become used to. They had regarded their privileges as rights that they could take for granted, but this was no longer possible. Second, they resented the undemocratic style of the government. They believed that the government was democratically elected and accountable to the electorate. In practice, this did not happen. In reality, the government was not a democratic body at all, but one that for many decades had acted in the sectional interest of the Afrikaners. As noted previously, Afrikaners trusted their *volksmanne* to rule in good faith once elected to office. To insist on accountability would have somehow smacked of an inappropriate lack of confidence. The Afrikaner farmers had felt comfortable with the autocratic way the government had run the affairs of the country as long as it served their interests. When they were no longer the central concern, they suddenly turned to democratic arguments to voice their protest. Rural whites and Afrikaner farmers felt neglected. Their insecurities reflected at the same time their disappointment with the traditionally benign, caring father figure of the government. As we will see, this disappointment turned to hate and rejection in certain cases.

Curiously enough, it was the issue of taxes and their appropriation that drew the greatest amount of resentment. As long as the farmers perceived tax money to be somehow channeled to serve the public (read "their") interest, they carried their tax burdens with patience. During the previous two decades, however, a gradual shift had occurred in the meaning of the notion of *public interest*. Public interest, in the eyes of rural conservatives, had come to mean mainly white interest. The National government, pursuing its "homeland" policy in the interest of keeping South Africa as white as possible, had to divert more and more public funds to the homelands and black development. More recently, in the wake of the repeal of some apartheid laws, government had broadened the domain of the public interest to include the whole population, regardless of race. The following quotation from a farmer not only illustrates his view of the in-group but also harks back to the era of white/farmer protection by a paternalistic government:

> *We* are taxed to over our ears. The other day it was published in one of *our* journals that *we* gave to the TBVC countries [independent homelands] 3,800 million rand from *our* taxes, of which 2,800 million rand comes out of *our* pockets, from the pocket of *our* salary earner. *Our* white universities' subsidies are being stopped by *our* government; note, *our* white universities. (emphases added)

He then cited the amount of taxes he is paying and observed that he still had to add to that at the end of the tax year:

> Where is that money going to? If that money is at least used to . . . if two-thirds of that money is used for *my* white prospects [*vooruitsig*], for the prosperity of the whites, then I would be satisfied—but it is being dumped [*ingevoeter*] into a bottomless pit by *our* government and as a result *we* get no dividend from it. I don't even have the money or cash to send my child to university. It is true, they are forcing the standard of *us whites* down in order to lift that of the black with *our* money, and he does not appreciate this. We get no dividends from this and this is why I do not support this government of *ours*. (emphases added)

The speaker's indignation was clear. He was expressing what the CP leader, Treurnicht, highlighted in the speeches discussed in Chapter 5: Whites are carrying an unduly large tax burden while the blacks, whose tax load is minimal, reap the greatest benefit. Blacks thus have an unfair advantage over whites.

After elaborating on the incompetence and failure of the homelands, frequently invoking notions of blacks' inherent inferiority, one affluent farmer expressed the opinion that the government was foolhardy in its failure to understand that blacks' standard of living did not improve regardless of the amount of money you allocate to them or to their areas. How was this foolhardiness to be explained, and what led the government to act disloyally toward its own people? Most informants agreed that the government was weak, that it could not stand on its own but bent over backward to appease foreign opinion and interests. In fact, it was held to be increasingly influenced by capitalist forces. In this respect, the leading figure in South Africa's mining and financial world was a symbol:

> But I can tell you now . . . the biggest poison in the country is Harry. Harry Oppenheimer. And his financial might is the stab of death for this our country. Should they hand him to me to do with him whatever I would like to do, I would hang him from a tree at the Limpopo as you would string up a crow to die. That's what I'm telling you. . . .
>
> Look, what I also want to know is what is P. W. Botha doing with a man like Harry Oppenheimer on his economic advisory council? In whose interest is Harry Oppenheimer going to act except in his own? I think Dr. Vorster, or John Vorster, did not want Harry Oppenheimer on his economic advisory council. But P. W. involved him. Therefore, I am telling you these government people of ours are lackeys of Oppenheimer.

The image of poison is important, for it gives meaning to the notion of a weakened government. Capitalist interests polluted and weakened the government. The notion of pollution and the symbolism of an endangered body (politic) recurred in a number of different contexts in this study (see Douglas, 1966). The suggested elimination of the "archcapitalist" also reminds one of a witch-hunt. Somehow, this informant thought that a watershed occurred in National Party politics between the presidency of B. J. Vorster and that of P. W. Botha. Botha, according to his view, was the inaugurator of the reform policy. Since the time he had embarked on implementing his reforms, the country had been weakened.

The pervasiveness of pollution as the reason for the government's weakness is further brought out by the preoccupation of informants with the combined strength of capitalism or capitalists and communism or communists. These were seen as debilitating agents. Many informants assumed that the government had actually been used by the United States. The following extended quote demonstrates this line of reasoning. The speaker is a middle-aged farmer who was interviewed in January 1989:

> Let me tell you this: We are too overly concerned with foreign opinion. . . . This America, . . . with their so-called show of force. America was too rotten bad to accomplish anything in Vietnam. Russia was too weak to make their mark in Afghanistan. Now—I am asking myself: How on earth will they fight us in a conventional way over here? In other words, this is how I see the matter. They use this Pik Botha [at the time minister of foreign affairs] and others like him to scare us with nice little words like "confrontation" and such things. In the meantime, they are looking whether they could change us on the inside by shoving this unacceptable element socially into our midst; and now, even shoving it into our midst in church matters in order to make us apostate [*afvallig*] at a certain stage, and thus one starts to undermine your own foundations, with the result that one becomes a people [*volk*] without pride. I will tell you the reason is that this America, as far as I am concerned—I think that the American government contains more communists than, than Russia—and they are not looking for, they are not interested in the little black [*swartetjie*] in South Africa. They want our country, pal, that strategic sea route, and they are looking for the minerals of our country— that is what they are looking for. And that is the reason that this Kissinger, in my view he is a communist—at that time, in Vorster's time he started to— he . . . they used Vorster very well in order to sell out Rhodesia. He engineered the fall of Mozambique and the same happened here to the other side, to Angola. Now they are busy with southwest [Africa] but the ultimate thing they are looking for is here at the southern tip of the continent. That is what they are looking for. They think we are too stupid to realize this, that we are laymen unable to realize this—but our government is apparently too stupid to understand this. Jonas Savimbi has more intelligence than P. W. Botha and his whole cabinet.

Though he accused the United States of communism, this informant held that the U.S. government is driven by greed in its conspiracy to engineer the downfall of (white) South Africa. Because, according to him, the United States is militarily inefficient, it has resorted to an undermining strategy, deviously changing (white) South Africans from the inside. This it is doing by introducing "unacceptable elements" into society. From the context in which the informant used this term, these elements apparently are the liberals. The choice of words is significant. The informant said that a foreign element has been "forced into society" (*tussen ons . . . indruk*). Read with the poison symbolism noted above, we again observe the symbolism of the intrusion of a harmful substance into the social body, affecting its well-being and integrity. This shrewdly engineered intrusion has the devastating effect of "apostasy." The religious connotation is not accidental; I take the speaker literally. As we have seen in previous discussion of right-wing political speeches, the people (*volk*) constitutes a religiously sanctioned entity. The word *afvalligheid* (apostasy) is used in the Afrikaans translation of the Bible to indicate the state of religious degeneracy of Old Testament Israel, which God punished by subjecting the Israelites to suffering. The farmer's fear is thus very real—apostasy results in a people's loss of pride.

The farmer quoted above believed that the government is blind to this undermining. It has been playing along without realizing that it is being exploited. However, not all Americans are seen as devious. In the eyes of one very successful farmer, American businessmen are a different category, to whom the speciousness of National Party leadership and government is clear:

When this disinvestment started, a number of American businessmen said they wanted to talk with the guys. They wanted government people, [representatives] of the National Party: government people, of the coloureds, of the Indians, and of the Conservative Party. Cas U. of the Conservative Party went over. Now these guys [*ouens*] then talked to the businessmen and consulted with them and informed them. In the evening, at a dinner, and it was the turn of Cas U., and they told him: "You shouldn't break down everything we tried to achieve, man. You have to think what you are going to say." Then he said [to himself]: "I can't bullshit these guys. They're not baboons over here. If I start singing that old ditty they would realize it was the old fabricated story." Then he, among other things, told them: "You Americans, if you try to change our skin color with your money, then we do not want your money." Then he explained the CP's policy. The businessmen gave him an ovation. To me it seems that if—, and if it happens, the CP takes over, there will be much more foreign capital because these guys, I believe, do not have confidence in P. W. Botha because he is a jellyfish [*slapgat*]—that's what I believe. You should put this on that tape and I will be happy if they put my words on television. I think he is a jellyfish and I think you Americans also think that way but if a guy, a strong guy rules again—because there is great potential in this country, then more money will be invested in this country. But now I want to know why do we never hear about the right-wing faction among the Americans. There is quite a number of right-wing or pro-right-wing Americans but the press suppresses the information [*doodswyg*].

This informant argued that businessmen were realistic. He curiously identified me, the interviewer, with the Americans. The Americans in general were also supposed to be realistic in their orientation. This is the same distinction farmers made with regard to (white) South Africans: There was the suspect, "unrealistic" government on the one hand and, on the other, there were the "realistic," trustworthy people.

This respondent's belief in the rationality of his argument and that of the party he supported is important. He had no doubt that "realistic" people would accept the rationality of the CP's economic approach. There were obstacles, however. The main problem was the government's suppression of information. Not only did the government-controlled media omit or ignore news about the conservative viewpoint, they also distorted the situation. They actively brainwashed the public, according to this view. One of the main distortions propagated by the media was that South African blacks constituted a unitary bloc within one common polity. By creating this impression, the government could convince the public that blacks were potentially powerful as a bloc and that they should receive the attention of policy makers because of this fact. This perspective of the government was held to derive from its view that South Africa is one country of which the black population is an integral part. To those farmers interviewed, blacks belonged to different ethnic groups and had political rights within their own areas. Any other view was a distortion of the "facts." This view, of course, harks back to the apartheid notions of the 1960s so popular during the reign of Verwoerd. The interest in perceiving blacks as a number of tribes derives from the otherwise unfavorable impression created by the numerical ratio of whites and blacks in the country. If blacks are split up into ethnic units, whites stand out as a much larger bloc:

But I do not agree with this business about the, the ratio between black and white. You have all these kaffir states—there are the Sotho, you have the Venda, there is the Xhosa and the Mashangaan, and they—maybe the Basotho have larger numbers than us whites—and maybe too the Zulus. But now these politicians of ours, they so willingly want to compare that global black force with us whites and, in reality, we are more than the Vendas; we are more than the Xhosas; we are more than the Mashangaans. But they want to—

maybe to their own advantage—compare for us the black bloc with the white bloc. Man, they are brainwashing us and that is the whole story.

The contrast between the notion of "us whites" and the various language communities listed is marked. Should one be led to think that these whites perceive themselves as an ethnic group *qua* whites? Later in this chapter we will look at perceived cultural differences as further features of these whites' ethnic self-perceptions. The assertion that the "politicians' " view of blacks is that of a "global black force" is also significant because of a basic contradiction contained in the view of right-wingers themselves. When it comes to the labor issue, blacks are indeed a "force" to them. The idea of a "black force" is thus very significant to them. When, however, it comes to assessing numerical strength, mostly when claims to land and territory are at stake, the tribal or ethnic argument is used.

BLACK LABOR:
DEPENDENCE AND RESENTMENT

With the exception of one Oranjewerker (see below) I interviewed, all informants were unanimous about farmers' dependence on black labor. Even those farmers who attempted to follow the Oranjewerkers' way of completely doing away with black labor on their farms confessed that they found it impossible. Black labor is an integral part of the day-to-day running of a farm. Beyond that, it is a prerequisite of operating a South African highveld farm. These farms are large and expansive and require a stable labor force on a year-round basis. Although farming is mostly based on corn production, mixed farming is practiced. Some farms have dairy cows and/or cattle raised for beef. Others combine animal husbandry with crops such as potatoes. The various activities have to be coordinated and are labor-intensive. Furthermore, white farmers have developed a farming style that engendered a dependence on black labor. During the first half of the twentieth century, black sharecroppers helped white farmers with their seasonal labor needs. White farmers also used their own sons' labor. However, since the 1950s, apartheid laws allowed blacks on farms only as laborers. Manual farm labor was labeled *kafferwerk,* with the result that farmers' sons would be more interested in managing labor and/or the mechanized aspects of farming.

Although black families may have lived on one farm for generations, the farmers interviewed saw them as temporary workers whose actual homes were in the black homelands. Most of the farmers believed it was unnecessary even to attempt to get by without black labor, because blacks would always be in supply—even in the future segregated dispensation the Conservative Party wished to reinstate. Notwithstanding their dependence on blacks, many farmers complained about the quality of blacks' labor. Some claimed that black labor is too expensive. This struck me as a remarkable assertion, because it is well known that black farm labor is ridiculously underpaid. Those who said it is too expensive gave as reasons the inefficiency and lack of productivity of black workers.

Black labor is seen as inefficient because farmers have to use many laborers. They stereotype black laborers as essentially lazy. The following conversation occurred between Servaas, a farmer, and Ernst, a businessman and farmer. Servaas had joined the Oranjewerkers and was trying to get rid of his black laborers; his father thought that this would be impossible. Servaas was very ambivalent about the issue of black labor. He agreed with the Oranjewerkers' principle that whites should not be dependent on black labor in the land they claim as their own. In practice, however, it was difficult. Asked whether a complete mechanization of the farm wouldn't be too expensive, he said:

> *Servaas:* Actually it is the other way around. I can go to my friend [who dispensed with black labor and who has expensive farming machines] and his things are impeccable. Eh, when you go to my stuff, you know, they are broken—in pieces. I think my capital outlay per surface unit and over time is much greater than his. Initially his might be greater. But it goes a longer way in his case. Thus I don't think it is financially [more expensive]— if you can manage to do it that way [i.e., to do all your work yourself] in a system that is based on black labor both on and off farms. If you could cope within [the system] then it will be financially advantageous. . . .
>
> Morally you have a problem. You know you could be schizophrenic but as far as they [Oranjewerkers] are concerned, if you subscribe to their principles and it is your desire [to do your own work], they won't object to your membership. You see, though, the setup here with us is that to my father this is unacceptable. I am not in a position to say, okay, the blacks can go now and my father has to drive the tractor.
>
> *Ernst:* But at this stage your farm isn't very economical anyway.
>
> *Servaas:* I know. I don't have enough to go it alone, to farm by myself.
>
> *Ernst:* That's what I mean. If you have too much to do, you can't go it alone.
>
> *Servaas:* No, but I have too little. One has to have enough to handle the situation by oneself.

Ernst: But if your father tells you now that he will work with you on the farm in the condition it is now.

Servaas: Yes, if you employ two additional whites . . .

Ernst: You'll have to have an alternative . . .

Servaas: I think it is wishful thinking that I could handle the whole farm, as it is, all by myself, but . . .

Ernst: You have nothing to start with. . . .

Servaas: No, if you look at the setup, eh . . . look, I made some calculations and I can give you some rough indications. Half of my farming income is spent on black wages. The moment they leave the farm I will be able to spend less than half.

Ernst: I don't think so. I saw figures at . . . that indicate that your smallest input on a macro basis in farming [is labor].

A discussion then followed on the way labor is calculated. Servaas persisted in his argument of the high cost of "black" labor.

Servaas: Let me tell you if you could do their labor yourself and you do not have them around, then you will have an extra amount available. If you fire them then there is one expense item less. You then have to decrease the surface you cultivate. But you do not have those expenses and your expenditure on wages and labor this week—and I'm not speaking of hidden costs because these could double the amount—and I'll tell you why in a moment—are between R 35-40,000 per year and your farm's income isn't quite R 70,000. Do you follow me? Thus if you could eliminate them and still do your own work, it will be easier. You are farming half the surface of your farm just to pay them.

Ernst: Are you now talking about economic considerations rather than ideological ones?

Servaas: No, my point of departure is an ideological one but an ideology is of no avail unless it is practically achievable. You know, it is meaningless. And we just discussed these two things.

He then elaborated on the hidden costs:

Servaas: Because of the blacks' backwardness [*agterstandelikheid*] eh . . . , on the one hand. You know he is not up to [*opgewasse*] [it], you, you have First World tools and implements to work with. Then you put a Third World operator on them.

Ernst: If you put me on that tractor then I'll be worse even. Will you then tell me I am also a Third World operator?

Servaas: Initially you'll be worse because you don't know anything but after a month you will do it better than he could ever dream to do. Then there is an additional factor and that is interest in the work. You know, he has no interest in farming, whether the enterprise is successful or not. He has no interest whether this tractor eh . . . whether money goes into it for repairs. He has no incentive.

Ernst: Wouldn't it be a solution to give it to him?

Servaas: No, no it makes sense to motivate him, to give him a stake but eh . . . you will understand it much better. I don't understand it very well. . . . The only way that is best is financial reward. Blacks are not interested in financial reward. This is really how it is over here. But I formulated it wrongly. I said he is not interested in [financial reward]. He is interested in it but it doesn't play such an important role with him as it plays with a Westerner. There are other additional things that come into play, eh, eh, responsibility—that can play a role.

Ernst: Let us go back in history a bit, the history of [a particular farm]. That time when these Bulldog Lanzes [name of a tractor] plowed here. If you arrived here at night—and everybody was talking about it—now that Ben [a black laborer] who worked for your father, plowed in the night. Why did that situation change? He and that old Karel were ideal workers. . . .

Servaas: No, there are still loyal blacks but, eh, their needs changed in the first instance, their thinking had been changed. You know Ben and Karel didn't even have access to a radio. He accepted the status quo as unchangeable, whereas the present ones don't accept it as unchangeable anymore. Your communication channels have become more direct. Currently most blacks see the white as an exploiter, and I wouldn't say without some justification but it is a fact. Karel considered my dad to be his father. You know, my father cared for him. That is why he had that attitude. Blacks currently look at me as a person that uses them for my own enrichment. You know, he considers his circumstances and he looks at mine. He compares how much work he does with how much I do—in terms of physical labor that is. Then he reasons that this is not right.

Ernst: How do you know that they look on the matter as you said?

Servaas: Well, conversations I had . . .

Ernst: Do you have problems?

Servaas: No, I have no problems but I hear of this from talks they have among themselves and when I ask them about something.

Ernst: So you said there is a greater distance between you and your blacks than between your father and Karel and Ben.

Servaas: No, that is definitely the case.

Ernst then reminded Servaas that he too had changed over the years and
that it was not so exceptional to have a different view of human relations
after decades. Servaas then asked Ernst what he thought was the reason
for the widening of the communication gap.

> *Servaas:* Do you know, my father, for example, bound that same Ben with a
> thong around his neck—the one who milked the cows—and beat him with
> a fan belt. I don't know [why] but he did something wrong. Y'know, that
> is the type of treatment the white meted out and the black accepted it—
> whereas I have never lifted my hand against any black in this place.

Ernst, whose orientation is more liberal, contested Servaas's economic
reasoning as well as his prejudice on the Third World character of blacks.
The above dialogue is interesting because Ernst challenged Servaas, who
then had to come up with rationalizations and justifications. Servaas's
vacillations about whether a farmer could not do without black labor or
whether he could cope alone revolved around the issue of hidden costs.
Servaas gave economic justifications for eliminating black labor: It was
a waste. His calculations did not make much sense. However, the racial
undertones of his argument were only thinly disguised. Blacks as a
category were stereotyped as incompetent by nature. This incompetence
was associated with the Third World. The Third World was furthermore
seen as inferior by nature. Since the times of the "docile" farm laborers,
the past two decades had been a time in which blacks developed a new
self-awareness. This seemed to have passed Servaas by. The stereotypes
he had of blacks blinded him to recent developments. The old form of
labor relations on the farms, paternalistic domination, was thus not possible anymore. The resistance he noticed among his laborers was simply
dismissed in racist terms and attributed to their backwardness or incompetence. All he noticed was the difference between the present black
generation and the "good," docile blacks of the past.
  The perception that black laborers are expensive and ungrateful is part
of the reason conservatives have striven to maintain a separate white
territory and economy. They believe an economy in which blacks receive
equal treatment will "slip back" into the Third World. Observations about
"good" blacks from olden times carry with them nostalgia for an age gone
by. The media ("more direct" communication channels) are blamed as the
culprits that changed blacks' minds. As a result of their activity, the new
breed of black laborers, with their Third World character, has become
dissatisfied with their situation and resents the relations that perpetuate it.

Yet they are not entitled to a share of the machines (see Ernst's question), nor would they "appreciate" higher wages.

Let us now follow the argument of a highly successful farmer, Jan. He and his friend Nic, also a farmer, spoke with me in Jan's small combined workshop and office behind his farmhouse. The farmhouse, built of stone, has been home to Jan's family for four generations. Except for the roof, the house survived burning by the British in the Anglo-Boer War.

Because this conversation raises a series of issues, the translated quote will not be interrupted by interpretation in order to demonstrate the associations and connections the speakers themselves made. I probed Jan's and Nic's views on the economic development of the "independent homelands." To them, these homelands demonstrate not only their Third World character but also the government's wasteful development strategies:

Nic: But why is our tax money being stolen; it is through absolute corruption . . . in the Transkei and this other one [homeland] that was in the news recently where he embezzled a couple of million rand. Why is there no control? Truly [*my magtig*], I cannot be independent but in the meantime I have to—I am still dependent on your money, but I am considering myself to be independent. And then money is pumped in without the recipient having to give back one cent in rand to the sponsor. That's not how it works, man. You just have to go and have a look at Lebowa with that Lebowa scum [*gom*; literally, "dirty, sticky glue"; here applied to black homeland officials]—where their government offices are. You just have to look there. The offices are empty, a whole wing, and there are thick carpets and air conditioning [a luxury] and everything of the best. Just look at the Mercedes Benzes in front of those buildings. Those things are paid for by us.

I know a guy over there and he tells me that they [blacks] were building a small bridge. There was a big concrete mixer, two tipper trucks, and a front-end loader and everything is there. But the bridge had to be built by hand. . . . They went to fetch the blacks. . . . They went at 8:00 to fetch them and they arrived at 9:00. Then they unloaded and they had to carry stones from a small hill nearby to build the bridge with. This business went on for months. The guy said with all that equipment one could have finished that thing within a week or maybe in four to five days. It is now more than six months. This is nonsense.

Jan: Our labor is going [disappearing]. They [the government] abolished influx control. Now he [the black laborer] moves away—this morning I happened to talk to a guy. The other day he spoke to the mayor of one of these locations [black townships near white cities]. The guy told the mayor, eh . . . the black mayor told the guy, "Really [*jislaaik*], you farmers are giving us a lot of trouble." The guy said, "Why, why—what makes you

think this way?" He said, "You, who [have] the people on the farm."
[From what followed, I realized that Jan was giving his own reconstruction of the situation.] You allow them to keep a few cattle and he [the laborer] has a lot of benefits. Then he goes and sells that cattle. And, you know, he has his cattle and then he receives a monthly salary and then after the harvest he receives a bonus and all these sorts of things. He [the mayor] said he then buys [sells?] his four cattle and he has R 4,000.00 and he takes that bonus and he goes here [into the homeland] and buys himself a stand. I think he buys a stand for R 180.00 and then he puts up a tin shack, you know, a corrugated iron *khaya* [dwelling] and he has that amount of money and he sits there and does nothing until the money runs out. Then he registers as an unemployed and then, my friend [*boeta*], I think they're getting now—I am not sure—I think they get approximately R 150.00 a month. That is what he gets and he sits there and does nothing. And we are beginning to have trouble [*teëspoed kry*] with our labor; we are not getting enough labor anymore.

I have a neighbor—and nothing is happening on his farm. He is not in debt but even if there is a bumper crop he wouldn't have any money because he has about no inputs. I think he is paying half the wages I am—if it is as much as that. But he always has too many because they are going to his farm and they are just sitting there because there is nobody to check on them. They work as they like to. They are working in the fields and . . . eh . . . you know, here with me, I expect that everyone should work. And I am telling you, he has too many and my wages are about double his. He [the black laborer] doesn't want to work. He will be satisfied with much less but he just wants to sit and do nothing.

I then asked him how he was recruiting and retaining labor under these circumstances:

Jan: You see I cannot—my farm requires—there is a lot of work on my farm. I cannot have them sit around not working. I considered many ways. I considered to build houses for them. Then I talked to another guy. He built some houses. Then, maybe, somebody dies in that house—a child, or somebody dies in that house. After a year or two, that family may move and then others refuse to live in that house. . . . We have a lot of problems in this regard. The guy saw that two or three of his houses were empty. They built again these mud huts of theirs. Those they built again. They refuse to live in that house [because] somebody died in that house. I think if that were the case with whites then all towns and houses must about be empty. . . .

Nic: But let us look at land that was bought in the area of Cullinan and those areas near Pretoria—beautiful houses that farmers left after their land was expropriated. No, my man, if they—if he [the black] reached the same level of civilization [*peil van ontwikkeling*] that I have, then he would have moved into that house and would have tried to improve his standard by living there. But no, the first thing he destroys are the window frames, which he sells—and also the door frames. It isn't long before he takes off the corrugated iron roof and then he starts to build a corrugated iron hut next to that house. And where does he make fire? He lights a fire in the bathtub in that lovely bathroom. That is his nature. Now, the Americans want to—I can't understand this—they don't really know our position— they [the blacks] don't have . . . [civilization].

Numerous stereotypes are present in these accounts. Basically, Jan and Nic believed that blacks could not be entrusted with running their own affairs in the homelands. These experiments were a waste of the white taxpayer's money, money that did not serve the (whites') public interest. Blacks, left to themselves, returned to a form of barbarism, sitting in the sun, doing nothing and wasting resources. They were unappreciative of efforts to help them. Even those efforts to give them decent housing were in vain because of their superstition or backwardness. Both speakers thought that a country ruled by blacks would be as chaotic and inefficient as the homelands they were talking about. Their images were formed and reinforced by selective observations made by themselves and others, probably white homeland officials. They cited with approval a mayor of a black township who condemned blacks as lazy and worthless. Jan tried to add legitimacy to his argument by quoting the mayor for essentially articulating Jan's own biases.

Jan and Nic resented the abolition of the apartheid law that regulated labor supply because it opened up the possibility for blacks to leave the farm and subsist on welfare in the homelands. The government's policies thus interfered with the farmers' labor supply. According to Jan, black laborers needed to be strictly controlled. Only under the strong command of the white man would they amount to anything. Jan had a reputation for treating his laborers harshly and punishing them severely and violently. While we were walking to the car, he explained to me that the only way to ensure their compliance was to instill the fear of death in them. If you treated them gently, they would lose respect and may challenge you. Other farmers told me that Jan had a very low turnover rate among his laborers.

Farmers like Jan hoped there would be an adequate and consistent labor supply in the future. The government, however, was seen as interfering with this vision. The relationship between farmer and laborer was one of mutual dependence. This dependence was hated by both sides.

DRAWING THE BOUNDARIES
BETWEEN BLACK AND WHITE

The rural whites interviewed for this study had a sharp awareness of the differences between blacks and whites. They drew solid physical and social boundaries between themselves and blacks. These boundaries were constructed and sustained by deeply held convictions and traditional values. On the surface, arguments emphasizing cultural and ethnic differences were used to justify treating blacks differently from whites. Sometimes, however, the whites' racism could not be disguised. The following quotation contains a very condensed set of boundary markers. I asked an influential farmer why power could not be shared with blacks in the same country:

There are thousands of examples. Here, at the beach in Durban: That John Rolfe helicopter they use for lifesaving was there all the time—and there are whites on the beach. I was there myself. The helicopter lands on the beach. When there is a problem it flies out to fetch the person. Then they [the city council] open the beaches to all races. Then they [the blacks] throw bottles at the helicopter. A civilized [*ontwikkelde*] person doesn't act that way. . . . That is life threatening. If those bottles strike the rotor there can be loss of life. That thing costs more than a million rand—but they are throwing bottles at it. I don't want to sound racist because I try my best to treat my workers well. If one comes up with a problem then I'll try to solve that problem to the best of my ability. But, do you know, before Christmas I was sitting here paying their wages and I was giving each a bonus. That day they took my truck to go to town in order to do their Christmas shopping. My wife told me, "Gee, you know they are mostly going to buy clothes for their children. You should have given them a bigger bonus." I then told them to come to the house after they fetched everybody. I then gave each an extra amount. Then I told my wife, "Look what is going to happen now." That night at twelve they called me. They were stabbing each other. One stabbed his brother-in-law and he stabbed some others. It was one hell of a fight. I can pay them R 1,000 a month and I guarantee to you that he will not improve his standard of living. He will gamble and drink and squander it and I am the one who will be damaged because I will get worse and worse labor from them.

Look, I grew up with them. Since I was a very small boy I played with them and grew up with them. I really know them well [*Ek ken hulle wragtig*]. I know them. Maybe there is one here or there who is different but even they . . . We made this Komati agreement with Mozambique. They [the blacks] scored much from the deal. They scored a lot. And we asked them not to let terrorists operate from their territory into ours. And this is how it went. He didn't fulfill his part of the deal. He is untrustworthy. No, what I say is that the thing culturally differs too much from us whites. I do not discriminate against him in this regard by saying he isn't human, but as I know the black and even the coloured, he would side with a show of force. That is why it is acceptable to the ANC to throw a bomb here or there. The reason why he does not respect us is because we have a sloppy government unable to act firmly and according to principle. What infuriates us Boers are these things we see around us each day.

This informant's three anecdotes all point in one direction: Blacks are untrustworthy. This lack of trust and sense of responsibility extends to them not only as laborers but as people in general. This farmer expressed the difference in cultural terms, yet he included all blacks in this category. This same person had previously objected to looking at blacks as a numerical bloc. Now, however, he lumped them together into one culture of treachery and violence. This informant talked of blacks in the third person and at one point even referred to the typical black as "the thing." He also denied that blacks have a sense of morality. He justified his views by pointing out that he considered himself to be knowledgeable, arguing that the fact that he grew up with blacks endowed him with a thorough knowledge of their character. Other informants indicated their beliefs that educating blacks would not change their "culture"—a high level of education would not eliminate their basic characteristics. This was held to be true for Africa in general; many informants pointed to independent African states as additional evidence of blacks' negative characteristics. They stated that training would not help either. According to their stereotypes, blacks were that way and nothing could be done to change their nature. Koos gave some examples:

A friend of mine works in Phalaborwa at a transport firm. He is still studying for his B.Com. degree. He is studying through UNISA [University of South Africa, a correspondence university], but there is a black director also [attached] to the so-called black bus service in Phalaborwa. Then there had to be brought in a black because there was black director—into the accounts section. And here comes *ta* [derogatory term for a black] with his B.Com. degree. Johnnie [Koos's friend] doesn't have a B.Com degree. He attended university for a year and then went farming. The farming wasn't a success and he went to work in town. He [Johnnie] says, when he leaves the office, when he leaves that boy alone, that boy stalls. He stalls so much that he can't even draw up a balance sheet. That is a B.Com black that cannot even draw up an ordinary little balance sheet. But, my friend, he gets the same salary.

Koos continued to expand his argument with reference to the prime farmland bought from whites for incorporation into one of the homelands. Fifteen years before, the government's development agency started training blacks to run the farm by themselves. However, Koos said that the farm is still run by white managers today. Another of his friends was training a black to run a chicken farm:

> They had this chicken farm where they trained a black. They reckoned that this, this boy [boytjie] could do this thing now [cope on his own], so they handed the farm over to him. I then saw my friend in Pretoria the other day and I said to him in amazement that it was strange to see him in Pretoria. He then showed me . . . that black went on for a few months. He went on [farming] and did not pay those people who supplied the chicken feed. He didn't have any money. Then my friend had to get another loan of R 20,000 to hand over to the black in order for him to pay his suppliers.

Koos was, of course, inconsistent in his reasoning. In the first case, Johnnie was a university dropout who had failed in farming. Koos somehow did not notice this or forgave him. However, he judged the obviously inexperienced young black graduate very severely.

These rural informants had face-to-face experiences with blacks on farms. From their limited experience, they generalized about blacks overall. They relied on rumor, anecdotes, and gossip for their information. The circles of friends and relatives from which they drew their information came from rural backgrounds and thus shared the experiences and interpretations of farmers. Some of these friends were working in one or another government-administered rural development agency. As white officials, they had farming experience and were employed on agricultural projects. Occupying the lower echelons of the bureaucratic structure, they exhibited a degree of envy if not resentment toward the blacks with whom they worked.[1] These individuals were sometimes aspiring farmers without land or farmers who had failed. It was not surprising that their views and those of the informants would converge.

The main way in which rural whites drew boundaries between themselves and blacks was to construct blacks as complete outsiders who had nothing in common with whites. Blacks were, however, not deemed to be strangers. The whites were familiar with blacks; they believed they had in-depth knowledge of blacks, their ways and their character, based on years of close contact and observation. It was extremely difficult to break through this barrier of self-righteousness. Notwithstanding their claimed knowledge and familiarity, they talked about "the black" in very anonymous terms. The vacuous term *the black [die swarte]* was used to typify all blacks. The black as type stood for virtually everything the white is not. It was a negative mirror image. It was almost possible to construct the ideal self-image of these whites simply by inverting what they had to say about blacks. The more extreme conservatives could see virtually no common humanity shared between themselves and the blacks.

SOME SELF-PERCEPTIONS OF RURAL WHITES

As noted above, the perception among whites was that a people's pride is essential to its survival and that the color of one's skin is important. In much of the interview material gathered in this study, the notions of skin color (i.e., race heredity and descent) and ethnicity or nationalism (i.e., tradition and culture) tend to blend into an undifferentiated construction of the in-group. In the previous section we saw how one farmer explained, "No, what I say is that the thing culturally differs too much from us whites." This is a perfect example of that blending. Racism confronts us in the guise of ethnicity, or, more specifically, as ethnocentrism. After discussing the ANC, Jan, one of the farmers interviewed, switched the topic abruptly to something different. The sequence was as follows. He first commented on the ANC as the enemy of the white, then he spoke about whites' reaction to Barend Strydom's mass murder of blacks in Pretoria, and then he and his friend Nic went on to discuss the position of the coloureds and their descent. Although these were three disparate topics, the undertone that unified them was that of race; race was the associative principle that connected them. Another connecting factor was the perceived "stupidity" of the government: its lack of reason and its inability to comprehend what really was going on. There was great hostility and emotion in his voice as he spoke:

Jan: I cannot understand all the whites. When this guy shot the blacks in Pretoria—I arrived at my sister's in Pretoria. She said, "Just look what this guy had done. Everybody saw it—how a white racist acted—and he acted out of hate or whatever in killing those blacks." She said, "Look what he did. This will only fire the hate of the blacks. Now you will see how they murder whites." Then I told her, "For how long have they been murdering the old [white] people? You must know this yourself. For how long were they doing that? Why is there no outcry about that? Why does nobody see this as hate that is fanned? But now, when this guy went and shot blacks he is a racist but nobody moans about all the old people killed on the farms."

Nic: Another thing that irritates me is the [argument about] the coloureds. Surely you must have read the same history books as I did.

Interviewer: . . . must be.

Nic: You know, these National Party politicians want us to believe that we were the creators of the coloureds. I am from the Cape, my pal, and the coloured we are talking about over there is surely not the creation of the whites. The so-called *baster* [literally, "bastard"], they never talk about—the politicians don't talk about the *basters* we know from the Cape where white blood was indeed involved. The polemic is not about them—they are fewer than the whites under your fingernails [?]. There are a few in Rehoboth in Southwest and here low down on the West Coast and in those [here the tape is indistinct] parts. But they are not part of the polemic. The polemic is about the coloured.

Jan: Where does the coloured get his so-called Afrikaans surname?

Nic: Those years when there was still loyalty—between the coloured and the white—he simply took his child's name from the surname of the white master [*oubaas*] on whose farm he had been living all those years. He took his child's name from him. Now I am asking who were the three yellow nations at the Cape when Jan van Riebeeck arrived? The Griqua, the Bushman, and the Hottentots—and later on there was a fourth yellow group imported, the Malay. Now, do you want to tell me they stopped breeding? They bred among themselves. You know, Julies [a coloured parliamentarian] told P. W. Botha in the Parliament, "Listen, I am not related to you [*Ek is niks van jou nie*—meaning 'I am not your relative']. When you whites set foot on this land my great grandmother was looking at you from the shore." In other words, he admitted that he was a nation on his own. Now, I am saying if the white did create the coloured, do you want to tell me that our creative urge [*skeppingsdrang*] was so weak, or that our creative—our genetic part was so weak that we could not breed their characteristics out of our midst, characteristics such as the head, that curly hair, those thick lips, and those blue gums [his voice filled with disgust]? I am telling you pal, they so badly want to lay the poverty of those nations at my doorstep for me to dip even deeper into my pocket in order to try and bridge the gap. Sorry, I am not doing this—I don't believe it.

Both the assertion about the condemnation of the racist killer and the excursus on the coloureds described the implicit assumptions Jan and Nic make about their in-group in an inverted way. Nic employed the term *nation* to indicate the distinctness and otherness of coloureds in a cultural sense, while at the same time using "genetic" evidence to support his argument. Jan did not exonerate Strydom's act of murder, but he was indignant about its being attributed to racism. He understood the murder of white elderly people on farms to be racial killings, and he was angry because the label of racism was applied one-sidedly. He did not condemn racism, however. The assumptions the speakers had about their in-group could thus be articulated as "We are not racist. We are a racially and culturally distinct nation."

As an aside, I was left with the impression that the mass killings of blacks were understood to be redress for the murders of whites. At the Monument celebrations in May 1990, this impression was reinforced by the talk I heard around the stalls where money was collected for the defense of the killer, Strydom. It was a disturbing thought that an in-group morality could possibly accommodate this sort of violence toward an out-group. In the years that followed, there were several instances of whites in rural areas shooting indiscriminately at blacks from moving cars. Some blacks were killed.

Apart from race or descent as markers for the white in-group, culture was also considered to be crucial. We will later notice how the cultural and racial arguments were telescoped into each other.

Servaas, who attempted to rid his farm of black labor but found it well-nigh impossible, was discussing the disadvantages of the melting pot idea with Chris, an urban Afrikaner intellectual with rural roots. Servaas wanted strict territorial separation because, to him, white domination was ethically untenable and practically impossible in any future South Africa. A [black] majority would also monopolize power. Servaas thought that a separate white territory would be the only solution. Chris challenged him, and the following discussion ensued:

Servaas: [Separate territory] . . . this is how I see the future for myself and for my children.

Chris: But that is when you take the [here the tape is indistinct] as your point of departure. If you take values people might share, for example, then I can share with many black people and coloureds—we can have the same basis. We can be Christians together, we can be members of the NG Church together, we can [share] democracy and whatever more there is to share. What happens to this business about minority and majority then?

Servaas: Chris, the trouble is, if . . . eh . . . if you consider yourself a white Afrikaner, or if you consider yourself a South African—these are two things.

Chris: —but why can't I be both?

Servaas: —because your Afrikanerness [*Afrikanerskap*] is defined by history in terms of certain principles—

Chris: —but those principles I am sharing with many other people.

Servaas: No, no you do not share your whiteness [*blankeskap*] with the coloured.

Chris: Okay, but I share my language and I share my faith with him.

Servaas: No, you don't share your language. A coloured speaks a different language.

Chris: [At an occasion] where there are coloureds and whites—if I turned my back I wouldn't know whether a coloured or a white was talking. . . .

Servaas: But anyway, these things are not important. What is important to me—and the reason I say it is unimportant is because I do not differ from you that you can share values with them like religion. Democracy—you will have a problem because he has a different idea about democracy than you. Some of them have the same idea about democracy that you have but the majority does not have that idea of democracy. And there are many things you know about, moral standards and other things, I can share with them. In politics power is at stake. Power is the definition of politics, and power is used. Power that isn't used isn't power anymore. In the beginning you will have the situation as soon as he gets power, he will use it to do unto the white what the white had done to him all those years. This is why I say you'll have a period that is not going to be nice. I am not prepared to go through that period. You know his objective will be to break the Afrikaner because the Afrikaner oppressed him, and he sees the Afrikaner as a threat, and his purpose will be to break the Afrikaner. That is how I see it. I am not saying it should be like this, but this is my view.

Chris: You are thus arguing that our dilemma is of our own making.

Servaas: Yes, but . . . eh . . . without having a sense of guilt about it. I don't have a sense of guilt because one has acted in terms of a certain upbringing and a certain perspective you had on life and I don't blame [*verkwalik*] myself for this.

In comparison with Jan and Nic, Servaas held a definition of the in-group that was less stark and, on the surface, less blatantly racist. Jan and Nic saw blacks as a disenfranchised labor force with roots and rights in their own territories. Their presence and behavior in "white" areas would be strictly controlled. Servaas, however, had ethical objections to *baasskap* (domination). He attempted to define the core of his whiteness and Afrikanerness with reference to both historically founded principles and language. When challenged, however, he dropped that strategy and locked on to the central point of power sharing and democracy. Chris was able, with a few questions and remarks, to shave away the ideology of culture, revealing the actual in-group, racial interests underlying Servaas's rhetoric. The realm of politics would, according to his view, ultimately determine the fate of the in-group. The only way to escape this was to have a separate territory. We will come back to this issue in the section headed "Fears and Visions," below.

For Servaas, the white Afrikaners were the in-group. He simply ignored the issue of sharing that Chris raised. An interesting switch occurred when he thought that points Chris raised were not important. He agreed verbally that "sharing" with "them," presumably the coloureds, was possible, but as soon as he turned to power and politics he started using the personal pronoun *he*. As in Jan and Nic's discussion, this "he" was the abstract generic black, appearing in this particular instance in the role of the vengeful majority seeking redress. It is also significant that Servaas had no sensitivity for the role whites played in bringing about such a situation. It neutralized his ethical qualms about domination, but was also indicative that he took for granted that the in-group in which he was a member was a racial one in the first place.

Returning to people like Jan and Nic, who supported white self-rule in the existing geographic entity of "white" South Africa, we see how they blamed the government for the deterioration of the quality of life and peace of whites. Foreign elements such as capitalists and communists intruded and changed the South African polity. The rural CP supporters wanted a restoration of the racial laws of the 1960s. They felt that the government was wrong in abolishing apartheid laws, because those laws served the purpose of preserving whites as a category. The ultimate fear was that blacks might get the vote and then "we will be voted out of our own fatherland." The reinstatement of laws such as the Mixed Marriages Act, the Immorality Act, the Group Areas Act, Influx Control (the Blacks [Urban Areas] Act), and laws proscribing political interference, especially the security laws, was essential for maintaining white unity and whites' control over their own affairs. They wanted reempowerment as a group. They wanted their fundamental right to self-rule in the existing geographic South Africa.

Many whites felt not only victimized but assailed. The rhetoric at the rally held at the Monument in Pretoria in May 1990 confirmed this.

Therefore, many of them adopted a militant stance and vocabulary. A particularly hated out-group were the "traitors," Afrikaners who were expected to show loyalty and solidarity but failed to do so. Instead, traitors took up the cause of the enemy. They were considered a powerful force because they bore the signs of their appearance and language and could thus effectively and unobtrusively move among the in-group. Traitors were singled out as the most dangerous category of enemies and, if it came to a revolution, these were the persons to be eliminated first. Since the death squads linked to the Civil Cooperation Bureau, a government agency, were exposed in 1990 and 1991, many right-wing organizations have been alleged to have had strong links with the killings of white liberals and dissidents such as the anthropologist David Webster and civil rights lawyer Anton Lubowski in Namibia.

FEARS AND VISIONS

Among those with an ideal of a separate exclusive white territory and those who hoped to maintain white supremacy in the present South Africa there was great apprehension about the possibility of a unitary state (*eenheidstaat*) shared by whites and blacks. In the eyes of these whites such a state would be a melting pot (*smeltpot*) that would ultimately lead to the disappearance of the Afrikaner and other whites in South Africa. In such a unitary state the whites would not rule themselves; they would be subject to a black majority rule. They would thus be powerless. This loss of power would lead to the loss of everything, because they would not be able to control their own fate. They were therefore prepared to make great personal sacrifices and to tolerate a significant drop in their standard of living as long as they could be assured of white autonomy in a white sovereign state. They were already suffering disadvantages because of the "unfairly bestowed favors" that the period of reform brought to blacks. This made them more apprehensive. They related numerous stories about what they considered reverse discrimination: stories about whites and blacks with equal qualifications on paper yet the blacks reportedly earned more, and stories about blacks with inferior qualifications earning the same as whites. The indignation of these white speakers did not so much deal with reverse discrimination as with equal pay for equal work, because they simply believed that blacks did not have the ability to do work equal in quality to that of whites.

Rural whites feared that majority rule would also bring the revenge of the black population upon them (as Servaas spelled out in the dialogue quoted above). Whites feared that blacks would mete out the same discriminatory treatment to them as they had to the blacks. It was especially feared that Afrikaners would be singled out for revenge because of their leading role in oppression. Whites' fears about a black takeover were also directly linked to their perception of how blacks governed states in Africa and how white residents were treated after these states became independent from their colonial masters. The worst aspects of African dictatorships—tyrants, state corruption, famine, genocide, and related phenomena—were cited. Knowledge about other areas of Africa that offered a less pessimistic picture was sadly lacking among informants. Rural whites tended to use antiquated names when referring to states in Africa, such as Congo (for Zaire; see below), Rhodesia (for Zimbabwe; see below), and Southwest (for Namibia; see below). These usages were current in the postcolonial periods of white exodus in the wake of internal unrest in certain black states. This perception of Africa was also consciously selective because it fit the pattern of the stereotype of black racial incompetence, inferiority, and depravity. Rural conservatives could not understand the current government's lack of insight into these matters:

> This one man, one vote: This will lead to the downfall of the white in this country as sure as the sun rises and sets. I thus have proof from all the countries in Africa. All the countries around form a list. If you give him power, then he has the military power. If he governs, he also has the military might and then it is finished with the white man in that country. What I mean is that we do not need to do experiments here. The experiments had been done north of us. Okay, maybe we can't compare everything on the same scale, but the experiments have already been done north of us. We only have to look toward the north. Then we'll see whether this thing [black government] is going to work over here, and it did not work over there. Everywhere where the white fled from Kenya or the Congo, where the white fled—here are people [in our town] I know who came from there and the country was ruined. But now I want to ask these intelligent people what they wish to achieve when they can see it did not work over there.

This speaker thus called on commonsense perceptions of recent postcolonial African history. He was unable to understand how the South African government could be so blind to the consequences of black rule. The resolution of these fears lay in the retention of white hegemony through a strong government. At the time of this particular interview, January 1989, a general election was still to be held. Many rural people were confident that the Conservative Party would win. This proved to be a false hope. The National Party carried the majority vote in September that year. As the National Party proceeded with its reform program, the right-wing Conservatives seemed to have gained ground in both rural and urban areas because their fears of future majority rule were fanned by the release of Nelson Mandela early in 1990 and the repeal of important apartheid laws in June 1991. Majority rule was the nightmare scenario for informants. In 1989 I confronted one farmer with the scenario of black majority rule. He reacted as follows:

> Look, we have to fight until the last and as a last resort one has to try violence. I think this is what is going to happen—this is what is going to happen last, because look, you have to think about this carefully. It is not easy to say it just like this, and then you don't do it, because it is going to be ugly—but I do think as a last resort. Look, we have no place to flee to. There is no place we could go to. We moved from the Cape to this area and the country is full of Rhodesians. There are Rhodesians who came here and now Southwesters will also come. They will come here. We have nowhere . . . eh we will, . . . look totally in the last instance we will . . . [*ons sal seker . . .*]. You hear somebody says so easily . . . oh . . . he just emigrates. Before I go to another country with a totally different—a nation with another culture and tradition, I will perish [*vrek*] here, but may I tell you one thing, the day I go I want to, I want to—if there is a revolution in this country—I guarantee you today—I will not shoot the kaffirs first. I'll shoot the liberal whites first because it is they who [forced?] me out. This I guarantee you.

Before he talked about emigration, this speaker hesitated and stuttered and then switched to the third person. Nevertheless, whether he made up his mind to leave under majority rule or after the revolution or not I do not know. What is important for this discussion is his feeling of being cornered, of having run out of options. Again and again, rural conservatives said "our only alternative," "our only option," "our only hope," or the "only solution" is either a separate territory or the continuation of the status quo. If these "only" options were impossible, the final resort would be violence. In light of some of the violent confrontations that have occurred between police and conservative rural whites, centering mainly on the paramilitary Afrikaner Weerstandsbeweging's resistance to reform, this alternative has proved not to be merely a theoretical one. We have seen how the fanatical right-wing opposition to the government led to violence in the Western Transvaal town of Ventersdorp, where three right-wingers were killed.

VALUES: RATIONALIZATIONS
AND CONTRADICTIONS

The rural white Afrikaners interviewed for this study saw themselves as friendly, hospitable people. They were Christians and members of Calvinist-based churches. They subscribed to their churches' doctrines. In their own eyes, they were decent, honest, and kind people who loved their fellow men.

> This farmer, this fellow who wanted to load five sheep onto his light truck—and he had there these two black men who were—the one was 70 and the other 80—very old people. They were so weak that they couldn't hold those sheep properly. They had to catch them in pairs. One then opened the tailgate of the truck . . . and he dropped it because the sheep jumped away—which they—which they were holding and then the farmer hit him full in the face so that the blood flowed. But those sheep they had to load were on their way to a church auction. Do you understand this? He [the farmer] . . . eh, was doing something so good. He was taking five sheep to the church and he still justified the whole thing. Now, it seems to me there is a certain area the fellow does not bring in line with his conscience.

Ernst, the liberal-minded rural Afrikaner, told me this story about a scene he had witnessed. We had been discussing discrepancies that existed between people's beliefs and their actions. He previously had told me he felt shame when talking about these things his fellow Afrikaners were doing to blacks. On occasions such as the one in this story there were usually onlookers, children, both white and black, and others. In this incident, when the truck tailgate was dropped it might have been slightly damaged. This was the trigger for the farmer to lash out, assaulting and humiliating the elderly black men who were loading the sheep. Ernst related that the farmer then went about his business as usual, not caring about what he had done. The farmer did not relate his "good deed" of giving the sheep to the church to the humiliation and violence inflicted on the old black men; he failed to make this rather blatant connection. It was as if the act of unbridled assault did not count in the context of his good deed of giving to charity. Furthermore, it was not exceptional for him or others to do something like this—not even before witnesses, not even in front of children in a community where the elderly are normally revered. Bluntly put: Did the white farmer consider these elderly blacks to be fellow humans, fathers or grandfathers? Did he regard them as lesser beings? Every indication is that the farmer did not deem his behavior abnormal or reprehensible. The blacks were regarded as dehumanized outsiders, without the needs, feelings, or dignity of whites. The fact that, to other white bystanders, such behavior was not unusual or outrageous is another indication of how thoroughly the farmer's unquestioned assumption was shared among them (with the exception of a person like Ernst). During 1991 the South African press reported that increased numbers of blacks were being randomly killed by rural whites (National Puplic Radio, August 22, 1991). White judges often responded to these incidents with lenient sentences.

Contradictions between the deepest held values of neighborly love and acts of hate did not enter into the consciousness of these actors. Tacit agreements about what one could do to blacks for the most part went unchallenged. Where they were challenged, processes of rationalization set in. The very denials that informants made concerning their racism and discrimination illustrate this point. We have seen the strategies they used to protect themselves from these accusations. They denied racism, covering it with the argument that their differential treatment of blacks was merely their expression of a desire to maintain and protect their own culture in their own territory, a right granted to black persons. Thus they translated the racial argument into a cultural one. The cultural rationalization, of course, could draw on worldwide support for notions such as "cultural pluralism" or "multiculturalism."

Apart from these *ideological rationalizations,* there were political rationalizations. In a long discussion, Ernst argued that the politicization of reality was a very damaging process. When asked why, he said:

Do you know what troubles me most is that the human being, and I'm sorry to say this, that the Afrikaner, the true Afrikaner [*regte Afrikaner*] has the greatest difficulty in determining what is right and what is wrong. I mean, regardless of politics all these things are jeopardized in the arena of politics, but at the end of the day something is right or wrong and I think the Afrikaner has difficulty in seeing the difference—what is right and what is wrong. There are things in me I have to fight against because I had to decide what is right and what is wrong. But I think my background and maybe my inborn differentiation between black and white make it very difficult to process certain things. If one decided what is right and what is wrong—it is the only way you can act. In my view, this has nothing to do with politics. But all these things are being coupled to politics. If you do something wrong you simply bring it into connection with politics because that road is prepared for you, [the road] that maintains you have to disallow blacks certain things. Do you understand? You don't need to decide whether it is right or wrong. All you do is to say it is politics. This nauseates me.

According to Ernst's argument, politics was being used to exonerate the individual from dealing with the situation in terms of his or her personal conscience. Politics is a preconfigured rationalization, and one need not consult it to decide on a particular course of action. This is a useful distinction, and it highlights the authoritarian nature of the attitude toward politics. The rationale behind the attitude is this: The leaders have thought about this, and in their wisdom they have come up with recipe solutions such as "No rights for blacks in 'white' territory." Conservative whites could then treat blacks in the spirit of this tenet without thinking about right and wrong. This is what I call the political rationalization, or rather the *authoritarian rationalization.*

Finally, there is the *rationalization of common sense.* Real-life examples of the incompetence of blacks, their inferiority, and a host of other negative characteristics were given by informants. The informants never regarded these as prejudice or interpretation; they were facts. The anecdotes had the ring of truth because they were not only produced by persons predisposed to see blacks negatively but they were formulated as accounts in the interactional field of people sharing those beliefs and experiences about blacks. Their very selective drawing upon the so-called chaotic state of affairs in African countries and the "lessons" that purportedly emanated from those countries to South Africa endowed the arguments attached to them with the claims of common sense and thus "irrefutable" truth.

In combination, the three forms of rationalization constitute a mode of reasoning that perpetuates itself through its constant use by people sharing these convictions. This combination approximates Max Weber's ideal types of emotional and traditional rationalization. The rural whites interviewed for this study prided themselves on their knowledge of blacks. They shared very strong in-group feelings, with accompanying senses of moral rectitude and insider intellectuality. They were members of a moral community whose insider morality stopped at the boundary of the racially other. The same rules did not apply to "them" and "us." The distance between insiders and outsiders was marked by a moral, not spatial, boundary separating immoral, irresponsible, incompetent outsiders from their white opposites. Sometimes physical appearance was perceived to be disgusting and symbolic of blacks' worth. Yet both whites and blacks were locked in this symbiotic relationship that could last only as long as the mastery of the white man was recognized by both parties. Anyone who wanted to change this system undermined its integrity. Such a person was perceived as an immoral being whose actions could destroy the moral community and who therefore may be worthy of elimination. Opposition to liberal politics and to the government, which appeared to be liberal, was therefore fierce.

I should insert a word of caution here. The particular area I studied may lead the reader to construct an image of an extreme type of conservative farmer. Yet, there was an undeniable pattern found that originated in the paradox of the simultaneous indispensability and unacceptability of blacks in white eyes. It was this paradox that the farmer quoted in the next section wished to bypass with his own solution of self-help and total exclusion of blacks from his world of work and experience.

EXCURSUS: A GOTHIC AFRIKANER
AND HIS FRAGILE UTOPIA

The Oranjewerkers are members of a movement that insists on having a separate territory for whites in which blacks would not be allowed. The main principle of the movement is that whites should become absolutely independent of black labor. Before the physical creation of such a social and geographic utopia, members of the movement advocate practicing the principle of *selfwerksaamheid,* or doing one's own work.

On a sunny day during the summer of 1989, I approached the farm of an Oranjewerker whom I will call Kobus. He and his family had a reputation for doing all their farm work by themselves. As I arrived, I saw how the ranch-style house's low roof was dwarfed by the huge barn close to it. There were no laborers' huts or houses to be seen. No luxuries such as flower beds or mowed lawns surrounded the house, near which some white children were playing. Kobus came out to welcome me. His face and arms were deeply tanned—more deeply than I have ever seen on a white. Kobus was welcoming and friendly toward me as a stranger. We went into the house, where the furnishings were simple but functional—many of them heirlooms. We sat down at the dinner table and started talking. I explained what my research was about and we discussed his ideas about the country, labor, and the future. He was a strong man, but he spoke in a cultivated voice.

He had a master's degree, and he argued from conviction backed up by study and experience.

Kobus's farm was near the town of Morgenzon, a small white settlement of about 500 people in the Eastern Transvaal. The town had received much publicity in the Afrikaans press and was ridiculed because of what journalists saw as the residents' wish to turn back the clock. Very few people in the Oranjewerkers movement were as consistent as Kobus in running their farms solely by themselves. At Morgenzon there were between 30 and 40 Oranjewerkers who met about once a month. All were trying to implement *selfwerksaamheid* by cutting down on black labor. In the town, some of the Oranjewerkers ran a fiberglass shop, a garage, and a clothing store. The others were mostly farmers.

Kobus and his wife owned some huge agricultural machines. The tractors dwarfed the house. Kobus had made electronically controlled multiple-row planters himself. He and his wife worked very long hours to cultivate their farm. They had very little leisure time. Yet, he said:

> *Kobus:* It isn't a problem to farm this way, but when one person does it this way, or when a few individuals do it this way, one encounters problems. There are no problems running a farm this way as a system. To start it is a problem. To run it here, like in Europe or America, isn't a problem. If I could mention an example: Prices of certain agricultural products will change. I would say if vegetables were produced by whites they will become more expensive. Grain will probably be cheaper. We will probably be able to produce grain along American lines and prices. If you produce something, a commodity, that requires a rise in price to make the whole venture possible, then you have problems to get out of the system.
>
> *Schutte:* Do you think that farming in this way, doing your own labor, will be exemplary to other whites?
>
> *Kobus:* I think it depends. . . . People will continue in their old ways until things become too hot, you know, but in the final analysis you break down resistance to this thing by practicing what you preach. Ultimately there are two choices in South Africa. We cannot maintain a system on institutionalized domination [*baasskap*]. There is no doubt about this. It is only a matter of time—but I think the Afrikaner has territorial rights he could exercise in his own area. The size and position are irrelevant as long as you agree on the principle. The problem in South Africa is this: You cannot accommodate Afrikaner nationalism in a black and coloured government. That is the problem and that is the fact of the matter. In other words, people are steering toward a tremendous problem. Even if you would normalize matters according to Western standards through democratization, you will

have immense clashes; you will have tremendous clashes because the Afrikaner proved himself and learned that, if he wants to cause trouble, he surely will. The problem here is, you know—to subject the Afrikaner to a foreign government is basically the same as the threat [*storie*] to subject the British to German rule. Do you know they [the British] were prepared to fight to the last man. The principle involved is the same: We will have to get something in South Africa that can accommodate Afrikaner nationalism, you know, and this is the only way, the only method to achieve a devolution of powers in order that nobody in the end—that there will no longer be a system of discrimination. There is no other way. It is no solution to replace white domination with black domination for the simple reason that they are the majority. This is not going to solve anything.

Schutte: Some politicians suggest that whites should have the choice between joining a common multiracial setup and a smaller exclusive Afrikaner state. What is your opinion?

Kobus: I think one has to keep in mind that you would not be able to have group protection in a mixed setup because group protection by its nature is also unacceptable because, you know, it boils down to a system of privileging one group. It is not possible to differentiate without discriminating in a unitary setup. In other words, hopefully there will ultimately be a democracy with one person, one vote on the surface. I say hopefully, because I mean that I hope it is not going to be some form of Africa socialism on the surface, or a dictatorship, a black dictatorship. In the last instance, there should be full devolution of powers and a man desiring to live there would be welcome to do so. You know, you would not be able to force anybody to the one side or to the other. It won't work. If one looks at our discriminating laws, the differentiating laws where a man was prohibited to marry a black woman. This would be absolutely meaningless [in a unitary setup] to prohibit such a man to marry a black woman. I think one should be sure of oneself and sure of the fact that white domination is going to disappear. All we have to look for is whether we can keep a territory [for ourselves]. In other words, [in a unitary setup] not one of these political parties like the NP or the KP [Konserwatiewe Party, or Conservative Party] would be able to maintain their policies of white domination.

Schutte: Would such a separate territory not be surrounded by the rest of South Africa? What would the relationship be between the white territory and the surrounding area?

Kobus: Look, I would say there are a few preconditions. It should be at least an economically viable state with preferably an access to the sea. In other words, it should be able to occupy a place among the nations of the world. It will be an economic part—it will be interdependent with the whole of southern Africa. By its nature it would not produce [use] every little thing it needs. It will trade like any other country in the world and its number-one trading partner will probably be the rest of the Republic of South Africa. Its number-two trading partner will probably be the rest of southern Africa. But it is very important to remember that it should be independent in the last instance. Otherwise, it would not be able to accommodate Afrikaner nationalism. I do not want to say "neutralize," but "accommodate," in the sense that the potential for conflict could be removed. In this way it should probably be a fully independent country. One could speculate of course about a canton system, that it [the white territory] could be a canton, but that will probably not work in the sense of . . . There is an inclination among especially the liberals, the English [speakers] and so forth, that we—you see—water down the power of the central government to such an extent that it would not matter whether it was a black government or not. That is essentially what they are saying. They want a weak government similar to that of Switzerland in order for them [the government] not to have any power. In other words, each individual has the maximum degree of freedom and [it is assumed that] there will be no problems. There will be no domination and there will be a bill of human rights. They think that will be successful but there are grave problems with this [assumption]. You know, the blacks will ask themselves why the whites had one of the strongest centralized governments when they ruled and why they made it as weak as possible when we took over. We won't accept that.

In the end, blacks will work out a system on their own. Whites cannot work out a system beforehand, saying, "Well, I am handing the reins of government to you but this system is not to be changed." You know, this has a potential for conflict. In my opinion this land [of whites] must finally be fully independent.

Schutte: Would such a country not be throttled by South Africa as with Lesotho?

Kobus: [Lesotho] is throttled economically, not geographically. We will have to be economically independent, otherwise we won't be independent at all. You know there are many countries in Africa that aren't economically independent. In the end theirs is an independence that doesn't mean a thing, you know. In other words we'll have to run a highly mechanized, highly automated, highly technological economy with our highly skilled people. One will have to have a Western, Third World [I think he meant First World] type of economy. I feel confident that we can ask people to create such an economy. I think the Japanese also proved to us that he isn't dependent on the land. He is not dependent on minerals, but he is dependent on human material. I think we have the human material to achieve our ends. This is one side of the economy. The other side is when we look at a unitary state. . . . One need not be an economist to understand that the greater the Third World component of your nation is, the closer you will be to a Third World economy. I don't want to speak in a discriminatory fashion. Whatever the facts of the case might be, we won't be able to sustain a Third World [?] economy in South Africa. We are witnessing it. You know, economically we are busy sinking; we are going down. In the end, I thus see no possibility that the rest of South Africa could squeeze us economically as we did with Lesotho.

Schutte: Would other population groups have access to such a territory?

Kobus: That is a matter of detail. One does not want a racial state in the first instance. I mean, we are a people's state [*volkstaat*]. We are talking of an Afrikaner people's state. It is not a white state. The detail of the thing is—we hope that once it is normalized, it could function in a normal way as any other country of the world. There are, however, specific circumstances that apply to us that do not apply to other countries. But eh, I would say we have to—if we—if the whole exercise need not be subtle we have to admit immigrants from countries of our origin/descent [*stamlande*]. You see a country such as America, and various European countries and so forth, can accommodate percentages [of] people of a totally different cultural and racial origin without encountering serious problems. In our case we will be a people—if we're lucky—of 1.5 million. You know we would simply not have room to accommodate 1.5 million blacks while maintaining our identity. In other words, we will definitely have to maintain it. As we acquired it and created it, we have to assert it [*handhaaf*].

Schutte: Tell me, how did you come to these conclusions about the future of the Afrikaner?

Kobus: I tell you, it was a long way I had to go, but I have to tell you that I realized about in matric [senior year in high school] that there was something that was not going to work out. That was in high school. Until I joined the Oranjewerkers I did not belong to any association. Nothing made sense to me. Up to the present, I have to tell you, the thinking of the Oranjewerkers has changed a lot. I don't know whether you realize that at one stage it was actually SABRA [South African Bureau of Racial Affairs] that petitioned the government to start white growth points. There was nothing else behind the initiative and SABRA had—at least the government did not agree with SABRA and their policy at the time and cut off all their funds. In that way the Oranjewerkers were weaned. I have to say that during the past 10 years the status quo in South Africa sank quickly and deeply, you know. We realized then, you know, that there was only one solution for the Afrikaner—the people's state. I don't know whether you've noticed that a philosophy underlies this [view]. We feel that from a general perspective people's states are faring better than the melting pots. You know—for example, Russia is an artificial unitary state in the process of falling apart. They definitely have extreme problems. America, of course, is a country that keeps on stirring the pot in order to prevent a situation from polarizing. As far as I am concerned I am not so convinced that the American system will ultimately be successful. So finally, I think that people's states are the most stable socioeconomic units because they are doing well economically and politically they are stable—and, you know, that is when you compare them with the melting pots of the world. In the last instance that is what laid the foundation for me in deciding that the only hope of the Afrikaner was to go for the people's state. Well, I am convinced that this is a relatively new idea among the Afrikaner. The Afrikaner never had a strong desire for a territory of their own. The trek to the North, and what happened thereafter, was mainly to avoid domination—but, you know, we all saw they had no problem with dominating others. At a certain stage political parties seriously debated the issue of a white territory or white territories, though there never existed any white territory, not even white residential areas. In the final analysis, if you strip off those peels and look at the matter in a straight and honest way you have to confront the issue and decide what you want to do and what you want to have.

We established contact with a number of, eh, people. I can't even remember, but you know the problem of Quebec—and then we had a few Bretons over here—they feel that their problems—if you consider that they are fairly close to each other in a cultural sense—for example, we might not have had such a problem if the Dutch suddenly took over the government. Should an Englishman, for example, consider himself to be ruled by India—it is more—it is closer to the cultural difference and gap, or the cultural shock the Afrikaner would experience under black majority rule. You know, in my opinion one doesn't even have to go into the moral considerations of the issue. It is a simple fact that it is not going to work. To submit the Afrikaner to black majority rule is not going to work. It will definitely generate conflict. This model of the National Party that argues for a system where everybody will have a say in the government on an equal basis and at the highest level means, if they are honest about it, black majority rule. And then, power; the political power will rest, in the final analysis, with a person from a specific race, from a specific nationality. That is the problem you know, and, in the end, I don't know whether a method exists for eliminating domination in a unitary state.

Schutte: Returning to your situation here on the farm: You are working very hard while many other members of your group lead an easy life without much manual labor and a lot of free time. Do you experience your lifestyle as a sacrifice?

Kobus: I won't—I won't say I always have the same attitude—have a consistent attitude to all of this. But, you know, I believe in this thing as the only solution and therefore we must practice what we preach. It is, however, more of a challenge to me than a sacrifice. The challenge pales somewhat when you have financial problems like the whole agricultural sector in

South Africa today. You know, one starts feeling that one doesn't need that challenge anymore. But I definitely do not take it as a sacrifice but rather as a challenge. I have been to America and I saw many places where people did not have lawns. The problem is that we want to prove something over here. We have to prove to these people that we also have lawns—that we have nice houses. Otherwise we have problems, and I saw over there [in America] that houses are not cleaned every day from back to front. But we have this situation over here that, when you look at the competition, then we have to keep our houses clean, et cetera. Then we have to devise all sorts of new plans and then it becomes a challenge.

Schutte: Americans of course have time-saving devices.

Kobus: We have the same in South Africa. I would say we have the same machines they have, but when I was over there I did not see them having anything of importance we do not have over here.

We left Kobus's home together, and he drove out to one of his fields. I stopped when I saw him turn off the road and approach his tractor and planter. It was already late in the afternoon, but he had decided to go back to work, to utilize what was left of daylight. The tractor started with a puff of black smoke. He waved as he moved off.

NOTE

1. This is based on personal observation made during anthropological fieldwork in the homelands.

9

Whites in Town I:
Conservative Perspectives

Duty

It was a land . . .
without the wheel, the lamp, a match to light a fire;
without a book, pencil, or pen;
without a blanket.
Nobody could make a button; no one could make a buttonhole to fasten his skins.
Superstition, plague, and famine threatened the land and dominated human life.
War and raids were the order of the day.
Human life was not appreciated.
Who has changed this?
Who brought about peace, progress, education, and modern medicine; the written
word, calculation, commerce, currency, banking, credit, transport, towns and
cities, ships and harbors, electricity, intensive agriculture, enough food?
Who was responsible for law and order, safety of life and property, respect for
other tribes and races?
Whoever was responsible for all these benefits has to sustain and preserve it.
Nobody else could.

A 65-year-old Afrikaner gave this quasi-poem written on a scrap of paper
to a research assistant, saying that these lines expressed his feelings about
South Africa and its future. He was one of the many urban whites interviewed
who drew very hard-and-fast lines between the inhabitants of the dark
barbaric continent, Africa, and the civilizing "white man." The boundary
was drawn in terms of perceived qualitative differences between white

and black. It tended to be rigid and did not allow for permeability. Civilization was furthermore a legacy of "whites" that had to be sustained/asserted (*handhaaf*) and preserved. It was they who brought enlightenment to Africa in order to save its indigenous peoples from the "barbarism" in which they were caught up. The whites were clearly painted in elevated moral terms and contrasted with blacks, who stereotypically did not care about human life.

Urban whites have less direct involvement with other population categories on an everyday basis than do rural whites. They are less plagued by the paradox of dependency and rejection. Blacks are more anonymous and transitory to their day-to-day existence. The typical bourgeois white views blacks with greater anonymity and less biographical involvement than does the typical rural white. The urban white is more dependent on the media and popular political discourse for information about blacks.

The whites interviewed for this study who had conservative orientations generally drew clear and solid boundaries. They were explicit in arguing their interest in preserving the existing racial divisions in South Africa and felt threatened by recent reforms. Within this category of urban conservatives, I make a further distinction between those who were in more secure and powerful positions and those who were not. This makes sense viewed from my original intention of examining the perspectives and views of people who shared comparable worlds of experience. Both subcategories resided in cities and in suburbia. Their interaction with the black population and other "nonwhite" groups was largely confined to the domestic sphere and rarely included face-to-face interaction at work or at leisure. This pattern of contact clearly differed from that in rural areas, where the whites interviewed interacted with blacks in both the home and the fields. The basic difference between the worlds of experience of the two subcategories can be found in their lifestyles. The richer, more powerful individuals had opulent, expansive lifestyles and a higher degree of financial and physical security than did those in the other category. In order to demonstrate the various concerns and perceptions of people within this broad category, I will document two interviews from each category extensively and then look at emerging themes contained therein. Subsequently, I will examine those themes in sequence, adducing additional material from other transcripts and observations.

CIVILIZATION: THE DIVIDING LINE

God Drew a Line

Dawid, whose poem is quoted above, lived in a middle-class suburb in Benoni on the eastern Witwatersrand and was a member of the Dutch Reformed Church. The interview was conducted, in Afrikaans, in January 1989, so the following excerpt includes references to realities and laws that have changed since that time. He was asked how he viewed the future of South Africa.

Dawid: If the present government persists with the political dispensation the white will be dominated by *the* black. The white is a minority and the blacks are multiplying. The future is dark. South Africa can be compared with Zimbabwe. The white has a very slim chance and South Africa is going to be as *uncivilized* as Zimbabwe. We have to act to prevent the blacks from dominating, because once they dominate, they will never share power with the whites.

Interviewer: Some people say that the Groups Areas Act [abolished in 1991] is to be amended. How do you feel about that?

Dawid: If that should happen and the Group Areas Act should even be abolished, the white would be *totally lost.* Everything then would have to be shared, including public amenities, just like in America. I have spoken to an American, and he told me that he moved from suburb to suburb. The American saw that wherever the black moved in, the whites moved out. The elderly cannot go for a walk in the evenings anymore.

Interviewer: Is that different from the past?

Dawid: The past was a different era. The new era doesn't make sense anymore. In the Bible, God drew a line that separates nations and peoples, and this stayed so to the end—why does it have to be different now? In the past the survival of the whites was not threatened/jeopardized [*bedreig*] by the black majority. The blacks knew their place both in and outside the workplace. The blacks were dependent on the white. The Voortrekkers civilized the blacks—educated them and taught them. Today there are houses and cars in Soweto you will also find in Houghton [a very expensive white Johannesburg suburb]. These blacks [who own expensive houses and so on] call the other blacks "kaffirs." In the past it was different. Blacks worked and lived on farms and received a little piece of land and some cattle as reward—and they were well-off. Today the blacks think that the white didn't treat them well. Today blacks also have better housing but they neglect their houses and demolish everything. Blacks also do not move into somebody else's house because the house is bewitched. The house would instead be demolished or abandoned.

Interviewer: What about personal safety today?

Dawid: Yes, I fear blacks today; I feel unsafe regardless of where I might live. I keep my doors locked and I have burglar bars on my windows to keep blacks out. I am taking these precautions because I am not looking for trouble, but my home feels like a prison to me. I heard on television that there were 462 assaults on senior citizens. Of these, 143 were murders. I was amazed that no extensive coverage was given to this. There was only a small item in the newspaper. For my personal safety I have a rifle and a pistol.

Interviewer: What about the future?

Dawid: I hope that white and black will be separate [*apart*] in the future. The Botha government failed to keep them apart and it is leading the country into perdition [*verderf*]. Since influx control has been abolished, 2.5 million blacks began squatting. Many were unemployed and millions of rand were spent on housing. Blacks should live in homelands, and influx control should be reinstated.

Interviewer: Can South Africa afford to send them back?

Dawid: All blacks don't need to go back because many were born in the cities. Those who are working here in the cities may stay but have to live separately, as in past years. Therefore more rigorous legislation is necessary. This is especially necessary with regard to the black townships [*lokasies*; an old term] because the blacks are owing money on their electricity bills and on their rent. The Johannesburg City Council should intervene. Blacks working in the mines have contracts of seven months. These blacks have to return to the homelands at the end of this period. That is not happening, and now they are bringing their families with them. A small handful of whites have to support the large majority of blacks. There isn't any money for this. Teachers' salary increases are paid for by the increased petrol [gasoline] prices. South Africa is bankrupt, and the gold reserves are low. The government tells blatant lies about finances. White boys are bored in the army instead of doing work. Blacks cannot be given all the work in business because they are unable to give the same service. Black cashiers are working at SPAR [a grocery store chain] and now SPAR is stuck with them. South Africa could do without blacks if whites were prepared to do the same work as the blacks. Blacks are mostly illiterate and can do work appropriate to their qualifications.

Interviewer: Where do you get your information from?

Dawid: I read *The Citizen, Beeld,* and the Conservative Party newspaper, *Die Patriot.* News reporting is very one-sided. Once you analyze the news, Allan Hendrickse [a "coloured" politician who defied the racial ban on mixed beaches] gets preferential treatment for his provocative swimming. The NP also gets a lot of television coverage. The opposition has no mouthpiece and is shot down by the newspapers. The newspapers govern our country.

Interviewer: Have you altered your political views since the recent changes?

Dawid: No, I have always been conservative, and I have not been in favor of changes that would cause white and black to integrate. God forbade that we, as the white people/nation [*volk*], be bastardized in 300 years.

Changes are occurring too rapidly and the tempo is being influenced by foreign countries [*die buiteland*]. I fear the Group Areas Act may be lifted before the next election. Blacks and coloureds have their own areas where they can do whatever they want to, where they can bring about many changes. In Boksburg the coloured area has better facilities, and the white municipal service is also provided to coloureds—for example, there are buses for coloureds going to Benoni [East Rand towns].

The current changes should never have occurred. Verwoerd, Vorster, and Malan disregarded foreign opinion. Sanctions will be good for South Africa, because the whites can stand on their own legs. Blacks, especially the impoverished, are vulnerable to communism, and this will make South Africa into a Third World country. South Africa will become like Mozambique, which turned communist. After the Portuguese left, Mozambique decayed into nothing.

The changes will cause conflict to increase because hate between white and black will intensify. It is especially the blacks who hate whites. Should communism get a foothold in South Africa, it will become a poor country in which there will be no room for the white.

Interviewer: What do you think will happen when there is "one man, one vote"?

Dawid: The whites won't rule anymore. Blacks will be in Parliament and we will have a black president. South Africa will then become a second Zimbabwe. The whites will be murdered one and all. Naturally, the whites will rebel, and I will fight on their side for the sake of my children.

Dawid constructed a definite boundary, if not a barrier, between black and white. To paraphrase his views: The existence of this boundary was sanctioned by God, and as long as it was maintained, there was peace and personal security. The boundary was also impermeable. It separated two clearly differentiated categories, one associated with civilization, the other with barbarism. However, the present is very different. The purity and clarity of relations between whites and blacks in the past has been corrupted through recent political changes by the government. Blacks do not "know their place" in white South Africa anymore. Though less competent, they compete with whites for jobs in "white" areas. A return to the past is therefore necessary if a racial conflict of cataclysmic proportions is to be averted.

Conservatives interviewed for this study held "civilization" to be the strongest dividing principle between white and black. The word *civilization* concealed a number of overtly racist assumptions and judgments. They were easy to detect because, generally speaking, civilization involves behavior that can be learned. The language and terms they used, however, indicated that many informants in this category viewed blacks' inferior state to be immutable.

In a more "reasonable" vein, a Conservative Party supporter explained to me that it was not the problem of exclusion and the denial of rights to nonwhite people that motivated him to support separate living areas and facilities. It was not nonwhites' inferiority that bothered him. Rather, it was the problem that assimilation into another group would eventually erode the identity of the white people. This was a variation on Dawid's view because it nonetheless retained the rigidity of the boundary between white and nonwhite. I spoke to this informant, Leon, about the fact that people from different population categories were now settling in Mayfair, Johannesburg. He opposed this development. He told me that a South African white who left the country permanently to settle in another country was bound to be assimilated into the host society. He drew a parallel with Mayfair:

> You will be assimilated into their culture—gradually. This is what happened to the Boers who went to South America.[1] It is a natural and logical process. What I'm fighting for is not because I have something against Ibrahim [an Indian] who bought [the house] next to me. To tell the truth I respect some of them but I don't know many of them because our cultures are so different. But those I know, I do respect. However, tomorrow, or the day after, Moosa [another Indian] may come. I am not against Dr. Moosa. But it so happens that I do not then feel free to chat over my fence with groups from my own culture. And this is when you really communicate; with groups from your own culture. And that's the reason I grant that man [his place], but I too am looking for a place in the sun, and their numbers alone are going to assimilate me.

Leon compared the situation of sharing residential areas with other groups to that of the self-imposed exile of Afrikaners and their "disappearance" because they were assimilated into their host societies. There is a strange logic to this argument, which is born of the fear of potential self-estrangement in the country of one's birth. Like Dawid, Leon drew a boundary between white and nonwhite that was rigid. As in so many other cases in this study, Leon drew the boundary overtly in terms of cultural criteria, but it implicitly carried with it a strong racial referent. Although Dr. Moosa may have been a learned man and might have assimilated much more of a Western lifestyle and value system, racial overtones still seemed to determine Leon's attitude.

Mud Hut, Lion Skin, and Blanket

Ockey, an English speaker in his 60s, had spent 33 years of his working life in South Africa as a butcher. He was born in Yugoslavia and is a Roman Catholic. The nature of his work brought him into daily contact with black laborers and clients. He was interviewed in a hotel bar in a somewhat depressed area of downtown Johannesburg by a research assistant. After some informal talk, the discussion turned to blacks, and the interviewer asked whether he could tape-record the conversation:

Ockey: As long as you don't ask my name and address.

Interviewer: I don't need your name and address.

Ockey: Now, you just ask me whatever you want and I'll give you [the information].

Interviewer: Do you believe in separate development [the old term for apartheid]?

Ockey: No, no [seriously], the coons can't develop. They're black. They're an ignorant nation that needs guidance. The coons need guidance.

Interviewer: Ya, okay, so with the help of the whites . . .

Ockey: No, the whites . . .

Interviewer: They're separate? You can't see them mixing?

Ockey: No, no, no.

Interviewer: Whites and blacks mixing . . .

Ockey: No, they're inferior. You see, what this one Afrikaner said is the gospel truth. He said, if it wasn't for the white man *the black guy will be still sitting there in his mud hut with his lion skin and blanket* [emphasis added].

Interviewer: Ya.

Ockey: That's what the white said.

Interviewer: Ya, and you don't think there might be a bit of trouble or . . .

Ockey: There will be trouble. Of course there will be trouble, Yes, of course, there will be trouble.

Interviewer: How would that affect the whites?

Ockey: Yes, yes, so they put a bit of fear in them. Of course they'll put fear in them. You see the African, they're a very unpredictable nation. Like about 15 or 20 years ago, Zambia was starving, and the South African government gave them 100 million metric tons of wheat, and they sold the wheat to the Russians, and they bought guns with that wheat. So, in other words, he would rather have a gun than a loaf of bread.

Interviewer: Where [do you get this from]?

Ockey: Oh, well, that's what I heard.

Interviewer: Do you think we'll be sitting like this in 10 years' time? Do you think there will be changes?

Ockey: No, no—he can never be on a par with a white—never. It's been proven in America.

Interviewer: Ya, I'm thinking in terms of escalating violence. Maybe the whites will have to . . . [the interviewer wanted to say "negotiate" but was interrupted]

Ockey: Yes, well, if he pulls a gun on me, I'll pull a gun on him [here the tape is indistinct]. It's a way of putting it. Yes, of course people get terrified you see. They're locking doors. You see before . . . about 20 years ago, 25 years ago before the rands and cents came in [decimalization of the currency in the 1960s] they used to get £1/10/0 a month. They used to get a bag of mealie meal. Then there was no trouble. There was no trouble at all. And now they've got everything and they want more. You see, they can sit in a bioscope [movie theater].

Interviewer: Ya.

Ockey: Well, they pay the same price as I do. The only thing that I say, you know, if he does the same job as me, I think he should get the same pay as I do. If you do the same work as I do, irrespective of color, you must get—pay the same wages.

Interviewer: But, we are separate, aren't we?

Ockey: He must be kept in his place.

According to Ockey, blacks thus need the permanent guidance of whites because they are inferior. As we will see below, some think that even university education cannot bring them to whites' level. Their ignorance supposedly cannot be eradicated. Ockey contrasted the good old times without unrest with recent times, when blacks began making more demands. The discussion continued about blacks' elevated standard of living in South Africa in comparison with other countries. The interviewer turned Ockey back to South Africa:

Interviewer: Getting back to [our] reality with this Boksburg . . . you know where they tried to enforce separate—eh, you know, the economic consequences . . .

Ockey: No, you must remember that these parks have been maintained by the whites. You see, let the white . . . You can't go and sit in Joubert Park, and go there to the Oppenheimer fountain. You cannot find a seat. All the blacks are sitting over there and the whites pay for the upkeep of these parks. The whites pay for that.

Interviewer: The blacks must have their own park?

Ockey: The black must have his own park. You see the blacks want to come and sit on a white bus. All right, and they say why do we react to that? What would their reaction be if I had to go and sit on the Soweto bus?

Interviewer: Tell me, what do you think it would be?

Ockey: No, you will be assaulted. They'll tell you [to] get on your own bus.

Ockey thus supported separation of public facilities. In the conversation that immediately followed, he took for granted that blacks would support white business in those areas that decided to enforce old-style apartheid. His one-sided perspective was further demonstrated by his observation that whites maintain the parks. Whites may pay the bulk of the property taxes used for maintaining the parks, but the work is surely done by blacks. Ockey had no sense of sharing. He could tolerate blacks' presence only when it was to the benefit of white business; when it led to crowding in parks, they had to disappear. He continued hammering on the inferiority of blacks as the reason for segregation. Talking about American blacks, he said:

Ockey: You can't compare an American black with a South African black. Ah, I'm sorry; that's unequal. . . .

Interviewer: They're different? What made that difference, would you say?

Ockey: Slavery originated from America. Americans invented apartheid. They invented apartheid.

Interviewer: But their blacks now, they are quite different to ours?

Ockey: Yes, of course. You see, they are more civilized.

Interviewer: And why would you say that?

Ockey: You see, they are allowed to go to universities. Well, I don't know. I haven't been there. I wouldn't know.

Interviewer: Do you think the same things [are] possible here maybe?

Ockey: No, no. You see they live their different lives. A Zulu lives one life, a Rhodesian lives one life, and you see, you cannot expect these guys that come from the tribe just to adjust to your way of life—no, they're primitive. Definitely primitive. The more the government gives to them, the more they want. You see they go to bars and they go to the bioscope. He can come and sit in any bar in Johannesburg. . . .

Interviewer: So, do you see this as an ongoing thing? The whites must give in just to keep him happy—or not, maybe?

Ockey: I still say, I'll say it now and I'll say it in 20 years if I'm still alive. A black can never be on a par with a white; he can never be on a par with a white. Never. They just lack that something.

Ockey foresaw violence in the future and a drop in his standard of living. It is important to observe that "primitiveness" to Ockey was connected to "tribal life." His comments on black demands for equality and the sharing of bars and theaters immediately followed his elaborations about blacks' primitive nature. His words not only expressed an aversion to physical proximity to blacks in public places, they also conveyed the image that "the black" was an insatiable "leech."

Ockey spontaneously raised the issue of the AWB, which he liked:

Ockey: I tell you why I like the AWB. You see—because they are on the whites' side. You see the government has deprived the whites of jobs and they've given the jobs to blacks. What do they expect the whites to do? That's why the AWB supports the whites. They only support the whites because the government took their jobs away, and they gave the jobs to the blacks—and they gave him half of the white man's salary. So you can't win [indignantly].

In his perception, the government was thus selling the whites out to the blacks by taking away their jobs. Blacks had an unfair advantage, yet they were demanding more. He resented their desire to be on equal footing with whites and the government's willingness to give in. He believed that blacks hate whites. Talking about his experience of blacks working for him, he observed:

Ockey: No, they've got a lot of hatred in them.

Interviewer: Why do you think that?

Ockey: Well, they want to be on a par with the whites. I suppose they are envious. It's a perfect example of Africa; what happened to Africa? Any guy in his right sense will see that there is disaster where the black man is. Mozambique: They're starving. They hate a white man and yet, in

Mozambique they said over there, the white man's money is always welcome in Mozambique. Very, very hard to understand.

The "leech" image, though not directly stated, appeared repeatedly in this interview. The more blacks were given, the more they demanded, and the results were disastrous, which you could see if you looked at other countries in Africa where independence had been given. It led not to prosperity, but to greater misery. Ockey thought that those forces working for the blacks were communist inspired, and that ANC members should be shot as murderers.

He Needs Another 50 Years' Education

In contrast to Dawid and Ockey, Mac, in his 50s, was a wealthy owner of a construction company. Although South Africa was economically depressed, he seemed to flourish; he employed about 100 blacks as semiskilled and unskilled laborers. He was generally optimistic about the future of the country. He also was less rigid in the boundaries he drew between black and white. Yet, in his talk, he sometimes revealed perceptions of harsh and deep-seated differences. At the beginning of the interview he spoke about the rather unburdened life led by liberal white students, but he soon adopted a serious tone when he addressed what was, to him, one of the main factors disturbing the peace in the country. It was not primarily the government that was to blame for the upsets, but the liberals:

> I've always said that there are a lot of problems in this country, but I'll go and shoot a few whites first . . . I know the ones. Did I tell you about my experience as security policeman? as a part-time policeman? [laughs] The list of the names I had was all people I used to [laughs] know . . . [laughs] You understand? People who were liberalists in outlook; the dangerous liberalists' outlook, the ones who could incite and cause trouble, and that's the thing you've got to be very careful about. . . . You must have creative discussions. . . . you must have knowledge from the beginning, the middle, and the end. . . . you mustn't take what you've heard and then add to it, you know, 'cause this is very dangerous . . . especially amongst our blacks you know. . . .

He admired the Afrikaners' achievements over the past two generations and maintained that they devised laws such as the Group Areas Act for their own protection. This was a law that even the Indians wanted but spoke against. He felt he didn't need that protection, because, see, it's a protection; not so much for me, 'cause whoever wants to buy a cottage next door to me is not serious because, first of all, what is he gettin' for the money he puts here? The average black—this wouldn't suit him. It's far too small for his half a dozen kids and his two or three wives and his girlfriends, you know. People forget all these things. So that's society as far as I'm concerned. A politician, as far as the blacks are concerned—*he needs another 50 years' education before he can come as a force in politics* and be able to . . . uh, vote for what he sees is right, not what he's told is right. So I think policy, as far as the blacks [are] concerned—I think they've been exploited, not so much by the white people, but by their own people, by uh, uh, the churches. (emphasis added)

Blacks were thus very far behind, and they had very different sets of needs. In comparison with whites, they did not have the same moral standards, such as beliefs in monogamy and marital faithfulness. They lacked the ability to decide for themselves, therefore they were easily exploited. Although he thought it was important to educate them, Mac viewed education essentially as a privilege that was abused by blacks who went to high school and university. The main culprits were those who used the church as their basis:

You know, if education is so poor in this country, how do these chaps [black church leaders and politicians] get these academic degrees? . . . I thought it was exact to say [that] I don't understand this unequal education [allegation]. I really don't understand it at all. I know that, if you've got your little farmer's school in the country, obviously, you can't afford to pay the same teacher who would teach in Johannesburg, and if you cannot afford [it] or if you've got no village [there's little chance] for higher education. I think education is a privilege, at this stage, for a lot of people. I think it's not just; you're entitled to it because it's abused by the ones that get it, and if I was an underprivileged person—as everybody calls these poorer people in this country—I would thank God that I had a chance to go to the university and look something over. But they destroy their lives with politics, and they're a long way away from being politicians, a long way away.

This very dense statement contains a number of assumptions and overlooks certain realities. The privilege of education is administered and distributed by whites. Mac was not aware of this, or, if he was, he was not able to express it. In an ironic way, almost immediately after this pronouncement, he said he would not be worried if his children decided to emigrate because they could be of benefit to other countries by applying their education: "Whatever you inherited in this country, you can only [be of] benefit wherever you go, because any person with a degree in this country and ability to work is an asset to any other country in the world." Their education would qualify them to maximize their opportunities in the wider world. Furthermore, he saw blacks as largely rural living, either on the farms or in tribal villages inside or outside a homeland. The "tribal" stereotype of all blacks nearly surfaced here. His resentment of the political use of education also overlooked the fact that education was used for political purposes by the National Party governments for many decades. Mac also did not appear to understand the relationship between power and education that he, as a businessman, must have been aware of. His thought pattern was fraught with inconsistencies and double standards. He gave an indication where his attitudes came from:

Mac: I'm a great believer in aristocracy. Really, I'm, you know—I'm basically a snob from that point of view. If you're a worker you're a worker, if you can evolve and pass it [okay], if you can't evolve, you must stay that way . . . and that's what I say with the underprivileged people: Why should we make eh, ehh, . . . a black person [attain] the same education as myself unless he can help that education. . . . I don't have to bring my standard down to give him a better parcel like they've done in America. And I'm quite sure that over here—that makin' things easier . . . in many cases . . . which is wrong. I think that, uh . . . first of all before we can go on with this situation in this country we've got to real-, realize that if the blacks want to be like us white Africans . . . they've got to live like whites. . . . they've got to have values like the white African. . . . they've got to work and keep the one wife . . . and they've got to pay for their home . . . and they've gotta pay the rent. . . . you know, they've gotta do all these things which they're not doing.

Interviewer: What about the idea of a white African becoming more African?

Mac: Oh, that, yeah.

Interviewer: Is that necessary?

Mac: I'm very open. I've got nothing against my black colleagues . . . but a lot against a lot of white colleagues. . . . I must be honest with you . . . eh . . . I say that a few of my type of people are not too fond of English people . . . are not too fond of Greeks, don't misunderstand me. You can erase this you see [laughs], eh . . . I'm not too fond of, but I'll accept them as South Africans, you understand? You know, you know, you understand what I mean? So it's not with me a color bar . . .

Interviewer: . . . no, its more a cultural . . .

Mac: . . . it's more my feelings for their color you see and I was brought up that way . . . and all during the wars I associate[d] with many people but

I was never really with them. I was with them as far as . . . this side was
going forward, so I went forward . . . you know . . . and [clears throat]
so . . . when there was too much, was too much [attention] drawn to
pigmentation in this country . . . and uh . . . the first thing a black person
does . . . soon as he makes a few rand, he leaves his . . . he doesn't go and
practice in his own kind, part of the world . . . he becomes a doctor, he
wants to eh . . . eh, doctor, uh, uh, rooms in medical center and deal with
this Mrs. van der Merwe and Mrs. Kavinsky. He doesn't want to go and
help his own people . . . and that's what I don't understand . . . so is there
a special education to . . . anywhere a special [here the tape is unclear]
you know I don't understand it . . . so when I listen to all these academics
and all these fantastic . . . intellectual people . . . giving their version . . .
which is [based] upon ideology . . . it's not a South African outlook. . . .
this is all really because in America they hear they do this.

Mac was struggling with the class/race distinction. At the beginning of
this exchange he confessed he had sympathies for aristocracy and class
divisions in society, presumably as a static arrangement. As a consequence, he thought, no special effort should be invested in black education. In this way he assured himself that society would remain very much
the same. He identified himself as a "white African" who set the standards
in the country. He defined those standards in terms of values and lifestyle—thus as cultural standards. However, his subsequent statements
leave great doubt whether blacks might find acceptance in "white African"
society at all, because, after stumbling unsuccessfully through a rejection
of the "color bar," he made it abundantly clear that well-qualified blacks
were still expected to serve "their own people." He thus set the boundaries
in an overt racial way. It is hard to see how an additional "50 years'
education" would make any difference in the acceptance of blacks as
equals. It was one of the remarkable features of many of these interviews
that respondents presented barely disguised contradictions one after the
other without realizing it.

Mac then turned to the importance of education, but observed that
blacks are undisciplined and backward. Turning to his employees, he
observed that they adhered to a lifestyle totally unacceptable to him. The
terms in which he described them are significant:

Mac: . . . now all the blacks that work for me, and I've got about a hundred, . . .
they've all got two or three wives.

Interviewer: Are they mostly from rural areas?

Mac: Oh yes, that's their homes. [They] stay here. The [hostel?] is their home and all these blacks of Soweto have their wives somewhere else too. The ones that live and work here . . . uh, the ones who don't have a place to go . . . 'cause they're bastard sons and they're bastard daughters . . . from another mother. . . . This is the tragedy other people don't understand. . . . You know this, uh . . . uh, all my boys say they're, uh, celibate. [One has] got a couple of children with some woman that works here . . . and uh . . . [another] has got a couple of children with some woman in Soweto . . . you know . . . now, that's only, eh . . . I'm only givin' you a couple of boys I know . . . and K. [a black woman] is a Bantu and that's a custom: they don't care. . . . Wherever—where my chaps go on construction . . . they [make women] pregnant; there's more children left there . . . and that's it . . . they move on. . . . Now, what I'm tryin' to say is . . . in a society that we live in you've got to be . . . uh, part of Western ideas.

Emphasizing the necessity of blacks' becoming part of Western ideas, he contradicted himself and finally relinquished the African part of his self-professed "white African" identity. He then acknowledged that there was diversity in the country but that one law should apply to all. There were difficulties, however. Mac characterized the black as wild, uncontrolled, and without fear. This characteristic made it difficult for the black to obey the law:

Don't underestimate the black 'cause he's the greatest [here the tape is unclear] in the world. But he hasn't got the fearing, . . . you know the, the God-fearing feeling that a Christian's supposed to have. It'll take many years for him to get that, because he was never brought up like that. Death to him was really nothing, uh, to appreciate. We don't like to die; we like work with the fear of death . . . 'cause that's how we've been brought up, but [the] African as such hasn't an ounce of fear . . . and it will be many, many moons before they get into that situation . . . so, there's all that to contend with, which takes time—and you must always remember somethin': The black lost the war, . . . and . . . the white man has taken over—he's a white African. He's here to stay; he's got nowhere to go. This is his home, he's not gonna give her away.

The idea that death and the fear of death are not strong emotional issues among blacks apparently prepared the ground for Mac's accepting the unequal application of the death penalty to blacks and, at worst, reducing the impact that deaths of blacks in riots and demonstrations had on whites. In fact, Mac made himself clear on this:

This is how you must look at it. So you have laws, . . . we are a South African country with a lot of Africans to contend with . . . but justice must be served in an African [way?] . . . uh, people talk about the hanging so I don't think people understand in this country . . . punishment is the only way they understand, maybe in a hundred years' time it'll be different, I don't know . . . but at the moment, if an African steals or a white master steals, . . . the punishment is slightly different from what they appreciate here. . . . You know, you've gotta go back to this, this, this 50 years ago in the home, in his home, how he was locked up when he stole and then was cast out of the village. . . . Do you understand? . . . And to him it was a . . . great sh . . . , crime, you know a terrible thing to be caught stealing . . . now there's still rumor Africans hung those themselves . . . and they don't want these boys coming from Soweto et cetera, et cetera . . . for that example and other vermin . . . so you've all that to take in consideration.

Mac's meaning is not always clear in this transcribed version of the conversation. One must read between the lines to understand. Mac justi-fied the differential application of the law to blacks because they were only halfway out of the tribal system or still immersed in it, where, he assumed, thieves were still being hanged. While discussing their "tribal state," he suddenly jumped to the "boys from Soweto." In other parts of the interview it was clear that Mac considered the *plaasboys* (farm boys) to be a much more acceptable, docile category of blacks. The urbanized black, however, was uprooted, unpredictable, and violent; Mac even de-scribed him as "vermin."[2]

After justifying censorship extensively in terms of the protection of the (white?) youth, Mac was asked how he viewed the future of South Africa from a global perspective. He strongly favored a federal system for the country. Notice how he was arguing that such a system would basically perpetuate a status quo in which "tribal" blacks would be confined politically to the former homelands and urban blacks would qualify for political rights only in a limited way:

Mac: Now [Ciskei] . . . it's gonna be Ciskei . . . and KwaZulu is gonna be KwaZulu . . . you know, and it's always been Kwaz- . . . It's not as though we've moved them there . . . , they've always been there . . . traditionally. . . . Zululand has been Zululand, . . . the Transkei has been the Transkei . . . for Basotholand's been Basotholand. . . . Swaziland is Swaziland . . . and the people who live in Swaziland are Swazis . . . and they speak a different dialect, you know. . . . So it's always traditionally been there . . . and the only way they got it to work in Nigeria . . . was to wipe out the . . . the

Ibos . . . they wiped them out, two and a half million of them [4-second pause] you know . . . uh . . . Good, Gotegia [I couldn't make out from the tape the correct spelling of this place; I presume it must be some ex-British colony in the East] . . . Gotegia today . . . is still the same as it was when I was there during the war . . . the poor are poorer . . . and the rich are richer . . . and the uh . . . *Ezhe mazul* [?] . . . it's rubbish, the peasants . . . the wogs as we call them and they're still called wogs . . . and the coolie is still called the coolie . . . now . . . whether that will ever be solved, I don't know . . . I mean as I remember, in Scotland a laborer was called an Irishman . . . [laughs] that's what it was: a bloody Irishman that digs the ditches . . . now they've got so- some other people doing it . . . you know [4-second pause] you see.

Interviewer: What would you do if you stay here . . . in South Africa if you would have a federation . . . and you had like Zulu people . . . being in Zululand and Xhosa being in Ciskei . . . whatever . . . Transkei. . . . What would you say then about urban blacks . . . about people who . . . ?

Mac: Well, the others like . . .

Interviewer: . . . consider themselves free and not tribal?

Mac: Well, well . . . the urban black who becomes a legitimate . . . citizen, in other words, . . . uh . . . you'll have to treat as an Irish, as a man with 17 children and 18 children in the family . . . you know, you got one street with 5,000 people . . . where you got a residential area with 500 people . . . where the 500 people are paying for the 5,000 people . . . so why should them 5,000 people be the same good as 500 people . . . you see . . . so, it's all, it's all a matter of sorting out . . . but . . . the thing is to educate the people to have one wife . . . and two children or whatever. . . . I mean these these, these . . .

Interviewer: The . . . wo-, would you go along with the idea of the qualified vote then?

Mac: Well, I would say . . . a qualified vote . . . that would be to a certain extent . . . a qualified vote to vote for what . . . vote for who?

Interviewer: To vote for the government of the country . . .

Mac: Ya . . . uh . . . what would you say the contribution of . . . ugh, Soweto, let's say . . . let's say this . . . eligible vote is 100,000—

Interviewer: Uh-huh. . . . Eligible, you mean over 18?

Mac: I would say . . . responsible citizens, uh, you know, let's say it's 100,000 of them out of a million and a half. Now . . . if they've got a legitimate guy . . . so you've gotta be very careful there . . . uh . . . Any guy who's stood for M.P. [member of Parliament] for a black in that Sowetoland . . . I don't think the problem that exists in this century. . . . I think they'd wipe him out. . . . You see what happens every time there's [an] occurrence in [Soweto?] land . . . people who're trying to come forward are going to get killed.

Interviewer: Why, though, why do they get killed?

Mac: Because there are a certain type of . . . you can agitate to do; to do that sort of thing . . . burn, *shesa* [Zulu word meaning "burn"] . . . *bulala* [Zulu word meaning "kill"] . . . that's their . . . international language they want to uh . . . *Shesa*'s to burn . . . *bulala* is to kill . . . you see . . . and this is all they do . . . and you've got plenty of boys who'll go and do it . . . I mean I can even send my blokes to kill if I wanted 'em to. It's so easy. . . . I can tell my boys wha—I want, want, uh, taken out, you know, and he'd do it. . . . it's so simple to do . . . so there's . . . you know, the average white guy . . . is not such a great guy but . . . through his sorta home life and his upbringin' . . . I'm not talkin' about some back-bustin' bunch of whites . . . , I'm talkin' about the average white . . . just like myself. I don't want any . . . uh . . . I . . . for me to kill somebody it's not right. I don't even want to fight anymore . . . you know, I let the proper order and sort it out . . . so . . . but it's, the average black's not like that . . . he hasn't reached that stage yet . . . there is exceptions.

Here, Mac's colonial mentality is revealed in no uncertain terms. In his perception, we can conclude, South Africa is some postindependent ex-colony in which colonial relationships between natives and colonials still prevail. The federal model for the future comes in handy because it not only has traditional justification, but in an unspoken way it serves the purpose of keeping the uncivilized out of sight and influence in the metropolitan areas, where the "civilized" would wield power. Mac was clear on the matter that blacks were numerically overrepresented in urban areas and that a qualified or weighted vote should keep their influence to a "deserved" minimum. Therefore, he estimated that about 1 in 15 should have a vote. He foresaw that no black politician would last very long anyway because of the existence of the violent black and the urban killer who only knew the laws of burning and killing. Therefore, black political power did not seem to be an urgent threat to white power. By their nature, blacks would sabotage their own political participation, which would be limited anyway by a highly selective and qualified vote. Mac was there-fore not worried about the future of South Africa. He did, however, as in the beginning of the interview, attach great blame to the liberals for the country's misery. Liberals had their priorities wrong and one-sidedly supported the case of the so-called underprivileged. They did a great deal of damage by influencing the international community against the country. Bishop Desmond Tutu was especially singled out as a culprit when people spoke about the "evil system" (of apartheid):

> *Mac:* [Apartheid] . . . the system . . . if it wasn't for that system . . . I don't like to call it that. . . . I called it the upper class, middle class, and lower class, that's what I call it. In order to belong to the South African clubs here, . . . was just, . . . no matter how much money you got, you could never become a member . . . and there's nothing wrong with that . . . is there? . . . Is there anything wrong with it?
>
> *Interviewer:* Well, it's certainly something different from apartheid.
>
> *Mac:* Just call it another name . . . you see its unfortunate with this Afrikaans language . . . on tape . . . it sounds bad. . . . this is the tragedy of it and, uh . . . the Dutchman said . . . he wants the separate race system . . . and that was the whole idea of comin' to this country . . . away from bloody Holland, you know. . . . Do you understand? . . .
>
> You sift the good from the bad. The future for whites in this country is fantastic. It's challenging, and it'll be difficult, but everyone knows they can't do without us.

Like so many preceding generations of National Party politicians, Mac proposed a name change, calling the system a "class" system. The National Party government had called its policy "apartheid," "separate development," and "constitutional development," but they all meant the same thing. Mac here tried to substitute "class" for "apartheid." There is very little, except the minute concession of a worthless qualified vote, that distinguishes his views from the old-style apartheid reality (not policy) of the 1960s. In fact, his rigid stereotypes of blacks did not allow for mobility in any meaningful sense. His conception of blacks' position was therefore much closer to that of a caste, with explicit racial overtones.

Mac's perception and projection of the future falls very much in line with those of Dawid and Ockey. Because of his financially secure position, he was not threatened by black crowding and competition for jobs.

POLLUTION, BODIES, AND BOUNDARIES

The boundary between blacks and whites was rigidly viewed by those informants quoted above as one between civilization and the lack of it. These men all represent an older generation of South Africans. We now turn to the views of some students in their 20s who made the same contrast. As I found in many interviews with whites of conservative orientation, bodily contact or the sharing of facilities with blacks was a problem for these informants. The views they expressed are reminiscent of those discussed in Chapters 7 and 8. In the following interview this theme is manifested in no uncertain terms.

A student at Rand Afrikaans University agreed to ask fellow students some open-ended questions I had formulated. I basically wanted him to ask how they viewed relations between blacks and whites, now and in the future. The interview developed into a discussion. Apart from what I perceive to be an artificially deracialized terminology used by the participants, the discussion was quite spontaneous. I have translated it here as fully as possible. Much of the anger and subdued violence of the language unfortunately was lost in the transcription and translation. This is a direct translation, and it does not always follow preferred English usage or lexical conventions. I have done this purposely, to emphasize and highlight the degree of emotionality the issue evoked from the respondents.

The discussion first centered on the violent nature of blacks and the killings of blacks by blacks that were taking place in rural areas:

> *Koos:* Brother is pitted against brother. Zulus fight each other. Now, what do you do? Our biggest problem in South Africa is international pressure and the different ethnic groups in the country, the different blacks, and really [*wragtig*], no single one agrees about the same thing. Now, what are you going to do, what? I mean, nobody really knows what we will do to keep the blacks happy because it is many, eh . . . it is not the blacks who moan about the business. There are whites behind it all.

> *Tom:* Okay, another thing that disturbs me are these boycotts by other countries. How many times have [we] done the people a favor. I refer to the nonwhites and other racial groups. At a certain stage . . . we [even] had a nonwhite person in the Springbok [rugby] team. It had no effect on the boycotts by other countries.

The students then discussed the mineral wealth of the country and their feeling that South Africa, as the "richest" country in the world, does not need other countries' economic support:

> *Tom:* It isn't worth our while to do the other race, those of a different color [*anderskleuriges*] favors [*gunse bewys*] all the time. Let's take the schools, for example.

> *Koos:* Yes, I know . . .

Tom: When they burn down the schools, they are just rebuilt again. If we do that, we will land up in jail. Another thing: Would you like it when your child had to sit in the same class with a nonwhite person?

Koos: Okay, okay, but you have to remember now—in my background [farming]—I cannot manage without those of a different color. Show me the whites who would do that kind of work.

Tom: Yes, but I am talking about academic things. Would you like your son or daughter . . .

Koos: Yes, yes . . .

Tom: . . . to attend one school? Never mind together [*saam*] in one school! What about dating [*uitgaan*]? You know, at a certain stage she will . . .

Koos: . . . but wait. This [is] where it is important how you raise your children.

Tom: the children are eth[ically] . . .

Koos: Now we're talking about the ethical side of life if you mention how you were raised [*grootgemaak*]. We were raised in a period where our foundations were formed in a time when severe racial discrimination existed. Okay, well, they are also human. Give them their rights, okay.

Tom: But only to a point.

Koos: . . . to a point. If I take it . . . eh. All right, we have coloureds on the farm. The laborers [*volk*] on the farm are coloureds. He has his people who sit in Parliament and all that jazz but what infuriates [*die hel in maak*] me is that those people don't have any clue about what is going on. It is of no use to explain to them because their, their standard is too low. They don't understand. But personally, I won't manage without these people because I need manual labor.

Tom: Yes, but you're talking about manual labor. There is a difference between manual labor and academy [meaning education]. Okay, he also has to . . . , he has to qualify, but I maintain he went to his school. Why does he have to join us, attend our schools. I don't believe this is worthwhile. I don't believe it is necessary.

Koos then related how he had made the acquaintance of a coloured attorney, a wealthy man, who maintained he wanted to live separately and that coloureds disliked whites as much as whites disliked them. The discussion then reverted to blacks as a bellicose and violent people who lacked the ability to govern even themselves. Tom said blacks would prefer whites to rule the country because blacks would oppose being governed by blacks from factions different from their own.

Tom: They themselves say they don't have the ability to govern the country. Remember, they are not on the same level as we are. They are about 30 years behind in general. I'm speaking of . . .

Koos: . . . the general level, or standard; the standard of living.

Tom: That's right, that's right. Take for example Mamelodi [black township near Pretoria]. They build new houses for them, beautiful houses, even better than the ones we whites live in. And, eh . . . they just fuck up [*neuk op*] those houses, breaking the windows, throw stones at each other. A human being won't do these things . . . or won't I . . .

Koos: Yes, this has to do with how they are raised. Look, they believe, many blacks still believe in this labolla [meaning *lobola*—bridewealth] which they have to pay for the woman [*meid*] in order to get her.

Tom: Exactly.

Koos: They don't marry as we do when we decide to marry.

Tom: Yes.

Koos: Should a man decide to marry—and this is where it applies. In our Western world the woman isn't as subservient to the husband anymore.

Tom: mmm . . .

Koos: In their world it is still like this. When the man tells them to jump, they jump. The *meid* [woman] then jumps.

Tom: Exactly. We men also treat our women too leniently because it is very clearly written in the Bible that the man should be the master in the h[ouse].

Koos: . . . the wife should be serving her husband. We are digressing now. The other question [on the list I gave the student] is: "What do you think about sharing facilities such as parks, universities, schools, and residential areas? Give the reasons for your answer."

Tom: Look, the first thing . . .

Koos: We have already mentioned the schools and universities.

Tom: . . . true.

Koos: Okay, leisure facilities such as resorts. Let's take a [place outside a particular town]—it has a thermal spring. . . . You know there was a doctor—and it was in the newspapers, everywhere that the—it was in this local newspaper—that the doctor treated a black woman [*meid*] for some vaginal disease. And this resort, by the way, had been opened to people of a different color. Now, she stealthily slinked [*sluip*] her way among the other people—a highly infectious bloody disease she is casting [*inneuk*] into the midst of the others.

Tom: Okay, but you have to remember; you have spoken about the nonwhite persons the doctor saw, or rather, the nonwhite person the doctor examined—

there may have been whites with the same problem doctors might have told them about.

Koos: Yes, but okay—just let me finish. Look, they . . . show me a woman, who, according to them, has her period . . .

Tom: [objecting] Who would do such a thing?

Koos: Okay, it is only a very few who would do such a thing.

Tom: A minimum of course. She [a black woman] will do this because she is not bothered—she is used to . . .

Koos: . . . She is used to it. That is how she grew up. They don't worry over these things.

Tom: That's right.

Koos: That's my problem—do you understand? They are talking about education—it, it is much lower than ours. . . .

Tom: . . . I saw something else, you know. In winter I see many little kaffirs and little black girls [*meidjies*] running around [deep breath] you know, without clothes sometimes. They sometimes wear only a shirt, sometimes just short pants—and it's winter—if, if we let our children out this way in winter they become deadly ill—and nothing happens to this small thing [the black child]—so this, this to me is a clear proof you know that we, we . . .

Koos: . . . that healthwise their resistance is much higher than ours—but their level of education—that is the point of the argument.

Tom: Yes.

Koos: Their level of education is much lower than ours.

Tom: No, that's true. No, I agree 100%.

Koos: . . . but, now look, eh, you have been on border duty too?—In Ovamboland and those places; I take it people, eh . . . right . . . eh, take the Himba, yes? He is the seventh underdeveloped race in the world. Imagine, that black gets the opportunity to come and live among you; among us.

Tom: . . . It's happening these days. I mean Hillbrow [Johannesburg] is a good example. Last night I went looking for an apartment—and a few of these apartment buildings were simply neglected—were mixed. The one I did get had it written into its lease: "Whites only." I thought it was a good thing they did. How can you integrate with such a person. I mean they want . . .

Koos: Yes, dammit, we have our standards that we now[adays] . . . We want to eat in a clean way.

Tom: Exactly. They're not . . .

Koos: They don't worry. Take for example, take that—I don't know what's his name—but that millionaire in Ovamboland. He's driving the most beautiful car and everything—and he has the most beautiful expensive suits he is wearing and everything. But then, just have a look where he is living. It is an old, small, mud hut [*kaia*; an inferior dwelling of blacks, from the Zulu word *ikhaya*] next to the highway.

Tom: Exactly, exactly.

Koos: . . . because he isn't . . . [I think he wanted to say "stupid"]. He is making money. He is [has] a brain for business . . . that black.

Tom: That's correct . . .

Koos: . . . but then he wants to live like that . . . because they are too tr . . . They are my . . . Okay, tradition is a good thing but you don't need to pull the dam from under the chicken, or rather, from under the duck [I'm unsure what this means—probably that it's not necessary to go overboard with tradition].

Tom: That's correct . . . No . . . the other evening . . . about a month ago they had this program on *Netwerk* [a television newsmagazine] . . .

Tom then elaborated on how blacks had overcrowded apartments in Hillbrow and how the buildings had become dilapidated. He and Koos then addressed the next question on the list.

Koos: [reading] "On what level would you feel comfortable associating with blacks? On what level would you refuse to associate with them? Why?"

Tom: Okay, on the level of associating with them is . . . eh . . . on the farm. You know the . . . I'm talking about the old farm black [*plaaskaffer*]. You know that one who still believes himself to be a kaffer. I, eh . . . you know, that he still lifts his hat when he says: "Good afternoon, boss [*baas*]" or whatever, whatever [his ways] are. This city, these things [*goed*] have become too white. I mean, they have almost turned into whites.

Koos: Okay, I can, I can—let me just give you one example, eh? What absolutely infuriates me—Okay, the, the . . . eh . . . that time, . . . the Immorality Act has been scrapped; all those things. You may now marry a black woman [*meid*] if you prefer to.

Tom: True.

Koos: Right, it then . . .

Tom: Look here . . .

Koos: The people who do these things are all foreigners. They haven't been born in South Africa. But what outrages me [*die hel in maak*] is, I have been to Checkers [supermarket] in Vryheid [a Northern Natal town] . . . I was walking behind some blacks and I can understand Zulu. This is what he told his mate in Zulu, "Look at that woman walking over there," and it was a beautiful girl—I estimate she was in standard 9 or 10 [eleventh or twelfth grade]—those pretty years they're in—the long-legged look.

Tom: [giggles]

Koos: And, man, was she bloody sexy! Then he said to his mate [*maatjie*] [in a denigrating tone], "Do you see that girl? I am going to get into bed with her."

Tom: [sighs] I think this is an ordeal [*stryd*].

Koos: No, to me, as a genuine Boer-Afrikaner [*stoere Boere Afrikaner*]—it makes me deeply unhappy.

Tom: It makes one mis[erable], unhappy. They . . .

Koos: They cause our women to become cheap.

Tom: Let us turn to the question on what level are we prepared to associate with them in order to get a better [perspective?]. One can associate with him best on the farm, where you could tell him, "Listen, Johannes," or whatever his name might be, "Do this for me. Do that for me." On that level I can associate with him. I will even associate with one such as him until the evening—and I'll tell him, "Now I'm going to dinner." He will sit outside. He does not enter my house but I will give him his plate of porridge or I'll give him coffee in his tin mug. This . . . eh . . . That is the level on which I can associate with him—under the normal working conditions. I mean on farms. Something that really troubles me—and that concerns Parliament. Most people who vote for the National Party—I really don't want to talk politics now, but let us bring this out into the open: This is—They see the nonwhite person working with them. He is in the office every day. He wears a neat suit and tie—the works—and that is the normal . . .

Koos: . . . educated black . . .

Tom: It is an educated black. But let me tell you one thing: Of that [bloated—he did not finish the word *opgeswelde*] . . . eh . . . educated black—let him go home one evening where he'll be with his mother, over there in the mud hut [*kaia*], there he too eats with his—with his hands. Then, that knife and fork business is gone. Give him some Zebra [brand name] kaffir beer—as we call it—and he will dance just like the others on the verandahs. Then that old culture returns. You will never get his culture out of him. And now they [list of questions] also ask: "On what level?"—How did they say?—On what level . . . ?

Koos: [reading] "On what level would you feel comfortable in associating with blacks? On what level do you refuse to associate with them? Why?"

Tom: Okay, I think we responded to that one; why I cannot associate with them. It is mainly a matter of culture.

Both Koos and Tom had rural backgrounds, and they shared many of the values and attitudes of the whites described in Chapter 8. Nevertheless, they were preparing themselves for careers in an urban setting. Their perceptions were relevant for their future relations with blacks in this setting and under more democratic circumstances. The interview opened with them making an association between black ethnic identity on the one hand and discord and violence on the other. They saw ethnic identity as a black problem. This notion of ethnic identity as a black problem was a page torn from the books of Verwoerdian apartheid. Its spirit was still alive in their minds. Ethnic identity in traditional apartheid was not viewed as a problem among whites. They were all lumped into one population category. It was blacks who were assigned to discrete and ascribed ethnic categories. Koos and Tom, however, saw ethnic identity as an intrinsic disadvantage from which blacks were suffering. This is what they took for granted. They were, however, inconsistent, because toward the end of the interview, they applied the notion of "culture" to blacks as a whole. "Ethnic identity" as a concept came in handy and was used in an ad hoc fashion to account for the violent nature of blacks.

During the rest of the interview, they treated blacks as an undifferentiated category, however. Blacks were an ungrateful lot who were unable to appreciate the concessions and giveaways of the government and the white taxpayer. Their schools were rebuilt by whites after they were burned down by black children. In order to placate overseas critics, whites "even" included a black on their treasured rugby team.

A series of contrasts underlay the boundaries Koos and Tom drew between whites and blacks. The first was the contrast between the ignorant black laborer and the educated white. Toward the end of the interview they briefly considered the position of the educated black, but soon found cultural reasons to lump him with the rest.

The second contrast was that between the low standard of living of blacks and the high standard of living of whites. The meaning they attached to the phrase *standard of living* was not, as we would expect, the socioeconomic standard. It was more a question of lifestyle resulting from a black tradition rather than from structural reasons of poverty. These respondents viewed the lifestyle of blacks as crude and inferior. Their remarks about houses and apartments in Hillbrow and Mamelodi bore out this attitude clearly.

The third contrast concerned white culture and black culture. Looking at this distinction very closely, Tom and Koos associated cultural differentiation with socialization—that is, that different groups "grew up" differently or were "educated" differently (e.g., see their remarks about *lobola*). However, this difference went beyond mere assertions about learning. They implied a rejection of blacks. This rejection was based on their perception of blacks' bodies and the way blacks treated their bodies, especially the women. Black women were mentioned in the context of their pollution of pools (formerly) used by whites (only). Tom's objection that whites may also have been a polluting factor was quickly overruled by further citations about bodily differences between white and black. Black women were presented as if they cared less than white women about such things as menstruation and infection. Immediately following these comments, they made a further comparison with black children. They viewed black children as robust beings with the ability to resist the extremes of winter and infections much more successfully than white kids. Black children are not fragile. I interpret this to mean that they are more animallike, and do not have the needs that children usually have, such as proper clothing, shelter, and health care.

Combining the utterances about the black woman and the black kids, a pattern of association emerges. The respondents referred to both black adults and children as "things" or "goods" (*goed*). On the face of it, they apparently constructed an opposition: white = culture, and black = nature. However, they did not deny that blacks have a culture. Blacks have customs, traditions, and are socialized, according to these speakers. Rather, I would argue that the "culture" here ascribed to blacks is pretty close to nature, if not positioned between nature and culture. We can argue that blacks were ambiguously situated between "the natural" and "the cultural." The ambiguity they presented to the informants typically gave rise to notions of pollution and danger (see Douglas, 1966). The solution to this ambiguity was to keep white and black apart. The abhorrence with which Tom and Koos viewed the possibility of sexual relations between a black man and a white woman was a further typical instance of potential pollution and the endangerment and devaluation of the young white woman. Apart from the fear expressed, the threat of black male sexuality was only thinly disguised under the extreme unhappiness both respondents expressed about the "ordeal" of the supermarket scene.

There were more inconsistencies in their argumentation that reflected the double standards they were employing. The Ovambo millionaire was presented as a case for the inferior lifestyle of blacks, yet he obviously made rational decisions, not only about his business or investments but also about the appropriateness of his clothing and transport. "Tradition" was given as the reason for black backwardness, yet Afrikaner "tradition" underlay much of which both Tom and Koos were saying, especially the reference to the *stoere Boere Afrikaner.* The use of double standards escaped both our discussants. Here and there mild objections to too-coarse stereotypes crept in, for example, when Tom tried to argue that whites also bring infectious diseases to public places. These, however, were rapidly plowed under by copious additional "evidence."

Blacks in Tom's and Koos's world of experience had their place—separate from whites and at a sanitary, safe distance from their superiors. Blacks who approached the stage of becoming like whites in the city were not true to their being but returned to their "culture" as soon as they left the educated (white?) world. To a large extent the students shared the views of the other interviewees quoted above. They based their attitudes on personal experiences with mostly rural black laborers but also cited an encounter with at least one sophisticated person of color. Both drew a definite and impermeable boundary between white and black. The evidence suggests that this boundary, on the surface described as "cultural," was in fact perceived more as a "natural"—that is, immutable—one. From a social scientific perspective, it is known that culture and socialization are, in principle, adaptable to change. "Culture" and patterns of "growing up" were viewed by these students as changeless and rigid.

On the question of "natural" boundaries, their views are echoed in the following exchange, which took place between two middle-aged English-speaking gentlemen on a bus traveling from the middle-class northern suburbs to downtown Johannesburg. They were overheard talking about the provocative behavior of an eminent black activist's son, who appeared in public with a white girlfriend:

> Man A: He felt safe because he had his white girlfriend there—never mind his wife at home. I don't care if the kaffir has a white girlfriend or not, but it was only for purposes of propaganda that they were there together. Any girl brought up in this or any country in their right minds—to find . . . to think there's nothing in color. There is something in color. I'd like the Lord to bring out a system where, if you intermarry against your color, that you get a black square or dots, to prove to us there's something wrong. Not that there's anything wrong with a man's mind . . . I think there's something wrong with a woman to think of having children. What are they in this country? The kaffirs: call them Bushmen. I can guarantee that most people of all races want to keep the Group Areas Act. Do you think Moslems want to blend with Hindus? No matter how liberal you are, black is black, white is white, Chinese is Chinese. Color is color.

> Man B: When races mix—you see what happens anywhere in the world. Those areas become slum areas. Look at the mixed parts of London . . . it's a direct result of mixing races. It's natural—think of Catholics and Protes-

tants, Arabs and Jews, et cetera. Keep people separate to keep harmony. Enforced integration makes whites unhappy, lowers standards, and blacks feel [they] lose identity.

These men saw racial mixing as an outrage; they associated it with socially undesirable and disorganized phenomena such as slums. According to Man A, racial admixture was "wrong" in the eyes if God, and the bodies of those involved in racial mixture should bear a recognizable stigma. Both men made strong appeals for "pure" categories. The same confusion occurred here as we have seen previously in the talk of conservative informants, between race and other categories, such as religious affiliation and membership in ethnic communities. To Man B, separation of these social categories was "natural" and also guaranteed harmony, happiness, and a sense of identity.

FEARS AND THE FUTURE

After decades of peace and security under National Party rule, white urban life became more and more precarious toward the end of the 1980s. The Sharpeville crisis of 1960 left a brief but sharp mark on the white public. Whites rushed to gun shops to buy firearms initially, but the anticommunist witch-hunt of the 1960s and the ban of the ANC convinced them that the government had taken adequate measures to regain control and to restore and guarantee their personal security. The economy boomed in the latter half of that period, reinforcing a sense of trust in the government and in the country as a whole. To conservative whites, the late 1960s were the "golden age" many of them yearned for early in the 1990s.

The renewed upsurge of black protest toward the middle of the 1970s, labor unrest, and, ultimately, the Soweto schools' revolt of 1976 made a deeper impact. Again, the strong-arm methods of the government succeeded in repressing black resistance. The media were heavily censored and whites were brought under the impression that the government was again firmly in control of events. Yet disturbing news filtered through to the white public. The Angola/Namibia border encounters could not be hidden. More young whites were conscripted, and more died. Toward the 1980s, black liberation movements shifted their attacks to "soft" urban targets, and a number of bombings of civilian targets followed that made a profound impact on the white public. Whereas issues concerning arable land, agricultural prices, labor, and taxes were crucial to rural whites, the main issue that led to the politicization of reality among urban whites was that of security. After the declaration of the first state of emergency in 1985, the security issue became a public affair. Authorities published elaborate documentation about explosive devices that could be used to blow up public buildings. All post offices and public buildings displayed large plastic sheets (approximately 6 feet by 4 feet) embossed with the images of the most-used limpet mines and land mines. Schoolchildren were taught emergency procedures. The media associated terrorism with the ANC and other liberation organizations. A whole generation of children passed through a political socialization process dominated by a terrorist scare blamed on certain sections of the black population.

In July 1989, I interviewed Hennie, a police officer. He was in his 30s and had considerable experience in police work. He lived in humble circumstances in a garden flat converted from the garage and outbuildings of a main dwelling in a Johannesburg suburb. There wasn't much furniture in his living room: a mattress on the floor and a television set. The kitchen had a table and some chairs. Hennie's fiancée, Jeanie, a trainee nurse, was present during the interview, and she joined in the conversation at times. At the time of the interview the state of emergency had been renewed for the third time. Hennie was on active duty during the 1976 Soweto revolt and took part in suppressing the waves of unrest during the 1980s. This interview was extensive, so I have paraphrased some of the material presented below. As a whole, it is illustrative of the confusion and despair this particular enforcer of the law experienced. Hennie told me:

> As far a I am concerned, we are going downwards. We aren't following the straight road. We are going downhill. There are more and more . . . if I could say it like this . . . there are more and more blacks going to universities . . . graduating. They know, it's either them or us. Thus they already made their decision . . . but eh . . . I really don't know. This can't be hidden anymore. We all wonder about this thing. Everybody knows about this. I mean it is only one of the things [troubling me]. As I told Jeanie: If I had to marry now I will not raise my child in this world. Definitely not, definitely not. It isn't because I don't want to have children, or that I'm funny, or something like that. What I encounter, what I see every day: I will never be able to raise a child in this life.

It is significant that Hennie perceived the deterioration of the country in the context of black educational advancement. I understood his remarks to mean that the face of the country was changing for whites. More qualified blacks would be involved in responsible positions and whites would have to compete with them. He spoke about his experience as a police officer, witnessing violence and death.

He went on to complain that many police officers were giving law enforcement a bad name. To the new recruits the police force was just a way of dodging their military service. They had no commitment to their profession. Furthermore, increasing numbers of police had been arrested for burglary. They were misusing the public's trust in order to gain access to private homes. It was very difficult to combat this phenomenon because the police were strained in responding to all the cases of unrest, car theft, and large-scale robberies. He was particularly emphatic about the dramatic increase in bank robberies:

> Let me tell you this . . . on a normal day there are robberies at at least 15 locations in town . . . people with guns and . . . they are blacks. It isn't white people. It is only blacks involved in these robberies.

He then elaborated on how well these robberies were planned and how the robbers obtained inside information in order to do a clean job:

Schutte: Why would you say this sort of crime increased so much?

Hennie: I'll tell you, heh. The ANC . . . these are the things we hear, which we take notice of. The ANC is running out of money. People inclined to rob are ANC oriented. They work for the ANC. If somebody approaches you and tells you, "Look I'll give you 10% of the money you take from the bank." You wouldn't do that if you take R 500,000 from the bank. Understand? But these people are blacks and this is what they are doing. They are collecting the money in order to do something with it or to buy weapons—or to do something else we don't know about. I reckon that 40 million rand is a lot of money. You can't bank that; you may take it physically out of the country. That money lies around somewhere because they are playing with [it]. That's their plan: they want to do something during the next election. I think we have tremendous problems ahead; very big problems.

Schutte: How do you mean?

Hennie: Definitely terrorism.

Schutte: From whose side?

Hennie: Bombs from the ANC. They are definitely planning something big.

Hennie's fears turned out to be groundless; the 1989 elections were relatively peaceful. His suspicions are relevant, however, because he established clear connections among robberies, the ANC, and terrorism. He also had the idea that blacks were prepared to accept only a percentage of the loot as reward and were thus acting less selfishly than other bank robbers. In the following passages he elaborated on the planning of bomb attacks and attributed a strategy to the ANC whereby non-ANC blacks were used to plant bombs. Often these people became victims of their own deeds. I tried to steer him to the topic of unrest he had witnessed in black areas. I discovered that he did active duty in the area of Pietermaritzburg in the province of Natal, an area notorious for the terrible toll the so-called black-on-black violence exacted. Long before the police were implicated in assisting supporters of one of the factions, Hennie's comments were significant:

> *Schutte:* These explosions are one aspect of violence; what about the other problem of unrest in the black residential areas? It looks like a terrible and endless matter.
>
> *Hennie:* No, I don't believe you'll ever stop it. I know for a fact that in Pietermaritzburg—I've forgotten the name of the black area, but it is in the area of Pietermaritzburg. We are called up to go there for three months. That is all they are doing over there: controlling unrest. That is what they were doing. . . . It was blacks against blacks—it is blacks who wish to exterminate [*uitmoor*] each other—for example, tribes, you know. They firmly believe that this or that area is their territory and if you [disregard] that, you are in trouble. This is what happens there—blacks among themselves—it is only blacks against blacks. We are just present to control—when maybe it gets out of control or such things. We are not meant to stop it. If those things become uncontrollable or it escalates then we'll stop the whole business, but we are there only to [here the tape is inaudible]. I mean you'll never be able to stop those people and if you stop them, they just continue again, they just continue—that's all that is happening—yes, we have a lot of unrest in South Africa.

The phraseology Hennie used contained the familiar notion that blacks are tribal and violent by nature. In his view of the role of the police, they did not have a mandate (or the initiative) to stop the slaughter, but only "controlled" it. It is the normal function of the police to protect the lives of all the citizens of a country. He seemed to be satisfied to let blacks "follow their nature" in exterminating each other. He talked about them as outsiders, beyond the protective reach of the law. As we will see in a later passage, the notion of "out of control" applied to the threat of unrest spilling into white areas. This self-perception of the role of the police is an extremely ethnocentric one. It reflects on the humanity, or lack of it, accorded to blacks. Hennie also suggested that blacks were destroying themselves, without it being necessary for whites to intervene. This was an attitude frequently encountered in white supremacist discourse at the time of the research. It was well known that many police belonged to right-wing political organizations.

As the interview progressed, Hennie wove a tight web of suspects who were extremely elusive and difficult to track down. The "tribal" black might have been the distant outsider, but the ones he feared most were mostly invisible, shrewd, and often white:

> They are very intelligent, they don't want to be [visible]. They operate in a gradual way. I mean, it is not only by way of bombs and terror. There are books and records—they are all meant, eh . . . I mean it is not only Communists that are communist oriented. They are doing it with books and pamphlets. I don't know whether you have been to Wits [University of the Witwatersrand]; I mean three-quarters of that campus is communist. I mean many people on television are communists. This [particular television interviewer] is the biggest communist you can imagine. You can't really do much against communists. You can't do anything against him unless he committed an offense, but the [police] know about him—[they know] she is the one who organizes things, distributing pamphlets. She is a very important communist in South Africa.[3] She is an important link to communism—you know, thus—eh . . . there are many people—really, I think—for example in Mondeor [suburb] and, ehm . . . in Meredale [village south of Johannesburg] and you will be astonished if you know where you live and who [in the area] are communists and who are not communists. You know, you get a fright when somebody comes to you and, eh . . . somebody who knows about these things and he takes you through the neighborhood and shows you who lives where and what [they are]. Then, you get frightened. But those people aren't, . . . they're not—they don't care much for [committing] terrorist acts. They don't want to commit terrorism; they're only—they work from below. The ANC does the thing [i.e., terrorism] and they [the communists] are just something like a sideline. They distribute books and all these sorts of things.

The tone in which he described the alleged communist television personality was chillingly reminiscent of the language describing targets in the dossiers of death squad operatives. Hennie was convinced about the guilt of this person; so were the death squads (Pauw, 1991, chap. 10). They eliminated people whose guilt could not be proved in the courts. Hennie adhered to the same theory and pattern of thought.

Hennie then elaborated on the atrocities of the ANC and the exchanges police had with them. He repeated many instances of alleged robberies committed by ANC members, the proof being their use of Russian and Czechoslovak arms. He lauded the role played by a black policeman as somebody he could trust:

> Last night I was doing duty at [a particular suburb] and I chatted with a guy from the robbery squad—he was a black man. I mean, I mean, I appreciate talking with such a man because that guy knows what he is talking about; you know, he knows his work. I mean, he is a black man [the tone of his voice dropped apologetically]. He doesn't care; he doesn't care about the color of his skin [*voel niks vir die kleur van sy vel nie—teenoor anders nie*] in the presence of others. Nothing; nothing. Look, this is his work. . . .

The black colleague was involved in tracing and engaging in street battles with ANC terrorist-robbers. Before we pursue Hennie's fear and his construction of the enemy, a short digression on his talk about his black colleague is appropriate. He accorded this black colleague features of almost superhuman courage, insight, and near invulnerability in his pursuit of "terrorists" and robbers. In his language use, Hennie also attempted to deracialize the brave colleague. In the sociology of race, the observation is sometimes made that racial differences, from the perspective of whites, and specifically conservative whites, seem to stand out more prominently when blacks are viewed as incompetent and failing. Where the opposite occurs, racial difference and distance are played down. However, this was not always the case in my research. The students whose dialogue is presented above thought that educated blacks reverted to an inferior cultural state and lifestyle as soon as they left their professional atmosphere. These students, however, lacked the close association with a professional black that Hennie had.

After talking about other black criminal "elements" in society whose minor illegal activities were tolerated by the police because they were considered useful in preventing major crime, Hennie turned to "terrorists" again.

> *Hennie:* You will always find criminals on the streets. I encounter them every day, I arrest them and lock them up. But you don't lock up . . . eh, catch an ANC terrorist or a communist just like that. Very, very seldom. Look,

I have locked up terrorists in the past but it isn't as if you deal with them on a day-to-day basis. It is not a fear of every day—jeez—I can work today and we are only dealing with terrorism, but I mean, I also have this fear on the job. I mean, it [anyone] could just be any person on the street or it could be a terrorist you meet on the street—having a gun, turning around and shooting at you. That fear is always there. It isn't as if I can just go out. I may never return. . . .

Schutte: What about the fear of whites who do not know where the danger lurks? They do not know whether it will spill over from Soweto into the [white] residential areas.

Jeanie: If you look at it closely, as his dad told us the other evening about Soweto—it lies straight in a line with that air force base. If they only try to make trouble those guys will take off and it won't be five minutes and Soweto is nailed. That is why it [Soweto] is built like that, for immediate action. He told us that here in Newlands—it wasn't Newlands at that time when he was a child—when the blacks marched, the whites shot them dead. . . . They [the blacks] will never be able to take the initiative in a march [on the white suburbs]. . . .

Hennie: Look, there is not even going to be—I mean, when we get information telling us the blacks are going to invade the city or something like that—no, there's no chance for them that those blokes would even get out of Soweto—never, never. They'll never make it regardless of how few we are. Soweto will be cordoned off—and Soweto is big. Look, there's no chance for him to get out of there. If he does get out of there he has to have a reason and that doesn't mean that he wants to go shopping. The only reason would be going to work—that's the only reason he'll get out of there.

Jeanie: The thing is, the whites—and I don't know whether everybody feels like me—but even if they come in their hundreds of thousands they do not have the firepower that the whites have. Us they will never . . . They are going to, they are going to—it is going to be a Blood River. If it ever comes to an armed invasion and there is war, they are going to lose. That's for sure.

Hennie: Definitely. If I tell you, as I told the others the other evening, those people do not make threats [meaning the ANC]. You always hear, jeez, the blacks from Soweto are going to do this or that. That day never comes. But we don't take it, eh . . . I mean we take it seriously and we act as if those people are really meaning what they say. They can always do it but we act in a serious way. We prevent it, in other words, whether they do it or whether they do not. It is my job to go and stand guard over there—even for three days on end. You have to be there in case something happens. But as always, they say they are going to do these things—they say they

do it but they never do it. But the ANC never say anything. They just do
it. [Those others] are dogs whose bark is worse than their bite.

The association between the ANC and terrorism was repeated here as
well as the fear of an unpredictable strike the ANC might launch. Subsequent to this interview, the ban on the ANC was lifted, of course.
However, this stereotype of the ANC as an unknown, extremely hostile,
and murderous movement was typical among conservatives during my
last visit to the country in June 1991. The specific passage quoted here
reveals further features of the concerns of conservative whites in general,
such as the fear of a spillover of black political activity into white areas and
the appropriate measures to counter it. A demonstrationlike spillover of
blacks into white areas was seen as an "invasion." Hennie saw the role of
the police as one of prevention, repeating the attitude expressed about the
role of police in the Pietermaritzburg area: controlling black-on-black
violence when it threatened to spill over into white areas. From his stand-
point, boundary maintenance between black and white was necessary, and
the security forces had a vital role to play in this regard. In a remarkable
assertion, he conceded that, in an unrest situation, the boundary was
permeable only for blacks crossing as laborers into white areas. He thus
confirmed what, to this category of whites, was the ultimate rationale for
black presence in "white" areas: their labor. Blacks moving en masse into
white areas implied the endangerment of white life and property. The
general and diffuse fear that blacks might arise as a bloc, looting, burning,
and raping in the white areas, was most pervasive notwithstanding the fact
that there was no historical precedent for such an occurrence. This fear
should further be understood against the background of conservative
whites' perception of blacks as uncontrollable savages bent on revenge.
Jeanie's words most clearly revealed a disposition to take to arms in a bloody
conflict at such an occurrence. She associated it with the last desperate,
but also symbolic, stand of whites against an overpowering black force at
Blood River in the 1830s, when the white minority, according to popular
belief, was miraculously aided by God in overcoming the black enemy.
   Hennie then related the panic that the so-called ANC terrorists inflicted
on the public and how the fear of terrorism and bombings in public places
increased over the last decade. He described how he had to clear a major
shopping mall in order to investigate an empty shoe box left behind by
somebody. He commented on how different the lives of young children
had become in this era of terrorism. As he spoke, I reflected upon the way

in which young children would view the ANC and black politicians in the future. The label "terrorist" attached indiscriminately to black activists evoked a deep suspicion. Both the formal political rhetoric of conservative politicians as well as the informal talk of adults at home made this connection. Hennie's fear of the resolute but surreptitious "ANC terrorist" was also indicative of a fear of the invisible, unpredictable and unsuspected occurrence of acts intended to kill whites. The "terrorist" can be any black (rarely a white). In the psychology of urban conservative whites I have spoken to, people said one would never know who is a terrorist—even some black you have trusted for many years may be prove to be a terrorist disguising himself or herself in such a way that even people most closely associated with him or her would not know. This talk and attitude reminded me of the classical image of the sorcerer as the undetected possessor of lethal power and substances intended for use against his or her enemies at the appropriate moment.[4]

Hennie despaired that the situation would ever improve, that peace would be restored. He believed that there were immediate problems to be addressed within the state of emergency. The whole face of crime had changed and, in his view of the role of the security forces (military and police), the ultimate use of violence against blacks as a category was justified. At this stage of the interview he became hesitant in his formulations but said enough to reveal how an ordinary police officer perceived the tragic events of the past and what his predispositions were concerning future encounters between black and white:

Hennie: But, to tell you honestly . . . eh . . . there is no solution. There will never be a solution—

Jeanie: [interrupts] But we also don't understand the implication of the state of emergency, or the political side of it. What does the state of emergency actually mean? It doesn't mean anything to me.

Hennie: [interrupts] Look, the state of emergency isn't . . .

Jeanie: [interjects]—shoot everyb . . .

Hennie: . . . the state of emergency isn't the thing. We now have to, eh, . . . people who steal cars. That is not criminally motivated. It is simply terrorism. Terrorism, communists. Communists come and do these things. Those things aren't criminal offenses or something of that sort. These acts are all based on the ANC. They are geared to the terror attacks by the ANC and it—this state of emergency which will prevent . . . eh . . . not prevent, but that is why it had been declared. . . . That is why they . . . when that terrorist is captured he cannot be let out like that guy who stole a car, I mean let out on bond. It is these things [that explain the state of emergency]. It is not, . . . it is why, it's why I mean—

Jeanie: But, it isn't. Isn't the state of emergency about your being able to shoot regardless?

Hennie: No . . .

Jeanie: I don't mean the guy that loses his nerve [meaning an individual nervous officer who might fire unauthorized shots]—

Hennie: Look, a terrorist, okay—

Jeanie: [interrupts] Is it only a matter of—eh . . . only a matter of terrorism. I don't know about these things. . . .

Hennie: The state of emergency was only declared because of terrorism. That's all.

Jeanie: What do the words *state of emergency* actually mean? What can you do to that fellow?

Hennie: You are not allowed—as a person you may do nothing to them.

Jeanie: But our country is—

Hennie: —people who—

Jeanie: —in a state of emergency in case something goes wrong—in case the bombs start falling . . .

Hennie: Then, for example, martial law will be declared—understand—then the government stands down and the [security] forces take over. Once it becomes as serious as that then the government doesn't have a say anymore—then P. W. Botha doesn't have a say; then the forces take over, then the army will take over; the police and the air force; all the forces in South Africa. They get together and, and they decide on a plan and execute it. Then nobody can say that either this or that political party is involved. They have to be neutral when we take over. That is why the state of emergency has been declared.

Jeanie: Then why are there these people who protested the other day when the state of emergency was reinstated—for the third time? Why then did they protest?

Hennie: Because they don't want there to be a state of emergency. They see . . . eh, how can I say. They are afraid because once the state of emergency is declared, okay . . . Look, I'm sure you know about martial law that reigned here in South Africa in, eh, 19 . . . eh . . . 1978—no—

Schutte: 1976.

Hennie: '76, okay. That was on exactly the same grounds that, that happened here in South Africa although it wasn't on such a large scale that one could say war erupted—it was mostly confined to Soweto and Sebokeng—all these places . . .

Jeanie:—to suppress them—

Hennie: Ya, you know they went out of control [*hulle het hand-uit geruk*] and they were shot at. The government was neutral. It couldn't say, Whoa, stop this anymore—don't shoot anymore. We decided—look we are shooting, even when many are killed and then we stop and so forth.

Jeanie: So you mean if Soweto now decides to march, decides to attack, then you may shoot them dead—this is what it means [emphatically].

Hennie: We may shoot them but then the government still has a say: "Stop; don't do this." But once martial law is declared—that day . . . [tone of anticipation and relish].

Jeanie: Yes, but I'm now talking about the state of emergency, that is what it is about in case they move against us now.

Hennie: That's correct, we may shoot them anyway, that speaks for itself, understand? We may not shoot whenever we like . . .

Jeanie: You have to stop whenever . . .

Hennie: . . . when we're told to—that is . . .

Jeanie: That is what the protest was actually about . . .

Hennie: They didn't want the state of emergency to be renewed.

Jeanie: They didn't want the state of emergency declared because they knew that if it happens . . .

Hennie: . . . because then they know; because they know . . . they know that they are much weaker than we are as far as weaponry [*wapenkrag*] is concerned.

Jeanie: . . . in case of . . . [here the tape is unclear]

Hennie: You know that is why they made the protest, because they are scared.

In all the talk between Hennie and Jeanie, they did not mention blacks by name, but the use of the pronoun *they* unambiguously pointed to either urban blacks or "ANC terrorists." The conversation was quite emotional, punctuated by constant interruptions. It was as if the couple had never before spoken about the topic in such detail. In its course, the conversation shifted attention from terrorists to black crowd control in general. First it centered on the state of emergency's suspension of certain rights, ranging from the posting of bond for car thieves to the use of ultimate force, that is, the shooting of people in crowd control. This shift is important. It occurred at the point where Jeanie started talking about bombs falling. It was the taken up by Hennie and the conversation shifted from martial law placing the "forces" in power to the use of firepower in crowd control. Again, Hennie and Jeanie shared the fear of blacks running out of control. Jeanie's language included terms such as *opmars* (march on), *opruk* (the movement of an army attacking), and *optrek* (march on). Her use of this terminology shows her assumption of military intentions on the part of blacks as a category. This fear, as pointed out above, ran very deep, yet it was not based on any precedent. It drew on a grossly exaggerated overestimation of the degree to which the urban black population was organized or mobilized. After the lifting of the state of emergency and the legalization of the ANC, whites like Hennie and Jeanie did not realize that the urban black population was divided on the strategies of the ANC. They found it necessary to perceive blacks as an undifferentiated and ominous unitary bloc.

Hennie at one stage seemed to confuse the state of emergency with martial law with regard to the use of lethal weapons against black civilians. During his hesitant argumentation, he was tense and illogical. He at one stage erroneously linked the suspension of political parties, and presumably constitutional rule, to the state of emergency. He also mistakenly assumed that martial law was declared during the Soweto unrest of 1976. He was on active duty during that unrest, in which unarmed youths marched in protest and were shot at by the police with fatal consequences. At no stage was there any real threat to the lives of the police. There was also no threat of the unrest spilling over into white areas. Yet he used the phrase *hand uitruk,"* which means *"getting out of control"* (the term also has a colloquial use referring to unruly behavior of children at school or at home). What the loss of control in this situation meant could not even be unambiguously established by the various commissions of inquiry that followed the bloodbaths of that time. The way Hennie was speaking, however, revealed his predisposition to the use of lethal force. The government had the power to stop the shooting, but Hennie made it clear that they, the forces, would shoot whenever they considered it appropriate for "gaining control." Reading between the lines of these utterances might be risky, but I want to suggest that the terms *gaining control* and *losing control,* as used by both police officers and civilians within the context of shooting talk, reveals a great deal about the justification for police violence when dealing with black crowds.

DISCUSSION

The urban whites interviewed for this study who had a conservative orientation to the present and future of South Africa desired, as the word *conservative* implies, a continuation of the old structures they were used to. In contrast to their rural counterparts, they had less intensive contact with blacks, not only at the workplace but in the domestic sphere as well.

Their contacts with blacks as professionals were relatively rare. Many urban whites shared their rural counterparts' biases toward black professionals as people who were only superficially Westernized. Once the veneer of Westernness was scraped off, the primitive, tribal black would be found beneath it. For black persons, ethnicity was seen as part of their crudeness and lack of civilization. Blacks were deemed to be violent and savage, permanently locked into fixed and primordial ethnic identities. Black ethnic boundaries were believed to be firm and unchanging. Whites saw a common denominator uniting all black cultures: their inherent crudeness. A Zulu, for example, would forever remain a Zulu, a Xhosa a Xhosa, and so forth. Here again, the deep racial and ethnic structuring of whites' apperception of the wider social world surrounding them is documented. In comparison with their rural counterparts, urban whites used the same ideological rationalizations that confuse race and culture. Ethnic groups, as defined by apartheid over many decades, have become the cognitive map by which these whites navigated reality and made sense of it. To some, the static concept of ethnicity even had a cosmological dimension.

Most informants believed there was an unbridgeable, or almost unbridgeable, gap in civilization between white and black. They saw blacks as not quite human. They perceived blacks as closer to nature, and therefore believed blacks' needs to be different from those of whites. For some, this difference justified treating blacks unequally before the law. Blacks' housing and other needs were related to their low level of civilization and culture and to their proximity to nature. Like their rural counterparts, these white urbanites thought that the government was doing too much for the black population, that blacks unjustifiably received handouts that they in no way appreciated. One could even say that these respondents judged blacks to be unworthy or undeserving of development aid or assistance. At best, blacks should have been left to themselves in their own areas. Their presence in "white" areas could be justified only as long as they provided labor to white homes and industries. The whites hoped that the black labor force would stay docile and not become "uppity."

The whites resented the changes that had been taking place in the wake of the government's reform policies. They were unable to understand the rationale behind the changes, because they deemed them unnecessary. Conservatives perceived their reality selectively. Some could not understand why public facilities and amenities had to be shared; such things had been separate for as long as they could remember. For them, segregation and the differential treatment of blacks were matters of common sense. The success of decades of apartheid socialization blinded many whites to the contributions blacks made to the system. Ockey, for example, thought that parks were maintained by whites and that they therefore deserved exclusive access to them. Changes to the apartheid system were frequently regarded in an extremely negative light. Dawid, for example, thought that whites would be "totally lost" after the abolition of the Group Areas Act. Leon, the "reasonable" Conservative Party man, thought that the disappearance of this law would lead to the assimilation of white people into the overwhelming nonwhite majority and thus doom white "culture" and sense of belonging to oblivion.

These conservative whites' sense of identity can be looked at on two levels. First, there was a deep identification with the country itself. South Africa was home, and there was nowhere else to go. Afrikaans speakers especially felt they were indigenous to the country, but English speakers also exhibited very strong attachment. Regardless of the language communities they belonged to, these whites all shared an awareness and sense of South Africanness. However, as soon as many were confronted with the South Africanness of blacks and blacks' sense of belonging, the informants became inconsistent, either repeating the old notion that "they" (the blacks) belonged to the (apartheid) national states or claiming that both black and white shared their South Africanness in special, but parallel and divided, ways. Blacks and whites had separate lifestyles in geographically separated areas. Mac maintained that he was a "white African." However, when he was pressed to elaborate on the "African" component of his identity, he changed the subject and drifted to another theme. His case raises an interesting question: In what sense do whites in South Africa perceive themselves as African? What does it mean when conservative whites make the assertion that they are African? The nature of this self-identification becomes clearer in light of what these informants had to say about Africa in general. Most of their statements about Africa were extremely negative. The examples they used to illustrate black mismanagement and incompetence in government and economic affairs all came from Africa. The "African" component of these whites' self-identification seems to have much more to do with geography, climate, animal and plant life, and white colonial lifestyles than with African culture.

The second level of self-identification, closely linked to the first, involved the notion of "civilization." We saw repeatedly how cultural difference was perceived to be something that set white and black apart. It was acceptable and morally justifiable to talk about cultural differences in order to distinguish categories of people. However, this cultural difference, viewed more closely, clearly harbored the judgment that "white culture" was superior to black culture(s). The transformation of the horizontal plane of cultural difference to the vertical plane of superiority and inferiority was achieved through the equation of "white culture" with civilization. A further transformation occurred when "civilization" was identified with whites, that is, with race. The negative symbolism attached to blacks' bodies and the pollution with which they were associated confirmed the basic racism inherent in these arguments.

Finally, as far as the future was concerned, a clear dividing line could be drawn between those urban conservative whites who were relatively well-off and those who were not. Mac is an example of a wealthier conservative. He realized that he would still be better off than most in a future integrated South Africa. He was convinced that the basic social structure of South Africa would be preserved. His wealth and other ties with the outside world provided him with an option to leave should the worst happen. His class position coincided with his racial status. The cases of Dawid and Hennie, the police officer, were quite different. They were more despondent and confused about the future. In Hennie and Jeanie's case there was a degree of despair on the one hand and, on the other, a willingness to reach for more violent means to preserve whatever they had.

Conservatives constitute a significant proportion of the white South African population. Their reactions and responses to democratization moves in the country will be crucial for the chances of a relatively peaceful transition from racial oligarchy to a representative form of government. In the referendum held on March 17, 1992, urban whites overwhelmingly supported the government's initiative to negotiate a new constitution for the country that would provide for power sharing with blacks. That result surprised many observers. The voter turnout of 85% was astronomically high, and 68.5% of the voters indicated that they supported the negotiation process (*Star,* March 19, 1992).[5]

Was this an indication of a radical change of heart by conservative whites? Such an assumption would be unrealistic. The National Party government took the CP opposition by surprise by announcing the referendum soon after the latter's success in capturing the Potchefstroom constituency in a by-election in February. Potchefstroom was a traditional stronghold of the National Party and, after it fell into the hands of conservatives, President F. W. de Klerk took the risk of testing the white electorate's support for his negotiations for a new constitution. He needed a mandate from his constituency and he acted from a position of strength, because his government had an almost complete monopoly over the media, which was useful in manipulating the electorate. The government also had the funds to engage a top public relations company, Saatchi and Saatchi, to run the campaign. The CP and their satellites made a poor showing in comparison. Both camps used scare tactics. The government's strategy was successful, for it divided the conservative whites in the towns. They had to decide whether to vote for or against their most feared scenario. The consequences of a no vote were depicted as disastrous. Worn out by years of economic recession, inflation, international isolation, and a pervasive sense of insecurity, many conservative voters were convinced that the government's course of action might minimize further losses and isolation. The glorious future of a "new South Africa" depicted by the media and the public impact of renewed sports contacts with the international community created a temporary atmosphere of euphoria and celebration.

However, some conservatives' swing toward favoring a negotiated future for South Africa rather than insisting on a restoration of the old apartheid system was neither an indication of a change in their attitude toward blacks nor evidence of a change in their hopes that their privileged position would be maintained. The only important shift that occurred was the idea that the future had to be negotiated rather than dictated by the minority. Whether "negotiation" to them meant equal partners coming to an agreement after a process of give-and-take is uncertain. It is also unclear whether those conservatives who voted yes were aware of what the consequences of their ballots might be if there truly was negotiation.

NOTES

1. After the Anglo-Boer War (1899-1902), a number of Afrikaners refused to live under British rule and decided to emigrate to Patagonia, in Argentina.

2. The violent attacks between black factions during 1990-1991 were largely ascribed to differences between supporters of Inkatha and the ANC. Looking at the opposing sides in this way reveals only a part of the real situation. For historical reasons, apartheid legislation created two categories of blacks: the "legal" urban resident and the rural and migrant laborer category. The rift between these two ran very deep. Risking some degree of speculation, I would argue that Mac's reasoning was typical of those police and armed forces members who allegedly cooperated with the largely rural-oriented Inkatha in its attacks on ANC supporters.

3. The person concerned was an Afrikaans-speaking woman with liberal leanings. She would never have survived the government's control of the media had she truly been a communist at that time.

4. I am here thinking of the distinction Evans-Pritchard (1963) makes between witchcraft and sorcery. Witches in some African societies were often unconscious of the harm they inflicted, whereas the sorcerer was the conscious, but secretive, agent of social and personal harm.

5. Some 75-85% of the voters in the metropolitan areas of the Cape Province, Natal, and Johannesburg voted yes. Pretoria and cities in the Orange Free State and the towns and rural areas of Western and Northern Transvaal polled yes at rates varying between 43% and 57%.

10

Whites in Town II:
Moderate Perspectives

You know, these Africans never learn! Just look at her! She doesn't understand that if they want to change and live like the white man, then they must speak English. They just don't want to adapt, yet they are the ones who want change.

It seems unfair to frame a chapter on more open, moderate visions and values among white South Africans by starting off with a quotation like this. Yet, as I will argue below, it gives expression to an important aspect of progressive perspectives. At first, I wanted to subtitle this chapter "Liberal Perspectives" or "Progressive Perspectives," but I realized neither would have been a fair reflection of the spectrum of attitudes and values I encountered. The most important difference between the attitudes and visions of white moderates and those of conservatives was found in the degree of rigidity with which white group boundaries were drawn.

Moderates also broadly acknowledged the inevitability of change. Some informants reluctantly acknowledged this fact, whereas others embraced it hesitantly. There were two basic ways in which moderates defined the direction that change was, or should be, taking. On the one hand, change could occur in the direction of a multiracial society with a dominant Western lifestyle and social values that would leave room for minority culture forms. On the other hand, change could occur in the direction of a nonracial society in which a new, unique, and syncretistic lifestyle would develop, incorporating and blending both African and Western cultural contributions. Very few of the moderates interviewed envisioned the latter. In academic terms, the difference between these two visions is basically that between pluralist and assimilationist perspectives. The reason it was difficult for informants to envision the assimilationist form of change had to do with the fact that progressive whites were unsure or vague about which cultural model would be the leading one—whether they were to be assimilated into Africanness or whether Africanness had to be assimilated into their culture. The following case illustrates this point.

LIVE LIKE
THE WHITE MAN

The words quoted at the beginning of this chapter were recorded during an unobtrusive observation made at a shopping mall in the affluent, politically liberal, and predominantly English-speaking suburb of Rosebank in Johannesburg. An elderly white man and white woman were sitting on a bench talking together. A well-dressed black woman and her child of about 5 years old walked past. Out of earshot of the mother, the man greeted the child in English. The child did not respond. The man persisted and drew the attention of the mother, who walked over to him. A conversation ensued:

> *Man:* You must teach your child to speak English.
> *Mother:* No, he's too young still [jocularly]. But you should learn to greet him in our language.

The man remained silent at this response, and the mother and child walked away. The elderly man and woman then had this exchange:

> *Woman:* You know, these Africans never learn! Just look at her! She doesn't understand that if they want to change and live like the white man, then they must speak English. They just don't want to adapt, yet they are the ones who want change.
> *Man:* They look so Westernized, though. But you know, they're all the same . . . they only know how to use money on their backs and in their tummies.
> *Woman:* Yes. But my girl—I offered her two of my dresses for Christmas. She told me that she doesn't wear secondhand clothes. I was surprised. She'd rather buy new ones. I thought—well . . . and these are our underprivileged people!
> *Man:* The Africans are changing in their attitude [toward whites?]. It's going to be hard for the government, because they have rightly given them more. But where can you stop? We must keep the standards up.

> *Woman:* I don't know how they'll manage. Our pensions are low enough as it is. The Africans don't even have the same overheads as us—taxes, rent, et cetera. No, . . . it's very difficult to know what's right.

The man and woman then said goodbye to each other and parted company.

The first thing that struck me in these exchanges were the forms of address. The white man spoke to the black woman in a very direct and commanding way. The tone he used was reminiscent of the way whites talk to their black servants: from a superior position, demanding obedience. The man did not use any kind of opening phrase, such as "Excuse me" or "Madam." According to white South African politeness norms, such an opening would have been appropriate in addressing a white woman, for example. Not so in this case. The black woman might have been a professional herself or married to a doctor or lawyer, yet the man spoke to her in a manner usually used with servants. This stereotyping was repeated by the elderly white woman, who associated the black woman with the general type of domestic servant ("my girl"). The black woman was apparently quite undaunted and self-confident, because she challenged the white man to use a black vernacular when addressing a small black child. She lacked submissiveness, and this prompted his remark that "Africans are changing their attitude."

Both whites took it for granted that blacks should adapt to the ways of whites, not only in regard to language issues, but in the whole spectrum of lifestyle ("live like the white man"). The speakers also generalized "Africans." In other words, regardless of the liberal discourse about non-racialism and individual rights propagated by the English-language press and the political parties dominant in this area, the speakers were lumping all blacks into one broad racial/laborer category. Blacks as an out-group were "all the same." To the man, it was confusing that they "look so Westernized, though." They thus appear Westernized but are, in fact, different in nature. They are irresponsible in money matters. The white woman confirmed this with reference to her domestic servant's refusal to accept used clothing from her. Blacks were thus regarded as the objects of charitable acts. As a category, they were the underprivileged, or the poor in need of handouts. Even the government was praised for giving them more handouts. The image of blacks held by these two whites evoked the colonial notion of "the white man's burden."

The discussion ended with the man's remark that standards had to be maintained. The woman understood this to mean their own living standard as pensioners. This use of the phrase *standard of living* stands in contrast to the way it was used by the students quoted in Chapter 9, who equated the black standard of living with an inferior lifestyle.

NATURAL SEGREGATION

Henry was a wealthy owner of a sizable company in Natal that employed many black laborers. He was opposed to apartheid and blamed the government for the economic ills that beset the country. He generally had an optimistic view of the future, but, as he revealed, he hoped for a future in which old divisions and boundaries would still prevail, albeit in a somewhat more diversified form. Henry was well informed and widely traveled, and he had served on a number of government and provincial commissions of inquiry. His interview was conducted in English by a research assistant:

Interviewer: What is your view of the future of South Africa with regard to the position of the whites?

Henry: It's obvious that they're going to have to live in a multiracial society. . . .

Interviewer: Do you think they will have to drop their standards . . . ?

Henry: Not necessarily, because what is happening—and I have this in my own company: we have blacks with daughters at St. Mary's—they are now reading up to the European level and I'm not saying this level we're at here [referring to himself], but they are improving their standard of living. The standard of living has gone down in South Africa not because of blacks but because of—stuff of the government. Our high inflation, everybody's standard of living has come down, definitively whites—not because of the blacks or coloured or anything like that but maybe because the government has totally lost control of the economy. . . . And another point people forget about: You look at living standards of coloureds and Indians. Now, everybody thinks that South Africa is just black, which I think is totally unfair. In actual fact it should be "nonwhites," and there is a very wealthy and stable Indian community—two times the population of whites in Durban—and in the Cape, you have a superb coloured population. Okay, you have your dregs. You have them in any society, but certainly, if we're going to have to put more money into black education we will see a drop in living standards.

Interviewer: With this multiracial society, do you envisage much intermarriage, or will whites remain a separate group?

Henry: No, I think you've just got to look at most of your sophisticated countries—Singapore's a classic—where the whites live together with

Indians, coloureds, et cetera. Poor black, white, and coloured will live in their ghettos.

You look at New York. People tend to live amongst themselves where you have a free right to go. I can imagine the Indians, in actual fact, will be very keen to live in white suburbs because that's the way they operate. But even then, the Indians like to keep to themselves. And then, of course, something else that people forget, you've got the Hindus and the Muslims who *always* live apart. You've got a *natural segregation* [emphasis added] that isn't forced upon anybody by group areas.

Interviewer: Do you think the present has differed much from the past? Do you see many changes?

Henry: Oh yes.

Interviewer: In what ways?

Henry: I think people are now realizing there's no way you can put people— I'm now talking about black people—miles away from the workplace where they've got to commute for hours, which is happening and happens all the time. Take Ezithebe [area in Natal]—a classic [case]. It's a black industrial area—a lot of large industries have moved up there and a lot of whites, in actual fact, are living [nearby]. So your pattern's got to change: Your workforce has got to be closer to their workplace. . . .

Interviewer: Do you feel your personal security has been threatened? Has there been any change in this?

Henry: I think the personal security of all South Africans is threatened at the moment, including blacks. The greatest confrontation at the moment—I sit on the [name of a committee]—the problem now is not black against white, it's black against black. That's totally political. You even heard in church yesterday where the priest said for the first time blacks have been able to get out because there haven't been boycotts against the whites because that was a white boycott [?].

Interviewer: Have you made any measures to safeguard your security?

Henry: Yes. I think we all have become security conscious: safety gates, better entrances, and facilities to get into your property. The whole of South Africa has become very security conscious. Your money is carried by security guards. But is it any different anywhere else?

Interviewer: Is there a disparity between your hopes for the future and what you can realistically expect?

Henry: Yes, what you're going to find is this: You have a very wealthy upper class, Indian and coloured. You have a middle class, Indian and coloured, and we're now breeding—it's something that no one can quantify—the black entrepreneur. You take your black taxi . . . 58,000 in all, this year already. You're going to create a middle-class black and you have your wealthy blacks. It happened in Soweto at his very stage, where they're segregating away from the riffraff. So, as I see it: Any massive population—you've got a huge peasant population—Durban's the fastest-growing city outside Mexico City—and you're going to have these peasants who are rural, they're gonna be squatters, they're gonna be no different to anybody else anywhere in the world—and they're multiplying at such a rate that they are going to stay poor. Now, what will happen is your other blacks are going to come up and, in actual fact, the black entrepreneur is now creating home industries employment for his own people, and they become *his* laborers. Now that is a totally different thing.

Henry then gave an example of 100 small farms run by blacks in Natal and continued:

Henry: . . . and as they become capitalists, their spending power increases. Don't forget the black normally doesn't save. He needs food, he needs clothes, so he becomes a spender.

Interviewer: You must have certain ambitions for yourself. Do you think that perhaps, with any big political changes in this country, these ambitions will be prevented from being realized for your sons?

Henry: Let me be quite honest about that. I have an international qualification. My age is probably the thing most against me there. I want all my sons to be capable anywhere in the world. I want to give them the opportunity for them to decide. The interesting thing becomes this: their own attitude is: This is the country they love.

    The problem on the education front—you probably haven't seen it at all. We've had the odd little bit of trouble at Natal University. . . . But at Westville University [originally an apartheid university for Indians, now open to all groups], which is Indian, white, and black, it's the blacks who caused the trouble. Now, this is a problem. It is—they are not going to be able to have this massive quick transition. If they really want to look at it—and you ask any American businessman especially—how many Negroes sit on the boards of top companies—and there aren't any. They're wonderful entertainers and middle management. And how can you then try and get a black who hasn't a clue? They're not managers. They're sportsmen and entertainers.

He then gave an example of a friend who asked an international company why it didn't have blacks on its board:

Henry: They say, "You don't understand, you're an Englishman—they don't make top management." He says, "I'm a South African." Then they said,

"You would understand." [At first] I didn't accept this. I spoke to an international businessman who said the exact same thing. Tokenism doesn't operate in America. They do it, you know—they've got to have it on the stage, theater. You've got to have a black, a Negro appear.

Interviewer: It'll be very interesting how this country works out. . . .

Henry: Well, what you've got to work on . . . you've got to say to yourself—and this is another crazy thing—who is going to be the black leader? People say, *What* black leader?' Which tribe is he gonna come from? . . . Are we going to have a civil war between blacks? They'll never work that one out.

I tell you what South Africa is close to—Canada. I gave an address in Canada and I did research. Their [per] capita income is higher than ours, miles higher, but you've got your French and your English. . . . They're two different cultures, two totally different people. . . . [The Indians] were very much like our coloured: They're ill treated, ugh, they live in very squalid surroundings, they are alcoholics. . . . Here the numbers are against us; there it is in their favor. And yet your greatest unemployment in America is amongst the Negroes.

He then went on to explain how he got much of his knowledge about the country's affairs from the various commissions on which he had served. When asked whether he saw any change in the country, he quoted his sister-in-law on a visit from Canada. She was originally South African and remarked how integrated the services in metropolitan South Africa were. Then:

Interviewer: Do you see parallels between South Africa and any other country—other than Canada?

Henry: The Canadian thing is the two cultures and two different cultures of whites. It wasn't a black thing. There is no country like South Africa. This is no country that has got this predominantly Afrikaans-speaking white population. Then you've got your English-speaking population and this massive population of Portuguese—that people don't realize how strong they are. Then you've got your tribal Africans and tribal stans [possibly short for Bantustans, an old term for the homelands]. [They] are very strong. Then you've got your Hindus, your Muslims, your coloured. I don't think there is any country like South Africa that I know of.

I'll give you a classic about that one—and this is on the beach problem. When I sat on this committee, they asked me what I thought about this [opening of the beaches to all races] and I said, "I believe in segregation on the beaches." They said, "But how can you?" I said, "I'll tell you why." My Indian clients tell me there's no way they can swim with the bloody kaffirs—they say "kaffirs"; it's peasants we're talking about—coming down here in their buses; same as we had there in the Transkei, when all the blacks came down. The coloureds don't want to mix with the kaffirs— I'm using that word just to make it [sound like the] rabble. So they want their own beaches. But then [my wife] and I swim on the international beach. You see superb black children, beautifully dressed, beautifully mannered; superb Indian children, no hooligans. And then you've got the beach for the Afrikaners, which is South Beach, always has been since I was a kid, and the Jews are on *that* beach. I'm serious. And the Durbanites go to Addington Beach. So, because of this complex situation we've got, integration must never be forced on anybody. Allow people the right to mix; allow them the right to their own cultures, to their own likes and dislikes, and give them the right to be able to use these without having those black gangs coming and robbing Indians on the beach, taking their clothes, beating people up. And also, I totally disagree with the whites who interfere with the Indians down at [?] and places like that. They're both wrong. They're both extremes. Whether it's black extreme or white extreme.

Interviewer: If we do get majority rule, how do you see yourself and your family?

Henry: I just have a theory that politicians are out for themselves [he then cited some examples of corruption]. The [only] change I can see is this, and it's going to take time. I think a long, long time. We know that in the year 2000 there'll be 11 blacks to every white in Durban. As one of these CP blokes who wanted me to join them [said]. I told him he was mad because he'd have to be the best football, hockey player with 11 people on one side and one on the other. They'll *swamp* you. So, if you work together now and try and work out a solution—the Indaba produces a solution because it protects the minorities—not only the whites, but the Indians and coloureds in Natal.[1] The largest tribe in South Africa is the Zulu. So you have got to have, like the American Constitution; so you have got to have protection for the people—so you'd have—if you just take a simplistic attitude here—if you have a proper free election of the City Council in Durban, you'd have, there'd be double the number of Indian city councillors to white, on proportion of representation. You'd have some coloureds. You can now move up to Stanger-Verulam [north of Durban]— there'd be very few whites, there'd be Indians, very few blacks. Now, move up to Ging[-gindlovu], Namatikulu [further north in KwaZulu], it'd be virtually totally black. So, if you then put together your provincial council or your Indaba, the black, because of numbers and because they have the greater ward area—they would have a greater say. But the *economic* power-wealth is in triangles like the Vaal triangle, or in the axis of Durban-Pinetown up to Cato Ridge. So, in a political sense, you'll have more blacks participating because they'll be looking after their population. But I don't see that it is going to make a hell of a lot of difference to us who live in Durban.

Interviewer: Have you recently experienced a change of heart in political matters? If so, what happened? Why did the change occur? [The research assistant wasn't satisfied with the previous answer.]

Henry: Well, you've got this tragedy, of course. There has been this CP . . . um . . . if you look at it this way, what you've really had. You take the South-West Africa situation. That is one of the greatest developments and that has come about by the Nationalist Party realizing that they can no longer live in isolation and it's also come about—make no mistake—by big brother America and Britain—and thank God for Reagan and Maggie Thatcher—because they, in actual fact, have put the screws on South Africa. . . . Now, the . . . um . . . er . . . this one is quite a vast one. . . . So, change has been forced upon us by superpowers and that change has made it a better place for people of Namibia and South-West Africa. The peace in Angola—I think it is very important because it means then we're protecting our *own* borders and you'll find *all* South Africans protect their borders, but they're not prepared to fight outside. So you get this, but there has been this other point: When you've got people who know nothing about our problem, especially Americans, this Dellums bill, a disaster, and they're now gonna apply sanctions. And you've got this prick, Tutu. Sanctions—who have suffered by sanctions? There's a factory in Ezithebe, Taiwanese. Because of sanctions 2,000 blacks in this sewing machine factory were fired. The *blacks* are suffering from sanctions. *America* is suffering from sanctions because all we're doing is exporting to other countries and they're [Americans] paying more for our goods. And they are driving us towards Russia. And [if] we do a deal with Russia, and then Russia and South Africa control the bulk of all strategic materials; that is more than cutting your nose to spite your face, it's cutting your bloody head off! So I would say the change . . . Change is a funny thing. . . . What's change? There has definitely been a more liberal outlook but we have this frightening thing: Afrikanerdom doesn't want to be totally split which it has been split. The other big change of course is with this Worral, Malan. I mean, the PFP have always, to my mind, [been] totally wishy-washy. Whatever anyone says, they say against it. They . . . ugh, very disappointing. But now, with these parties coming together—they come together and they start working and forming a *united* opposition. You'd find that you then get into a position where *South Africans* are working together and we now come to the point that I was very involved in: that was the drawing up of the future of South Africa. And the future for South Africa is in actual fact a federal system identical to that in America, where you have a federal parliament. It's been presented to the government and cabinet ministers. I was on the . . . presented it to them, drawn up by two

brilliant Afrikaans people: one's a deputy governor of the Reserve Bank—
Lombard—it was the Lombard Report. And there you bring *back* into
South Africa, the Transkei, the Ciskei, but they stay as Transkei and Ciskei,
but they become states of South Africa, and then we have a multiracial
parliament which will not only represent the Cape politicians, it will
represent the Ciskeians and the Transkeians and the Venda.

At this point the interviewer's tape ran out; after it was changed, the
interview continued:

Henry: [We] won't have this building fancy airports at Umtata, you don't have
to go through border posts to go through South Africa. So, South Africa
of the future as I see it—and it can happen because if you really take it,
you've just got to listen, the Afrikaner will not give up South Africa. Make
no mistake. They can't say it is comparable to Rhodesia. There were
250,000 whites in Rhodesia, we've got hundreds of thousands, millions
of Afrikaners who are very highly equipped with the most sophisticated
weaponry and, as Buthelezi said, it would be a bloodbath, and nobody
would win. But if you work on that system where we have this *multiracial,
separate*—ya, America is separate, you've got your states and they've got
their different legislation in the different states in America—go[ing] back
to my constitution law studies. You've got different tax acts in the states;
so you do exactly the same here. Ciskei can have a free port. So you can
encourage that. Their tax system is different. There's nothing stopping
you from doing that. But you bring everybody together into a central . . .
like a bunch of schoolchildren: If the headmistress and masters are all
sitting in a common room and the kids have got the run of the school they're
gonna ruin it. But if you bring everybody into a system—and I believe
that will be the future of South Africa. Whether, . . . and this is one I don't
know: you could have a white state up with the CP in Pietersburg and,
I'm afraid that is the one thing that worries me. But it doesn't worry me
to the extent that I can ever see them becoming a government. I think they
are radicals. They are gonna cause a lot of trouble. But I think they're gonna
lose so much face once the whites and blacks and everybody pulls together
that they'll be seen as a lost white tribe. I can't equate it to any other
[thing]. They're Nazi, neo-Nazi, political white fanatics and yet they have
black people working for them, which is ludicrous. And I think what'll
happen there is you'll get these fanatics: because they believe that that
type of Afrikaner will accomplish [?] for them. But what'll happen is that
they'll become smaller, because what'll happen is that, if you take Boksburg,
once they become economically starved, once nobody supports them, and
that is happening, this is the first *major* boycott—in the past we've had
boycotting OK Bazaars—now you boycott those people and once the

whites start boycotting them, there's no way the Afrikaner's gonna keep that or the CP is gonna be able to keep themselves together. So, I think what'll happen, they could become a tightly knit little bunch up in Potgieters-rus, or up there. And delimitation [remapping], of course, is gonna kill them too. And what we're doing with this new delimitation: The votes are loaded. In fact, the *platteland* [rural areas] would say the NP would come to power—and that will go against the CP. Oh, they'll become a force but I don't believe they'll become a worrying force.

Interviewer: . . . make a future here? There's nowhere else to go . . .

Henry: . . . let's take that one step further: Just look at my brother-in-law [in Canada]. At [his kid's] school in Canada you're not allowed to win prizes because that means somebody's better than somebody else. You can go to school with long hair, torn pants, because the teachers are not allowed to interfere with the children. Discipline doesn't mean a thing. Their standard of education is disgraceful. When they go to college, the first year is to orientate themselves, stupid subjects, total bloody waste of time instead of getting on.

At first the idea of "natural segregation" noted by Henry created the impression that ethnic groups would spontaneously cluster in whatever society he might have thought of. There were also passages in which he used class as a distinguishing and differentiating factor between and within groups. Thus blacks would develop a middle class with whom Henry seemed to be happy to share "international" beaches, for example. However, the overall framework of his argument was an ethnic one. Ethnic group membership was not only the principle underlying beach usage but was equally the organizing principle for all groups, especially for blacks.

His remarks about blacks in management revealed a blatant element of racism. He confined their competence to the worlds of entertainment and sport while assuming that they lack the capabilities to handle leadership in business. In addition, he implied that affirmative action policies in the United States are merely ploys to give them visibility, to place them "on a stage." It thus boiled down to tokenism and window dressing. Henry thus had very little confidence in black leadership. He believed that South Africa's future political map would display a number of "states" similar to those in the U.S. federal system. The country would be politically decentralized. The homelands would continue as federal states. Blacks would exercise their political rights in these regions, where "they'll be looking after their [own] population" without making much difference to those (whites) in Durban. He contrasted economic and political power with great emphasis. He wasn't explicit about it, but implied that economic power would remain in the hands of whites in the metropolitan areas. He was of course inconsistent, because those metropolitan areas also contained an overwhelming majority of blacks whose future exercise of political rights might have dramatic consequences for the white wielders of economic power.

The decentralized, federal model Henry was working with not only froze most blacks to their territories but also provided him with a solution to the worrisome Afrikaner right-wing problem. Under a decentralized system they might be confined to localities where they could stew in their own broth. The notion of regionalism or federalism matched his view on the multiracial nature of the country. His perspective excluded the idea of nonracialism. He accepted the persistence of existing ethnic and racial groups and failed to consider an alternative in which groups could change or amalgamate. He saw segregation into discrete groups as a "natural" phenomenon. He believed that, in contrast to apartheid's legal enforcement of segregation, it would occur of its own accord.

The theme of natural segregation also arose at an informal function I attended. I had a discussion with Marie, an Afrikaans-speaking woman from an affluent suburb to the north of Johannesburg. She was telling me how Afrikaners of her background tend to associate more freely with blacks than do English speakers (an observation that is contestable). She mentioned how her daughter was the only one to ask a black girl to play with her at a tennis party of teenagers from different backgrounds. The black girl was ignored by the English-speaking whites present. Marie said she herself had no scruples against meeting blacks socially. When asked how she would feel if a male black teenager were to ask her daughter for a dance at a social occasion, she replied:

> Well, I teach my children that the laws of the . . . eh, of the . . . of humanity are not made by humans. They are appropriately made by nature. I told my kids; when they play with black kids on our farm—with these black kids. Toward evening my kids say: "Mom, can't X sleep at our place tonight?" Then I took them and told them: "Kiddies, you have to look into nature. Nature sets laws to humans [*Bepaal vir 'n mens wette*]. Look at the birds and the animals during daytime. They graze together. They rest together. When it becomes night, though, the dove goes to the doves and the sheep go to their corral and so do the cattle. I would like you to understand: Humans are humans, do mix with them, but when night falls, come back to your own people." Indirectly, I am telling them, "Please, if you choose your companion for life, do so from the ranks of your own people." This, I believe, is a biblical injunction [*voorskrif*] that we should [stay?] with our own. I said—

"because it is the will of the Lord that we should not cross over—and I would like you to live in harmony with everybody, but, if one day you would like to—at night—where you wish to sleep together, where you wish to marry— you have to think very carefully because then you have to go with your own people according to the Bible."

I had asked Marie a simple hypothetical question about a black teenager inviting her daughter to a dance at a social occasion, and the response she gave invoked not only "laws of nature" but also the Bible for rejecting any relationship that goes beyond the public daytime context. The question had nothing to do with children's slumber parties, sexual relations, or marriage, yet Marie responded as though asked about all those issues. Her response demonstrated her deep concern, if not anxiety, about group boundaries. It differed from the conservative response, which would exclude social contacts. Her invocation of "nature" and the Bible to justify her views disregarded both the fact that in "nature" humans are one species and the fact that racial intermarriage occurred in biblical times. Yet limitation of the interaction between black and white was rigidly set because both nature and Scripture did not allow exceptions. There could thus be no objections to public interaction with members of other races in a social fashion, but there were definite and firm limits beyond that. From a very different angle, Marie shared with Henry the idea of a "natural" residential segregation. As the evening wore on, Marie philosophically declared that humans, like animals, were different. Each species had its own beauty. The leopard was beautiful in its way, but so too was the warthog. I wondered which image she applied to herself. She repeated her equation of the difference in black and white human visibility and specieslike differences between animals.

A NONRACIAL DREAM ISLAND

The following is a transcript of an informal discussion recorded in January 1989 at a street café in Yeoville, which is situated near downtown to the northeast of the Johannesburg city center. Its population consists of a fair proportion of young single professionals and students as well as young couples. At the time of the research, members of other population groups had settled in this suburb. Its social atmosphere was vibrant. In contrast with Mayfair, further to the west, in Yeoville the racial mixing had been harmonious. This discussion took place among four white friends: my research assistant; Fiona, a graduate student who at the time was living with a black boyfriend; Nestor, an artist; and Len, a set builder. All were in their 20s.

Assistant: Knowing the political situation of today, where do you see your future? What do you think is going to happen as far as you, the whites, are concerned?

Fiona: Well, I don't know. It worries me that things are going to escalate. I can see a pattern of things polarizing at the moment. People are getting more radical either way. Blacks are getting more militant. Not only blacks. Some whites are getting more militant. Left-wing as well as right-wing. And that situation is quite *kak* [shit] because then people like me are left in the middle and you don't really have much of a say. You're just basically farting around.

Assistant: You think it's quite a powerful movement from the radical left and the radical right?

Nestor: It's powerful on both sides.

Len: It's on the right.

Fiona: It's powerful on both sides.

Assistant: It's going to influence the outcome of the future of the country?

Fiona: Of course.

Assistant: In what way?

Fiona: Because the thing is, there is no negotiation for starters. There's no communication between these people at all and the government's totally to blame for that, because they created an atmosphere and environment of no negotiation and people who try to negotiate, people who try to step out and go and talk to the ANC, they paint a picture of them as total radicals. I mean, even black businessmen who really are not politically committed one way or the other just want to see a future for the country and go and talk to the ANC, they give a whole big spiel and like say these people are radical and paint a picture of them as militant.[2]

Nestor: But the government feels it has to do that!

Fiona: Yes, of course, but that's *kak.* The government is destroying this country but it's protecting its own interests.

Nestor: Any government would do that. It's inevitable that they must do that.

Assistant: So the government is protecting its own interests, which I agree is what is happening. What do you think that is going to lead to?

Nestor: Well, it is going to lead to a lot of dissatisfaction in the people. In the people that don't agree with it.

Len: There is dissatisfaction as it is.

Assistant: How do you mean dissatisfaction?

Len: [here the tape is unclear] hatred . . .

Assistant: Warfare, violence?

Fiona: Yes, you see, that's the thing. Because basically the only way you can get a message through is by putting a gun in somebody's face and blasting his brain away.

Nestor: But in the other extreme, that makes people that are against that more opposed to that.

Assistant: Okay, so it's going to boil down to violence.

Fiona: Yes. Well, I tell you I want to pack off and go and live in Zimbabwe.

Len: Don't be a fucking sell-out.

Nestor: There's a time for change for everything and I don't believe that the change is going to be for the worst. I really don't believe that.

Assistant: Okay, so it's going to be for the better. How do you see it being for the better?

Len: Well, you can't get any worse.

Nestor: Well, you look at this country now as opposed to five years ago. There's a hell of a change.

Fiona: Oh please man! It's much worse than it was. There's so much oppression now than there ever was before.

Nestor: But it's because people have suddenly become aware of [civil rights? unclear] and as soon as people become more aware they become more reactionary to it.

Fiona: So what are you trying to say? It's worse?

Nestor: No. People have to react to it in order to make the change.

Len: It's got to get worse to get better.

Fiona: We are all trying to react to the system in one way or another. The way we act, the way we dress, or whatever,—but the actual changes of society—that means fuck-all. The only way you're going to change this government . . . is by violence.

Nestor: But Fiona, you're silly. You are changing it. Merely by living with the people you are changing it.

Fiona: I don't believe that.

Nestor: You can't change something overnight.

Fiona: You know what's changed. The only thing that's changed is that people have become more radical on both sides.

Nestor: And you have to have that in order to implement the change.

Assistant: So, who's responsible for change then? The government? You think they're being pressurized?

Nestor: It's the public that have changed. The government is pressurized by the change in the public because suddenly people are becoming more aware of issues. Outside influences have forced the people to become aware of these issues and that's what makes the government aware of them.

Fiona: The government doesn't care.

Assistant: Pressure from both sides. Which way do you see the government's going?

Nestor: It's trying to keep a middle base.

Assistant: Can they do it?

Len: They will fuck out.

Nestor: No, I don't think they will.

Assistant: Okay, how [are] they going to fuck out? Are they going to give in to the left or the right?

Nestor: I don't think it's them that's going to give in. It's the public that's going to make the change.

Assistant: What do you mean, the change?

Nestor: I really feel that education is really important. To say one man, one vote, is not the answer because the black person is a person who's always been conditioned to rule in a tribal way.

Len: He's been told he's a child.

Nestor: No, no, no. You're thinking more recently [of] white society. Before that he was used to ruling in a tribal way, which was one leader and that was it: You followed the leader. But now you've got to realize you can suddenly think for yourself: This is right, and this wrong.

Len: We're all following P. W. Botha. Not by choice, by force.

Assistant: Okay, given the situation that you've got a black government, would you feel secure?

Fiona: Definitely.

Len: How can you say definitely?

Fiona: I'm not saying just because he's black I'd feel secure. But, for instance, when we were in Zimbabwe I really felt very at home in that environment. Harare was like a culture shock. It was so mellow. My experience of that was that I'm not against trying it out [in South Africa].

Len: I was trying to find my brother in Harare. I phoned the hospitals; it took like 5 times 20 cents down, 20 times being transferred to this department.

Fiona: Ya, okay, it's bureaucratic.

Len: No, it's not bureaucratic. It's fucking shit.

Fiona: Do you think it's because they're black?

Len: No, it's not because they're black; it's because they're slack.

[tremendous laughter] . . .

Assistant: So basically you people are the same as the other people I've been interviewing. You actually see no future for South Africa?

Len: You can't see what is going to happen.

Fiona: The reason why we're being so shortsighted is because we are so bloody censored. We don't have access to the kind of knowledge that is going to give us a vision of the future.

Len: I agree.

Fiona: We sit here waffling about bullshit, because we just don't have access to the knowledge. We have to fight to know what's going on in this country, and, and that's why I think it's so important going into the [black] townships because it just keeps you in touch in some way. But then, in other ways you don't know what riots are going on over there.

Assistant: What would you say the ANC's support is in the townships?

Fiona: 40%.

Nestor: I feel that the ANC is as radical as the Broederbond.

Fiona: But what percentage?

Nestor: I couldn't care. You need a compromise between the two. You have to. You've got two sects that you're dealing with and, unless you get a compromise, you're not going to get a change [here the tape is unclear]. Everybody agrees that violence is inevitable.

Nestor: Violence is inevitable because people react like that.

Assistant: Violence when?

Fiona: What do you mean when? It's happening all the time.

Assistant: But it hasn't changed anything.

Nestor: It has.

Assistant: Has it?

Fiona: Violence has definitely made people more aware. This is why I say there is no place for me in a way. Because I cannot relate to people who are violent—white or black radicals. I understand his [the radical black's] position a lot more than I understand the Dutchman's position, but I can't relate to it and I've accepted that as a fact. Because, when I was in the left, you know; these lefties act as if they're so, like you know, they're really into it and they're really committed to the struggle and they're like at one with Umkhonto weSizwe [military wing of the ANC] and all this shit, but meantime they are not. They're kidding themselves, because when it really comes down to it, they are white soft liberals that come from middle-class backgrounds [grunts of agreement] and it's very easy for them to say they're part of the struggle, because they're not really putting their lives in danger, because they're white. And I'm not into that, and you know what the trouble is? I can't even find my niche. I can't because there's just no niche for me. PFP, I mean please! They're a bunch of wimps. They don't represent me. They also waver in between here and there. Okay, I waver too, but I don't say I commit myself to one thing and then waver. I do support the UDF in many ways, but where are their leaders? They're all sitting in detention and in the meantime, there are a bunch of hooligans running around in the townships. That is my impression. You know why I get that impression? At one stage when the uprising started, everything was in control; it was fantastic, it was democracy in action. There were street committees, you know, area committees—it was amazing; it was incredible. The people were so organized and it was working right up to the top. It was working and the government and the police one by one eliminated all these leaders and eliminated all the area committee members and eliminated and eliminated, and eventually you were left with a bunch of kids who didn't really know what direction they had. All they knew was that they were frustrated and angry and just wild and they, you know, once everybody had been detained and murdered and whatever, these people just went on the rampage. That is my experience, and they made a lot of township residents do a lot of things that were very cruel. They did a lot of very cruel things, and they did a lot of very unjust things without any democratic consultation. I have experience of this [gives an example]. A lot of township residents are stuck between the cops and the comrades.[3]

. . .

Fiona: In this society the government has worked everything out so absolutely brilliantly that we are split in every possible way. You know, when you talk about blacks; I mean, the American perception of "the black" is one huge clump of people who all have one big thought, but it's not true. There are just so many opinions like among whites. People are polarized.

. . .

Assistant: The ANC will get in?

Nestor: I see an absolute disaster. You cannot have radicalism like that.

Fiona: [turning to the assistant] What do *you* see [happening in the future]?

Assistant: I see that eventually the Nats and ANC will realize that they've got to sit down and talk to each other.

Fiona: No, that's much too idealistic. I wish you were right. The thing is, you see, it's a matter of pride. The Afrikaner has got this thing—God and his land. The Afrikaner was promised this land by God and they made their little vow on the day of . . . the vow with the Zulus and they won and now it's God and the people and their land and they're not going to give in. Because it's God's duty to like, fight till the day they die. You know a Dutchman's brain is 10 inches thicker that anybody else's.

Nestor: Ah, come on—stop speaking shit.

Fiona: Ach, I'm just being racist.

Len: The Afrikaner will die [for his land]. The little Afrikaner number will not come along fast enough for the change [?].

Fiona: Yes, that's true.

Nestor: There was a lot of change the last five years.

Len: The CP is a natural reaction to change.

Assistant: But that's not helping the situation.

Nestor: It is helping. It is showing you the two faces. Suddenly these people confronted with the other face which is totally opposite to them. They'll suddenly think, What am I doing through the generations . . . ?

Assistant: Have we got generations?

Nestor: No, we haven't.

Fiona: But Nestor, you're saying everything is going to change. Do you think it is going to change for the better? Do you think it's just all going to work out?

Len: No, it's not.

Nestor: Well, I do.

Fiona: Well, bully for you because I don't.

Nestor: What do you think's going to happen in this country? Dissolve in a bomb? Is that what you really think?

Fiona: No, I don't think it's going to dissolve in a bomb. I just think it's going to be very, very violent. There'll be bombs going off every day.

Nestor: There's bombs going off every day now.

Fiona: But it'll get worse.

Len: It'll get worse.

Fiona: . . . get much worse and then maybe if we survive the big bomb that'll blast the whole [here the tape is unclear]. The government has made us believe that we are so fundamentally different from the next man, that I am so fundamentally different from the black man and the black man's so fundamentally different from the coloured and the coloured's so fundamentally different from the Indian that he's sowed the seeds of his own destruction. Because the thing is, now, in a time when unity is so vital, people are so fucked in the head that they don't actually know how to unify. And that's why I am living in Yeoville. It's a little haven. There are people here that just mix. It's wonderful.

Len: It's just a shop window. It's bullshit. They will melt when the rest of the country wakes up. Yeoville will fuckin' fade into nothing.

Assistant: You don't think the rest of the country can take a lesson from Yeoville maybe?

Len: Ach, what's Yeoville got to teach?

Nestor: Yes, I think they could.

Fiona: Yeoville's a model example of racial harmony.

Len: The only reason Yeoville's existing is because it hasn't got the rest of the country, the rest of the people.

Assistant: Given a model of the country—Boksburg or Yeoville—where do you think people would look to?

Nestor: I really believe the majority will look to Yeoville but the majority is too fucking slack to vote.

Fiona: Man, voting's got fuck-all to do with it. Voting is irrelevant.

Nestor: No, it's got a hell of a lot to do with it.

Fiona: Listen here [turning to assistant]. The point is that people live in suburbia and they never get a chance to experience things like that [Yeoville]. They live in their little paranoid lives and they just never get a chance to come out and really experience life like this. They never want to. They never want to go to the township because they think they'll be murdered on the spot. And they don't want to try.

Nestor: But that [fear] is spread by the media.

Fiona: Yes, that's true, but the thing is that once you break out of that there's so much hope. There is so much hope because there are people who are willing to reconcile themselves.

Assistant: So, there is hope now? Violence is not necessary?

Fiona: Yes. You see in one sense. This is why I live in this little insular world. In my insular world there is hope. Because here in this environment where we sit, the places we go to, there is racial harmony. People communicate, people don't stress out, people are cool. You know, it's not a hassle. That's why I don't even like to step out of it. That's why I can't be realistic, because I'm happy in this little environment of racial harmony that we're trying to breed. And that's why we're so pathetic, that's why we can't give you an answer [about what's going to happen].

Len: You can't live in Yeoville and say, wah, wah wah [speculate about the wider world?], because actually fuck it. Yeoville's a little . . . a fuckin' fart in a thunderstorm.

Fiona: I know it's a fart in a thunderstorm.

Len: Well, there's it. You can't actually say anything.

Nestor seemed to be slightly more optimistic than his companions about the future of the country. He also alluded to the fact that blacks were not quite ready for universal voting rights. All seemed to agree, however, that education and, above all, uncensored information were crucial. A general mood of pessimism pervaded the discussion, however. Fiona feared the polarization and foresaw violence. She felt alienated in the situation because of her rejection of both radicalism and violence. Unlike the majority of informants, she viewed Zimbabwe in a positive light. To her, people couldn't form a picture of the future because they lacked enough knowledge because of government censorship and control of information. Knowledge about other groups in South Africa was further impaired by the success the government had in making the South African population believe that vast differences separated them and that black areas were dangerous to visit. Whites were thus prevented from gaining firsthand experience of other groups. The high hopes Fiona had about grassroots democratic initiatives in black townships were stymied and killed by the government, thus her pessimism. However, she and her companions praised the island of difference they had found in their neighborhood. It was as if Yeoville were a microcosm that crystallized their hopes for a future racially harmonious existence. Yet they realized that its significance was tiny, and that its continued existence and tolerance was fragile.

These young people fall into a category of whites who comb the political spectrum for alternatives and programs. Fiona could find no one to identify with. The UDF had some promise, but it was not allowed to continue at the time of the interview. They thus felt powerless, being dragged along with events that seemed to plunge the country progressively into more and more violence. They had found an island where they could express and experience their ideals of nonracial relationships and lifestyles, but, at the same time, they realized how insignificant, even specious, it was. Finally, the tone of the discussion conveyed a sense of pessimism, powerlessness, political loneliness, and uselessness among highly sensitive individuals.

The above discussion took place at a time before the ANC was legalized and before certain key apartheid laws were abolished. These young people were right about government censorship and control of information, because they had no idea about the insider politics that was preparing the way for authoritarian reforms from above at that time. Yet we can imagine that their insecurities and doubts have not been totally removed by recent events in light of the track record of the government and their unallayed doubts about the ANC.

WHITE AFRICANS:
NO GRAY AREA TO ESCAPE TO

A number of subjects expressed their rootedness in Africa in unambiguous terms. In contrast to the colonial white African identity of somebody like Mac, moderate whites were more open to finding a new identity. How this was to be achieved was unclear to them, however.

Viv and Diane were a couple in their late 30s. Viv, from an Afrikaner background, was a businessman; Diane was an English speaker from the Eastern Cape. They had two children. They planned to emigrate permanently in 1982, but after 18 months in Britain they returned to South Africa. They lived in the middle-class Johannesburg suburb of Parkhurst, where they employed a part-time domestic servant.

The interview, conducted at the beginning of 1989, started off at a point where the couple were reviewing the various political parties and their programs. They agreed that they did not feel very happy with the liberal option provided by the Progressive Federal Party in the past. Viv confessed that he voted "tactically" for the PFP, and not because he had faith in the party. He and Diane also doubted whether the new Democratic Party that had formed at the time of the interview would actually contribute to change in South Africa.

> *Diane:* Yes, . . . ah . . . I just, I just don't bloody know . . . that's the . . . see, that's the awful situation we're in . . . in that . . . yes, we are frightened. . . . You don't feel secure, you don't feel happy.
>
> *Viv:* You can't stand it.
>
> *Interviewer:* What about children when you left S.A.?
>
> *Diane:* At this stage I don't really worry because they're so young. Another thing: As far as I'm concerned, I'm African, and I want to stay here, I want to be part of it.
>
> *Viv:* We enjoyed Europe . . . but as I say, you know, [when] that airplane landed back at Jan Smuts . . . we knew we were home. I mean it. . . . I-I don't know, I-I'm, it might sound ridiculous . . . but . . . if living here had to become unbearable . . . I would probably go to Zimbabwe . . . or, or Botswana . . . or wherever, . . . but I mean, . . . I'd even considered going to Mauritius before going to Europe or the [United] States or . . .
>
> *Diane:* I think there are quite a number of people who emigrated who are coming back.
>
> *Viv:* Yes, I don't know . . . but let me just draw an analogy with . . . if you take what happened . . . in Zimbabwe . . . let's take the state of unrest, the . . .

the civil war, and all the rest . . . that, let's take that level that Zimbabwe reached. Now . . . I may be wrong, but I don't think S.A. will ever get to that stage . . . because of the . . . infrastructure and uh, it's far more developed . . . the, the greater strength of the SADF . . . a lot of things . . . kind a . . . Part of me says, "Well . . . if the worst it gets is what happened in Zimbabwe . . . then I can still live here. . . . then I'm still prepared to be here to play my part . . . and . . . kind of, work towards a new South Africa." . . . So, I think, at the end of the day, I don't ever think it'll ever be that bad . . . if I always believe it will be, will be livable . . . over that period of change, but, when that period of change does happen . . . we've got to, we just have to adjust accordingly . . . but, I mean, I don't see it that every black in the street will be running around cutting the throat of every white person. . . .

The couple thus agreed that they preferred living in Africa even if they had to make sacrifices owing to political and economic instability. They were willing to adjust to a "new South Africa." What this would mean wasn't quite clear to them. The point is that they were committed to the country and were prepared to change their lives. They spoke about the media's representation of South Africa in Britain and shifted the conversation to censorship. Diane was asked whether she thought there was censorship in South Africa:

Diane: Oh, yes, without a doubt. . . .

Viv: . . . and the government controls the media. It's totally government controlled somehow, the press restrictions I think play upon . . .

Diane: . . . it's probably a good thing, the way the press turns things around . . .

Viv: . . . but, like what?

Diane: [4-second pause] . . . like wars and, say, violence. Yes, perhaps there are things that we just shouldn't know: violence, necklacings, we've got young children growing up in this country who don't need to know these things.

Viv then observed how South Africans were shown more of the violence in Northern Ireland than the British saw, and vice versa, British television showed more about South African violence than the South Africans saw on their television service. Recollection of what they had seen of South African violence on British television filled them with abhorrence:

Viv: While they were burning, people went and got a huge rock . . . and carried the rock . . . and dropped it on top of the burning body, on its head . . . to as . . .

Diane: It's so barbaric . . . but I don't know, I mean . . . and everyone here might say, God that shows you . . . the bitterness there is against the whites because that shows you that, eh . . . but they were burning their own people . . .

Viv: . . . because, because he was an informer . . . that is why . . . uh . . . It could be taken as the other way . . . it shows you that hatred [toward] the whites . . . and that's where they need to brutalize their own kind just because they're informers . . . but to me one has to make, become . . . so no human being should behave like that in our world.

Viv thought that black informers were burned as an expression of hatred toward whites. Informers were assumed to have supplied whites with information about black activists. It is significant that Viv spoke of "their own kind." Throughout the interview he was struggling with the problem of inclusiveness, that is, whether he felt he was part of the nonracial community. The couple recoiled from the memory of what they had seen on British television. From the tone of their description, it was clear that the kind of violence they had seen made them feel more insecure in South Africa. Diane even advocated some censorship—rare in liberal circles— in order to protect (her) children. It was almost as if she was trying to repress the thought that in the country of their future such incidents could happen; if they did happen, she would rather they not be known. In a hopeful tone, Viv went on:

But, I [6-second pause] I went to the Johnny Clegg [formerly Juluka, now with band Savuka—ethnic Zulu/pop music] concert last Saturday . . . in P.E. [Port Elizabeth]. Well, the gist of it, let me see. . . . He makes a, he makes a very strong political stand. . . . It's very, very strong . . . and he makes a point and says that the problem with S.A. is that we've got this huge . . . block in front of us called apartheid. In Zulu, uh . . . uh . . . mythology. . . . In Zululand they say, "If there's a rock in front of you . . . you don't look at the rock . . . you look around it or beyond it." It is a problem that we as South Africans have. We just see the rock, we don't look around, and we don't look beyond it . . . and his kind of plea to 10-, 10,000 people . . . uh . . . who were kind of all youngsters . . . under, kind of, 32 plus or minus. [The point] was to look around that rock, look beyond it, don't look at the rock, because you'll never get past it. . . . I mean everybody just shared and . . . support was incredible.

Immediately, however, this hopeful tone was replaced by another worry that entered the conversation: The right-wing Afrikaners were identified as the working class who had much more to lose than the English speakers. Viv and Diane feared that right-wingers might cause the clock to be turned back to the apartheid era. However, looking at Zimbabwe, they thought that life there continued normally for white workers after democratization.

Political rights for blacks were important, but Viv wondered whether the black middle class might lose out under a one person, one vote system. It was important to have a strong economy. The present poor state of the economy was a cause for concern. The government was not doing enough to stimulate growth by creating more employment opportunities. A strong economy would also help improve the quality of black education. The government needed to relax some of its bureaucratic rules in order to stimulate the informal sector. Viv went on:

> But the government will have to act by promoting the informal sector, for example, because, as the unemployment figure gets higher and higher, then you find revolution taking place. This move is necessary not only for political reasons but also for [relieving] sheer hunger and desperation. As yet, blacks have enough comfort to keep them from being really desperate. But the trend is there . . . with South Africa's gold sales down . . . there are repercussions for the economy of the homelands where each miner supports 18 people. There are staggering implications. If we have to close mines down . . . For every miner unemployed, there are 20 people without visible means of support. . . .
>
> To me, looking around the rock—if you look at southern Africa . . . shit—we are powerful! In a world sense, in terms of minerals, raw materials, people . . . we are a very powerful subcontinent. Where we've been really ripped off by the rest of the world is that we're not net producers in Southern Africa. For example, Zambia . . . copper. . . . We export everything at raw material price and reimport the finished goods. If the whole of Southern Africa were to become net producers . . . they are milking out our raw materials, and we don't produce. Even if we don't 100% agree politically with our neighbors; and the black African tribes might never do, if we could work together on a common market—that could really help growth.

Viv then suddenly switched his theme to the fact that he had no other passport. It was as if he was saying, I *have to* make it over here. At the same time, he lauded the quality of life in Africa. There was a degree of ambiguity in the switch he made. He was being forced to stay, but at the same time he liked it:

And the other side, I think I have got no chance of getting . . . any other passport . . . and . . . What I have to do, if I want to go to Britain with you, I've gotta, I've gotta go with uh, I've gotta be there for five years before . . . for immigration, because I am . . . a South African and that is it. . . . I don't have an uncle or an aunt or a grandfather or a grandmother or anything so that I can demand another passport. Now, I believe that is it . . . you are . . . you're South African and [7-second pause] from a quality-of-life, quality-of-life point of view [4-second pause] even if life here had to disintegrate, . . . I'd prefer to stay. I'd rather have that quality of life here in Africa . . . than go and live in a little two up and two down in Europe or . . . [9-second pause] I just wish, . . . I wish I could give the girls . . . an option. . . . I wish I had access to a British passport for them . . . for, if they wanted it, so that they . . . could so that, when they're 16 and 17, . . . they were terribly . . . eh. I tell you what, by that stage, when it, if I really believe in what I believe in, then hopefully . . . it won't be necessary. And the other thing I think we've got to . . .

Viv stuttered more than before when he talked about this. He was in some conflict because he really desired a foreign passport as a back door of escape if necessary. If he could not obtain such a document himself, he seriously desired it for his children.

Diane and Viv collectively reviewed the problems South Africa faced: race relations, different languages, nationalism, economic downturn, labor unions, unemployment, devaluation of the currency, and inflation. South Africa had just about every problem other countries faced to a much lesser extent. To Diane this was worrying and a major source of insecurity:

Diane: There is a sense of insecurity. You're living in it, you have to think of politics all the time. Our daily existence is born of insecurity.

Viv: I disagree. This big change we are going through . . . makes us acutely aware of what's around us. This huge wave of change in South Africa is far greater than elsewhere in the world, it makes us aware of these issues, of our surroundings. In England you are only called upon to think about issues every five years.

Actually, Viv did not disagree with Diane about the overall politicization of life in South Africa (this phenomenon has been pointed out among other categories of whites in previous chapters). Her assertion that their daily existence was born of insecurity is perhaps the most graphic description of the situation. They observed how younger people were now faced with these serious problems at a much earlier age than they had been. The mere fact that political candidates also tended to be younger illustrated this. They said that their 10-year-old child had a basic awareness of "how to treat Africans," something Diane and Viv never had at that age. They felt that the education system therefore should tackle these "cultural" problems at a very early age. At this point Viv switched to talk about Africa in general:

> Africa is a continent of extremes—everything is black or white, but there's no gray on another level . . . and the rest of the world . . . is kind of . . . maybe sound more black and white, but they've been about long enough and there's a huge gray level, a big, huge gray area. . . . No, what I said, what about color? [Diane laughs in the background]—it's everything here whether it's wrong—right it's black, white, red, blue. . . . Well then you take it's good, it's bad . . . we, we, we, we're a continent of extremes [all three people here are talking simultaneously and unintelligibly and then laughing]. Kenya and Nigeria, Congo, all of them . . . and that, that is the very nature of Africa, and we *don't have this gray area that we could escape into.* (emphasis added)

These words require some interpretation. Viv was correcting himself after the other two people present laughed about his reference to colors. He maintained that he was talking about culture and not about race. The rest of the world, especially the United States, has a long enough history in race relations to have developed a gray area. I understand this to mean that a domain of cultural and everyday life exists that is exempt from, or undetermined by, racial considerations—a neutral ground, so to speak, where one's membership in a certain racial category is not significant, where it does not count, and where, in a racial sense, one can disappear. Viv found Africa different. He felt that he was always on stage as a white and felt the need to escape into a gray area, where, I presume, he could relax. The gray area he was looking for is that area of normal day-to-day life where a person would not, in the first instance, be seen as a member of a racial community. Although he tried his best to get away from the notion of color, I presume that he meant that his visibility as a white would inevitably and always put him into the camp of whites.

In the discussion that followed, the interviewer, a white South African graduate student, suddenly joined in and explored what the "gray area" might entail. All agreed that a common ground should be created. Learning each other's languages, such as Zulu, English, and Afrikaans, was important, but so too was African history.

Viv regained his confidence and asserted that white South Africans had a unique understanding for Africans. He went into a long anecdote about his experiences during a course he took in Britain. Also taking the course were a number of Africans. They were absolutely ignored by the English, American, and Australian participants. Viv realized that the Africans, whom he called "Afs," were totally "out of their element." Viv was the only one who appreciated their problem and talked to them. Toward the end of the course, Viv and the Africans went on a weekend trip together, and when they returned, they made fun of a national costume party they had attended. The organizers of the course mistakenly had anticipated a conflict between the South African white and the black Africans, yet they were the greatest of friends. To Viv this was proof that there was a greater understanding between South African whites and Africans than there could ever be between Africans and Europeans or Americans. Imitating an Afrikaans accent, Viv said:

> I mean it's like the old nationalists thing, . . . "The complexity of this situation will never be understood by anybody else, therefore, we must do something to help ourselves."

Who Viv was thinking of as "we" is open to interpretation. The next passage reveals an inclusiveness, that is, that the understanding he spoke about did not necessarily reflect only the white South Africans' insight but that it was indeed an understanding shared by black and white to go forward in the reconstruction of the country:

> I feel the same way Diane does. I think there's going to be political alliances . . . there's gotta be change . . . and I think change brings anxiety . . . changes to . . . the law of the people, but I believe that there's gonna be a very prominent change, I believe there is future hope and, in fact, all of us will work together as South Africans, be it black, be it white.

The peculiar structure of thematic sequences during this interview should be pointed out. Themes of hope and despair followed each other. The opening cue about insecurity was followed by a description of Africa as home, that is, security. An elaboration on violence followed, before the hope of peering past the rock of apartheid was described. When unemployment was mentioned, the country's economic strength was raised immediately afterward. Remarks about the inability to get a passport were followed by comments highlighting the quality of life in South Africa, and the notion of Africa as extremes was counterbalanced by the notion of an understanding shared by black and white. This vacillation between themes of hope and despair was indicative of the internal struggle Diane and Viv were going through. They had gone through the traumatic experience of attempting to emigrate, and yet they were not happy doing so. Both engaged in internal conversation with themselves, trying to come to some convincing synthesis that would allow them to accept their situation in peace. This did not happen. Viv's remark about the lack of any gray area to escape to is telling; it becomes understandable only against the backdrop of Diane's comment about the politicization of all areas of life. This couple's world was rent asunder by politics, and they were left with the hope for a society that would be truly nonracial, in which all would cooperate regardless of race.

DISCUSSION

The cases I have selected to represent visions of the present and future among moderates are typical of the spread of cases I recorded. All of the moderates interviewed accepted the fact that change was inevitable. Within that acceptance, there were three distinct positions taken.

First, those who were financially secure were aware of their class position. The spontaneous ethnic groupings they foresaw pertained more to the lower classes. Henry was typical in this regard. To him, upper-class blacks posed no threat. Because of his stereotypical notions about the leadership and managerial abilities of blacks, he believed they would never be a substantial numerical factor and therefore would not constitute a great deal of competition for whites. Those nonwhites who did manage to reach the top would, in any case, maintain a standard of living and a set of values close to his own. Socially, he felt comfortable mixing with them. He did not elaborate on affectionate or marital liaisons or other involvement with people belonging to a different racial group than his own. His class position would be guaranteed by economic strength and the political and ethnic division of the masses.

Henry and Marie shared the view that ethnic differentiation occurs along spontaneous lines. They saw it as, so to speak, a natural phenomenon. Marie was more outspoken than Henry in drawing a definite boundary between whites and other groups. She refused to accept any possibility of the erasing, or blurring, of the boundaries between her group and people of different races. Had I asked her whether English-speaking children would be allowed to sleep at her house, she surely would not have objected in the same terms she did when the hypothetical children were of a different color. Marie's position was more extreme than that of the elderly whites at the mall. They, like Henry, insisted that "civilization"—that is, their way of living—was the important marker for rendering blacks assimilable. In both Henry's and the elderly people's cases, class apparently was the social boundary drawn between them and the majority of nonwhite people. The notion of "class" is, however, thinly disguised as "race." Upper-class blacks still fall into the "they," or out-group, category.

Fiona and her friends from Yeoville in Johannesburg were typical of respondents taking the second position. They were young professionals or students who generally liked the racially mixed microenvironment in which they were living. Its insularity was attractive and provided an escape from the day-to-day oppressive realities of racial prejudice and violence. Yet they were aware of the speciousness and fragility of their lifestyle. They were, in a sense, paralyzed and waiting for the rest of the country to wake up. They were filled with insecurity and the fear of a major outbreak of political and racial violence. They did not really know how or where to engage themselves politically. They found no acceptable political organization within the spectrum of political possibilities with which they could identify.

The third position was taken by Diane and Viv. Their sense of insecurity was acute. They had young children growing up in a country on the brink of a new era. Nobody knew in which direction it was going politically. They hoped that some form of synthesis would occur in which race would be of lesser or no significance. However, they despaired that this would ever be possible because of the prevailing and pervasive cognitive schema ascribing everyone to membership in a racial group. In distinction to Fiona and her friends' confession to an insular existence, Diane and Viv hoped for an existence shared by black and white.

Among whites with a moderate, or relatively progressive, orientation toward the future, there was thus a greater openness to change than was found among conservatives. For some, such as Henry, the future society would be a multiracial one in which he could preserve his class position. Younger and less settled people hoped for a future of nonracialism. It was only within the last category that there was an indication that some whites were prepared to accept Africa as their home on conditions other than solely their own. Viv asserted that white South Africans have an "understanding" of Africans not shared by Westerners. This "understanding," I conclude, is fundamentally different from the understanding claimed by conservatives. Conservatives and right-wingers interviewed for this study pretended to understand blacks in terms of their innate inferiority to whites. This "understanding" is little more than naked prejudice. Viv, I believe, hoped for an understanding shared by black and white because it is born of mutual respect and a concern for Africa and its problems. Yet this form of understanding, tragically, lacks a realistic base in the life experiences shared by blacks and whites. Too many decades of legal apartheid stand between them.

NOTES

1. *Indaba* here refers to the KwaZulu/Natal Indaba (*indaba* is a Zulu word meaning "deliberation"), in which all population groups were represented, which proposed that a joint administrative and economic region be established for the homeland KwaZulu and the province of Natal. The group right of whites would, inter alia, be protected. The government at that time rejected the proposals because they did not "adequately protect white interests" (SAIRR, 1989, p. 509).

2. The ban on the ANC has since been lifted.

3. *Comrades* here refers to black youths involved in organizing resistance and boycotts in black townships, sometimes enforcing complicity through ruthless means such as "necklacing."

11

Race and Discourse

During the past decade, members of the white population of South Africa have had to respond to a tremendous set of demands. For centuries, they occupied a privileged position in all spheres of social life, but in the 1990s they stand at a point in history that faces in the direction of a long period of adjustment to majority rule—a road that will not be without conflict, strife, and alienation. Whites will have to adjust to the economic realities of their country. For most, this will mean adjusting to lower living standards, harder work, and, above all, a new self-concept that will allow them to mesh with a new life world of legally sanctioned racial equality. It will entail the experience and acceptance of relative deprivation in comparison with their previous lifestyles and standard of living. For most, it will also mean a redefinition of their "white" selves in African terms. On the other hand, South African whites might just as easily be facing an embittered attempt to restore their comfortable lifestyles and perceived ethnic identity through a series of strategies that could lead to conflict and bloodshed.

THE MORE THINGS CHANGE, THE MORE THEY REMAIN THE SAME

Since the inception of the fieldwork in August 1988 to the final write-up stage of this study in April 1992, the white electorate's sympathies seem to have shifted remarkably. The four years that marked the symbolic identification of Afrikaners, at one end, with the justification of their presence and predominance in their "own" South Africa at the Great Trek celebrations ended with the resounding white support of the government's initiative to negotiate a new constitution for the country that would give political rights to the black majority in a common country. In May 1990 the massive rally of white conservatives at Pretoria seemingly indicated a shift toward right-wing white political attitudes. Some by-elections, apparently, reinforced this impression. However, within a month of the National Party's defeat at its traditional stronghold in Potchefstroom, the government found the support of more than two-thirds of the white voters for its role in the negotiation process. Was this a shift in white political allegiance? If not, how can it otherwise be explained? I have indicated some of the factors at work at the conclusion of Chapter 9.

One of the reasons for the unequivocal popularity of the conservative point of view was the noticeable convergence between the public discourse of the Conservative Party and its satellites, on the one hand, and private views, opinions, and meanings on the other. In terms of our distinctions, the interpretive schemes derived from and communicated by the traditional structure of South African social reality harmonized with the subjective expectations and hopes of a broad stratum of whites. There were similarities with regard to their respective definitions of social and ethnic boundaries and their conceptualization of the causes of the current crisis in the country. Regardless of the referendum outcome, these similarities and convergencies have not disappeared. They continue to exist in the unspoken realms of interests and hopes for the survival of white identity, privilege, and separateness, although they have received less publicity in recent times. Initially there was great support for the Conservative Party as a means for achieving these goals, but its track record was poor in effecting prowhite changes. Whites, especially Afrikaners, were split on whom to support in the referendum. The conservative support the government did receive from Afrikaners, I would suggest, derived from their authoritarian expectation that the white and Afrikaner-led government would pull through on their behalf, if not in terms of maximizing their interests in a new dispensation, then at least through minimizing their losses. The voting patterns during the CP-favoring by-elections, I gather, were thus largely protests to shake up the paternalistic government so that it would heed the calls of its ward. Blood was thicker than water.

Those I have labeled as moderates, however, did not consistently agree with the dominant public discourse of government, industry, and intellectuals. Henry, the Natal businessman, an expert in his own right, went along with an economistic, rational view. Other subjects in this category were much more vague about policies and the future they were moving toward. They had inadequate information because of the government's elitist and secretive approach to public discourse, historically emanating from its practice of letting a well-informed "inner circle" make decisions on behalf of the electorate, who were was mostly kept in the dark. In recent years that inner circle has turned into a "scientifically" informed cadre of experts: economists and politicians. The "moderates" at large were expected to accept these policies and interpretations at face value, with very little opportunity for debate or participation. The tone and thrust of the National Party political meeting in Melville, described in Chapter 6, provide a good example of this. Forced to make a crucial decision whether to support the government's negotiation process or not, moderates voted yes, as the referendum results in the major urban areas demonstrated. Moderates did not support a no vote for the obvious reason that it would have meant a step backward into support for obsolete white ethnocentrism.

Paradoxically, Conservative Party politicians were successful in communicating the meanings, fears, and aspirations of a broad public that did not support them. Moderate politicians, on the other hand, in the guise of the National Party, were talking over the heads of the public and yet received the public's support. The support for the National Party government seemingly emanated from very diverse, if not contradictory, motives.

First, in terms of the social boundaries whites drew between themselves and nonwhites, the conservative public had the intention of maintaining clear racial and ethnic boundaries. A yes vote in the referendum was no guarantee of that. Second, the moderate public made no such clear-cut distinctions. Moderates' views varied from nonracial attitudes that refused to set boundaries to those advocating "natural," multiracial, boundaries coinciding with race or class. A yes vote would not necessarily have meant a nonracial future for the country either. Yet both moderates and a majority of conservatives supported the referendum. The only possible conclusion this leads us to is that the government received the support of a crisis constituency that was geared to minimize its losses. There was no guarantee that a no vote would not have worse consequences than a yes vote. In addition, the government, imbued with its instrumental rationality and assisted by the latest public relations means, created a euphoric climate. Nevertheless, the surprise with which it received the news of the outcome of the referendum is a further indication that the government had no clear idea of what was actually happening, or what to expect. In some circles it openly conceded that the outcome was a gamble.

Sociologically, it is important to elucidate the social conditions that gave rise to the symbolic white unity expressed in the referendum. The voting pattern, though ex post facto, confirmed the initial proposition of this investigation, that a solidarity exists among whites that transcends many historical, cultural, and linguistic boundaries. The unity expressed in the referendum was thus not based on the same premises that the dominant discourse of the government and related parties hoped for. They were, and are, in search of a clearly defined public that supports them in terms of their technocratic rationales. The outcome of the referendum did not provide them with this. They would be mistaken to assume that a white public was supporting them in terms of their changed conceptualizations.

What now, in sum, are those uniting features? Let us follow a negative procedure by first examining the diversity of constructions of white solidarity and the social differentiation of South African society among conservatives and moderates, respectively, before exploring what might unite them.

ARTICULATION OF THE NEW DOMINANT DISCOURSE WITH EVERYDAY DISCOURSE

I will argue that the everyday discourse practice of conservatives on group relations reflected, on a subjective level, the dominant discourse of the decades before 1990. The dominant discourse established an objective reality that justified its perspective on human relations, politics, and the future by appealing to realism. Its views on ethnicity were claimed to be in accordance with the universal and natural human tendency to care for one's own and live with people of one's own kind in a discrete territory. The search for autonomy was deemed to be not only natural but in accordance with Scripture. This view resonated with the subjectively held conviction of conservatives that diversity and national autonomy were religiously rooted, and that boundaries were "natural" and at the same time divinely ordained. They thus reasoned from conviction in the first instance, assuming the existence of natural laws. Breaking these rules was not only immoral but blasphemous. To disregard them would amount to what some informants described as apostasy. Boundaries between groups were thus sacrosanct and inviolable. In terms of Max Weber's distinction, conservatives could thus be said to be guided by the ethics of conviction or ultimate ends (*Gesinnungsethik*) in constructing a political future for the country. Their tendency to harp on the fact that their solution was the *only* solution underscores the point.

In both everyday and public discourse, conservatives distinguished their "realistic" efforts to restore white privilege, either in a common or separate country, from the lack of realism on the part of the reformist white government, the "liberals," the "communists," and the "capitalists." The list of outsiders was comprehensive but highly contradictory. It was difficult to determine what common denominator ran through the list. The outsiders did all seem to have the same effect on South Africa: They all politicized and made problematic what was previously simple and uncomplicated. They distorted "reality" for their own gain. Local liberals played into the hands of foreigners who wanted to take the whites' birthright away. In light of recent developments, there is less and less probability that conservatives will be able to restore the past. Their specific interpretive scheme, with its emphasis on the purity and primordial nature of the in-group, will have to give ground to a more flexible group-way-of-thinking or lapse into sectarian separatism in order to uphold their purity. Conservatives may thus join up with moderates.

Moderates, on the other hand, were not so clear in their definitions as conservatives. To some, interracial communication and the blurring of old group boundaries seemed desirable, but the many decades of apartheid had seriously impaired their ability to cross racial barriers. Some treasured the island of communication and nonracialism they had discovered. Others lived in the realization that they would never be able to rid themselves of their white racial visibility and ascriptive identity in their quest for human solidarity regardless of color. Some therefore tended to withdraw into privacy behind the high walls of their suburban existence, waiting apprehensively for better times, hoping, perhaps tacitly, that on a high level of power, decisions would be made that would create the conditions in which they could realize their ideals—which, in itself is an authoritarian tendency.

Yet, barely hidden under the surface of everyday discourse lurks the interpretive scheme of a group-way-of-thinking that subjectively installs civilization, democracy, and Western values as boundary markers. This subjective reality posits and internalizes a Eurocentric reality with its own tradition. The ideal of Africanity and the identification with Western values constitute the field of tension in which many moderates find themselves.

Moderates found they could support the government's initiatives for negotiating a new future for South Africa. The idea that the official discourse of the government and its allies was much more geared toward the ethics of responsibility (*Verantwortungsethik*) than toward the ethics of conviction, in Weberian terms, was also acceptable. However, this posed a problem, because action geared toward responsibility inevitably involves accountability. Given the authoritarian pretensions of inner-circle decision making, accountability under these conditions would give in to trust by, rather than rely on the test of, followers. The type of rationality encountered in official discourse relied on scientific reasoning. Because the means-ends relationship is crucial to scientific reasoning, it is in principle testable. The question is, by whom? The government, in conjunction with its business and academic partners, therefore had to rely on the accountability of scientific reasoning to a community of initiated experts. Not their followers, but a national and international expert community would have the capacity of judging whether the government acted responsibly or not. From the perspective of its followers, it was a matter of trust—that is, of conviction—that legitimated the government's activities.

Responsibility, in the particular meaning it acquired here, was denuded of its humanity. What might be good for the economy and orderly social relations might thus not always be good for the individual humans it was supposed to serve. This is where the instrumentality of scientific and technical reasoning revealed itself in great clarity. Decisions were to be made about what was good for the system. Individual aspirations and feelings were to be subjected to the requirements of the system. In the extreme case, individuals and groups, regardless of race, might have to make sacrifices. Under the new definition, these sacrifices and hardships would no longer be the result of exploitation or domination in the interest of the white minority, but the exigencies of an objective system supposed to serve the polity as a whole. Perhaps this strategy might convince foreign investors in the short run, but it would hardly create confidence among moderate whites who were concerned about humanitarian issues. In future, the official discourse, of course, hopes to become the dominant discourse, acceptable to the majority of parties in the country.

The official discourse of the government defined itself as a reasonable and rational approach. It was devoid of "ideology." Ideology was essentially irrational, ineffective, and counterproductive. Thus the traditionalism of the right-wing political parties, emphasizing the predominance of the white group, the socialist inclination of certain intellectuals, and the ANC's nonracialism and opposition to privatization and decentralization were all rejected as failures compared with the scientific approach of the government.

In the realm of group relations, the dominant discourse took recourse to the "facts" of the universality of ethnicity and the plural character of modern nations. It also took into account the internationally accepted requirements of equality and human rights. It consequently devised a schema for a future South African society in which its "plural" nature would find recognition within the context of legally sanctioned human rights. Under the guise of facts, scientific reasoning, and internationally accepted legal principles, it created in an instrumentally rational way (*zweckrational*), a canopy under which it could accommodate a diverse set of white expectations and aspirations conceived of in a value-rational way (*wertrational*) (see Weber, 1978, p. 24). On one level, it left space for white, Afrikaner "ethnicity" to rally and consolidate on the principle of association. On another level, it reconstructed the dominant white section as a powerful minority among others that would negotiate its political interests from a position of strength. Its strength, in the final analysis, would be guaranteed by the predominance of its members in a privatized economy it was setting up in the last decade of the twentieth century. If successful, these transformations of South African society, which could preserve much of its power structure and racial makeup, would be achieved through a shrewd scientification of social reality and policy. It would be difficult for adversaries to counter these strategies on rational rather than moral grounds.

Although all whites could not go along with all the instrumental rationales the government provided for a negotiated future on the level of dominant discourse, the government captured their hopes and aspirations for the opportunity and space it provided for expressing their group-way-of-thinking, their interests, and their sense of identity, whether closed to or open to Africa on the level of everyday discourse. By enshrining the principle and prevalence of the group, if successful, a future order would perpetuate racism much more assiduously than one based on the principle of individual rights. In order to anticipate arenas of potential conflict in the future, let us review some of the ways in which the whites interviewed for this study drew boundaries between themselves and blacks.

BLACKS IN WHITE
DISCOURSE PRACTICE

Conservatives were most consistent in drawing boundaries. The primary boundary set between black and white was very rigid and impermeable. Blacks were viewed as outsiders. Although the nonracist pretense of conservatives led them to define blacks in terms of different cultures and ethnic groups, it soon became evident that they viewed blacks as a bloc; they asserted that blacks shared the same characteristics in many contexts. However, conservatives also objected to blacks' being viewed as one bloc, because their numbers might then justify viewing them as an overwhelming group entitled to political rights vis-à-vis whites. They therefore argued that blacks were minorities and different peoples. But when it came to white fears and resentment, blacks were evidently viewed as one entity, and this entity was defined in unambiguous racial terms. Farmers resented their dependence on black laborers—not their dependence on Zulu or Sotho speakers as laborers. Conservatives' aversion to a unitary state was motivated by their fear of being overwhelmed by blacks as category, not by various black nations.

When one examines the notion of cultural diversity as a reason for distinguishing the peoples of South Africa as discrete ethnic units, one is soon struck by the way the conservatives interviewed for this study applied the term *culture* to blacks. They associated cultural difference with a difference in civilization. A new opposition resulted, namely, civilized culture versus uncivilized culture. Examining the use of the word *civilization* more closely, another element arises, namely, that uncivilized people's practices with regard to their bodies were seen to differ from those of civilized people. From here it was only a small step to attributing differences in the treatment and care of the body to the "nature" of the group. This reasoning completed the transformation of "cultural" categories into "natural" or "racial" ones. Evidence from interviews revealed that some conservative whites did not define blacks purely in terms of nature or, for that purpose, as animals; rather, they saw blacks as occupying a position between humans and animals. Blacks were more robust than whites, but also more savage and wild, requiring white control. Blacks needed to be kept apart from whites because too close a black presence, especially if it involved bodily contact or the sharing of facilities that involve the body, was perceived to be polluting or infectious. In this sense blacks constituted a confusion of categories situated between "nature" and "culture." In the anthropological literature this confusion of categories has been described as a source of pollution and danger in the eyes of a group preoccupied with rigid group boundaries.

A negotiated future that, in effect, preserves white group rights and solidarity would assist in perpetuating these boundaries and the definitions upon which they are based. The boundary is essentially a racial one and is based in deep-seated beliefs and values that could effectively be preserved in a closed group context.

Among whites with a more moderate orientation there was much more flexibility. Perhaps the most accurate general comment that can be made is that the moderates found blacks to be socially acceptable as long as they adhered to civilized standards in their behavior and lifestyle. The less civilized, according to this view, would automatically and spontaneously distance themselves. This might be achieved through class differentiation. The scheme of reasoning in this case was a social Darwinist kind rather than a racist one. Assimilation of blacks would occur at the top end of society, and at the bottom there would be poverty and ethnic differentiation.

Nonracialist orientations were relatively rare. Social relations they may give rise to, I imagine, would thrive as a result of individual initiatives exploiting the niches of social tolerance that may open up.

THE BASIS OF
WHITE SOLIDARITY

I have argued that a pervasive white group-way-of-thinking not only underlay whites' setting of boundaries between themselves and other groups but was also constitutive of their visions of the future. In many respects, my argument has followed the contours of this way of thinking by tracing the negative definitions of the "other" or the "outsider." In this way I have shown how important the "we" group was in terms of "culture," "civilization," and "class." Some of these distinctions were barely disguised as racial self-definitions.

I have presented abundant evidence of the convergence in the visions of English and Afrikaans speakers, whether conservative or moderate in orientation. Whites in South Africa have largely shared the same life world, a world of similar experiences. They appropriated this world socially in terms of conventional everyday language and social practice. Their life world has been their "home" for many generations, and it is now changing. This idea filled many with uncertainty and fear. If there was one factor that favored a self-protective sense of solidarity, it was that of fear.

Fear of the unknown was common among respondents. Their knowledge about nonwhite groups had been mediated by a tradition that depicted those groups as dangerous and unpredictable. The stock of knowledge whites have been drawing on has made it difficult for them to see the racially other as partner for the future rather than as a threat. Commonsense typifications about postcolonial black rule have only reinforced whites' worst fears. Surviving apartheid structures also inhibited whites from building up personal acquaintance with blacks and other groups in order to move beyond seeing each other in anonymous and stereotypical terms. There was also fear regarding a future for which no clear direction could be found, either in an existing stock of knowledge or in historical precedents in other countries. Looking back on the past of the South

African population as a whole, one cannot document a democratic tradition that has the potential of coping with present exigencies. The authoritarian sectionalism of whites has not provided much experience to draw upon for the future. On the other hand, blacks have been excluded from meaningful democratic decision making all along. The black public therefore also has very little tradition or experience to draw upon. This does not bode well for the future. In addition, the violent ethnic conflicts in various parts of the world in the past two decades have only enhanced whites' apprehensions.

Those with a conservative orientation also suffered from fear of a potential loss of identity. If we look at his concern more closely, we soon realize that it is not simply a fear of loss of ethnic identity, but a fear of loss of prestige-identity. Those in the lower strata of the white population were more dependent on prestige-identity defined on the basis of their race than were those who were better educated and more affluent. Now that such privilege is bound to fall away, these whites had become anxious. To overcome the sense of alienation that may accompany the loss of this form of prestige, it will be important for South Africans to cultivate a new work ethic that will break the racial barrier and cope with competition and cooperation regardless of race (recall that certain categories of work have been defined as low prestige and not worthy of whites).

THE FUTURE?

The issue that will make or break future South African politicians will be that of how to accommodate, manage, or contain in-group orientations in the "new South Africa." These orientations may be expressed in cultural, ethnic, or class terms. As far as whites are concerned, we can anticipate that their leaders will increasingly face a crisis in legitimation as they fail to satisfy the hopes and value orientations of whites. The emerging polarization between the affluent managerial expert class and a broad middle class that finds itself under increasing psychological and economic pressure is worrying and may prove disruptive. Any future government will take cognizance of these tendencies and will engage in policies designed to reeducate all groups, but paying special attention to the unique problem posed by the white minority. At the end of the twentieth century, whites may find themselves to be the problem—a complete reversal of the situation after more than three centuries.

12

Whites in American Race Relations: A Comparison

> Although America's apartheid may not be rooted in the legal strictures of its South African relative, it is no less effective in perpetuating racial inequality, and whites are no less culpable for the socioeconomic deprivation that results. (Massey & Denton, 1993, p. 15)

Massey and Denton make this observation in their book *American Apartheid.* The authors are writing in the last decade of the twentieth century, 130 years after Lincoln's Emancipation Proclamation of 1863. Despite the continuous struggle to incorporate African Americans into a more egalitarian society since Reconstruction, racial inequalities have persisted in American social life and have solidified institutionally. In recent decades, the high ideals of a nonracial society posited by Martin Luther King, Jr., and other civil rights leaders have been contradicted by social practice. Tremendous efforts have been expended on the legal/constitutional level to correct inequities. Yet Massey and Denton document the phenomenon of "hypersegregation" in the major cities of the United States (p. 10). Hypersegregation has created black underclass communities that suffer from deprivation and a diminution of life chances. Recent statistics on socioeconomic status, health, education, housing, incarceration, and political participation present a bleak picture. Huge gaps exist between black and white and, in certain cases, black disadvantage is even on the increase.[1] Viewed from a structural perspective, racial inequality still seems to be well entrenched in U.S. society. Within the scope of this chapter, only a scant review can be given of this vast and copiously researched area. In this section I will focus more on the problematic aspects of open and hidden white ethnocentrism and racism in the United States, without losing sight of the continuous and Sisyphean efforts of many whites to create favorable conditions for a more egalitarian and peaceful society.

The purpose of this discussion is to look at race and ethnic relations in the United States from the perspective developed in the chapters of this volume concerned with South Africa. I will therefore present evidence of white ethnocentric attitudes and constructions on the everyday and commonsense level. Structural racism in the United States has perhaps been best documented in recent times. Structural discrimination can justifiably be taken as evidence of underlying attitudes and values. A comparison with South African constructions may illuminate American processes of racial boundary construction and the premises upon which they are based. In making these comparisons, we should not lose sight of the historical, demographic, and social structural differences between the two societies.

Comparisons between race relations in South Africa and the United States are not new. Perhaps the best known is George Frederickson's (1981) historical work on white supremacy. Studies based on everyday life experiences, however, have been few and far between. This may be because of the heavy emphasis given to structural factors in U.S. studies. In the introduction to the second edition of his *Portraits of White Racism,* Wellman (1993) makes two important observations. He first records that much less attention is given to prejudice among whites in American studies because of an increasing focus on the institutional rather than the psychological context in which African Americans find themselves. Second, racism as a sociological concept has been discredited and replaced by such nonracial notions as "economic dislocation," "moral character," and "victim-focused identity" (p. 3).

The structural approach is perhaps best exemplified by the work of William J. Wilson, which has had tremendous influence on the American sociology of race relations. In *The Declining Significance of Race* (1978), Wilson makes economic factors crucial to his explanation of African Americans' social position. He relegates "race" to the domain of the irrational, making "class" the privileged explanatory concept. In later work, he corrected some misappropriations of his concept of the "underclass" (Wilson, 1987). These misunderstandings tended to look at the underclass phenomenon in cultural terms, thus having the effect of blaming the victim. In a coauthored article, Loïc J. D. Wacquant and Wilson (1989) reinstate race and class as factors contributing to the structural entrapment and impoverishment of blacks in urban ghettos. The structural approach, however, does not take adequate account of the discrimination suffered by the

African American middle class and, more seriously, neglects the dimension of experience and the racial construction of the other.

Wellman (1993) contrasts the structural approach, which minimizes the importance of "race," with the "cultural" or "ideological" angles, which tend to maximize it. They look at racism as an "ideological construction that is based on misrepresentation or 'false knowledge' " (p. 8). Essentially, then, it seems that such views take an outsider perspective that measures ideological constructs made by racists against some norm of universal rationality or "truthful" knowledge. They furthermore do not take adequate account of the structural embeddedness of ideologies.

The perspective from which I have conducted this study, and from which I am making this comparison between the United States and South Africa, calls for an understanding of the meanings white people attach to the phenomenon of the racially other and of the motivations that lead them to act in ways, or establish structures, that have discriminatory consequences. Wellman maintains that the sociology of (American) racism has become bifurcated between the structural and cultural approaches and pleads for an integration of the two in a perspective that "sees racism as a system of exclusion and privilege, *and* as a set of culturally acceptable linguistic or ideological constructions that defend one's location in that system" (p. 25). This formulation sounds acceptable as long as one refrains from prematurely specifying the motive or the rationalization for whites' acting in a racist way. In the South African study described in this volume, I attempted to let whites speak for themselves so that I could arrive at a valid interpretation. In my view, Wellman overemphasizes whites' social organization of racial advantage or privilege. His stress on the maximization of benefits may lead one to narrow one's focus to utilitarian considerations. The in-group, whether expressed in terms of racial, ethnic, or other identities, may construct meanings that may precede or go beyond the calculus of advantage or privilege. I have attempted to demonstrate this in the South African case by exploring wider parameters of ethnocentrism. A too-narrow focus obscures other important dimensions of racial constructions.

SOME IMPORTANT DIFFERENCES

In comparing whites' racial and ethnic constructions in South Africa and the United States, I will concentrate on black-white relations. In both countries there are numerous other ethnic and racial groupings as potential objects of white racial thinking. My decision to stay with black-white relations is guided more by considerations of space than by the perception that they are of greater significance than others. In any event, black-white relations are more visible than other combinations. Below, I will consider the differences in racial boundary setting between the two societies. A simple comparison that looks for parallels and analogies without considering some very important differences between the two societies cannot be justified. First, I will address the way historical differences between the two countries have affected race relations; I will then explore structural differences in the two societies as well as differences in the dominant discourse pertaining to race.

Historical Processes

The first important historical difference between the United States and South Africa, as far as black-white relations are concerned, has to do with the way in which black presence was established. In South Africa, the black population is indigenous. Blacks were slowly pushed off the land they originally occupied and later were conquered by the white settler population. Traditional languages, cultures, social structures, and, to a certain extent, political structures, though modified through processes of change, remain identifiable and constitute important resources for a sense of identity among the black population. In contrast, the black population's presence in the United States was brought about by involuntary immigration. Africans were stripped of their cultural resources as their communities of memory were destroyed. They were divided by a particularly humiliating system of chattel slavery that had no place for the preservation of kinship or any other social structure. Whites' perceptions of blacks in the two societies have thus been thus fundamentally different. South Africans have tended to view blacks much as white Americans have perceived Native Americans. They are "nations" and thus worthy of recognition and negotiation; they can be enemies or allies. Of course, the indigenous peoples of South Africa were eventually conquered and transformed into laborers, but they were never enslaved. They always had a cultural heritage that gave meaning to their blackness, even in the eyes of whites. That is one reason some whites try to express differences between blacks and whites in cultural terms.

South African whites thus tend to look at blacks as members of linguistic and cultural communities—as Zulu, Tswana, Xhosa, and so on. In the United States, however, whites tend to look at blacks in an undifferentiated way, without perceiving much cultural variation among them except perhaps for their geographic distribution in the North or South. Similarly, their descent has been genetically defined according to the rule that one drop of "black blood" makes a person black (Davis, 1991, p. 5).

A second important historical difference lies in the fact that South African blacks have been associated with rural hinterlands, later called homelands. Of course, many urbanized blacks have refused to accept ascription to a homeland, but of concern here is the widely distributed perception among whites. This perception has also been reinforced by the dominant discourse and entrenched in legal practice. The situation in the United States is completely different. African Americans have never had a homeland or "reservation" in the United States. Historically they have been associated with the South and, beyond that, with Africa. Generally, the white American public has a vague and undifferentiated view of Africa as the country of origin of blacks. The idea of Africa as a homeland to which African Americans can return has never been a serious thought among a broad spectrum of U.S. whites. African Americans, therefore, cannot be wished away to some homeland but are a permanent presence and, for many whites, a perennial problem within the shared country.

The third historical difference centers on the problem of labor. Once South African blacks were conquered, white politicians and entrepreneurs engineered a system for extracting labor from the reserves where they were initially concentrated. Through various push and pull factors, blacks streamed to the cities to be employed in the lowest skill categories. They were either temporary laborers or achieved a degree of permanent residence. Overall, as the preceding chapters demonstrate, they were viewed as blue-collar, manual laborers. This status was also expressed and perpetuated by a legislative apparatus until deep into the 1980s. In the United States, the prime and only reason for the original Africans' presence was that of labor. After emancipation, African Americans entered the urban labor market as free men, but at the lowest levels. They had to compete with European immigrants, who already had a head start. African Americans' status, however, was not persistently associated with blue-collar work, nor was their legal status fixed in labor. They could freely compete in the market, but their disadvantages and racial status caused them to be overrepresented at the lower income levels.

Finally, the historical profiles of the white populations in the two countries differ substantially. Not only are the numerical proportions radically different, but there are certain cultural differences that cannot be ignored. Earlier, I indicated how the Dutch East India Company discouraged large-scale immigration to the Cape of Good Hope. The number of Dutch was thus kept low and was augmented by only a few French Hugue-nots in the late seventeenth century. In that period there was a degree of admixture with the slave population. In the nineteenth century, the British boosted white immigration in order to settle and "pacify" the frontier with blacks. The white population grew slowly and mostly through natural increase. Except for a small, cultured English enclave at Cape Town, most whites engaged in subsistence farming. Those in the Afrikaner segment of the population were puritanical in their orientation, but in a unique way that combined an Old Testament ethos with that of their Dutch Calvinist heritage. It was only with the discovery of diamonds and gold in the late nineteenth century that the white population was significantly enlarged, mainly through English-speaking immigrants. Industrialization and urbanization occurred much later and on a much smaller scale than in the United States. It centered on the mining industry of the Witwatersrand area and was characterized by an English commercial culture.

The mostly rural Afrikaners entered the new urban economy in competition with blacks. Legislation during the early decades of the twentieth century favored white Afrikaner labor at the expense of blacks. National-istic fervor and chiliastic expectations helped the Afrikaners to "reclaim" their "promised land" politically and to carve out an important niche in the economy. After the political triumph of Afrikaner nationalists in 1948, the debate on race relations was dominated by an exchange between liberal English speakers and nationalist Afrikaners. The English speakers argued for fairness and reasonableness toward blacks, and appealed to a form of rationality in race relations that would both favor capitalist entrepre-neurs by stabilizing the black labor force and accommodate some of their aspirations. The Afrikaners, on their part, appealed to the reason of ethnic nationalism in defining both themselves and the variety of black "nations" they discerned. Their arguments were deeply rooted in a unique Calvinist tradition that, unlike its European counterpart, did not exhibit a natural affinity for capitalism. The debate between Afrikaners and English speak-ers endured for almost 40 years and, despite its acrimonious nature, the two sides seemed to achieve a common end: the entrenchment of white privilege. Apartheid proved to be good for business and agriculture. As indicated previously, English speakers' and Afrikaners' appraisals of the racial situation have undergone a convergence in recent years. It was especially the Afrikaner intellectuals and political elite who embraced the notion of a free market economy, with its "natural" concomitant social differentiation of class. The conservative whites persevered in their use of ethnic nationalism for making sense of the racial situation.

In summary, then, South African whites have contended with the racial situation as an ideologically and historically divided minority. This minority protected its privileges and advantages by legal means and justified them through two different ideologies of entitlement: entrepreneurial reward and ethnic descent.

The development of the white majority in the United States is quite a different story.[2] The territory the United States now comprises has a long history of conflicts and negotiations among colonial settlers, indigenous peoples, and other settlers. The sharpest difference between the United States and South Africa is found in the tremendous scale of European immigration and the near total decimation of the indigenous population. The settler population thus rapidly advanced to become the numerical majority. Among them, the white Anglo-Saxon and Protestant group prevailed over other European colonists, such as the Dutch, French, and Spanish. When they established themselves on the eastern seaboard, they brought with them a set of strong puritanical values and attitudes shaped by religious conflict and the delegitimation of secular authority in the land of their origin. Pioneer English settlers had a robust sense of independence and social solidarity that enabled them to throw off the yoke of British rule at an early stage.

Their numbers were vastly greater than those of their South African colonial counterparts, and, instead of massively dispersing toward the frontier, they formed various communities and settlements that remained culturally in touch with Britain and Europe. During the seventeenth and eighteenth centuries, settlers in South Africa were much more cut off from European influences, partly because of the tremendous distance involved and the fact that the Cape was more a way station than a destination. American settlers established schools and centers for higher learning. The South African frontiersmen had no such experience; a facility for higher education was established only in the nineteenth century.

American whites had early and intense exposure to the Enlightenment in its pragmatic form. It led to the establishment and distribution of higher learning on a wide scale. Confidence in scientific rationality and the ingenuity of the inventive mind led to rapid technological advances. These orientations, combined with puritan work habits, made for huge strides in the economy and the rapid industrialization of the nineteenth century. The industrial North and its dominant ideology prevailed after the Civil War. Whites consolidated their power and cultural character to the extent that it could assimilate great waves of European immigration during the nine-teenth century and the beginning of the twentieth century. Although assimi-lation occurred at differential rates for immigrants from northern and southern European areas, it nevertheless resulted in the dispersal of immi-grant communities among the broader white population. Religious, lin-guistic, and cultural differences were accommodated in an overarching white American identity.

Unlike whites in South Africa, U.S. whites were not as ethnically divided among themselves in the twentieth century, nor did a part of them struggle for recognition and power as the Afrikaners did. The most solid ethnic boundaries they drew were in relation to African Americans, Hispan-ics, and Asians. The ethnic stratification that existed early in this century was in part attributed to ability and effort. This filled white Anglo-Saxons with a sense of entitlement to their dominance. They held that it was through their effort that a great industrial country had been built up. The doctrine of individual freedom further postulated that, under the conditions of freely available opportunity, anybody could make a success. Those who lagged behind lacked either ability or effort and were thus responsible for their own position in the economic and status hierarchy. Stratification therefore was "natural," and effort could be linked to innate ability. This social Darwinism was sometimes accompanied by scientific racism. The causes of poverty were attributed to the poor themselves, and poverty happened to be concentrated among African Americans and Hispanics.

Afrikaners had no such view of poverty. At worst, they saw it as an accompaniment of blacks' laborer status in a white country. Opportunity was available to blacks in their separate homelands. Whites' privilege was their birthright. Liberal English speakers saw apartheid as the cause of poverty and believed in a free economy in which class stratification occurred. In theory, their attitude was nonracial. In practice, class divisions coin-cided with race.

In summary, thus, white Americans in this century found themselves at an advantage over other groups. They did not need to entrench their privilege by legal means. It was historically established and symbolically expressed in the distribution of wealth. In their eyes, their entitlement to the major share of resources was a matter of their record of performance.

Structural Differences

South African social reality was legally constructed. This legal construc-tion was directly responsible for the unequal distribution of life chances in that society. Apartheid legislation affected every part of every population group's life. White supremacy was entrenched in numerous ways. This legal construction also determined the country's physical structure and segregated various groups, assigning them status and relevant wealth. Apart from skin color, blacks physically appeared poorer, did certain work, and lived in impoverished circumstances and areas. The structures imposed on them had the effect of reproducing white stereotypes of them. Recently, certain key laws have been abolished, but their structural effects linger on. Blacks are still poor, separate, landless, and of low status, and they have much shorter life expectancy than whites. The new black majority government will have to deal with these effects and structures.

In the southern United States, Jim Crow legislation constructed a legally segregated social reality. Although not as tightly knit and pervasive as the South African system of a few decades later, Jim Crow laws nevertheless had comparable devastating effects on the life chances and status of blacks. The civil rights era and its aftermath aimed at the legal dismantling of segregation and racial privilege. Discriminatory practices have been identified and dealt with by law. Segregation and racial inequality have been addressed by a series of equalization policies ranging from school desegregation to elaborate affirmative action strategies. Yet a glance at recent statistics reveals that there are still significant and disturbing gaps between the life chances of blacks and whites in the United States.

Taking secondary structural assimilation as an indicator of progress toward a formal inclusion of African Americans in the American way of life, income and employment patterns reveal that, in the 1950s, black family income remained at about 55-60% of white family income. After a slight rise above 60% in the late 1960s, it dropped to 58%, where it stood from 1974 to 1990. Between 1959 and 1992, the unemployment ratio of blacks to whites stayed more or less constant at 2.2 (Feagin & Feagin, 1993, pp. 233-234). Many other parameters could be used to trace patterns indicating greater or lesser inequality. The discrepancies between black and white in the United States are not as blatant as those in South Africa, but they nevertheless have not been significantly reduced, even after four decades of desegregation and equal opportunity policy making. Structural inequality remains an undeniable and visible feature of American life. It is visible, for instance, in educational attainment. After the proportion of African Americans with four-year college completion rates had risen steadily to 12%, it remained there between 1980 and 1991. The comparable figure for whites is 25%. High school completion rates for blacks lies within 5% of those of whites at 82% (Marger, 1994, p. 257).

Liberal whites anxiously monitor the degree of secondary structural assimilation, looking for signs of a decrease in residential segregation and trends toward greater occupational similarity. Yet even positive signs are sometimes deceiving, as statistical evidence is often constructed in such a way that the real situation is cloaked. McLemore (1994, p. 331), for example, documents a rapid fall in the occupational dissimilarity between black and white males from an index score of 43 in 1940 to 24 in 1980. For women the figures are even more dramatic: from 63 in 1940 to 18 in 1980. He concedes, however, that these statistics may not mean much because of stratification within each occupational category listed. That is, within each category, blacks are more likely than whites to be represented in the lower positions as far as pay and prestige are concerned. Even if the index of occupational dissimilarity were zero, occupational assimilation would still be incomplete.

Primary structural assimilation as an indicator of the informal inclusion of African Americans in American life is also revealing. Structural assimilation at the primary level is measured by residential distribution, intermarriage, friendship patterns, and club membership. Taking residential patterns first, the phenomenon of urban segregation is overwhelming.[3] Massey and Denton (1993) found that in the North

> the prevailing pattern during the 1980s was one of stasis: the average index changed by only 2.3 percentage points (compared with 4.4 points during the prior decade). . . .
>
> As of 1990, eight northern metropolitan areas (Buffalo, Chicago, Cleveland, Detroit, Gary, Milwaukee, New York and Newark) had segregation rates above 80, indicating an extreme separation of the races. (p. 221)

Residential separation of blacks and whites has definite consequences for free association between the groups. At the height of school desegregation in the period 1964-1975, the University of Michigan's Institute for Social Research reported a rise in interracial contacts beyond the classroom (McLemore, 1994, p. 338). The fact remains that blacks and whites are largely separated in their interpersonal relationships. A more recent study of more than a million high school friendship pairs found evidence of only a few hundred friendships across racial barriers (Hallinan & Williams, 1987; cited in McLemore, 1994, p. 339). At school and university levels, clubs and associations tend to be segregated. In the area of institutionalized religion, black churches have a distinct identity and social basis. The most significant test is perhaps the incidence of interracial marriage. Regardless of all the liberalization that occurred in the 1960s, blacks had the lowest out-marriage rate of 32 ethnic groups studied in 1978 (Gurak & Kritz, 1978; cited in McLemore, 1994, p. 339). Although the out-marriage rate among blacks increased to 0.4% in 1990 from 0.14% in 1963, it is still far lower than that of any other minority group. Although we must allow for the likelihood of spontaneous preferences exercised by blacks in the choice of marriage partners, we must also leave room for the possibility that these choices occur within the context of racial rejection and prejudice. Opinion surveys have found that whites are far from unanimous on the question of whether interracial marriages should be declared illegal (Marger, 1994, p. 276).

The overall structural picture of black-white race relations in the United States demonstrates disadvantage and separation of the black minority. Segregation and lack of interracial contacts are the breeding and feeding ground for prejudice and negative stereotypes. The association of African Americans as a category with poverty, unemployment, low-status jobs, and violence gives rise to stereotypes. These stereotypes are the result of a vicious circle in which structural factors marginalize a large section of the African American population, which is then defined in those terms and shunned or avoided out of fear and disgust. Structural factors come into play in helping to reproduce white race consciousness. This mechanism has been demonstrated with regard to South Africa. The United States proves that segregation need not be enforced by law to have similar effects.

The American case exhibits a strange anomaly. Opinion polls conducted over the past few decades show consistent decreases in prejudicial attitudes among whites. In 1989, 93% of white respondents favored school integration. Asked whether whites had the right to keep blacks out of their neighborhoods, 78% replied in the negative (Marger, 1994, p. 276). The National Conference of Christians and Jews reported in 1978 that the prevalence of seven negative stereotypes had been consistently declining since 1963. Stereotypes such as "Blacks tend to have less ambition than whites" and "Blacks are inferior to white people" declined by as much as 16 percentage points. Can we conclude from this evidence that prejudice is on the decline? We can hardly respond in the affirmative in view of the structural evidence. This anomaly points to a deeper-seated source of prejudice that opinion polls simply cannot capture. There is a wide discrepancy between how people respond in surveys and how they act in reality. With regard to South Africa, I have argued that this source may well be located in patterns of thinking about the racially other. We will come back to this point later in this chapter.

The Dominant Discourse

It is in the area of dominant discourse practice that the deepest differences are found between South Africa and the United States. The most salient difference involves the importance attached to group identity in the two societies. In the United States, the emphasis is decidedly on individuals and their maximization of opportunity. Among whites in South Africa, in contrast, Afrikaners attach great importance to group identity and group self-protection as a means of survival. Because of their history as a numerical minority surrounded by a powerful imperial force and confronted by a massive black population, Afrikaners had to consolidate themselves as a group in terms of ideologies of a shared nationalism and a primordial ethnic identity. More recently, the sentiments of Afrikaners and English speakers have converged around issues of economic survival in the name of civilized values.

Historically, Afrikaners have defined themselves as a group with a special mission and calling on the subcontinent. In fulfilling this mission, they have believed that they are entitled to the country, that South Africa is theirs. They have projected the importance of group identity onto African groups and thus elevated the importance of group identity over individual identity on a countrywide basis. Only in recent decades has there been a major rethinking on some of these assumptions that has led more enlightened segments of Afrikaners to the realization that all whites are in the same boat. Through various means indicated previously, whites have identified with a universalist notion of scientific rationality not only as the way to pull the country through difficult times but also as a means to preserve an elite culture of white manager-experts. The group-way-of-thinking has undergone a transformation from its ethnoracial (Afrikaner) reasoning to its manager-expert form. Instead of the exclusiveness of primordial ethnic identity, with its strong overtones of race and descent, the new elite group sets its boundaries less rigidly and is more open to the inclusion of people qualified in terms of their competence in a world driven by scientific rationality. The preservation of this rationality coincides with the preservation of civilized values in a country largely characterized by Third World realities. An individual's assimilation into this elite group depends on his or her identification with and expression of those values.

At first glance, the new dominant discourse appears to favor class formation over anything else. However, the composition of this class is mostly white and will probably remain so for a long time, as control of the situation still rests with those with the most resources (i.e., capital).[4] It will be in the interest of the white entrepreneurial elite to co-opt enough blacks to enhance their credibility and legitimacy. What the new black majority government will do about this remains to be seen. Their future role in the economy of the country is crucial, although the dominant discourse may change in the direction of democratic egalitarianism.

Compared with the United States, South Africa displays some important differences and similarities. Shortly before majority rule became law in South Africa, the country's dominant discourse looked very similar to that in the United States. Scientific management was held to be the key to a smooth and peaceful government in both countries. The important difference lies in the way the two countries have reached their present positions. In South Africa, the old group-based ideologies wreaked havoc on the economy. The government made an about-face and adopted the language of business and technocracy. Individual merit instead of group membership would determine the individual's position in society. The United States, in contrast, has a long tradition of pragmatic and scientific means of running the country and dealing with its economic and social problems. This tradition was not born of the crisis of group-based ideologies; rather, it is rooted in a philosophy of individualism and freedom. This philosophy is taken for granted and held as self-evident. Individual merit and performance are supposed to count, rather than membership in a class, family, status group, religious community, or ethnic group. Group membership is a private matter, and so is adherence to a cultural tradition (in South Africa both have been public and official matters). This is the officially sanctioned position that is evidenced in equal-opportunity statements, position announcements, and policy declarations of both private and government bodies.

However, the distinction of individual merit and merit as a member of a group has proved to be problematic. The credibility of the nonracial (i.e., merit) and egalitarian assumptions of the dominant discourse suffered after the civil rights era in the face of incontrovertible evidence of the continued and intensifying racial disadvantage of African Americans and Hispanics as groups, not as individuals. An important shift was occurring, from the point where race as a social and cultural entity was capable of melting with other such groups into an overarching identity to the position where it was not. In this sense it assumed the character of a fixed, "unmeltable," and biological group identity. This shift has occurred in both the dominant discourse and in the self-conceptualization of African Americans. As a social concept, "race" membership was cultural and changeable. Race membership was much less fixed and static than where people attached increasing value to its biological overtones.

The dominant discourse in South Africa has avoided defining blacks in terms of race as an immutable biological and inferior identity. Rather, it has adopted discourse strategies based on cultural and ethnic distinctions. However, as we have seen in the close examination of conservative whites' everyday constructions of blacks in Chapters 8 and 9, it is clear that they nevertheless attribute permanent racial differences to blacks. In South Africa the privileged segments of the population have thus attempted to hide their racially based claims behind the decency of cultural difference. This is visible on both the dominant and everyday discourse levels. In the United States, the disadvantaged have realized that the egalitarian rhetoric of the dominant discourse brought them nothing. Instead, group membership has become the basis for achieving a degree of power from a position of disempowerment. I agree with Outlaw (1990), who notes that "for the past twenty years, however, 'race' has been the primary vehicle for conceptualizing and organizing precisely around group differences with the demand that social justice be applied to *groups* and that 'justice' be measured by *results,* not just by opportunities" (p. 60).

The dominant have had to adjust to this and give expression to the redistribution of justice through a shift in emphasis from the elimination of discrimination against groups in affirmative policies to a redress of the imbalances in society that favor certain groups. The dominant discourse has become increasingly preoccupied with the issue of group rights—an issue that has perennially bedeviled South African politics. The problems of ethnic districting, whether applied to schools or to elections for political office, are test cases for an emerging shift in official discourse in the United States. The shift toward group rights in the dominant discourse will have to take account of some of the assumptions the notion of group rights is based on. Is it simply based on some primordial and biological notion of race membership according to which membership is fixed by birth and endures forever? Such an assumption could eventually lead to a castelike construction of U.S. society not unlike that envisaged by the Population Registration Act of South Africa in 1950. Currently, the official discourse is unclear on this. Official forms and documents vacillate between social and biological definitions, some demanding information about "heritage" (the social definition of race/ethnicity) and some wanting to know "race" (the biological side). The intent in making these distinctions official, of course, is to make possible the redress of inequality and not to sustain it as in South Africa (until recently). However, this practice engenders the group-way-of-thinking that has been explored in this volume in the South African context.

Davis (1991) maintains that the so-called one-drop rule, according to which an African American is any person with any known black ancestry, is taken for granted by people involved in the dominant discourse, such as affirmative action officers and judges (as well as black protesters and Ku Klux Klansmen). In addition to the factors mentioned, the persistence of the one-drop rule adds the further concern that racial thinking may be endemic to the dominant discourse.

PUBLIC DISCOURSE

If the group-way-of-thinking—or, in the United States, "thinking along racial lines"—is a characteristic feature of the dominant discourse, it is even more true of public discourse. In both public discourse and everyday talk, "race" is a reference schema according to which the social world is interpreted and given meaning. Used by whites, the term *race* is applied to minorities. It is a term applied to the out-group rather than to the in-group. This is different from South Africa, where the equivalent reference is *ethnic group,* used to indicate the in-group of whites as well as various out-groups. Of course, such a use of *ethnic group* is political too, because it divides the black majority by splitting them up into various "ethnic" minorities.

During the past two years, I have asked the students in five American university classes to list the "races" found in the United States. In four cases they defined every minority as a "race" except for whites. This is no isolated instance; the in-group is taken for granted and is not problematized. The terms *ethnic, minority,* and *race* are indicators not only of out-groups, but of social formations problematic to mainstream society. Public discourse on race is therefore indicative of how social boundaries are constructed through the problematization of the presence of identifiable racial groups. In a negative way, the white in-group defines itself by lumping all out-groups into one overarching category of "people of color." Many groups caught up in this defining net object to the label, especially people of Hispanic and Asian origin. "People of color" are problematized either as disadvantaged or unfairly privileged.

Liberal-minded whites perceive "people of color" as the collectively disadvantaged. They construct therapeutic programs to help these people empower themselves. However, outside the context of empowerment and disadvantage, these whites still use their constructions of minorities in ways that assign to the ethnically or racially other an identity that is irrelevant to the situation. This carryover from one context to another can cause resentment. Some minority people complain of being fixed into a permanent victim stereotype that hinders their sense of inclusion in informal gatherings, where well-meant victim stereotyping stifles their spontaneity. At more formal occasions, such as committee meetings, professional roles of "people of color" are often restrained or obscured by this form of stereotyping. It is not difficult to imagine that minority members tend to cluster socially at universities because of the embarrassment of being victim stereotyped out of context. Victim stereotyping of "people of color" also disregards those numerous cases to which neither disadvantage nor color visibility applies.

The South African material presented in this volume does not provide clear comparative instances of this phenomenon. Liberal-minded South African whites would tend to act paternalistically when dealing with less educated, poorer blacks, but would treat "civilized" individuals equally as long as they follow the rules and priorities set by white middle-class convention.

In the United States, conservative whites monitor equal-opportunity and affirmative action programs closely in order to determine whether "people of color" are receiving any unfair advantage or privilege. Their central concern is to uphold publicly the principle of individual merit against that of group entitlement. Their fear of unfair advantage crystallizes around public debates on "quotas" and "reverse discrimination." Former President Bush claimed that the Civil Rights Bill of 1990, which was intended to address discrimination in the workplace, contained quotas. He vetoed that bill and then signed the 1991 version only after lengthy negotiation and many compromises. When President Clinton nominated Lani Guinier to head the Civil Rights Division of the U.S. Department of Justice, the *Wall Street Journal* successfully labeled her a "quota queen." In view of the anticipated opposition to her nomination, it was withdrawn even before the candidate was given an opportunity to clarify her views. In justifying resistance to quotas, appeals are made to fairness and balance. Teun van Dijk (1992b) quotes a congressional debate: "It is neither fair nor sensible to give employers of our country a difficult choice between using quotas and seeking a clarification of the law through costly and risky litigation" (p. 54).

Opposition to quotas and the defense of publicly shared values involve the denial of racism or racial thinking. Denial helps to obscure the problem and creates the impression of correctness and racial innocence. Denial is the art of impression management in the face of contradicting evidence. In countries where discrimination and racism are officially banned and where norms against race hate have developed, denial takes a prominent form in public discourse. Furthermore, van Dijk (1992a) argues, "the denial of racism also has a prominent role in the very reproduction of racism" (pp. 95-96). It can take various forms, from isolating an incident or a remark as an aberration or misunderstanding to blaming the extreme right or white supremacists. Through various mechanisms the mainstream (white) society exonerates itself. In South Africa, the government media (like most whites interviewed for this study) have gone to extraordinary lengths to deny racism. In the face of overwhelming evidence of inequality and differential treatment of blacks, they maintained that the country practiced only fair ethnic and cultural politics or followed sound business practices.

In view of the denial of racism in the United States, it is not surprising that the media and commercial world still contain an inordinate amount of negative stereotyping of blacks that is simply not noticed or ignored as trivial. Images from the American racial past crop up in new guises in advertisements, trinkets, motion pictures, and other representations. The image of the docile, servile, sexless, overweight, bandanna-wearing mammy still crops up in sanitized versions on syrup bottles. Certain rice products carry the image of a black person that evokes the picture of "uncle," an old, docile, subservient, harmless, "good" black. Most adult whites grew up reading comic books and watching cartoons with similar images of the mammy, the uncle, "pickaninnies," "Topsy," "Sambo," and black cannibals, to name but a few. Their racial socialization, which was perhaps influenced by visual representation more than in any other society, was further enhanced by Hollywood material that portrayed blacks as either savage (both in Africa and the United States) and devious or subservient and dependent. In recent times the cineast Donald Bogle (1989) has observed that modern depictions of male blacks perpetuate, in an updated form, the image of the loyal servant who is denied a strong sexual identity (cited in Lyman, 1990, pp. 71-72). On the other end of the spectrum, blacks are depicted as characters more savage and unbridled than any of their white counterparts.

The press is another agency with an important but implicit function in perpetuating racial stereotypes. In many urban centers local news reporting focuses on problems in predominantly black and, sometimes, Hispanic neighborhoods. The public gaze is directed to drug trafficking, drive-by shootings, child abuse and neglect, family violence, rape, and burglary with blacks as perpetrators and victims. This daily fare on local networks cannot fail to make an impact on viewers. Blacks become associated with social deviance. Rarely is this representation balanced by comparable reports on crime and deviant behavior in white neighborhoods, nor is there enough informed commentary to frame deviance in a sociopolitical context. Further, the hiring practices of newspapers and television companies favor the white middle class. Regardless of affirmative action policies, more than 60% of all U.S. newspapers do not employ a single black journalist. Van Dijk (1992b, p. 43) reports that the U.S. media employ only carefully selected token minorities. In this way, minority perspectives are underrepresented and white prejudices remain unchallenged and uncorrected, retaining their plausibility for viewers and readers.

Whereas white Americans receive distorted information about African Americans, South African white journalists have been knowingly or unknowingly hamstrung in their reporting by language and segregation barriers that have led to both distortions and omissions. Television channels and newspaper editions have been racially and linguistically separated. As a result, blacks have been less visible in the white public eye. Images of blacks as largely tribal and uncivilized have been common, however. In recent years political unrest brought prominence to black affairs in white communities. Reporting on this unrest was done within the context of white fear, with the result that the stereotype of the black savage became more general.

EVERYDAY DISCOURSE

White Americans' experience of African Americans and other minorities is molded by a unique history born of the tension between opposites, such as exclusion and inclusion, domination and empowerment, and exploitation and co-optation. Historical experiences are mediated by official renderings of the past, which usually document a movement toward greater democratic participation and a serious concern for eradicating and solving persistent social problems. The overall tone of self-perception is an optimistic one couched in glowing terms, praising the greatness of the country, its institutions, and its international leadership. The dominant and official discourse affirms this positive image with regard to human relations. The official discourse of government strains itself to sustain the impression of the United States as an egalitarian, just, and free society and goes to extraordinary lengths to make plausible its efforts to keep it that way. The structural evidence—proof of government successes—falls short, however. Phenomena such as ghettos, riots, poverty, and rampant crime and other social problems persist and even become worse. Rarely does the government, in its quest for trust and plausibility, accept responsibility for creating these or contributing to their development. In addressing the problem of inequality, official discourse responds in the characteristic way, by devising scientifically and technically "responsible" solutions. In the process, it has to avoid and distance itself from the "bias" of social group interests and perspectives. Yet it falls into the trap of adopting socially defined concepts, giving them official validity by bureaucratizing them. In return, this circular process creates the impression among the citizenry that government categories are "objective" and stable. Above, I noted how "race" membership has become fixed in a biological, objective conceptualization of group membership. The official categorizations have a symbiotic relationship with those in public use. The categories of public discourse are more elaborate and incorporate historical predicates in the form of stereotypes and other popular typologies that attach themselves to official categories. They are endowed with respectability by being purified of the blatant denigrations of their counterparts of the past. Assisted by the relative isolation and social distance between whites and minorities, these popular typologies remain largely unchallenged by empirical evidence.

In a cumulative way, then, historical representations as well as official and public discourse structure whites' everyday experience of "racial" groups. They not only structure experience but also selectively focus and direct attention on aspects of behavior and appearance that are relevant and important for interaction. In this way, role expectations and self-presentations are constructed. These constructs enable and convince individuals to "do the right thing" in everyday life. The constructs are self-evident and taken for granted. The actions they frame and direct are "moral" and "responsible." The same applies to the group they belong to, the dominant Anglo-American group. Where evidence of racism appears, white individuals and groups engage in a number of strategies to sustain their own respectability. These strategies include denial, trivialization, exceptionalization, and attribution to misunderstanding.

Except for white supremacists, few American whites, even the clearly prejudiced, will sacrifice respectability by being openly racist or by publicly using racist language. In fact, there is a genuine desire to be generous and fair, even to be antiracist. The quest for racial innocence is widespread and strikes the outside observer as a phenomenon quite peculiar to the

United States. There are, of course, those who say that blacks are of little concern to them as long as they have no direct involvement with blacks (Wellman, 1993, p. 217).

In their self-presentations, whites thus tend to be nonracist. Yet, as we have seen, their experience of blacks and other minorities is racially structured. A remarkable tension exists between the racial way of thinking and the nonracial self-presentation. This same tension was found among moderates in South Africa interviewed for this study; for example, see the case of Henry in Chapter 10. If members of other racial groups assimilated to his values and lifestyle, Henry said that he would have no objection to integrating with them as individuals. The qualitative evidence Wellman published in 1977 and augmented in 1993 points in a similar direction. He was amazed to find that, regardless of their class positions, his subjects claimed to be remarkably "liberal" (p. 208). Some maintained that if blacks would play by the rules of the dominant society, adhering to the principle that individual performance and merit are the only considerations in the distribution of reward, then U.S. society would be much more egalitarian. They saw America's problem not as one of racism but as one of blacks' failure to conform and adhere to (white) rules in pursuing goals. The responsibility was thus taken away from whites and attached to blacks, who were either not motivated enough to work hard or did not care because they were "happy, soulful and musical."

Wellman's subsequent research confirmed that white self-exoneration took much the same form 15 years after his first study. An investigation among white students at the University of California in Berkeley demonstrated the way they defended their group privilege without introducing "race" as an argument. In their criticism of the affirmative action policies of the university, they emphasized their unreasonableness by considering minority status as an admission criterion. Some saw this action as an insult to minority students and a procedure that worked to their disadvantage. In the case of Asian students whose academic merit was beyond question, white students objected to admitting them on a representative basis because they were academically one-sided. They maintained that it was well-rounded "people like us who belong at the university" (Wellman, 1993, p. 236). These rationalizations indicate how the white students took their advantaged position for granted, without questioning their lack of sensitivity to the problem of equality. The South African students in the present study were much more open in their racial thinking. They also tried to cloak their arguments for racial exclusion in terms of differences in civilization and culture rather than "race," but their expressed disgust toward physical features of blacks clearly revealed their racism.

In the working-class area of Bensonhurst, New York, white youths have also employed nonracist language in defending their attitude that blacks should be kept out of their neighborhood. In 1989 a gang of youths attacked black teenagers who were looking to buy a used car in the area. One of the black youths subsequently died of his injuries. A follow-up investigation among white youths found that they, and the community they lived in, considered their initiatives to keep their neighborhood homogeneous (white) acceptable. The view they were expressing was culturally approved because it stressed the value of community. Blame for incidents of violence was laid at the door of uppity blacks, who were considered to have an unfair advantage. The whites therefore did not need to contradict American principles of freedom, nor did they need to use racial or genetic language (Wellman, 1993, pp. 240ff.). Like the students at Berkeley, Bensonhurst youths skirted the issue of their relative advantage and privilege over blacks. The issue of equality was neatly swept under the carpet in morally and socially acceptable rhetoric. In both cases the tension between the classical American values of liberty and equality was resolved in favor of an ethnocentrically conceived communal freedom that allowed the community to decide for itself who its members were.

The perception that blacks and other minorities have an unfair advantage did not crop up in the same form in the South African material. Conservatives drew a rigid line between black and white and justified it as divinely ordained (Dawid; Chapter 9). Although the criterion of "civilization" was used to justify further the separateness of whites, it could just as well be substituted for "race," as I have indicated. Interestingly, Leon justified separation culturally as a strategy against assimilation of the white minority by the numerical black majority. In both cases there was a similar tendency to mask, with less success, the language of racism.

The nonracial self-presentation in racial talk seems to be of recent origin in the United States. Kovel (1970, pp. 187-212) has developed a psychohistorical typology of racism in the United States in which he distinguishes "dominative" from "aversive" racism. Dominative racism is racism characteristic of the antebellum South and was originally associated with slavery in a plantation economy. Blacks and whites were locked into one economic system run by, and dictated by, whites. Their domination was complete in slavery. Aversive racism is more a feature of the North in the postemancipation era; it has spread to other areas. *Aversion* implies not only avoidance but also rejection of black "inferiority." This form of racism has attained prevalence since the basis for dominative racism was destroyed. Adding my own interpretation to this typology: Whites and blacks in the South lived more in a common world of experience than those in the North. They shared a life world characterized by the domination of whites and the submission of blacks. This was a close though distorted relationship in which each party built up a degree of intimate knowledge of the other. The people involved not only were known to each other as master and slave in the domestic and work sphere, but paternalistic concern, sexual attraction, and other informal relationships seem to have brought black and white closer than was possible or desirable in the North.

The shading off of the Reconstruction era into the era of Jim Crow and "separate but equal" doctrine was an indicator of the shift toward the aversive form of racism. There was greater personal distance between the races, as well as a greater degree of rejection and symbolic distance. Separate facilities were emblematic of this aversion, and pollution ideas served as reinforcements for whites to remove themselves even more. Whites who were able to break through these barriers joined in the civil rights struggle.

In the post-civil rights era, a new form of racism appeared, which Kovel (1970) calls "metaracism":

> Metaracism is a distinct and very peculiar modern phenomenon. Racial degradation continues on a different plane, and through a different agency: those who participate in it are not racists—that is, they are not racially prejudiced but metaracists, because they acquiesce in the larger cultural order which continues the work of racism. (pp. 211, 213)

Metaracism partially typifies the everyday racial attitudes described above, more so in the case of the Berkeley students than for the Bensonhurst youths. It also characterizes the agents. However, given the foregoing discussion of the tension between self-presentation and style of reasoning, it is now possible to say that the agents are not racist in self-presentation. They provide enough evidence, however, that they think, or reason, along racial lines. The agents of metaracism engage in that group-way-of-thinking explored above, but in a much more covert fashion. It is covert because the way humans reason in the world of everyday life is taken for granted. The avowed liberal is not a racist in his or her own eyes. This is true of both Americans and their South African counterparts. It would be grossly irresponsible to assert that a racial way of thinking is so generally distributed that few escape its clutches. I am referring only to those cases where this curious strain between self-presentation and style of reasoning occurs.

South African whites have, of course, engaged in dominative racism for centuries. Domination was not only built into the economic, legal, and political system but was also part of most whites' everyday world. In both the domestic and work spheres, whites were the "bosses" whose commands brought strict obedience from blacks unless they wanted to place their jobs (or even their lives on certain farms) at risk. Domination, in this sense, is nowadays receding. The ethnographic material presented in this volume illustrates experiments with integration, such as those sketched in the dialogues in Yeoville (Chapter 10). In general, aversion and domination tended to occur simultaneously. As legal segregation is becoming something of the past, aversive strategies are coming to the fore. Conservative urban whites and some moderates interviewed for this study were prone to such reasoning. Clear parallels with metaracism are, however, difficult to find. The main difficulty lies with the problem of the "Africanity" of moderate and liberal South Africans. When "Africa" stands for backwardness and lack of "civilization," whites present themselves as nonracial and justify the setting of boundaries along nonracial lines. The boundary of inclusiveness thus runs along a line of civilization relegating Africa, and most blacks, to the realm of the "less civilized." In setting the boundary in this way, whites use a set of values that is peculiar to themselves and to a few blacks. The social framework of these values is that of the white segment of the population, that is, a minority. They fail to find legitimation in the broader social framework of the country. This is different from the United States, where whites involved in metaracism appeal to a set of values widely distributed among the numerically and politically dominant section of society. In the United States, this set of values is the "norm." Such values are considered normal; they are not white values. In South Africa, the "civilized" values set by whites cannot but be associated with the white way of life.

There are, of course, those like Diane and Viv (Chapter 10), who lament the absence of a "gray area" into which they can escape. Diane and Viv presented themselves as nonracial, but felt that a "white" identity was inescapably thrust upon them in a period of political turmoil when everybody had to take sides. Their case illustrates how implausible a nonracial self-presentation becomes in the rapid transformation of contemporary South Africa.

CONCLUSIONS

From the outset, in conducting the study reported in this volume, I avoided prejudging its subject matter as that of racism. Rather, my theme was how whites achieved social solidarity in different ways over a period of time. In South Africa there were times when the ethnic group, the nation, the "chosen people," class, and the civilized were all expressions of that solidarity. Except for extreme right-wing whites, "race" was not made an explicit basis for solidarity. Yet, after examining a substantial amount of evidence, especially recent material documenting the convergence of interest among various white groups, "race" seems to be the unexpressed binding factor. I use quotation marks around "race" here to distinguish it as a social construction, regardless of the tendency for this social construction to include biological references. "Race" as a social marker has very little to do with race as descriptive indicator of gene frequencies.

As a social construction, "ethnic group" would imply less emphasis on the biological makeup of a person than "race" by bringing out culture-specific features. "Race" would fix the identity of a group as immutable, whereas ethnic group would leave room for change and social incorporation of members not related by descent. American official discourse has been shifting its definition of "race" identity from mutable ethnic group connotations to biologically fixed "racial" connotations. Everyday discourse also contains evidence of this meaning of race. In South Africa the term *race* is shunned as group identifier. In recent everyday and public discourse, the term *civilization* has been used, because it coincides with the central values and lifestyles of the white segment of the population.

The Collective Self in Two Societies

"Race" as an interpretive schema of the social world may have a referent to the speaking subject and to the other facing the subject. In the United States, "race" is less used as a self-identifier by whites. White supremacists are an exception, but they are marginal to public discourse. Both in the forms of aversive and metaracism, "race" is implicit in consciousness and thought. "Race" describes the exception rather than the normal. The white collective self is the normal. Its way of life is normal and unquestioned. In a descriptive sense it is simply there, taken for granted, highly prized and worthy of emulation. The system it governs the country by and the way it organizes social and economic life are based on

rational and objective considerations and are thus "correct." The preservation of the system is a matter of course and there is no reason to change
or adapt its concomitant lifestyle in order to redistribute resources and
equalize life chances.

South African whites also shun "race" as a self-descriptor. Subsequent
to the convergence of Afrikaner and English-speaking group identifica-
tions, the collective identification with civilization became largely syn-
onymous with "race." Identification with civilization was explicit, and in
some elite and affluent quarters it indicated an open system to which
blacks could be admitted on the condition of their adherence to the rules.
In contrast to the American way of life, which was established and unpre-
carious, "civilization" in South Africa was fragile. There was a certain
"oughtness" about it. It was still being, or was to be, implemented. To many
others, whites as a group were the bearers of civilization and were thus in
need of group preservation.

In this case, "race" thus was a schema or reference. The persistence of
inequality was inevitable as long as blacks remained uncivilized. To the
elite this was a long way off; to the others, inequality may be permanent.

The Collective Other in Two Societies

The collective other is racialized in the United States. The other comprises "people of color," who carry with them ineradicable racial identi-
fiers. They are the exception to mainstream culture and way of life and
are therefore defined in a special way. Some of these "racial" groups are
marginalizable. Mexicans, for example, could have guest worker status
attributed to them. People assume they have a homeland in Mexico—they
therefore could return. African Americans cannot be marginalized in the
same way. They are here to stay. Mexican and Asians are potential outsiders;
African Americans are not. They have a peculiar status. They are insiders-
as-outsiders. Their presence is permanent, yet they are what white America is not. They are physically present, but "racially" different. Insiders-
as-outsiders occupy an eminently ambiguous position. They may be victims
at the same time they are disloyal rebels. Insiders-as-outsiders are out of
place at the same time they are present. Their otherness contrasts and gives
features to what racially thinking whites think they themselves are.[5]

In South Africa today, the racial other cannot be marginalized. Official
policy marginalized blacks literally to the homelands and the outskirts of
the cities. On an everyday level, blacks were peripheral in the consciousness of whites. They were outsiders temporarily "inside" the country. This

has changed radically in the past decade. The collective other, the "racially" other, has been indisputably installed as insider and at the center of shared social space. The centrality of the collective other will cause a crisis in the self-concept of South African whites who now will have to decide whether to remain in the fold of the diminishing and marginal "civilized" group or redefine themselves inclusively as part of a common society. The latter can occur only when they abandon the group-way-of-thinking, their xenologic reason.

NOTES

1. The income gap, for example, has widened since 1975. The gains in educational standards up to the mid-1980s tended to level off, and some even tended to decline (Marden, Meyer, & Engel, 1992, pp. 225, 227).

2. I am fully aware of the danger of overgeneralization and the existence of regional differences in whites' peopling of the United States. The purpose here is to bring out some general differences between the U.S. and South African cases.

3. There seems to be some confusion in the literature. McLemore (1994, p. 337) reports the findings of Harrison and Weinberg, who found decreases in residential segregation. He observes, however, that a pattern of suburbanization among African Americans could create an appearance of residential desegregation that does not reflect the real social situation.

4. In 1991 only 2.2% of managers in South Africa's top companies were black (Adam & Moodley, 1993, p. 172).

5. Wellman (1993) notes that the evidence indicates that "more than 100 years after the abolition of chattel slavery, the American Self is still defined by who it is not" (p. 245).

References

ABC News. (1990, February 13). *Nightline* (transcript). New York: Journal Graphics.

Adam, H. (1971). *Modernizing racial domination*. Berkeley: University of California Press.

Adam, H., & Giliomee, H. (1979a). *Ethnic power mobilized: Can South Africa change?* New Haven, CT: Yale University Press.

Adam, H., & Giliomee, H. (1979b). *The rise and crisis of Afrikaner power.* Cape Town: David Philip.

Adam, H., & Moodley, K. (1986). *South Africa without apartheid: Dismantling racial domination.* Berkeley: University of California Press.

Adam, H., & Moodley, K. (1993). *The negotiated revolution; Society and politics in post-apartheid South Africa.* Johannesburg: Jonathan Ball.

Adorno, T. W., Frenkel-Brunswick, E., Levinson, D. J., & Sanford, R. N. (1982). *The authoritarian personality* (abridged ed.). New York: W. W. Norton.

Afrikaner Weerstandsbeweging. (1988). *Sweepslag, Mondstuk van die AWB.* Pretoria: Author.

Auerbach, F. E. (1965). *The power of prejudice in South African education: An enquiry into history textbooks and syllabuses in the Transvaal high schools of South Africa.* Cape Town: A. A. Balkema.

Barth, F. (1970). *Ethnic groups and boundaries: The social organization of cultural difference.* London: Allen & Unwin.

Berger, P. L., & Luckmann, T. (1972). *The social construction of reality: A treatise in the sociology of knowledge.* Harmondsworth: Penguin.

Blauner, B. (1990). *Black lives, white lives: Three decades of race relations in America.* Berkeley: University of California Press.

Bogle, D. (1989). *Toms, coons, mulattoes, mammies and bucks: An interpretive history of blacks in American films.* New York: Cunningham.

Boonzaier, E., & Sharp, J. (1988). *South African keywords: The uses and abuses of political concepts.* Cape Town: David Philip.

Boshoff, C. W. H., Jooste, C. J., Marais, M. R., & Viljoen, D. J. (1989). *Die Volkstaat as Afrikanerbestemming.* Pretoria: South African Bureau of Racial Affairs.

Bot, A. K., & Kritzinger, M. S. B. (Eds.). (1925). *Letterkundige leesboek.* Pretoria: J. L. van Schaik.

Bozzoli, B. (1990). Intellectuals, audiences and histories: South African experiences, 1978-88. *Radical History Review, 46,* 237-263.

Bruwer, P. F. (1986). *Die derde vryheidsoorlog woed: Ons kan wen* [The Third War of Liberation is being waged: We can win!]. Pretoria: Oranjewerkers Promosies.

Bundy, C. (1986). *Re-making the past: New perspectives on South African history.* Cape Town: University of Cape Town, Department of Adult Education and Extramural Studies.

Cameron, T. (Ed.). (1986). *An illustrated history of South Africa.* Johannesburg: Jonathan Ball.

Claasen, G. N., & van Rensburg, M. C. J. (Eds.). (1983). *Taalverskeidenheid: 'n Blik of die spektrum van taalvariasie in Afrikaans.* Pretoria: Academica.

Coetzee, A. J. (Ed.). (1981). *Hulsels van kristal: Bundel aangebied aan Ernst van Heerden by geleentheid van sy vyf-en-sestigste verjaardag op 20 Maart 1981.* Kaapstad: Tafelberg.

Cohen, A. (1974). Introduction. In A. Cohen (Ed.), *Urban ethnicity.* London: Tavistock.

Collinge, J., & Niddrie, D. (1990, July). Keeping the right image: The mainstream media in South Africa. *Southern Africa Report,* pp. 3-7.

Collins, P. (Ed.). (1989). *Thinking about South Africa: Reason, morality and politics.* New York: St. Martin's.

Crapanzano, V. (1985). *Waiting: The whites of South Africa.* New York: Random House.

Cronjé, G., Nicol, W., & Groenewald, E. P. (1947). *Regverdige rasse-apartheid: 'n Diep-dringende beligting vans ons blank-nieblank verhoudinge teen die agtergrondsituasie van kontak, integrasie en/of segregasie van die kleurgroepe.* Stellenbosch: Christelike Uitgewers Maatskappy.

Davis, F. J. (1991). *Who is black: One nation's definition.* University Park: Pennsylvania State University Press.

Dean, E., Hartmann, P., & Katzen, M. (1983). *History in black and white: An analysis of South African school history textbooks.* Paris: UNESCO.

de Klerk, W. A. (1976). *The puritans in South Africa: A story of Afrikanerdom.* Harmondsworth: Penguin.

de Klerk, W. J. (1991). *F. W. de Klerk: Die man en sy tyd* [F. W. de Klerk: The man and his times]. Cape Town: Tafelberg/Jonathan Ball.

de Villiers, M. (1988). *White tribe dreaming: Apartheid's bitter roots as witnessed by eight generations of an Afrikaner family.* New York: Viking.

Dooyeweerd, H. (1935). *Wijsbegeerte der wetsidee* [Philosophy of the idea of law] (3 vols.). Amsterdam: H. J. Paris.

Douglas, M. (1966). *Purity and danger: An analysis of concepts of pollution and taboo.* London: Routledge & Kegan Paul.

du Bruyn, J. (1982). F. A. van Jaarsveld: Afrikaner historikus en vernuwer. *Historia, 27*(1).

Dugard, J. (1980, Fall). South Africa's "independent" homelands: An exercise in denationalization. *Denver Journal of International Law and Policy, 10,* 11-36.

du Plessis, H., & du Plessis, T. (Eds.). (1987). *Afrikaans en taalpolitiek.* Pretoria: HAUM.

du Plessis, L. J. (1951). *Letters of a farmer.* Manuscript published privately.

du Preez, J. M. (1983). *Africana Afrikaner: Master symbols in South African school textbooks.* Alberton: Librarius.

du Toit, B. M. (1974). *People of the valley.* Cape Town: A. A. Balkema.

du Toit, S. J., Hoogenhout, C. P., & Malherbe, G. J. (1877). *Di geskiedenis van ons land in di taal van ons volk* [The history of our country in the language of our people]. Cape Town: Genootskap van Regte Afrikaners.

Essed, P. (1991). *Understanding everyday racism: An interdisciplinary theory.* Newbury Park, CA: Sage.

Evans-Pritchard, E. E. (1963). *Witchcraft, oracles and magic among the Azande.* Oxford: Oxford University Press.

Feagin, J. R., & Feagin, C. B. (1993). *Racial and ethnic relations.* Englewood Cliffs, NJ: Prentice Hall.

February, V. (1991). *The Afrikaners of South Africa.* New York: Kegan Paul International.

Finnegan, W. (1986). *Crossing the line: A year in the land of apartheid.* New York: Harper & Row.

Finnegan, W. (1988). *Dateline Soweto: Travels with black South African reporters.* New York: Harper & Row.

Franken, J. L. M. (1953). *Taalhistoriese bydraes.* Cape Town: A. A. Balkema.

Frederickson, G. (1981). *White supremacy: A comparative study in American and South African history.* New York: Oxford University Press.

Giliomee, H., & du Toit, A. (1983). *Afrikaner political thought: Analysis and documents: Vol. 1. 1780-1850.* Cape Town: David Philip.

Giliomee, H., & Elphick, R. (Eds.). (1979). *The shaping of South African society 1652-1920.* London: Longman.

Giliomee, H., & Schlemmer, L. (Eds.). (1989). *Negotiating South Africa's future.* Johannesburg: Southern.

Glaser, B. G., & Strauss, A. L. (1967). *The discovery of grounded theory: Strategies for qualitative research.* Chicago: Aldine.

Goldberg, D. T. (Ed.). (1990). *The anatomy of racism.* Minneapolis: University of Minnesota Press.

Gordon, S. (1988). *Under the harrow: Lives of white South Africans today.* London: William Heinemann.

Gramsci, A. (1971). *Selections from the prison notebooks* (Q. Hoare & G. Nowell-Smith, Eds. and Trans.). New York: International.

Green, P. (1990, July). Afrikaner women: Breaking the mould? *Femina,* pp. 60-65.

Grobbelaar, J. (1990). *Vir volk en vaderland: A guide to the white right.* Durban: Indicator Project of South Africa.

Gurak, D. T., & Kritz, M. M. (1979). Intermarriage patterns in the U.S.: Maximizing information from the U.S. Census Public Use Samples. *Public Data Use, 6,* 33-43.

Hallinan, M. T., & Williams, R. A. (1987). The stability of students' interracial friendships. *American Sociological Review, 52,* 653-664.

Hamilton, C. (1992). *The real goat: Ethnicity and authenticity in Shakaland.* Paper presented at the Wednesday Seminar of the Institute for Advanced Study and Research in the African Humanities, Northwestern University, Evanston, IL.

Heese, H. F. (1984). *Groep sonder grense (Die rol en status van die gemengde bevoling aan die kaap, 1652-1795).* Belville: Wes-Kaaplandse Instituut vir Historiese Navorsing.

Horowitz, D. L. (1991). *A democratic South Africa? Constitutional engineering in a divided society.* Berkeley: University of California Press.

Human Sciences Research Council. (1972). *The teaching of history at South African secondary schools: A condensed version of a survey in the year 1966* (C. R. Liebenberg Report No. 0-11). Pretoria: Author.

Humphries, R., Schlemmer, L., & Slack, L. (1990). White politics: Constraint or opportunity? *Politikon, 17*(1), 11-27.

Joubert, C. J. (1979). *History for standard 10.* Johannesburg: Perskor.

Kallaway, P., & Adler, T. (Eds.). (1978). *Contemporary South African studies: Research papers* (Vol. 1). Johannesburg: University of the Witwatersrand, Faculty of Education.

Kane-Berman, J. (1990). *South Africa's silent revolution.* Johannesburg: South African Institute of Race Relations.

Konserwatiewe Party van Suid-Afrika. (1989, July). *CP election news.* Pretoria: Author.

Kovel, J. (1970). *White racism: A psychohistory.* New York: Pantheon.

Landman, J. P., Nel, P., & van Niekerk, A. (1988). *Wat kom na apartheid? Jong Afrikaners aan die woord* [What happens after apartheid? Young Afrikaners speak out]. Johannesburg: Southern.

Lelyveld, J. (1985). *Move your shadow: South Africa, black and white.* New York: Times Books.

Lévi-Strauss, C. (1969). *Totemism.* Harmondsworth: Penguin.

Louw-Potgieter, J. (1988). *Afrikaner dissidents: A social psychological study of identity and dissent.* Philadelphia: Multilingual Matters.

Luckmann, T. (1978). Preface. In T. Luckmann (Ed.), *Phenomenology and sociology: Selected readings.* Harmondsworth: Penguin.

Luckmann, T. (1983). *Life-world and social realities.* London: Heinemann.

Lyman, S. M. (1990). Race, sex, and servitude: Images of blacks in American cinema. *International Journal of Politics, Culture and Society, 4*(1), 49-77.

Machover, K. (1980). *Personality projection in the drawing of the human figure: A method of personality investigation.* Springfield, IL: Charles C Thomas.

Malan, R. (1990). *My traitor's heart: A South African exile returns to face his country, his tribe and his conscience.* New York: Atlantic Monthly Press.

Marden, C. F., Meyer, G., & Engel, M. H. (1992). *Minorities in American society* (6th ed.). New York: HarperCollins.

Marger, M. N. (1994). *Race and ethnic relations: American and global perspectives* (3rd ed.). Belmont, CA: Wadsworth.

Massey, D. S., & Denton, N. A. (1993). *American apartheid: Segregation and the making of the underclass.* Cambridge, MA: Harvard University Press.

McLemore, S. D. (1994). *Racial and ethnic relations* (4th ed.). Boston: Allyn & Bacon.

Moodie, T. D. (1975). *The rise of Afrikanerdom: Power, apartheid and the Afrikaner civil religion.* Berkeley: University of California Press.

Murray, M. (1987). *South Africa: Time of agony, time of destiny: The upsurge of popular protest.* London: Verso.

North, J. (1985). *Freedom rising.* New York: Macmillan.

Olzak, S. (1990). Report to the Human Sciences Research Council. *South African Sociological Review, 3*(1), 62-68.

Omond, R. (1986). *The apartheid handbook.* Harmondsworth: Penguin.

Operation South Africa. (n.d.). *The threat is red: Our answer* [pamphlet]. Kempton Park: Author.

Oranjewerkers. (1990). *Afrikaneroorlewing-Waar?* Morgenzon: Author.

Outlaw, L. (1990). Toward a critical theory of race. In D. T. Goldberg (Ed.), *The anatomy of race.* Minneapolis: University of Minnesota Press.

Pauw, J. (1991). *In the heart of the whore: The story of apartheid's death squads.* Johannesburg: Southern.

Phelan, J. M. (1987). *Apartheid and media: Disinformation and dissent in South Africa.* Westport, CT: Lawrence Hill.

Pirie, G. H. (1990). Dismantling bus apartheid in South Africa, 1975-1990. *Africa Insight, 20*(2), 111-117.

Ponelis, F. A. (1987). *Die eenheid van die Afrikaanse taalgemeenskap* [The unity of the Afrikaans language community]. Unpublished manuscript, Stellenbosch University, Department of Afrikaans and Dutch.

Posel, D. (1987). The language of domination, 1978-1983. In S. Marks & S. Trapido (Eds.), *The politics of race, class and nationalism.* London: Longman.

Raath, A. W. G. (1990). *Selfbeskikking en sesessie: Die saak vir die Afrikanervolk.* Pretoria: Stifting Afrikanervryheid.

Reader's Digest Association of South Africa. (Ed.). (1989). *The Reader's Digest illustrated history of South Africa: The real story.* Pleasantville, NY: Reader's Digest Association.

Republic of South Africa, Bureau of Information. (1990, May). *This is South Africa* [pamphlet]. Pretoria: Government Printer.

Republic of South Africa, Bureau of Information. (1991). *Address by the state president, Mr. F. W. de Klerk, DMS, at the opening of the third session of the ninth Parliament of the Republic of South Africa, Cape Town, 1 February 1991.* Pretoria: Government Printer.

Republic of South Africa, Central Statistical Service. (1988). *Demographic statistics, capita selecta.* Pretoria: Government Printer.

Russel, M., & Russel, M. (1979). *Afrikaners of the Kalahari.* Cambridge: Cambridge University Press.

Saunders, C. (1988). *The making of the South African past: Major historians on race and class.* Totowa, NJ: Barnes & Noble.

Scholtz, G. D. (1954). *Het die Suid-Afrikaanse volk 'n toekoms?* [Does the Afrikaans people have a future?]. Johannesburg: Voortrekkerpers.

Scholtz, G. D. (1957). *Die gevaar uit die ooste.* Johannesburg: Voorwaarts.

Scholtz, G. D. (1961). *The origins and essence of the race pattern in South Africa.* Pretoria: South African Bureau of Racial Affairs.

Scholtz, G. D. (1964). *'n Swart Suid Afrika?* Cape Town: Nasionale Boekhandel.

Schoonees, P. C. (Ed.). (1991). *Woordeboek van die Afrikaanse taal* [Dictionary of the Afrikaans language]. Pretoria: Staatsdrukker.

Schutte, G. (1989). Afrikaner historiography and the decline of apartheid: Ethnic self-reconstruction in times of crisis. In E. Tonkin et al. (Eds.), *History and ethnicity.* London: Routledge.

Schutte, G. (1991). Racial oppression and social research: Field work under racial conflict in South Africa. *Qualitative Sociology, 14,* 127-146.

Schutz, A. (1973). *Collected papers I: The problem of social reality.* The Hague: Martinus Nijhoff.

Schutz, A. (1976). *Collected papers II: Studies in social theory.* The Hague: Martinus Nijhoff.

Schutz, A., & Luckmann, T. (1974). *The structures of the life-world.* London: Heinemann.

Sharp, J. (1988). Ethnic group and nation: The apartheid vision in South Africa. In E. Boonzaier & J. Sharp (Eds.), *South African keywords: The uses and abuses of political concepts.* Cape Town: David Philip.

Simmel, G. (1971). *On individuality and social forms: Selected writings* (D. N. Levine, Ed.). Chicago: University of Chicago Press.

Smith, K. W. (1988). *The changing past: Trends in South African historical writing.* Johannesburg: Southern.

South African Advertising Research Foundation (SAARF). (1990). *All media products: survey and trends 1985-1989/90.* Sandton: Author.

South African Institute of Race Relations (SAIRR). (1989). *Race relations survey 1988/89.* Johannesburg: Author.

South African Institute of Race Relations (SAIRR). (1990). *Race relations survey 1989/90.* Johannesburg: Author.

Spier, J. M. (1950). *Inleiding in de wijsbegeerte der wetsidee.* Kampen: J. H. Kok.

Stals, E. L. P. (1974). *Die verhouding tussen blankes en nie-blankes in die Suid-Afrikaanse geskiedskrywing.* Johannesburg: Rand Afrikaans University.

Stein, H. F., & Hill, R. F. (1977). *The ethnic imperative: Examining the new white ethnic movement.* University Park: Pennsylvania State University Press.

Stengel, R. (1990). *January sun, one day, three lives: A South African town.* New York: Simon & Schuster.

Stigting Afrikanervryheid. (1990). *Besetting van die Broeipunt.* Pretoria: Author.

Strauss, A. L. (1987). *Qualitative analysis for social scientists.* New York: Cambridge University Press.

Surplus People's Project. (1983). *Forced removals in South Africa* (5 vols.). Cape Town: Author.

Thompson, L. (1985). *The political mythology of apartheid.* New Haven, CT: Yale University Press.

Trust Bank of Africa Ltd. (1990, March/April). *Ekonovisie: Oorsig* [Bimonthly economic overview]. Johannesburg: Author.

UNESCO. (1972). *Apartheid: Its effects on education, science, culture and information* (2nd ed.). Paris: Author.

van Biljon, P. (1947). *Grensbakens tussen blank en swart in Suid-Afrika: 'n Historiese ontwikkeling van grensbeleid en grondtoekenning aan die naturel in Suid-Afrika.* Cape Town: Juta.

van der Merwe, H. J. J. M. (1961). *Segregeer of sterf.* Johannesburg: Afrikaanse Pers Boekhandel.

van Dijk, T. A. (Ed.). (1985). *Discourse and communication: New approaches to the analysis of mass media discourse and communication.* Berlin: Walter de Gruyter.

van Dijk, T. A. (1987). *Communicating racism: Ethnic prejudice in thought and talk.* Newbury Park, CA: Sage.

van Dijk, T. A. (1992a). Discourse and the denial of racism. *Discourse and Society, 3,* 87-118.

van Dijk, T. A. (1992b). Text, talk, elites and racism. *Social Discourse, 4,* 37-62.

van Jaarsveld, F. A. (1964). *The Afrikaner's interpretation of South African history.* Cape Town: Simondium.

van Jaarsveld, F. A. (1971). *Afrikaner, quo vadis?* Johannesburg: Voortrekkerpers.

van Jaarsveld, F. A. (1979). *Die evolusie van apartheid.* Cape Town: Tafelberg.

van Jaarsveld, F. A. (1984). *Omstrede Afrikaanse verlede: Geskiedenis, ideologie en die historiese skuldvraagstuk.* Johannesburg: Lex Patria.

van Wyk, J., Conradie, P., & Constandaras, N. (1987). *Suid Afrika in poësie.* Pinetown: O. Burgess.

van Wyk-Louw, N. P. (1972). *Die pluimsaad waai ver of bitter begin.* Cape Town: Human en Rousseau.

van Zyl Slabbert, F. (1985). *The last white Parliament.* Johannesburg: Jonathan Ball.

Vatcher, W. H. (1965). *White laager: The rise of Afrikaner nationalism.* New York: Praeger.

Viljoen, G. van N. (1978). *Ideaal en werklikheid.* Cape Town: Tafelberg.

Wacquant, L. J. D., & Wilson, W. J. (1989). The cost of racial and class exclusion in the inner city. *Annals of the American Academy of Political and Social Science, 501,* 8-26.

Weber, M. (1978). *Economy and society: An outline of interpretive sociology* (G. Roth & C. Wittich, Eds.). Berkeley: University of California Press.

Wellman, D. T. (1993). *Portraits of white racism* (2nd ed.). New York: Cambridge University Press.

Wilkinson, I., & Strydom, H. (1978). *The super-Afrikaners: Inside the Broederbond.* Johannesburg: Jonathan Ball.

Wilson, M., & Thompson, L. (1969-1971). *The Oxford history of South Africa* (2 vols.). Oxford: Oxford University Press.

Wilson, W. J. (1978). *The declining significance of race: Blacks and changing American institutions.* Chicago: University of Chicago Press.

Wilson, W. J. (1987). *The truly disadvantaged: The inner city, the underclass, and public policy.* Chicago: University of Chicago Press.

World Apartheid Movement. (1990). [Untitled pamphlet]. Pretoria: Author.

Wright, H. M. (1977). *The burden of the present: Liberal-radical controversy over Southern African history.* Cape Town: David Philip.

Yetman, N. R. (Ed.). (1991). *Majority and minority: The dynamics of race and ethnicity in American life* (5th ed.). Boston: Allyn & Bacon.

Index

About the Author

Gerhard Schutte (Andries Gerhardus Schutte), author of numerous articles on African religion, social change, and the sociology of knowledge, was born in Pretoria, South Africa. He studied anthropology and theology at the University of Potchefstroom. Between 1966 and 1967, he conducted ethnographic fieldwork on a Dutch Reformed parish in Soweto that was later published in *Swart Doppers?* (Black Calvinists?). He did his graduate studies at the University of Heidelberg in Germany, where he completed his Ph.D. in 1970. His dissertation looked at nativistic movements as social processes. After serving as a Lecturer in Anthropology at the University of Potchefstroom, he became Senior Lecturer in Social Anthropology at the University of the Witwatersrand in Johannesburg in 1971. During the years following that appointment, he did ethnographic fieldwork in Soweto on a number of healing groups, and later in the area of Venda, Northern Transvaal, on regional cults.

In 1977, the German Von Humboldt Foundation awarded him a grant to investigate the problem of sociological interpretation across cultural boundaries at the University of Constance. He returned to South Africa as Professor and Head of the Sociology Department at the University of the Witwatersrand. His research at that time focused on socioeconomic issues and the life worlds of black migrants. In 1980-1981 he was elected President of the Association for Sociology in Southern Africa.

Political turmoil made ethnographic research in black communities virtually impossible after 1984, and he departed for the United States in 1987. After lecturing at the University of California at Santa Cruz, Loyola University in Chicago, and Northwestern University, he was tenured at the University of Wisconsin at Parkside, where he is teaching today.